DICKENS STUDIES ANNUAL

Essays on Victorian Fiction

DICKENS STUDIES ANNUAL
Essays on Victorian Fiction

DICKENS STUDIES ANNUAL

Essays on Victorian Fiction

VOLUME
40

Edited by
Stanley Friedman, Edward Guiliano,
Anne Humpherys, Talia Schaffer, and Michael Timko

AMS PRESS, INC.
New York

Dickens Studies Annual
ISSN 0084-9812

Dickens Studies Annual: Essays on Victorian Fiction welcomes essay- and monograph-length contributions on Dickens and other Victorian novelists and on the history of aesthetics of Victorian fiction. All manuscripts should be double-spaced and should follow the documentation format described in the most recent *MLA Style Manual*. The author's name should appear only on a cover-page, not elsewhere in the essay. An editorial decision can usually be reached more quickly if two copies of the article are submitted, since outside readers are asked to evaluate each submission. If a manuscript is accepted for publication, the author will be asked to provide a 100- to 200-word abstract and also a CD-ROM containing the final version of the essay. The preferred editions for citations from Dickens's works are the Clarendon and the Norton Critical when available, otherwise the Oxford Illustrated or the Penguin.

Please send submissions to The Editors, *Dickens Studies Annual*, Ph.D. Program in English, The Graduate Center, CUNY, 365 Fifth Avenue, New York, NY 10016-4309. Please send inquiries concerning subscriptions and/or availability of earlier volumes to AMS Press, Inc., Brooklyn Navy Yard, 63 Flushing Avenue—Unit #221, Brooklyn, NY 11205-1073, USA.

Dickens Studies Annual: Essays on Victorian Fiction is published in cooperation with Queens College and The Graduate Center, CUNY.

International Standard Book Number
Series ISBN-13: 978-0-404-18520-6
Series ISBN-10: 0-404-18520-7

Vol. 40 ISBN-13: 978-0-404-18940-2
Vol. 40 ISBN-10: 0-404-18940-7

All AMS books are printed on acid-free paper that meets the guidelines for performance and durability of the Committee on Production Guidelines for Book Longevity of the Council on Library Resources.

AMS PRESS, INC.
Brooklyn Navy Yard, 63 Flushing Avenue–Unit #221
Brooklyn, NY 11205-1073, USA
www.amspressinc.com

Manufactured in the United States of America

Contents

Preface

Just as every era produces its own translations into English of Homer and Dante, so every period desires its own interpretations of the literary past. We continue to receive submissions offering studies of Dickens and his contemporaries that we and our reviewers find informed and stimulating, essays that add to our comprehension of work that is becoming ever more distant in time.

As always, we are indebted to the Victorian writers who created fiction of enduring interest, to the scholars and critics who submit their articles to us, and to our outside readers who generously use their time and expertise to guide us and our contributors.

This volume contains discussions of novels written during different stages of Dickens's long career, as well as a scholarly edition of his initial literary efforts. We offer special thanks to Robert C. Hanna for his edition "Before Boz: The Juvenilia and Early Writings of Charles Dickens, 1820–1833" to Duane DeVries, who graciously assisted with the copyediting of this material, and to Natalie McKnight, who prepared an insightful, comprehensive survey of Dickens studies published in 2007.

Again, we have benefited from the practical assistance given by various academic administrators: President William P. Kelly, Provost Chase Robinson, Ph.D. Program in English Executive Officer Steven F. Kruger, and Nancy Silverman, Assistant Program Officer, Ph.D. Program in English, all of The Graduate Center, CUNY; and President James L. Muyskens, Dean of Arts and Humanities Tamara S. Evans, and Department of English Chair Nancy R. Comley, all of Queens College, CUNY.

We also express appreciation to John O. Jordan, Director of The Dickens Project at the University of California, Santa Cruz; JoAnna Rottke, Project Coordinator for The Dickens Project; and Jon Michael Varese, the Project's Research Assistant and Web Administrator, for placing on the Project's website the tables of contents for volumes 1–27 of DSA, as well as abstracts for subsequent volumes. (These items are included in a link to Dickens Studies Annual on the Project's website, which can be reached at <http://dickens. ucsc.edu>.)

Gabriel Hornstein, President of AMS Press, has continued to express strong interest and to provide generous support; Jack Hopper, retired Editor-in-Chief at AMS Press, still gives valuable assistance to DSA; and David Ramm, Editor-in-Chief at AMS Press, offers quick and resourceful help in solving numerous problems. We are also very grateful for the many tasks efficiently performed by our editorial assistant for this volume, Brett Kawalerski, a Ph.D. candidate at The Graduate Center, CUNY.

In starting to prepare this issue, we decided to replace the Editorial Board and the Advisory Board with one Editorial Advisory Board, a group that will have rotating participants and includes fewer members than the two previous boards. Because of new professional responsibilities, Professor Talia Schaffer, who has been our valued colleague, will no longer be serving as an editor for future volumes. We thank her for her editorial contributions, and we are pleased that she will continue her association with *Dickens Studies Annual* as a member of the new Editorial Advisory Board.

—The Editors

The Editors are happy to announce that in preparing future volumes they will be joined by Professor Natalie McKnight, of Boston University, a distinguished scholar who has published important studies of Dickens and other Victorian novelists.

Notes on Contributors

JAN ALBER is Assistant Professor in the English Department at the University of Freiburg in Germany. He is the author of a critical monograph entitled *Narrating the Prison: Role and Representation in Charles Dickens' Novels, Twentieth-Century Fiction, and Film* (Cambria Press, 2007), and the editor or co-editor of several other books, including *Stones of Law, Bricks of Shame: Narrating Imprisonment in the Victorian Age* (University of Toronto Press, 2009). Furthermore, Alber has written articles that have been published or are forthcoming in such journals as *The Journal of Popular Culture*, *Short Story Criticism*, *Storyworlds*, and *Style*. He has contributed to numerous edited collections as well as to the *Routledge Encyclopedia of Narrative Theory* (2005) and the *Handbook of Narratology* (forthcoming). His new project focuses on unnatural (that is, physically or logically impossible) scenarios in postmodernist novels and plays. In 2007, he received a scholarship from the German Research Foundation (DFG) that allowed him to spend the 2007–08 academic year at Ohio State University doing research under the auspices of Project Narrative.

PHILIP V. ALLINGHAM is an Associate Professor, Secondary English Curriculum and Instruction, and Chair of Undergraduate Studies in the Faculty of Education at Lakehead University in Thunder Bay, Ontario. He serves as the Canadian Contributing Editor to Professor George Landow's Victorian Web and editorial consultant to *The Dickens Magazine*. After completing a doctorate on the dramatic adaptations of the Christmas Books of Charles Dickens at the University of British Columbia (Vancouver), Philip Allingham served for three years as a coordinator in the B.C. Provincial Examinations Branch, Victoria. He has previously published studies of illustrations for Dickens's works in volumes 33 and 36 of *Dickens Studies Annual*.

KAREN BOURRIER completed a Ph.D. dissertation at Cornell University in 2009 on disability and masculinity in the mid-Victorian novel. She has work on Charlotte Yonge forthcoming in the special issue of the *Victorian Review* on disability.

ROBERT C. HANNA is Professor of English at Bethany Lutheran College, Mankato, Minnesota. He is the author of *The Dickens Family Gospel*, *The*

Dickens Christian Reader, and *Dickens's Nonfictional, Theatrical, and Poetical Writings: An Annotated Bibliography, 1820–2000*. A frequent contributor to *The Dickensian*, he recently published ''Bardd Cymraeg Anhysbys Ymhlith Cydnabod Charles Dickens A Thomas Beard Yn 1834'' in the University of Wales's literary journal *Llên Cymru*.

MICHAEL KLOTZ received his Ph.D. in English Language and Literature from Cornell University in 2007 and is currently a visiting faculty member in the department of English at Wake Forest University. He has previously published articles on material culture and domestic space in Charlotte Brontë, Charles Dickens, and Charlotte Perkins Gilman. He is currently at work on a study of the relationship between nineteenth-century vital statistics, probability, and narrative.

JOHN KOFRON is a Ph.D. student in the English Department at Indiana University. He completed his M.A. at the City College of New York (CUNY) in 2007. This essay is drawn from his master's thesis, ''Dickens, Collins, and the Aesthetics of Arctic Exploration.''

NATALIE MCKNIGHT is Chair of Humanities at the College of General Studies, Boston University. She has published numerous articles and two books on Victorian fiction: *Idiots, Madmen and Other Prisoners in Dickens* (1993) and *Suffering Mothers in Mid-Victorian Novels* (1997), both with St. Martin's Press. She is currently working on *Literature in Context*, an anthology of art and literature, and a book on Victorian fathers.

STEPHANIE PEÑA-SY is writing her Ph.D. dissertation, ''Virginia Woolf and the Domestication of Philosophy: Gender, Intellectual Labour, and the Common Reader,'' at the University of Toronto. Her work considers British Modernist intellectual history with particular interest in the identity politics of work. Her current writing projects include articles on the domestic servant in Katherine Mansfield's fiction and maternity as labor in the fiction of Edith Wharton. She completed this article while she was a research affiliate at the Institute of the Humanities at the University of Manitoba and would like to thank the Institute for their support.

PAUL SCHACHT is Associate Professor of English at the State University of New York at Geneseo, where he teaches British literature, humanities, and writing. He holds an A.B. in English from the University of Michigan and a Ph.D. in English and American Literature from Stanford University. He has published essays on Charles Dickens, Charlotte Brontë, Mark Twain, and humanities computing. He is currently exploring Dickens's relationship to the idea of intellectual property.

VICTORIA FORD SMITH is a Ph.D. candidate in nineteenth-century British literature at Rice University. Her research interests include children's literature, book history, and authorship.

ROBERT TRACY is Professor Emeritus of English and of Celtic Studies at the University of California, Berkeley. He has been Visiting Professor of American Literature at the University of Leeds, of Russian Literature at Wellesley, and of Irish Literature at Trinity College, Dublin. His publications include articles on Dickens, Trollope, Seamus Heaney, and Brian Friel; *Trollope's Later Novels* (1978); editions of works by Synge, Trollope, Le Fanu, and Flann O'Brien; *Stone* (1981), a translation of Osip Mandelstam's *Kamen*; and *The Unappeasable Host: Studies in Irish Identities* (1998). He is President (2008–09) of the Dickens Society.

In Pursuit of Pickwick's Hat: Dickens and the Epistemology of Utilitarianism

Paul Schacht

Hats often serve as a comic prop in Dickens's novels, but they are mentioned with unusual frequency in Pickwick Papers. *The reason has as much to do with the evolution of Dickens's social philosophy as it does with the devices of his humor. As the quixotic leader of a club modeled partly on the utilitarian Society for the Diffusion of Useful Knowledge, Pickwick is a mind seeking to know the world. The hat is both an object-in-the-world and a natural metonym for the perceiving mind. In* Pickwick, *it participates in a play of signifiers—including heads, feet, boots, and spectacles—through which Dickens discredits utilitarian assumptions about the relationship between mind and world. To this exposure of utilitarianism's misguided epistemology,* Oliver Twist *would add a retort to its reductive psychology and* Hard Times *an assault on its impoverished moral calculus. Thus, to pursue the hats of* Pickwick *is to better understand the intellectual continuity that runs through these three novels. It is also to confront the contradictions that inhabit that continuity and bedevil Dickens's politics.*

"There are very few moments in a man's existence when he experiences so much ludicrous distress, or meets with so little charitable commiseration, as when he is in pursuit of his own hat." Thus begins one of the best known comic moments in Dickens's *Pickwick Papers*, a moment that finds a hapless and hatless Pickwick in competition with the wind for both his headgear and his dignity:

Dickens Studies Annual, Volume 40, Copyright © 2009 by AMS Press, Inc. All rights reserved.

The wind puffed, and Mr. Pickwick puffed, and the hat rolled over and over
as merrily as a lively porpoise in a strong tide; and on it might have rolled, far
beyond Mr Pickwick's reach, had not its course been providentially stopped,
just as that gentleman was on the point of resigning it to its fate.   (121)

Hats often serve as a comic prop in Dickens's novels: think of the hat-juggling
Joe of *Great Expectations* or the "air of goblin rakishness" produced by
Smallweed's skullcap in *Bleak House* (*GE* 169–72, *BH* 262). But hats are
mentioned in *Pickwick Papers* with a frequency that is large even by Dicken-
sian standards.[1] Why? The answer has as much to do with the evolution of
Dickens's social philosophy as it does with the devices of his humor.

Beginning with *Pickwick Papers*, and continuing through *Oliver Twist* and
Hard Times, Dickens would explore a set of questions about utilitarianism:
Why does utilitarianism fail epistemologically as an account of what and how
human beings know? Why does it fail psychologically as an account of human
motivation? Why does it fail morally, socially, and politically as an algorithm
for decision-making? In *Pickwick*, Dickens focused mainly if not exclusively
(and, to be sure, casually) on the epistemological failure of utilitarianism
through a loose satire of an amateur scientific society and its leader. That
leader, a modern-day Don Quixote in quest of truths about humanity, is a
mind seeking to know the world. And the hat, in addition to being rich in
comic possibilities, is both an object-in-the-world and a natural metonym for
the perceiving mind.[2]

The hat-play in *Pickwick Papers* participates in a larger play of signifiers—including heads, feet, boots, and spectacles—through which Dickens
made his first significant attempt to discredit the relationship between mind
and object assumed by the utilitarians. Dickens's critique of utilitarianism
grew by accretion, maintaining and expanding this analysis of epistemological
failure even as it added, in *Oliver Twist*, a retort to utilitarianism's reductive
psychology of self-interest and, in *Hard Times*, an assault on the felicific
calculus. To pursue the hats of *Pickwick* is thus to gain a fuller appreciation
of the intellectual continuity running from *Pickwick* through *Hard Times*. It
is also to gain a better understanding of the contradictions that inhabit that
continuity and bedevil Dickens's politics.

A Tip of the Hat: The Career of Pickwick

As both comic prop and symbol, hats help define the broad arc of Pickwick's
career. Granted, Dickens himself only discovered this arc as he inscribed it,
having at the outset no detailed overall plan for this or indeed any of his
novels before *Dombey and Son*, first published in 1846–48 (Butt and Tillotson

90–113). The arc is one that takes Pickwick from object of mild satire to object of deference and even admiration, one that Dickens would defend in the 1847 introduction by observing that, in real life, it is only after long acquaintance with a "whimsical" character that we finally see past his "peculiarities and oddities" to discover "the better part of him" (45). If Dickens did not plan Pickwick's transformation, he could not have planned to mark it symbolically by means of hats; however, he could, and probably did, choose separately to mark first Pickwick's absurdity, and later his new moral respectability, in this fashion. Indeed, as a way to bring home Pickwick's change to the reader, the second choice would have been naturally recommended by the first.

Through most of the novel, Pickwick's numerous struggles with various supracranial accoutrements serve mainly to symbolize his helplessness before adversaries and circumstances. As at Rochester, "ludicrous distress" is the keynote of these struggles: in the crowd at Eatanswill, where "Mr. Pickwick's hat was knocked over his eyes, nose, and mouth by one poke of a Buff flagstaff" (250); in the inn at Ipswich, where a wrong turn in the night leads him to the wrong bed and the embarrassment of being "almost ready to sink, Ma'am, beneath the confusion of addressing a lady in my night-cap" (393); at Dingley Dell, where, after a fall through the ice while skating, his "hat, gloves, and handkerchief" are "all of Mr. Pickwick that anybody could see" (501); at Bob Sawyer's, where Pickwick's host must caution him to " 'take care of the glasses' " because he has "put his hat in the tray" (525); in the warden's room at the Fleet, where Pickwick's nightcap is rudely "snatched from [his] head" and "fixed in a twinkling" on that of a drunken man as a "practical joke" (673). In each instance our main impression is of that utter incompetence in worldly and practical matters which leads Sam Weller to tell his master, after the Ipswich incident, " 'You rayther want someone to look arter you, sir, wen your judgment goes out a wisitin' " (395). Sam has been perfectly equipped for this role by an "eddication" in the streets that has made him "sharp" (353) and given him the control over his movements and his destiny that Pickwick lacks, a control that Dickens suggests in his initial description of Sam wearing a "bright red handkerchief . . . wound in a very loose and unstudied style round his neck, and an old white hat . . . carelessly thrown on one side of his head" (197) and in subsequent descriptions of which the following is typical: "Sam Weller put on his hat in a very easy and graceful manner, and thrusting his hands in his waistcoat pockets, walked with deliberation to Queen Square, whistling as he went along" (586).

The ludicrous distress of Pickwick is starkest in the episode that finds him awakening from a blissful, alcohol-induced slumber to the jeers of a mob that has gathered around him in his sleep. The mob pelts Pickwick with "a turnip, then a potato, and then an egg," followed by "a few other little tokens of the playful disposition of the many-headed," and greets his confused ejaculation of " 'Where are my friends?' " with the taunt, " 'You ain't got no friends. Hurrah!' '' In the depiction of this scene, titled ''Mr Pickwick in the Pound,'' Dickens's illustrator Phiz (Hablot K. Browne) adds a number of emblematic details not mentioned in the text, such as pigs rolling in the dirt and an ass braying in Pickwick's face. Though Dickens does not himself mention Pickwick's hat, Phiz depicts it knocked to the side of Pickwick's head. Above Pickwick, at dead center along the fence surrounding the pound, a boy leads the mob's ''Hurrah!'' with a waving hand, and to the right of this boy, another performs the same gesture hat in hand.[3]

If the mockery in this scene is less than severe, it is because by this point in the novel Pickwick has established himself as a bumbling but harmless, indeed lovable, innocent, immunized against more corrosive ridicule in no small part by his willingness to laugh at himself, as he does, for example, as soon as his friends have rescued him from the pound: ''Do what he would, a smile would come into Mr Pickwick's face; the smile extended into a laugh; the laugh into a roar; the roar became general'' (342). But Pickwick might have turned out a different kind of character altogether; Robert Seymour's illustration of the novel's opening scene—''Pickwick addresses the Club''—shows a rather sourfaced pedant discoursing with outstretched arm, a posture later adopted by the hypocritical preacher Stiggins (see Phiz's illustration, ''The Red-nosed Man Discourseth,'' 728) and by Stiggins's descendant Chadband of *Bleak House* (1851–53; see ''Mr. Chadband 'improving' a tough subject'' 319). The eponymous scientific club addressed by Pickwick, author of ''Speculations on the Source of the Hampstead Ponds, with some Observations on the Theory of Tittlebats'' (67), satirizes both Lord Henry Brougham's utilitarian Society for the Diffusion of Useful Knowledge (established 1826) and the British Association for the Advancement of Science (established 1832) on Swiftian grounds that with science in general, and amateur scientists in particular, abstract speculation too often trumps common sense, reason, and evidence (Patey).[4] Thus ''the immortal Pickwick'' of the novel's opening sentence has at first all the appearance of a busy old fool representing a contemporary version of immortal human folly—a ''humbug,'' as the one disgruntled club member, Mr. Blotton, angrily styles him (71). Not until Blotton introduces the face-saving linguistic talisman that bears the self-important club chairman's name, restoring good fellowship merely by conceding that ''humbug'' must be understood in a ''Pickwickian'' sense, are we certain, as readers, that we will have to calibrate our emotional response to Dickens's hero at a level well above contempt.

For the emotional fine-tuning required of *Pickwick*'s readers, the standard point of comparison is *Don Quixote*. Washington Irving drew it as early as 1841, observing that with both protagonists, ''we begin by laughing at him and end by loving him'' (Dickens, *Letters* 269n).[5] Yet, in the case of Pickwick's career, if not Quixote's, Irving's description fails to capture two crucial facts: first, that we begin by laughing at *and* loving a character whose very name has the power to dissolve conflict in chapter 1, and whose childlike innocence is plain by chapter 2; and second, that we end by laughing at him still, loving him more deeply, but having developed, only gradually, and increasingly in the novel's latter pages, an additional attitude: respect. This change has everything to do with Pickwick's entanglement in the legal system and immersion in the miserable world of the debtor's prison, experiences that open his eyes to a new reality. Dickens both signals Pickwick's new perspective and redirects our own through the symbolic use of hats.

Pickwick's distress in the debtor's prison is anything but ludicrous, even if the events that produce it partake of the absurd. In one of the novel's most famous passages, Pickwick witnesses the results of the "just and wholesome law which declares that the sturdy felon shall be fed and clothed, and that the penniless debtor shall be left to die of starvation" (686). Turning these sights over in his mind, gradually working himself "to the boiling-over point" as he reflects on the injustice they reveal, he stumbles with a new kind of absentmindedness into a room where he is stunned to discover, of all people, the swindler Jingle: "The general aspect of the room recalled him to himself at once; but he had no sooner cast his eyes on the figure of a man who was brooding over the dusty fire, than, letting his hat fall to the floor, he stood perfectly fixed, and immoveable, with astonishment" (687). "Astonishment"—Pickwick's very reaction to the mortifying gaze of onlookers in the pound—is here a reaction to the public degradation of a fellow human being who, however doubtful his morality, deserves better merely by virtue of his humanity. Phiz's illustration dutifully represents the hat upon the floor, a detail that here seems an emblem of Pickwick's perplexity and outrage rather than, as earlier, his bumbling incompetence.

As Pickwick's astonishment develops into a new sense of responsibility for his fellow creatures and a new determination to meet that responsibility through charity and patronage, the respect that other characters bear him shows itself repeatedly in conventional gestures of deference involving their own hats. Jingle and Job Trotter, the former dressed in clean linen supplied by Pickwick's benevolence, both remove their hats before him (731). Winkle, in a scene illustrated by Phiz as "Mr Winkle returns under extraordinary circumstances," kneels before Pickwick, hat in hand, when he announces his marriage to Arabella Allen while apologizing for his "imprudence" and belatedly seeking his leader's approval (756). Tony Weller punctuates Sam's declaration to remain with his master "vages or no vages, notice or no notice, board, or no board, lodgin' or no lodgin' " by "wav[ing] his hat above his head, and [giving] three vehement cheers" (887), in marked contrast to the hat-waving of those boys whose "Hurrah!" mocked Pickwick in the pound.

The image of Pickwick with which the novel's final paragraph leaves us marks the completed transformation of Dickens's hero with a last tip of the hat: Pickwick, we are told, "is known by all the poor people about, who never fail to take their hats off, as he passes, with great respect" (898).

Quixotic Metonymy: The Hat as Head

Thus, the play of hats in *Pickwick* tracks the reader's developing attitude toward the novel's protagonist, an attitude that in turn tracks the moral turn in Pickwick himself toward awareness and responsibility. The transformation is preeminently a mental or perspectival one, a matter of seeing and understanding. It takes place in the head, even if what matters most, as usual in Dickens, is its impact on the heart. The hat-play of *Pickwick* evokes this transformation metonymically.

Dickens's hat-for-head metonymy is highly conventional—hardly less so than that by which, in ordinary speech as well as literature, "head" itself substitutes for "mind." But it also has a specific antecedent in Cervantes, for when Don Quixote memorably dons an ordinary barber's basin, insisting that it is the "golden helmet of Mambrino," he not only takes on a ludicrous appearance that anticipates that of Pickwick in pursuit of his hat; he also expresses symbolically his imprisonment by delusion. Indeed, when he concedes to Sancho that the golden helmet has a basin-like appearance, but explains that this appearance must have resulted from an earlier owner's decision to melt most of the original for the sake of the gold, he expresses a deeper theme of Cervantes's novel, and one that would preoccupy Dickens, too: the human power and impulse to cling to error in spite of, and even by appeal to, inconvenient truth. Dickens would pursue this theme ruthlessly in his political satire of those he called "philosophers": adherents of an abstract theory of political economy that reduced all human motivation to self-interest despite obvious and copious evidence of human selflessness, a theory that forecast social happiness from laissez-faire policies which were already producing irrefutable, unconscionable misery. That Dickens had originally conceived Pickwick as a symbol of free-market quixotism is evident from his early references to the Society for the Diffusion of Useful Knowledge. Though in the ensuing numbers Pickwick's persistent immunity to simple fact receives a complicating overlay of romanticism (consistent with the nineteenth-century revisioning of Don Quixote himself: see Watt 193–227), the decision to force a confrontation between Pickwick and social reality in the Fleet—"This is no fiction" (686), the narrator insists of the injustice Pickwick finds there—nonetheless represents a return to the original conception of Pickwick as philosopher-fantasist as much as Pickwick's consequent benevolence and dignity represent a departure from the original conception of Pickwick as fool.

Or perhaps it would be truer to say that the philosopher-fantasist Pickwick never disappears from the novel, while the context of social misery that gives this conception political meaning must wait for its first appearance until close to the novel's end. Through most of *Pickwick Papers*, in other words, Pickwick symbolizes a generalized quixotism rather than the specific delusions of political economy. To this general stance, Sam Weller is the Panza-like foil. Appropriately, just as Pickwick's mentality is symbolized by his hat, so Sam's is reflected in his occupation. He is a polisher of shoes: a "boots."

This up-down polarity is a running joke of the novel, enacted not only through incident and plot but also through imagery and rhetoric, repeatedly reinforcing the contrast between, on the one hand, Pickwick's high-minded apriorism and inflexible adherence to lofty principle, and, on the other, Sam's down-to-earth respect for facts and circumstances. The sort of person who knows which end is up, Sam is not easily put in the position of the landlord in chapter 49, who is, as Sam gleefully puts it, "gammon[ed]" by a one-eyed bagman " . . . till he don't rightly know whether he's a standing on the soles of his boots or the crown of his hat" (773). By contrast, we are never surprised to find Pickwick in the position described in chapter 30: fallen through the ice, with nothing solid beneath his feet, and thoroughly submerged save for his "hat, gloves, and handkerchief," which, "floating on the surface," are now "all of Mr. Pickwick that anybody could see" (499–501). Nor should it surprise us that when Sam abandons Pickwick in the Fleet (as Pickwick fears, at least), it is Sam's boots that mark his absence:

> "Sam!" cried Mr. Pickwick, calling after him, "Sam! Here!"
> But the long gallery ceased to re-echo the sound of footsteps. Sam Weller was gone.   (692)

By his boots ye shall know him. Not that Sam's hat does not signify, but it is the sign of a mind that works in ways altogether different from his master's, a canny mind, a grounded mind. We know that he is not really abandoning Pickwick because of the way he departs, "fix[ing] his hat on his head with great precision and abruptly [leaving] the room" (692), clearly with a plan in mind. By this point we are well acquainted with Sam's capacity for planning, a capacity of which we have been reminded within the last few chapters because of his reunion with the "smart and pretty-faced servant-girl" Mary (421). In this reunion, one of the "tokens" that "one kiss or more, had passed between the parties" is the fact that "Sam's hat had fallen off a few moments before" (638), just as it had done over a dozen chapters earlier at the home of the justice Nupkins, where he and Mary first met, and where the two of them had discovered their mutual affection while recovering Sam's "mislaid" hat from a dark corner of the kitchen on their hands and knees (440).

The intentional fall of Sam's hat comically re-enacts the originary human fall into corporeality and sexuality, a fall that Dickens typically takes as a fact to be accepted rather than bemoaned. Sam and Mary, together with the various philoprogenitive men and women who inhabit Dickens's subsequent fiction (such as the Toodleses in *Dombey and Son*), are Henry Fielding's descendants fulfilling the longings of nature within parameters of legitimacy set by Samuel Richardson, and they represent a standing rebuke to what Dickens saw as the unnatural, unrealistic, and hypocritical program of sexual restraint preached by Malthusian advocates of Poor Law reform. The many unintentional falls of Pickwick's hat inscribe a different but not unrelated arc from pretense to reality, arrogance to humility and even humiliation, an arc repeated over and over in Dickens's works as the fall that pride inevitably goeth before; and this arc, too, had been traced by Fielding, himself directly inspired by Cervantes.[6] Fielding developed a mock-heroic idiom in which to perform both kinds of fall linguistically as the rhetorical counterpart of his narrative action, an idiom adopted at times by the narrator of *Pickwick*:

> The birds, who, happily for their own peace of mind and personal comfort, were in blissful ignorance of the preparations which had been making to astonish them, on the first of September, hailed it no doubt, as one of the pleasantest mornings they had seen that season. Many a young partridge who strutted complacently among the stubble, with all the finicking coxcombry of youth, and many an older one who watched his levity out of his little round eye, with the contemptuous air of a bird of wisdom and experience, alike unconscious of their approaching doom, basked in the fresh morning air with lively and blithesome feelings, and a few hours afterwards were laid low upon the earth. But we grow affecting: let us proceed.
>   In plain common-place matter-of-fact, then, it was a fine morning.
>   (327–28)[7]

Down comes the narrator's elevated style with a bump; and as he lampoons his own pretension, he establishes the credibility he will need to mock that of his characters.

Before Fielding, Alexander Pope had satirically juxtaposed the elevated and the mundane through a rhetorical gesture, known as *zeugma*, which links two nouns—one abstract, the other concrete—through a single verb.[8] Dickens adopts this device as well, but with the order of the nouns reversed (concrete preceding abstract), the number of nouns permitted to exceed two, and, in *Pickwick*, space reserved for hats. The effect may be simply comical, as in this example—''At length Mr. Stiggins, with several most indubitable symptoms of having quite as much pine-apple rum and water about him, as he could comfortably accommodate, took his hat, and his leave'' (456)—or pointedly satirical, as in this—

> Mr Pickwick stood in the principal street of this illustrious town [Muggleton], and gazed with an air of curiosity, not unmixed with interest, on the objects

around him. . . . There were, within sight, an auctioneer's and fire-agency office, a corn-factor's, a linen-draper's, a saddler's, a distiller's, a grocer's, and a shoe-shop—the last-mentioned warehouse being also appropriated to the diffusion of hats, bonnets, wearing apparel, cotton umbrellas, and useful knowledge.

(161)

Here Dickens punctures the claim to utility of Lord Brougham's "useful knowledge" simply by making it the culminating member in a catalogue of genuinely useful everyday items, where it seems as out of place as a hat in a shoe-shop.[9] Note that this final example of *Pickwick*'s characteristic rhetorical movement from the sublime to the sublunary satirizes the pretensions of Brougham's society in yet another way. Hats, shoes, shops, offices—all alike are "objects . . . within sight" of Pickwick's curious and utilitarian gaze as he stands in the center of Muggleton, enacting the quixotic attempt of the utilitarians to comprehend the human spectacle from a scientific perspective, a perspective that reduces everything, including knowledge itself, to the level of object. It is precisely this perspective that Pickwick must give over in order to free himself from error. At first blush this may seem an odd claim, since steady, empirical—that is, Wellerian—attention to the world of objects might appear the antidote to rather than the cause of quixotic hallucination. But the apparent contradiction is resolved when we recall that Pickwick views the human spectacle through spectacles of his own. Pickwick's spectacles stand metonymically for his head in a way that complements the symbolism of his hat.

"Bein' Only Eyes, You See, My Wision's Limited"

As noted earlier, Pickwick's quixotism does not take on a decidedly political cast until very near the end of Dickens's novel, when he discovers a world of misery beside which his own comfortable world of sport, punch, and parties stands starkly revealed as "fiction" (686). Even here, of course, the political message is blunted, partly by the fact that Pickwick returns to the dream-world of the Wardles and Dingley Dell but partly by the fact that Pickwick is, after all, only tenuously connected to utilitarianism.[10] Yet as we have seen, this tenuous connection has existed since the beginning of the novel in the tie between Pickwick and the utilitarian Society for the Diffusion of Useful Knowledge, and the connection is reinforced from time to time in slight but significant ways—for example, in the identification we have just witnessed between Pickwick the social investigator and Muggleton the avatar of laissez-faire (where "zealous advocacy of Christian principles" goes hand in hand with "a devoted attachment to commercial rights" and settled opposition to "any interference with the factory system" [161]); or in the repeated references to Pickwick as a "philosopher," references that invoke a contemporary synonym for utilitarianism: "philosophic radicalism."

The tenuousness of the connection is appropriate insofar as Pickwick takes an educated amateur's, a clubman's, interest in the amassing and diffusion of useful knowledge, not an ideologue's. He is, in other words, an altogether different intellectual and social type from Thomas Gradgrind of *Hard Times*, Dickens's most famous philosophic radical. In *Pickwick Papers* and in *Oliver Twist*—which began running concurrently with *Pickwick* after January, 1837—Dickens wields his satire directly against well-meaning men of means such as Pickwick and Mr. Brownlow, who, in trusting books over experience, are the kind of men easily duped by ideologues.[11] He wields it directly and more angrily against unthinking functionaries of ideology such as the workhouse board, who are "very sage, deep, philosophical men" (25); or the "elderly female" in charge of the "branch-workhouse" where Oliver is "farmed" until his ninth birthday, who proves herself a "very great experimental philosopher" in unabashedly pursuing her own self-interest by appropriating most of the weekly stipend intended for the maintenance of the children "to her own use" (20); or, most memorably and most extensively, the parish beadle Mr. Bumble, who, "snapping his fingers contemptuously," complains to the undertaker Sowerberry that juries are " 'ineddicated, vulgar, groveling wretches . . . [with] no more philosophy, nor political economy about 'em than that' " (38). He wields it most angrily—but only indirectly—against the ideologues themselves: indirectly insofar as this class of individuals goes unrepresented in the novel. *Oliver Twist* has no equivalent of Thomas Gradgrind. Dickens addresses the ideologues not through satire but through diatribe:

> I wish some well-fed philosopher, whose meat and drink turn to gall within him; whose blood is ice, whose heart is iron; could have seen Oliver Twist clutching at the dainty viands that the dog had neglected. I wish he could have witnessed the horrible avidity with which Oliver tore the bits asunder with all the ferocity of famine. There is only one thing I should like better; and that would be to see the Philosopher making the same sort of meal himself, with the same relish.   (41)

The duped and abstracted are a more dangerous class, arguably, than the propagators of ideology, if only because they are greater in number. For the same reason, however, their minds are better worth contending for. And more likely won: the moral awakening of a Pickwick, a Brownlow, even a Scrooge, carries more plausibility than that of a Gradgrind for precisely this reason. If only the duped and abstracted could be made to *see* the consequences in practice of ideas they accept as rational and necessary in theory, Dickens supposed, they might recognize the error of those ideas, or at least be moved to act with decency in spite of them, as does the bespectacled magistrate whose "gaze encountered the pale and terrified face of Oliver Twist" in the course of searching for the pen with which to consign Oliver to certain death as a chimney sweep, and whose consequent refusal to sanction the boy's indentures amounts, like his silencing of Mr. Bumble, to a "moral revolution" (34–35).[12]

Thus, about a year after Pickwick's being voted a pair of gold spectacles by his eponymous club in recognition of his learned efforts in the affair of the mysterious "inscription of unquestionable antiquity," the arrangement of marks and letters discovered by Pickwick on a small stone and explained by him in a "Pamphlet, containing ninety-six pages of very small print, and twenty-seven different readings" (227–28), Dickens would place Mr. Brownlow, a "respectable-looking personage, with a powdered head and gold spectacles"—Pickwick under another name—at a London bookstall, and describe him in the moments before his handkerchief was to be abstracted from his pocket by the Artful Dodger:

> He had taken up a book from the stall, and there he stood, reading away, as hard as if he were in his elbow-chair in his own study. It is very possible that he fancied himself there, indeed; for it was plain, from his abstraction, that he saw not the book-stall, not the street, not the boys, nor, in short, anything but the book itself: which he was reading straight through: turning over the leaf when he got to the bottom of a page, beginning at the top line of the next one, and going regularly on, with the greatest interest and eagerness.   (73)

The state of abstraction that makes possible the Dodger's act of abstraction is a state in which imagination takes precedence over reality, a state in which Brownlow can "fancy" himself to be somewhere other than where his boots are planted. That is precisely the state in which Pickwick pens his pamphlet on the stone, the state in which "three old gentlemen" who read the pamphlet cut off their eldest sons for doubting its veracity, the state in which "one enthusiastic individual [cuts] himself off prematurely, in despair of being able to fathom its meaning," the state in which the Pickwick Club not only awards the gold spectacles to Pickwick but expels Pickwick's nemesis Mr. Blotton—he who at the novel's opening had accused Pickwick of being a "humbug"—for daring to challenge Pickwick's fanciful scholarship with a dose of fact. Having bothered to track down the man who had sold Pickwick the stone, Blotton had learned that the inscription, carved by the man himself, said nothing more or less than, "BILL STUMPS, HIS MARK" (228).

The state of Pickwickian abstraction is a visionary state, one in which the eye, guided by an inner light, ranges far and wide, taking in everything but the material reality directly before it. The antithesis of Pickwickian abstraction is a determination to remain focused on that material reality and to abjure all knowledge claims not grounded in it, a determination best exemplified by Sam, during the trial of Bardell v. Pickwick, when challenged by Serjeant Buzfuz on his assertion that he did not witness Mrs. Bardell faint in Pickwick's arms. '' 'Yes, I have a pair of eyes,' '' replies Sam, '' 'and that's just it. If they wos a pair o' patent double million magnifyin' gas microscopes of hextra power, p'raps I might be able to see through a flight o' stairs and a deal door; but bein' only eyes, you see, my wision's limited' '' (573). Extended over an entire population, the consequence of Pickwick's wandering and abstracted gaze is at best absent-minded blindness to social suffering, at worst theory-mad denial of it. The consequence of Sam's ''limited'' but more concentrated vision, Dickens hoped, would be recognition of social suffering, followed by anger and action. The path to larger human sympathies lay, for Dickens, through a narrower and humbler conception of human knowledge and understanding.

So Wellerian empiricism turns out to be the antidote to quixotic hallucination after all. As Dickens sees the matter, utilitarianism's error, the error of reducing all things human to the status of ''objects,'' springs not from attentiveness to fact but from the distorting lens of utilitarianism's theoretical presuppositions, the ''gold spectacles'' through which it contemplates the human scene. It is a theoretical and not a mere methodological move to consider human beings, as utilitarianism does, apart from their own self-understandings, as we might consider hats, bonnets, cotton umbrellas, or the motion of the planets, because it is a move that puts human beings and their actions in the same class as these other phenomena. This classification then produces the relevant facts to be observed—''agents,'' ''actions,'' ''pleasure,'' ''pain,'' etc.—while providing no language for, and thus no means to observe, the entire realm of humanly constructed meanings, of the agent's experience as meaningful experience. The theoretical perspective of utilitarianism brings into focus a world from which the facts of experience—understanding ''experience'' as a horizon of meanings—have simply vanished.[13]

Needless to say, Dickens does not formulate his critique of utilitarianism in precisely the terms just used, the terms of such latter-day critics of positivist social science as Charles Taylor, Alasdair MacIntyre, and the coauthors George Lakoff and Mark Johnson, all of whom have absorbed the post-Dickensian vocabulary of Heidegger, Dewey, and Wittgenstein. Yet if the terms of his critique are different, the substance is notably similar, particularly in *Hard Times*, the novel in which Dickens comes closest to engaging utilitarianism and laissez-faire capitalism at the level of first principles. *Hard Times* memorably exposes not merely the callousness, but also the irrationality, of understanding and evaluating human affairs without reference to human meanings:

''And I find (Mr. M'Choakumchild said) that in a given time a hundred thousand persons went to sea on long voyages, and only five hundred of them were drowned or burnt to death. What is the percentage? And I said, Miss;'' here Sissy fairly sobbed as confessing with extreme contrition to her greatest error; ''I said it was nothing.''

''Nothing, Sissy?''

''Nothing, Miss—to the relations and friends of the people who were killed. I shall never learn.''   (48)

Of course, in form as well as theme, Dickens's fiction represents one vastly extended representation of the realm of meaning, his characters moving in a ''thoroughly nervous universe,'' an environment whose ''mode of existence is altered by the human purposes and deeds it circumscribes,'' a physical milieu ''impregnated with moral aptitude,'' so that his fiction recommends itself naturally to the type of critical effort to detail a ''Dickens World'' undertaken by Dorothy Van Ghent or J. Hillis Miller (Van Ghent 424–27). But it is in *Hard Times* that Dickens insists most directly and explicitly on the point—already adumbrated in *Pickwick*—that because philosophic radicalism as theory ignores the way human beings experience the social conditions it creates as practice, philosophic radicalism's conception of both human behavior and social relations is a flight of fancy, a triumph of the head over facts on the ground.

Gold Spectacles, Golden Helmets, and Iron Laws: Dickens and Imagination

Hard Times presents itself as a moral fable in which the ''man of facts,'' Thomas Gradgrind (8), learns the hard way that humans cannot live without ''fancy.'' It is framed by the image of Louisa gazing abstractedly at the fire—abstraction here representing an inevitable, life-preserving rebellion against her father's prohibition of wonder. It ends with a depiction of Sissy Jupe ''grown learned in childish lore; thinking no innocent and pretty fancy ever to be despised; trying hard to know her humbler fellow-creatures, and to beautify their lives of machinery and reality with those imaginative graces and delights, without which the heart of infancy will wither up'' (219). And yet, as we have just seen, *Hard Times* carries forward, while filling out and intensifying, a critique of the way abstraction and fantasy were perverting the social attitudes and policies of Victorian England, a critique that gradually took shape in *Pickwick* partly through the influence of the concurrently unfolding *Oliver Twist*. These two positions on the relative value of fact and fancy would appear to be in contradiction.

Catherine Gallagher has noted that *Hard Times* "exhibits a distrust of its own metaphors at the same time that it explicitly recommends them" (Gallagher, *Reformation* 160). In a more recent rhetorical analysis, she has also found paradox in the novel's treatment of work and play (Gallagher, *Body* 62–85). In analyzing these contradictions, she has emphasized their relationship to stylistic practices and thematic concerns peculiar to *Hard Times*, such as the use of metaphor to affirm and deny, simultaneously, an analogy between family and society, and the attempt to ground the legitimacy of novel-writing, as pleasure-producing entertainment, in its character as painstaking work.

Yet these paradoxes may also be explained as particular instances of the more fundamental fact-fancy paradox of *Hard Times*, a paradox that is by no means peculiar to that novel but rather already evident in *Pickwick*. For, as noted earlier, Pickwick-as-Quixote is never a simple object of scorn but is from the beginning lovable in spite of his blithe indifference to reality and even, like the romanticized Quixote of nineteenth-century criticism, because of it. When we are informed, in the account of the ridiculous Bill Stumps affair, that the name of the humbug-dispelling Mr. Blotton "will be doomed to the undying contempt of those who cultivate the mysterious and the sublime" (228), the voice of the informer does not come across as entirely ironic; it is, at some level, a voice in training for Dickens's most forceful denunciation of those who treat the mysterious and sublime as "humbug," published less than a decade later at Christmas of 1843. In the pages that follow the Pickwick Club's symbolic awarding of gold spectacles to their fearlessly fact-defying leader, numerous references to Pickwick's beaming, sparkling eyes (e.g., 469, 499, 578, 635)—inevitably conjoined with reminders of his cheerfulness and leading up to the final image of him, "his countenance lighted up with smiles," surrounded by his "visionary companions" (896) whose "every face shone forth joyously"—serve to remind us how much a true perception of reality depends, for Dickens, on the possession of an inner light. Thus, *Pickwick*'s critique of abstraction is in permanent tension with its romantic celebration of the imaginative and visionary. Nowhere is this tension more evident than in Dickens's angry narratorial declaration about conditions in the Fleet: "This is no fiction" (686). By the very force of its denial, this declaration highlights Dickens's investment in imagination as a mode of knowing: the fiction that he has devoted months to writing, and we to reading, must be valuable or neither of us would have come this far. Yet it necessarily revalues that mode of knowing as luxury, perhaps even dangerous luxury, rather than necessity. We interrupt this novel, it says, to bring you the following important news.[14]

In the end, the paradoxes that Gallagher identifies in *Hard Times* may have less to do with the particular narrative and metaphorical strategies of that novel than with Dickens's general inability to transcend the false dichotomy between reality and imagination, an inability that leaves him trapped in a language that posits fact and fiction, the literal and the metaphorical, work and play as distinct and often opposing categories. In our own time, philosophers and cognitive scientists have coined terms such as "constrained constructivism" (Hayles 27), "dynamic objectivity" (Levine 41) and "embodied realism" (Lakoff and Johnson, *Philosophy* 44) to represent variously nuanced versions of the view that human subjectivity and objective reality are mutually implicated in a deep and complex way.[15] Not only were these terms unavailable to Dickens, but the thought they attempt to capture is far from intuitive and, even for its adherents, conspicuously difficult to articulate. Under these circumstances, Dickens is more successful than one might have expected in dramatizing the interdependence of world and mind in all human understanding. Of the various titles that Dickens considered for the novel ultimately named *Hard Times*, one of those he rejected—*A Mere Question of Figures*—best reflects his perception of this interdependence, punning as it does on a word that can mean either "numbers" or "tropes" (Butt and Tillotson 201).[16] Gradgrind's dictum concerning facts—"Plant nothing else, and root out everything else" (7)—is itself a figure of speech, and his disciple M'Choakumchild attempts to teach the first principles of political economy through figurative tales about shipwrecks and starvation. These men of hard fact lapse into metaphor and narrative with good reason, some philosophers would argue, since for human beings the world is knowable only through such imaginative resources, and the social world is largely constituted by them.[17]

Largely, but not entirely. The hard men of fact also stand accused by Dickens of spinning narratives that distort the world they are meant to explain. That world contains the smoke of Coketown's factory chimneys, the "black canal," the river running "purple with ill-smelling dye" (22), the "killing airs and gases" bricked in by the "narrow courts upon courts, and close streets upon streets" (52) where Coketown's workers live in one-room dwellings too cramped for the mismarried to "live asunders" (in Stephen Blackpool's phrase) as the mismarried "great fok" do, and the law that prevents all but the moneyed mismarried from obtaining a second chance through divorce (59). The novel's title invokes these hard facts as surely as it does the hard attitude of the men who justify the facts' existence as natural and inevitable, and who propagate what Dickens calls the "popular fictions of Coketown": for example, "What one person can do, another can do," or "Show me a dissatisfied Hand, and I'll show you a man that's fit for anything bad" (90, 138). If one of Dickens's insights in *Hard Times* is *no knowledge unmediated by imagination*, another is *no knowledge through imagination alone*. And a third—worthy of Marx—is that those who disrespect the first of these truths provide the clearest demonstration of the second, blindly reifying golden desire as iron law.

Dickens holds these insights unsteadily, to be sure, and his periodic retreat from them is certainly disappointing. When he writes of imagination's capacity to "beautify" reality or, worse, of the need to cultivate in the working classes the "utmost graces of the fancies and affections, to adorn their lives so much in need of ornament" (219, 123), he clumsily positions imagination in a decorative rather than constitutive relationship to reality. Moreover, he does so in a way that mirrors his retreat from his own best intuitions about the social order's radical shortcomings. His call to let imagination ornament the hard lives of the working class echoes his exhortation to the captains of industry to grant their workers "some relaxation, encouraging good humour and good spirits, and giving them a vent—some recognized holiday, though it were but for an honest dance to a stirring band of music—some occasional light pie in which even M'Choakumchild had no finger" (24). Both these formulations permit Dickens's bourgeois readers to indulge the fantasy that a little adornment and an occasional holiday might compensate for industrial capitalism's denial of the worker's human need to exercise the transforming power of human imagination through work itself. Both smack of the bourgeois social-novelist's dispiritingly typical condescension, and both are clearly related to Victorian literature's equally dispiriting success at imagining the social body in ways that helped sustain bourgeois power.[18]

The philosophical and political failures of *Hard Times* are undoubtedly connected, then, and connected at a depth that is best described as a general failure of vision. This failure must be weighed against what Dickens, at his best, saw clearly and represented powerfully: the poverty, indeed the impossibility, of a stance toward the world in which, as subjects, we imagine ourselves to be disconnected observers of an "objective" reality. In assessing Dickens's achievement as a political writer, we are often admonished (by Richard Rorty, for example) to remember George Orwell's famous words about the face behind Dickens's novels: "the face of a man who is always fighting against something, but who fights in the open and is not frightened, the face of a man who is *generously angry*" (Orwell 460; qtd. in Rorty, "Philosophers" 15). This appeal to Dickens's good intentions, compelling as it may be, diverts our attention from Dickens's accomplishment as a critic of the positivist pretensions central to both utilitarianism and Victorian political economy. It invites us to look *at* Dickens rather than with him. We might do better to remember Dickens's own words about Pickwick at Muggleton. As we noted earlier, Pickwick gazing "with an air of curiosity, not unmixed with interest, on the objects around him," including the shoe-shop "appropriated to the diffusion of hats, bonnets, wearing apparel, cotton umbrellas, and useful knowledge," satirically evokes utilitarianism's aspiration toward a leveling, objectifying, disinterested point of view (161). It is this point of view, we said, that Pickwick's moral education requires him to abandon. But just as Gradgrind and Bounderby would unwittingly drop that point of view in turning to narrative and metaphor, so Pickwick here already betrays it by allowing his "curiosity" to be mixed with "interest." To be interested in that which one observes, notes Dewey (in a work plainly influenced by *Hard Times*), is to be "bound up with the possibilities inhering in objects . . . on the lookout for what they are likely to do to him; and . . . on the basis of . . . [this] expectation or foresight . . . eager to act so as to give things one turn rather than another" (120). Dickens saw that there is no other way to look at the world, even for supposedly disinterested utilitarians. He understood that it is not the fact of disinterestedness that does harm, but the fiction.

NOTES

1. Taking a Gradgrindian view of the matter, it is noteworthy that the 179 mentions in *Pickwick* constitute 17% of the total mentions in Dickens's fifteen novels (by comparison, *Pickwick* accounts for just under 8% of the novels' total word count), and represent more than twice the mean number of mentions per novel, 72. This analysis is based on word-incidence statistics from the *Victorian Studies Literary Archive Hyper-Concordance*. The *Concordance* was queried for incidences of the word *hat* only, not of related words such as *cap*, *night-cap*, or *headpiece*.

2. Though not concerned with Dickens, Fred Robinson's sophisticated treatment of the hat as literary and cultural symbol has influenced the present essay by example.

3. In his representation of the scene in which Pickwick pursues his windswept hat, Dickens's first illustrator for the novel, Robert Seymour, uses the same interplay of hats to underscore Pickwick's embarrassment and the spectators' delight at it. In "Mr Pickwick in chase of his hat," behind the central figures of Pickwick and his hat, there are three onlookers with hat in hand, one of them in much the same celebratory posture as the boy on the fence at the pound. Between the Seymour illustration in the second number and the Phiz illustration in the seventh, another Phiz illustration, placed in the third number, also makes prominent reference to hats, this time faithfully reproducing Dickens's mention of Pickwick's hat while supplying an unmentioned hat for Mr. Wardle. "Mr. Wardle and his friends under the influence of the salmon" places Pickwick on the left, "with his hands in his pockets and his hat cocked completely over his left eye" and Mr. Wardle in the center, his Phiz-provided hat cocked completely, and symmetrically, over his right eye (175). A moment later in the text, Pickwick, "taking off his hat and dashing it on the floor, and insanely casting his spectacles into the middle of the kitchen," offers up a joyful " 'Hurrah!' " (176). The hat-play of Phiz's "pound" engraving thus repeats—perhaps intentionally—that of Seymour's illustration for the "chase," while providing a neatly ironic contrast to that of Phiz's own "salmon" engraving and its narrative context. For extended

discussions of the relationship between text and illustrations in *Pickwick*, see Patten, "Boz, Phiz" 575–91, and Steig 24–50.

4. Dickens lambasted the British Association again in the "Mudfog Papers," published in *Bentley's Miscellany*, 1837. On Dickens's attitudes toward the SDUK, its founder Lord Henry Brougham, and the utilitarianism that informed the SDUK's activities, see Patten, "Portraits," and Newsom. On Dickens's attitude toward science in general, see Nixon.

5. Juliet McMaster notes that "The familiar comparison of Pickwick with Don Quixote began with the earliest reviews, and hasn't stopped yet" (75). For additional discussion of Pickwick and Quixote see Easson, Potau, and Welsh.

6. The title page of *Joseph Andrews* describes the novel as "written in imitation of the manner of Cervantes, author of *Don Quixote*."

7. Compare Fielding: "Now the Rake *Hesperus* had called for his Breeches, and having well rubbed his drowsy Eyes, prepared to dress himself for all Night; by whose Example his Brother Rakes on Earth likewise leave those Beds, in which they had slept away the Day. Now *Thetis* the good Housewife began to put on the Pot in order to regale the good man *Phoebus*, after his daily Labours were over. In vulgar Language, it was in the Evening when *Joseph* attended his Lady's Orders" (37–38).

8. E.g., in Pope's *The Rape of the Lock*, "Here, thou, great ANNA! whom three realms obey,/ Dost sometimes counsel take—and sometimes tea" (Dobrée 84).

9. See Preston on the origin of Dickens's Muggleton.

10. "Dickens may be trying to show innocence coming into a knowledge of the real world but Dingley Dell surely triumphs in the end, and the real world is held at bay while innocence nods happily" (Hardy, *Moral* 99).

11. Houston provides a detailed examination of the overlap between *Pickwick* and *Oliver Twist*.

12. "The generosity of Dickens', Stowe's, and King's anger comes out in their assumption that people merely need to turn their eyes toward those who are getting hurt and notice the *details* of the pain being suffered, rather than need to have their entire cognitive apparatus restructured" (Rorty, "Philosophers" 16).

13. "There is no such thing as 'behavior', to be identified prior to and independently of intentions, beliefs and settings" (MacIntyre 129). "The standard of utility or pleasure is set by man *qua* animal, man prior to and without any particular culture. But man without culture is a myth" (MacIntyre 161). "This is what is involved in seeing man as a self-interpreting animal. It means that he cannot be understood simply as an object among objects, for his life incorporates an interpretation, an expression of what cannot exist unexpressed, because the self that is to be interpreted is essentially that of a being who self-interprets" (Taylor 75).

14. Sean C. Grass treats this sentence not as an interruption of the novel's fictionality but rather as a continuation of those rhetorical devices, including the novel's title and the narrator's pretended status as a mere "editor," which insist on the novel's authenticity ("Pickwick" 25–26). Though *Pickwick* does abound in such devices, they are from the beginning plainly meant in jest and thus as part of the fiction. If they were not, and if "This is no fiction" were not meant to represent a break

with novelistic illusion, the rhetorical force of Dickens's exclamation would be largely lost.

15. Levine borrows the term "dynamic objectivity" from Evelyn Fox Keller.

16. Dahmane examines at length the interplay of literal and figurative speech in the novel as it relates to Dickens's critique of utilitarianism.

17. Influential claims for the epistemologically constitutive role of metaphor include those of Lakoff and Johnson (*Metaphors*) and Rorty (*Philosophy*). Claims for the constitutive role of narrative include those of MacIntyre (133) and Hardy ("Poetics" 5).

18. See, for example, Jaffe, "Spectacular Sympathy," and D. A. Miller. However, the conclusion of the present essay regarding Dickens's general epistemology points away from Jaffe's characterization of *A Christmas Carol* as a text that "turns its readers into spectators and positions them outside everything" (259).

WORKS CITED

Butt, John, and Kathleen Tillotson. *Dickens at Work*. London: Methuen, 1957.

Cervantes, Miguel de. *Don Quixote*. Trans. John Ormsby, ed. Joseph R. Jones and Kenneth Douglas. New York: Norton, 1981.

Christ, Carol T., and John O. Jordan, eds. *Victorian Literature and the Victorian Visual Imagination*. Berkeley: U of California P, 1995.

Dahmane, Rahzak. " 'A Mere Question of Figures': Measures, Mystery, and Metaphor in *Hard Times*." *Dickens Studies Annual* 23 (1994): 137–62.

Dewey, John. *Democracy and Education*. 1916. New York: Dover Books, 2004.

Dickens, Charles. *The Adventures of Oliver Twist; or, The Parish Boy's Progress*. Ed. Fred Kaplan. New York: Norton, 1993.

———. *Bleak House*. Ed. George Ford and Sylvère Monod. New York: Norton, 1977.

———. *Great Expectations*. Ed. Edgar Rosenberg. New York: Norton, 1999.

———. *Hard Times*. Ed. George Ford and Sylvère Monod. 2nd ed. New York: Norton, 1996.

———. *The Letters of Charles Dickens*. Ed. Madeline House and Graham Storey. Vol. 2. Oxford: Clarendon, 1969.

———. *The Posthumous Papers of the Pickwick Club*. Ed. Robert L. Patten. New York: Penguin, 1972.

Easson, Angus. "Don Pickwick: Pickwick and the Transformations of Cervantes." *Rereading Victorian Fiction*. Ed. Alice Jenkins and Juliet John. Basingstoke: Palgrave, 2002. 173–88.

Fielding, Henry. *Joseph Andrews*. Ed. Martin C. Battestin. Middletown: Wesleyan U P, 1967.

Gallagher, Catherine. *The Body Economic: Life, Death, and Sensation in Political Economy and the Victorian Novel*. Princeton: Princeton UP, 2006.

———. *The Industrial Reformation of English Fiction: Social Discourse and Narrative Form 1832–1867*. Chicago: U of Chicago P, 1985.

Grass, Sean C. "Pickwick, the Past, and the Prison." *Dickens Studies Annual* 29 (2000): 17–39.

Hardy, Barbara. *The Moral Art of Dickens*. London: Athlone, 1985.

———. "Towards a Poetics of Fiction: 3) An Approach through Narrative." *Novel: A Forum on Fiction* 2.1 (1968): 5–14.

Hayles, N. Katherine. "Constrained Constructivism: Locating Scientific Inquiry in the Theater of Representation." *Realism and Representation: Essays on the Problem of Realism in Relation to Science, Literature, and Culture*. Ed. George Levine. Madison: U of Wisconsin P, 1993. 27–43.

Houston, Gail Turley. "Broadsides at the Board: Collations of *Pickwick Papers* and *Oliver Twist*." *Studies in English Literature, 1500–1900* 31.4 (1991): 735–55.

Jaffe, Audre. "Spectacular Sympathy: Visuality and Ideology in Dickens's *A Christmas Carol*." *PMLA* 109 (March 1994): 254–65.

———. *Vanishing Points: Dickens, Narrative, and the Subject of Omniscience*. Berkeley: U of California P, 1991.

Lakoff, George, and Mark Johnson. *Metaphors We Live By*. Chicago: U of Chicago P, 1980.

———. *Philosophy in the Flesh: The Embodied Mind and Its Challenge to Western Thought*. New York: Basic Books, 1999.

Levine, George. *Dying to Know: Scientific Epistemology and Narrative in Victorian England*. Chicago: U of Chicago P, 2002.

MacIntyre, Alasdair. *After Virtue*. 2nd ed. Notre Dame: U of Notre Dame P, 1984.

McMaster, Juliet. *Dickens the Designer*. Totowa, NJ: Barnes and Noble, 1987.

Miller, D. A. *The Novel and the Police*. Berkeley: U of California P, 1988.

Miller, J. Hillis. *Charles Dickens: The World of His Novels*. Cambridge: Harvard U P, 1958.

Newsom, Robert. "Pickwick in the Utilitarian Sense." *Dickens Studies Annual* 23 (1994): 49–71.

Nixon, Jude V. " 'Lost in the Vast Worlds of Wonder': Dickens and Science." *Dickens Studies Annual* 35 (2005): 267–333.

Orwell, Sonia, and Ian Angus, eds. *The Collected Essays, Journalism and Letters of George Orwell.* Vol. 1. New York: Harcourt, 1968.

Patey, Douglas Lane. "Swift's Satire on 'Science' and the Structure of *Gulliver's Travels.*" *ELH* 58 (1991): 809–39.

Patten, Robert L. "Boz, Phiz, and Pickwick in the Pound." *ELH* 36.3: 575–91.

———. "Portraits of Pott: Lord Brougham and *The Pickwick Papers.*" *The Dickensian* 66 (1970): 205–24.

Pope, Alexander. *Alexander Pope's Collected Poems.* Ed. Bonamy Dobrée. 2nd ed. London: Everyman, 1956.

Potau, Mercedes. "Notes on Parallels between *The Pickwick Papers* and *Don Quixote.*" *Dickens Quarterly* 10.2 (1993): 105–10.

Preston, Edward G. "Notes on Muggleton and the Muggletonians." *Dickens Quarterly* 3.3 (1986): 129–31.

Robinson, Fred Miller. *The Man in the Bowler Hat: His History and Iconography.* Chapel Hill: U of North Carolina P, 1993.

Rorty, Richard. "Philosophers, Novelists, and Intercultural Comparisons." *Culture and Modernity: East-West Philosophic Perspectives.* Ed. Eliot Deutsch. Honolulu: U of Hawai'i P, 1991. 3–20.

———. *Philosophy and the Mirror of Nature.* Princeton: Princeton UP, 1979.

Steig, Michael. *Dickens and Phiz.* Bloomington: Indiana UP, 1978.

Taylor, Charles. *Human Agency and Language: Philosophical Papers.* Vol. 1. Cambridge: Cambridge UP, 1985.

Van Ghent, Dorothy. "The Dickens World: A View from Todgers's." *Sewanee Review* 58 (1950): 419–38.

The Victorian Literary Studies Archive Hyper-Concordance. Ed. Mitsuharu Matsuoka. 30 July 2004 <http://victorian.lang.nagoya-u.ac.jp/concordance>.

Watt, Ian. *Myths of Modern Individualism: Faust, Don Quixote, Don Juan, Robinson Crusoe.* Cambridge: Cambridge UP, 1996.

Welsh, Alexander. "Waverly, Pickwick, and Don Quixote." *Nineteenth-Century Fiction* 22.1 (1967): 19–30.

The Erotics of *Barnaby Rudge*

Natalie McKnight

The eroticism of Barnaby Rudge *has been undervalued. In this novel, Dickens plays both with and against Victorian gender norms to heighten sexual tensions between Dolly and Hugh, Dolly and her father, and Emma and Haredale. Dickens further fuels the eroticism of these relationships by aligning it with the violence of the Gordon Riots and the tensions between numerous gendered polarities, such as the urban and the pastoral, parents and children, and past and present. Phiz's suggestive illustrations extend Dickens's erotic descriptions. Barnaby, however, seems devoid of erotic charge, which may explain why the eponymous novel failed to tickle the fancy of many readers.*

In a *Dickens Studies Annual* article in 1996, Brian McCuskey made the outrageous statement that *The Pickwick Papers* is "one of the sexiest of Victorian novels" (258).[1] I would like to offer a similarly outrageous thesis: *Barnaby Rudge* deserves the claim as the most erotic Dickens novel. The novel's energy owes so much to eros, in fact, that I frankly wonder why it hasn't been more popular with scholars and the general readership (although I will suggest some reasons for this by the end of the essay). Eros has never been considered Dickens's forte as a writer. Humor, pathos, sentiment, linguistic pyrotechnics, strong rhetorical passages, a journalist's eye for detail, biting criticism of wrongheaded institutions, richly metaphoric atmospheres—these qualities are what we usually celebrate about Dickens. Relatively little critical attention has been paid to the erotic energy of his narratives. But it *is* there, and Dickens uses it not just for the sake of creating

---

interest and titillation, but also for connecting the romantic plots to the Gordon Riot plot and for analyzing the dangerous nature of sexual desire and rigid, stereotypical gender roles.

In this essay, I would like to examine how Dickens plays with and against Victorian gender norms in order to heighten the eroticism of certain scenes and characters, particularly scenes involving Dolly, Hugh, Joe, Varden, Emma, and Haredale. By heightening contrasts between peace and violence, the pastoral and the urban, weakness and strength, Dickens also heightens the contrasts between male and female and thereby creates an erotic charge based on polarization and magnetism. The contrasts suggest that Dickens locates sexual energy not only in the traditional distinctions between masculinity and femininity but also in danger; conversely, in the absence of such danger, eroticism dissipates. In *Erotic Faith: Being in Love from Jane Austen to D. H. Lawrence*, Robert Polhemus traces similarities between Dickens and Freud in this tendency to ally eroticism with the forbidden and to see virtue as having "inhibiting effects" on desire (152). He notes in particular the role of incest in promoting aberrant desires in *Great Expectations*. Similarly, in *Barnaby Rudge* eros sparks only when the object of desire is forbidden either by incest taboos or differences in class.

Dickens establishes numerous bold contrasts as he builds an erotically charged atmosphere: the snug and somnambular Maypole crew vs. the wildly violent rioters; the dark streets of London that present "at every turn some obscure and dangerous spot wither a thief might fly for shelter" (137; ch. 16) vs. the quiet meadows that Barnaby traverses where "nodding branches seem to bathe and sport [and] sweet scents of summer air breath[e] over fields of beans or clover" (372; ch. 45); the immaculate Chester vs. his brutish bastard Hugh; Protestant vs. Catholic; fathers vs. sons. John Bowen in his introduction to the Penguin edition of *Barnaby Rudge* states that the "novel is constantly drawn to vivid contrasts" (xviii) and offers as examples the polarities of order and disorder, good and evil, innocence and guilt (xxviii), "inside and outside, the past and present," (xxix); Bowen also points to contrasts between the novel itself and the magazine, *Master Humphrey's Clock*, that it originally appeared in, and ultimately between the genres of historical fiction and melodrama, differences which, as Bowen asserts, create a conflict that in part accounts for "the book's continuing and disturbing power" (xix). The only other Dickens novel that emphasizes contrasts so forcefully happens also to be the only other historical fiction that Dickens wrote, *A Tale of Two Cities*, with its famous opening that introduces an extended series of contrasts, beginning with "It was the best of times, it was the worst of times."

Perhaps the contrast between past and present that naturally occurs in any historical fiction nudged Dickens toward thinking in terms of contrasts in general. In *Barnaby Rudge* these tend to align themselves around the polarities of masculine and feminine, with the dangerous streets of London, the violent mob, the tyranny of fathers, and the seriousness and intellectual weight of history all resonate with stereotypical maleness; while the pastoral scenes, the wombish Maypole Inn, the relative helplessness of children, and the emotional excesses of melodrama suggestive of stereotypical femininity. The Gordon Riot scenes derive a great deal of their energy and excitement from the conflation of these polarities, their mating, if you will: the dangerous criminality of the city seethes into the country, children rebel against their parents, women behave as badly as men, Catholics join the anti-Catholic riots, and history shows itself to be, at some points, no different than melo-drama. The moment that most vividly captures this meeting and mating of polarities is the attack on the Maypole Inn, in which the mob thrusts the pole through the inn's windows, an image that symbolically conflates sex and violence, and as such, I would argue, serves as the central metaphor of the novel (454; ch. 54).[2] In this image, a kind of architectural rape scene, the city has forced itself on the country, the violent on the peaceful, the guilty on the innocent, a symbol of maleness (the pole) on a symbol of femaleness (the window).

Dickens asserts the connection between sex and violence in much more human, more erotic, and more metonymic ways, however. Hugh's accosting Dolly in the woods, the subsequent kidnapping of Dolly and Emma, Miggs's farcical fears/hopes of being molested, and the general orgy of the riots offer the best examples. In order to appreciate the eroticism of Hugh's encounter with Dolly, we must first focus on Dickens's initial sexually charged descriptions of Dolly. John Carey describes her as one of the most "succulent" of Dickens's heroines, with few others offering any serious competition (167). Perhaps because of her succulence, Dolly Varden raised more interest than most of the other characters in *Barnaby Rudge*: a much-edited version of the novel came out around 1870 called "Dolly Varden: The Little Coquette," and there was a Dolly Varden vogue in fashions in the 1870s, "stimulated by the Christie's sale of W. P. Frith's portrait of Dolly, painted for Charles Dickens in 1843 and sold at auction in July 1870" (Rice 41–43). The fashion in turn inspired a host of Dolly Varden comic songs. John Bowen points out that she also lent her name "to a buffer on a railway tender, as well as a species of trout and a kind of horse" (xxxi). While some have seen this Victorian fascination with Dolly as dated quaintness, I think the interest is hardly surprising as Dickens invested her with significant sexual energy. To begin with, her given name sets the erotic tone since, according to the *OED*, it has been used for centuries to refer to prostitutes and mistresses. Then, consider Dickens's description of her in chapter 19:

As to Dolly, there she was again, the very pink and pattern of good looks, in a smart little cherry-coloured mantle, with a hood of the same drawn over her head, and upon the top of that hood, a little straw hat trimmed with cherry-coloured ribbons, and worn the merest trifle on one side—just enough in short to make it the wickedest and most provoking headdress that ever malicious milliner devised. And not to speak of the manner in which these cherry-coloured decorations brightened her eyes, or vied with her lips, or shed a new bloom on her face, she wore a cruel little muff, and such a heart-rending pair of shoes, and was so surrounded and hemmed in, as it were, by aggravations of all kinds, that when Mr. Tappertit, holding the horse's head, saw her come out of the house alone, such impulses came over him to decoy her into the chaise and drive off like mad, that he would unquestionably have done it, but of certain uneasy doubts besetting him as to the shortest way to Gretna Green.

(165–66; ch. 19)

It's not just that Dolly is pretty—she's provokingly pretty, tantalizing, sexy, with all the bloom of youth, innocence, and virginity mixed dangerously with conscious attempts to attract. It's the consciousness of these attempts that inspires Dickens to use words such as "provoking," "cruel," "malicious," and "wicked" in reference to standard items of feminine dress of the late eighteenth century. As Patricia Ingham points out, the description suggests that "this is not only how male eyes see her but also how she sees herself and how she wishes to be seen. For her, as for her admirer, clothes have equal status with her body as the weapons of provocative cruelty" (23).

Of course, the metaphoric aspects of Dolly's outfit emphasize the eroticism, particularly her "cruel little muff." "Muff" has been a well-known slang term for female genitalia since the seventeenth century; Dickens's reference to Dolly's "cruel little muff" actually makes more sense on the slang level than it does in reference to haberdashery. (The word later becomes a slang term for a prostitute but, according to the *OED*, did not have this meaning until the early twentieth century). In illustrating Dolly in this outfit, Hablot Browne, who usually followed Dickens's instructions quite closely, chose to ignore the adjective "little' " in Dickens's description of the muff and instead portrayed the fur as large and prominent—fully one-fourth the size of Dolly, in fact (fig. 1). The word "cherry," repeated twice in this passage, also carries erotic overtones as it has been used to describe lips since the Renaissance, and probably before (e.g., the *OED* refers to Sidney's "Opening the cherrie of her lips") and by extension has come down into slang usage as a reference to virginity and female sexual anatomy. Consider also the point of view of this description of Dolly: one could argue that the third-person narrator is taking on the perspective of Simon Tappertit when he writes how provoking and cruel her beauty was, but he doesn't bring Simon in until the end of the passage. It seems as if the narrator, and by extension Dickens, feels provoked by the eroticism of her description and then later attributes the provocation to Simon.

Dickens presents, then, a highly eroticized portrait of Dolly—again, not just a pretty one as is the case with his descriptions of Kate Nickleby or Rose Maylie, both of which suggest loveliness without much sexual charge. Dickens's description of Rose Maylie offers comparatively few concretes; in fact, Dickens hardly establishes any physical attributes for her, and she seems poised to ascend to heaven at any moment: "Cast in so slight and exquisite a mould, so mild and gentle, so pure and beautiful, that earth seemed not her element, nor its rough creatures her fit companions. The very intelligence that shone in her deep blue eye and was stamped upon her noble head, seemed scarcely of her age or of the world" (235; bk. 2, ch. 7). As Patricia Ingham notes, many of Dickens's young female characters are defined by their "lack of physicality" (18). Kate Nickleby is cut from the same cloth: like Rose, she is "slight" and "beautiful" and around "seventeen" (36; ch. 3). Their age is the most specific aspect in both their descriptions, and it allies them with Mary Hogarth, Dickens's sister-in-law, who died in his arms at the age of seventeen. In a letter dated 17 May 1837 he wrote that he had loved her, after his wife, " 'more deeply and fervently than anyone on earth' " (qtd. in Johnson 1: 197). Rose and Kate, therefore, are objects of veneration, not ones to be invested with sexual energy. Dolly, clearly, is another story.

Having established Dolly as the embodiment of eros, Dickens confronts her in the woods in the two chapters following her description with Hugh, a creature as much beast as man, whose animalistic behaviors and appetites are emphasized repeatedly. As Barbara Stuart points out, "he spends most of his time in the barn" and refers to himself as a " 'steed' " (30). Dickens describes him as "a dreadful idle vagrant fellow . . . half a gipsy . . . always sleeping in the sun in summer, and in the straw in winter" (88; ch. 10); one who "has never lived in any way but like the animals he has lived among, [and] *is* an animal" (100; ch. 11). With little to lose in terms of status or respect, Hugh expresses his sexual desires openly to Dolly, a freedom not shared by middle-class characters. Brian McCuskey, in his essay on *Pickwick Papers*, demonstrates how Dickens displaces eroticism onto domestic servants; in *Barnaby Rudge*, Dickens moves it out into the stables with Hugh.

So Dolly and Hugh, the two most sexually charged characters in the novel—perhaps anywhere in Dickens—are brought together abruptly and alone in the woods as night is coming on. Dolly at first utters Hugh's name with relief and pleasure as she had thought she was being stalked by a stranger, but then the "coarse bold admiration in his look" terrifies her. "He stood gazing at her like a handsome satyr" Dickens writes (176; ch. 21). As John Carey points out, in Dickens's fiction nothing enhances a girl's attractiveness so much as fear: "the male appetite needs to be whetted by the fearfulness of its prey," he argues, and certainly this seems to be the case with Hugh (167). Dolly bolts past Hugh, but as he catches up to her, and she can feel his breath on her neck, he draws her arm through his, and then puts his arm around her waist. Dickens emphasizes the contrasts between them—Hugh's "strong grasp," Dolly's smallness that makes her seem like "a bird" (178; ch. 21). Dickens seems to delight, as does Hugh, in Dolly's vain efforts at resistance: " 'Ha ha ha! Well done mistress! Strike again. You shall beat my face, and tear my hair, and pluck my beard up by the roots, and welcome, for the sake of your bright eyes. Strike again mistress. Do. Ha ha ha! I like it!' " Soon, she is "panting" in Hugh's "encircling arms," and he's stealing kisses from her, only to be stopped by the arrival of Joe (178–79; ch. 21). It's the stuff of bodice-ripper romances, although the diction is finer, of course. Her later capture by Hugh and the mob really *is* a bodice-ripper, as Dickens tells us explicitly that her dress is ripped and her bosom heaving from her violent struggles with Hugh (491; ch. 59), which, he again, of course, enjoys (fig. 2).

To turn to Phiz's first illustration of Hugh and Dolly again (fig. 1), we can see how he further plays with the scene's eros by turning the figures away from each other, but provocatively: Dolly turns her backside to Hugh but glances over her shoulder, while Hugh leans back, pelvis thrust Dolly-ward. The branches of the trees above them interlock, even if the man and woman do not, the one above Dolly pretty with greenery, the one above Hugh, bare and bent toward Dolly and her tree like a threatening hand.

Both these scenes play on what Freud would argue are widespread masochistic and sadistic impulses in human nature, indicated by the prevalence of the "child is being beaten" fantasy that so many of Freud's patients reported to him. Dickens's scenes play out two stages of the fantasy that Freud's patients described: in the first stage, the patient fantasizes that she is being beaten by the father or the father figure and associates the image with a feeling of pleasure, followed by guilt; Freud sees this as a regressive fantasy in which the girl punishes herself for early sexual urges. In later stages, the child (and the fantasy occurs in both girls and boys) fantasizes that another child, almost always a male, is being beaten by some male authority figure. Freud notes that witnessing real beatings produces no sensation of pleasure at all in these patients, just the opposite, and so the fantasy is exclusively a psychological construct, leading in adults to tendencies toward masochism, sadism, or both, although usually masochism in women ("'A Child'" 172–82). Along the same lines, feminist Sandra Bartky writes that "standard heterosexual desire in women has often a masochistic dimension," and "male power [and] male dominance itself [are] erotically charged" (47). Psychoanalyst Helene Deutsch argues that masochism has probably evolved as a necessary aspect of female sexuality since women must endure so much physical pain "in menstruation, the initial sex act, and childbirth" (qtd. in Bartky 53). Women also have a tendency toward masochism, Bartky argues, because they

Fig. 1. Hablot Browne's "Hugh Accosts Dolly Varden"

Fig. 2. Hablot Browne's "Dolly in Hugh's Arms"

are taught to be more repressed and guilty about sexual desires, so that "pleasure must be inflicted upon [them]" (53). Widespread tendencies toward masochism and sadism in adults of both sexes can help to explain the appeal of the Dolly and Hugh scenes: they have a little something for everyone—sadism, masochism, and raw heterosexual energy, and since no one really gets hurt, it's a guilt-free sexual fantasy; not a bad bit of eroticism for the author of hearth, home, and Christmas to pen.[3]

The power differential between Hugh and Dolly, which is an important characteristic of the scenes' eroticism since it underscores distinctions between males and females, gets echoed in sexually charged father/daughter scenes, particularly ones between Dolly and her father, Gabriel Varden.[4] Dolly is a classic example of what Freud called the "erotic libidinal type," which he describes as "persons whose main interest—the relatively largest amount of their libido—is focused on love. Loving, but above all being loved, is for them the most important thing in life" ("Libidinal Types" 248). Dolly's main mode for interaction with others is flirtation, even when that "other" is her father. Dickens first introduces Dolly with a "roguish face" as she leans out her window to hush her father below, "pointing archly to the window underneath" to indicate that her mother is still asleep (40; ch. 4). "Roguish" and "archly" both suggest a flirtatious affect, as does her next line, a playful scolding of her father: " 'How cruel of you to keep us up so late this morning, and never tell us where you were, or send us word!' " (40; ch. 4). The fact that she presides over the breakfast table instead of her mother in this chapter adds to the impression that she is more like a young wife than a daughter to him, one of several father/daughter pairs in Dickens, as Patricia Ingham argues, who experience a "dissolution of conventional kinship patterns [that] involves the development of unorthodox sexual bonds" (126). Clearly, Sim feels jealous of their relationship, and the third-person narrator once again takes this apprentice's perspective when he states,

> Fathers should never kiss their daughters when young men are by. It's too much. There are bounds to human endurance. So thought Sim Tappertit when Gabriel drew those rosy lips to his—those lips within Sim's reach from day to day, and yet so far off. He had a respect for his master, but he wished the Yorkshire cake might choke him.   (43; ch. 4)

If the kiss had no erotic charge, and seemed purely parental, Sim would hardly feel such jealousy and hatred toward Varden at this moment. Dickens hastens to suggest the erotic connection between father and daughter by having Sim react to it in such a manner. By putting the reaction in the third-person narrative voice and not immediately indicating that it's Sim's interior monologue being expressed, Dickens seems once again to validate and share, at least in part, Sim's perspective. Yet, as author/authority, Dickens can also be seen as the ultimate father of the novel, the father behind Dolly's father. In his repeated enjoyment of the tantalizing details of Dolly's dress and manner, Dickens allies himself with both the petted, adored father and the jealous would-be lover.

Hablot Browne, always quick to pick up on cues from Dickens, underscores the erotic connection between father and daughter in two illustrations.[5] The first occurs in chapter 41 (fig. 3). At first glance, it is difficult to discern what Dolly is doing bent over with her head at the level of her father's midsection. Consulting the text, one finds that she is tying Varden's sash as he prepares for a parade of the Royal East London volunteers. But the composition of this scene is almost embarrassingly suggestive, with the odd position of Dolly's head (does one really need to bend over so far to tie a sash?), and her hands holding the sash up to her face (although the shadowy nature of the middle of the illustration makes it difficult to discern what she is holding). Adding to the suggestiveness of the scene, Miggs and Mrs. Varden look on disapprovingly, and the sword, a rather redundant phallic symbol in the picture, parallels the position of the dangling sash. One need not be Freud to find the imagery here sexually provocative.

The second illustration appears in chapter 71, as Varden, Haredale, Joe, and Edward rescue Dolly and Emma from their captors (fig. 4). In this picture, also by Hablot Browne, Dolly kisses Varden on the lips, and Emma faints in

Fig. 3. Hablot Browne's "The Locksmith Dressing for a Parade"

Haredale's arms, while the men who are supposed to be the lovers hover in
the background, seriously disgruntled as the father figures get all the good
body contact that they themselves want. Both Joe and Edward look as if they
feel just as Sim did in the breakfast scene—threatened by the overly intimate
father/daughter relationship. Hablot Browne did not project his own interpretation on this illustration; it simply captures what Dickens describes in chapter 71, with the young men hanging around in the background of the reunion
like "strangers" and only being brought into the scene "after a long time"
(596; ch. 71).[6]

The power differential between the fathers and daughters in these scenes
heightens their eroticism. Fathers naturally serve as authority figures in their
families, but Haredale's and Varden's power seems strengthened by their
positions as jailers: Varden, a locksmith, has the keys to Newgate and keeps
Miggs locked up in the attic during the riots; Haredale virtually imprisons
Emma in his estate, spying on her and intercepting her letters.[7] In *The History
of Sexuality* Foucault analyzes the intimate connection between pleasure
and power:

> the pleasure that comes of exercising a power that questions, monitors, watches,
> spies, searches out, palpates, brings to light; and on the other hand the pleasure

Fig. 4. Hablot Browne's "A Joyful Meeting"

> that kindles at having to evade this power, flee from it, fool it, or travesty it. . . .
> Capture and seduction, confrontation and mutual reinforcement: Parents and
> children, adults and adolescents, educator and students . . . all have played this
> game continually. . . . These attractions, these evasions, these circular incite-
> ments have traced around bodies and sexes not boundaries not to be crossed,
> but *perpetual spirals of power and pleasure.*   (45)

Foucault's analysis of the insidious erotics of power overlaps with Freud's
analysis of the insidious erotics of familial bonds; Dickens portrays the erotics
of both.

By showing the eros of power influencing family dynamics, Dickens draws
a thematic connection between Dolly's "wicked" and "malicious" entice-
ments, the power of fathers, and the violent orgy of the riots, where men,
women and children gorge themselves on scalding spirits while they burn
down seats of power. They aren't the same, of course, but they are in the
same spectrum. The sexual energy of the Hugh and Dolly scene in the woods
is like a spark that contributes to the raging fires of the later riots. Consider
how Dickens describes the rioters as exhibiting a lust for violence: "There
were men who rushed up to the fire, and paddled in it with their hands as if

in water; and others who were restrained by force from plunging in, to gratify their deadly longing. . . . But of all the howling throng not one learnt mercy from, or sickened at, these sights; nor was the fierce, besotted, senseless rage of one man glutted'' (462; ch. 55). The passions are all of a piece, it seems—''the drunken energy of life turning into a frenzied dance of death,'' as Steven Marcus writes (210). Sexual and violent passions share elements of danger, abuses of power, and destructiveness, and there is no end to trying to satisfy them. Everyone who is susceptible to sexual desire, Dickens seems to imply, is susceptible to losing control of that energy, becoming violent, abusing power, or letting oneself be abused by it. As Polhemus writes, Dickens ''can imagine sex only as a quick burst of flame that throws people into hideous conjugal postures and leaves them in agony and weakness'' (159). For Dickens, ''the sexual libido was the disruptive enemy of fidelity and religious idealism''; left unchecked or repressed too long it can provoke as much violence as the worst social injustices. In his view of the dangers of unchecked or overly repressed sexual energy, he prefigures Freud's notion that the sex drive undermines civilization and that the greatest achievements of humans come from its sublimation, which is not the same thing as its repression (Polhemus 160).

In relation to the power erotics described above, Barnaby truly seems an ''innocent'' in every meaning of the word; his idiocy enables him to escape in part both gender norms—those polarities that ignite sparks—and, therefore also escape desires for sex and violence. With effeminate accessories—feathers, lace, ruffles, and ribbons (35; ch. 3), and the occasional intuitive insight usually attributed to women, yet the physical strength and courage in the face of death usually attributed to men, Barnaby is a wonderfully androgynous hero, a particularly addled Jack Sparrow. But while Dickens had the courage to make an idiot his main character, he didn't have the stomach to make him sexual. At no point does Barnaby suggest any erotic impulse; in fact, he never even appears in any of the erotic scenes mentioned above, not even in the erotically charged mob scenes, although he does take part in the riots. Barnaby seems to be asexual, or pre-sexual, although Freud would argue there's no such thing. He truly is the sexual innocent that McCuskey shows Pickwick is *not*. Since Dickens relates erotic desire with power differentials and violence, the lack of eros in Barnaby truly does free him from any guilt in the mob's attacks or in the subtler power abuses in the novel. But the absence of sexual energy may have also freed him of much interest for Dickens's readers. The eponymous hero's disengagement from the novel's troubling but exciting erotics may be one of the reasons the book failed to earn a large, enthusiastic readership. The sexually charged Dolly offered readers much more pleasure.[8]

NOTES

1. McCuskey argues that traditional perceptions of Pickwick's sexual innocence miss ways in which the novel amplifies "the scope of bourgeois sexual experience," first in the below stairs realm of servants that offers "alternative forms of erotic expression" and second in the homoeroticism of Pickwick's and Sam's relationship (246–47, 261–64).

2. Barbara Stuart reads this moment as "Hugh's unleashed sexual vitality intent on destroying his restrictions" (34).

3. Dickens portrays Miggs and Sim Tappertit as a comic inversion of Dolly and Hugh, with Miggs playing the sadist role to some extent. While Dolly is plump and blooming, Miggs is wizened. While Hugh is strong and animalistic, Sim is a little dandy who seems more enamored of his own shapely legs than those of anyone else. Miggs plays the aggressor and wielder of power in her relationship with Sim—locking him out of the house in chapter 9 to exert some influence on him.

4. Patricia Ingham observes how Dickens repeatedly puts fathers and daughters "into the place conventionally filled by girl and lover," in *Dombey and Son*, *Little Dorrit*, and *Bleak House* most notably (119–20, 125–26). Similarly, Polhemus comments on "the interpenetration of filial and parental desire with erotic desire," particularly in *Great Expectations* (155).

5. As J. R. Harvey points out, in *Victorian Novelists and Their Illustrators*, Browne developed a new, more realistic style of illustration for *Barnaby Rudge*, one that suited historical fiction but still maintained an element of the grotesque for characters such as Dennis and Gashford. Harvey finds Browne particularly skilled in capturing through "dense crowding, tumultuous movement, and variety of action" the "violent ecstasy" of the riots (126–28).

6. It is important to note that Dickens always worked closely with Browne in the illustration process, giving him suggestions for illustrations and approving or emending the initial sketches (Patten 58–59).

7. John P. McGowan asserts that "Haredale and Varden stand in symmetrical relation to two of the evil fathers, Chester and Rudge," because the evil fathers have married the women the supposedly good fathers had courted (47). The parallel is indeed there, but it is complicated by Haredale's and Varden's authoritative actions and the unsettling eroticism of their relations with their daughters. As McGowan remarks, all the novel's fathers, good and bad, tend to "obstruct the natural sequence of time" by "preventing the younger generation's ascension to adulthood, an obstruction most obviously revealed by parental opposition to their children's desire to marry" (44).

8. I am indebted to members of the Dickens Society in attendance at the Dickens Symposium in Belfast (August 2006) for their comments on an earlier version of this essay.

WORKS CITED

Bartky, Sandra Lee. *Femininity and Domination: Studies in the Phenomenology of Oppression.* New York: Routledge, 1990.

Carey, John. *The Violent Effigy: A Study of Dickens's Imagination.* Boston: Faber, 1973.

Dickens, Charles. *Barnaby Rudge.* Ed. John Bowen. New York: Penguin, 2003.

———. *Nicholas Nickleby.* Ed. Mark Ford. New York: Penguin, 1987.

———. *Oliver Twist.* Ed. Philip Horne. New York: Penguin, 2003.

Foucault, Michel. *The History of Sexuality.* Vol. 1. Trans. Robert Hurley. New York: Vintage, 1990.

Freud, Sigmund. " 'A Child Is Being Beaten.' A Contribution to the Study of the Origin of Sexual Perversions." 1919. *Collected Papers.* Vol. 2. Trans. under supervision of Joan Riviere. London: Hogarth, 1953. 172–201.

———. "Family Romances." 1909. *Collected Papers.* Vol. 5. Ed. James Strackey. London: Hogarth, 1971. 74–78.

———. "Libidinal Types." 1931. *Collected Papers.* Vol. 5. Ed. James Strackey. 247–51.

Harvey, J. R. *Victorian Novelists and Their Illustrators.* New York: New York UP, 1971.

Ingham, Patricia. *Dickens, Women and Language.* Toronto: U of Toronto P, 1992.

Johnson, Edgar. *Charles Dickens: His Tragedy and Triumph.* Vol. 1. New York: Simon and Schuster, 1952.

Marcus, Steven. *Dickens: From Pickwick to Dombey.* New York: Basic Books, 1965.

McCuskey, Brian W. " 'Your Love-Sick Pickwick': The Erotics of Service." *Dickens Studies Annual.* 25 (1996): 245–66.

McGowan, John P. "Mystery and History in *Barnaby Rudge.*" *Dickens Studies Annual* 9 (1981): 33–52.

Patten, Robert. "Hablot Knight Browne." *Oxford Reader's Companion to Dickens.* Ed. Paul Schlicke. New York: Oxford UP, 1999.

Polhemus, Robert M. *Erotic Faith: Being in Love from Jane Austen to D. H. Lawrence.* Chicago: U of Chicago P, 1990.

Rice, Thomas Jackson. *Annotated Bibliography of Barnaby Rudge.* New York: Garland, 1987.

Stuart, Barbara L. "The Centaur in *Barnaby Rudge.*" *Dickens Quarterly* 8.1 (1991): 29–37.

Reading Laura Bridgman: Literacy and Disability in Dickens's *American Notes*

Karen Bourrier

Laura Bridgman, billed as the first deaf and blind girl to learn to read and write, was one of the most popular tourist attractions in Boston in the 1840s. Dickens paid a visit to her in January of 1842, and subsequently wrote about and excerpted the widely reprinted annual reports about her in American Notes. *I read this narrative as the story of Bridgman's entrance into literacy, arguing that Dickens's account of the staged spectacle of the young girl with diary in hand, surrounded by her schoolbooks, mobilizes sentiment in his audience by emphasizing both her proximity to able-bodied young white women and her distance from them. On the one hand, she is a paragon of the artless innocence of girlhood because her blindness and deafness supposedly preserve her from more dangerous forms of knowledge. On the other hand, the capacity to learn, especially English, is needed to prove her humanity. Bridgman thus crystallizes Dickens's radical ambivalence about the value of knowledge: he sees learning to read as both a humanizing and a threatening endeavor. Situated among the Lowell factory girls, whose literary pursuits prove their gentility for Dickens, and debates on slave and working-class literacy, Bridgman's story raises questions about literacy, consciousness and self-consciousness, and the boundaries of the human.*

When Charles Dickens visited the United States in January of 1842, one of his first stops was a visit to Laura Bridgman, the famous deaf and blind girl

Dickens Studies Annual, Volume 40, Copyright © 2009 by AMS Press, Inc. All rights reserved.

whom Boston doctor and philanthropist Samuel Gridley Howe had taught to read and write. Although, unlike most visitors, Dickens received a private audience, a stop to see Bridgman was not unusual for a mid-century visitor to Boston. As Elisabeth Gitter points out in her biography, throughout the first half of the 1840s, Laura Bridgman became Howe's star pupil and attraction, luring thousands of visitors to the Perkins Institute for the Blind on exhibition days (5). Articles in newspapers, magazines, and tourist guides all marked her as a site—and sight—not to be missed. As a tourist attraction, Bridgman's cultural significance stretched far beyond the limits of her own situation. She had to be authentically American, despite, or perhaps because of, her multiple disabilities. How does a young girl, deaf, blind, and almost devoid of the senses of taste and smell, come to represent all that is American in the British imagination?

The Boston Evening Transcript offered one answer. After a poor showing in the Great Exhibition of 1851, the editor of the newspaper suggested that there was one thing that America could have sent to the Crystal Palace that would have topped all the other exhibits as a monument to American ingenuity. That monument was none other than Laura Bridgman, who would have shown the Old World the transformative power of the New World's democratic commitment to educate all of its citizens, no matter how humble their station. "The heart of every American, and particularly every Bostonian," wrote the editor, "would throb with true pride on beholding Laura in that rendezvous of the nations . . . her sweet, expressive countenance radiant with joy and beaming with light—her restless fingers writing letters or braiding net work, or interlaced with a friend in rapid telegraphic talk, or tracing the word of God upon the printed page" (2). Although her "expressive countenance" would seem to need no words to communicate its joy, the skills that the editor imagines Bridgman performing—fingerspelling to her friends, writing letters, and reading the Bible—are those of literacy. Bridgman never did give such a performance in London, but she regularly appeared before crowds in Boston (Gitter 106). For spectators, her literacy acted as a guarantor of her humanity. If she could read and write, she was not an animal. Furthermore, if she could read novels and write in a diary, she was much the same as any other middle-class white woman. Dickens's account of his visit with Bridgman mobilizes sentiment in his readership by underscoring both her proximity to and her distance from able-bodied young women. On the one hand, the scene of Bridgman writing letters home from the Perkins Institute approximates that of an able-bodied young woman writing letters home from a boarding school. On the other hand, Bridgman turns out to be a better reader and writer than young women who can see and hear, because her deafness and blindness have supposedly preserved her purity from more dangerous forms of knowledge. The spectacle of a deaf and blind girl reading and writing thus becomes an education for her audience in proper sentiment.

What Bridgman had to teach was not the alphabet but how to feel. As Martha Stoddard Holmes's recent work in disability studies has shown, for the Victorians, the disabled body was a site of affect. In her work on melodramatic discourses and disability in Victorian culture, she argues that "Emotional excess makes and marks the distinction between able and disabled bodies" (31). Bridgman's body was certainly staged and managed in order to elicit an affective response from diverse audiences. For those who visited the Perkins Institute, the sight of what Stoddard Holmes would call Bridgman's "picturesque affliction" provided a moral uplift (23). Indeed, Bridgman was only one stop on what often seems a Dickensian tour of affective bodies, from the "strained attention" on the faces of prisoners in solitary confinement in Pennsylvania, to the "half-naked" and "dusty" bodies of slaves on plantations in Virginia (*AN* [2000] 121, 152). As Julia Miele Rodas points out in her recent work on Dickens and disability, Dickens's desire to see the Perkins Institute "is certainly of a piece with his greater interest in social and educational reform," but his "emotional reaction" to the school is "at least as strong as his interest in system and management" (60). Perhaps even more so than the phrenological tour of someone like George Combe a few years earlier, Dickens's tour of the U.S. seems organized around his emotive readings of bodies.

Dickens's meeting with Laura Bridgman is emotionally complex, evoking pathos and, perhaps more unexpectedly, a radical ambivalence about the value of knowledge. Representing as she does a kind of fantasy of transparency for Dickens, Bridgman is at once a disquieting and alluring figure. Dickens's visit with Bridgman evokes questions about the value of literacy as a means of revealing character, and about how well we can know another human being, or how well we would want to know another human being if all could be revealed. One of the things that is so appealing about Bridgman is that her deafness and blindness have supposedly made her completely unselfconscious: she is the epitome of that artless and innately good girlhood represented elsewhere in Dickens in Little Nell or Florence Dombey. Her lack of self-consciousness means that her thoughts are supposedly immediately accessible to sighted observers. Bridgman crystallizes the author's profound ambivalence about literacy: learning to read and write is not always an unmitigated good in Dickens, as we see in Pip's education in *Great Expectations* (1861), for example. The visit to Laura Bridgman provides a powerful instance of Dickens's feelings on the topic. On the one hand, he excerpts at length Howe's description of how the young girl learned to read and write, and praises the doctor who has devoted his life to such "Noble Usefulness" (53). On the other hand, Dickens is much more taken with Bridgman's beaming countenance, "radiant with intelligence and pleasure" (40), than he is with anything she writes or fingerspells—in fact he does not record any of the written communications, taken by many to be the proof of her humanity and intelligence, that take place during their brief visit. Bridgman's supposed artlessness speaks to the Victorian mistrust of self-consciousness, especially in women, but the project of teaching her to read and write is also the project of proving that she has the capacity for such forms of consciousness.

Dickens's meeting foregrounds this tension and offers a window into the Victorian concepts of the mind and body, and to the limits of the human. Recent work in disability studies has drawn attention to the critical interest of such scenes. Most obviously, disability studies offers a way of understanding the diverse bodies that populate *American Notes*, illuminating the processes through which certain corporeal characteristics, such as whiteness or blindness, are coded as morally relevant in Dickens's work. Thus, a discussion of the way Bridgman was supposedly brought out of darkness and back to humanity through literacy has broader implications for questions about slave literacy, working-class literacy, and the limits of the human in the mid-nineteenth century. Indeed, one of the most useful contributions that disability studies can make to Victorian studies is to show how social practices highlight certain corporeal traits—whether on the basis of race, gender, class, sexuality, or ability—in order to render the body a legible text. An analysis of Dickens's visit with Bridgman also shows that disability studies offers a way of thinking about Victorian concepts of consciousness and how it is embodied.

In this essay, I argue that there is a tension in the writing about Dickens's visit to Laura Bridgman between the imperative to become literate that is evident in Howe's *Annual Report*, which Dickens excerpts at length in *American Notes*, and the passages that Dickens himself wrote which focus on the lively signs of intelligence and humanity that are so evident in her countenance without recourse to writing. My main argument is not that Howe was more interested in the progress of Bridgman's education in humanizing her, while Dickens was more interested in presenting her as innately human, though this may be the case. Instead, I argue that to be seen as fully human, Bridgman had to be seen as both educable—or capable of reading and writing English, since sign language was seen as being on the borderlines of human language—and already innately human before her education began. Dickens's encounter with Bridgman thus represents a fantasy of total transparency that sits uneasily with the imperative to become literate. Bridgman needs to read and write to communicate with the outside world and prove her humanity, but Dickens seems much more taken with her in the moments when she is not performing her humanity through literacy but simply radiating pleasure. The tension between the mission to civilize Bridgman and the desire to see her as innately human becomes evident in considering her significance as a tourist attraction. Bridgman was an especially good tourist attraction because her deafness and blindness supposedly preserved her from awareness of her celebrity, making her a particularly authentic spectacle. In Laura Bridgman, Dickens found a carefully orchestrated tourist attraction who was paradoxically staged as a paragon of girlish innocence and artlessness. Howe needed to prove that Bridgman had the capacity for certain forms of consciousness, but it was all the better if she was completely unselfconscious. The emotion that Bridgman evokes for Dickens and other tourists is exemplary of a larger cultural anxiety about the desirability of literacy, which holds the dual potential to corrupt and to humanize. Bridgman's story shares the narrative arc of contemporary slave narratives, in which the moment the protagonist learns to read is the moment that he or she becomes human. She also shares a set of problems seen in many British debates on working-class literacy, which is often seen as less worthy object than other forms of labor for men, but as a means of social mobility, if a suspect one, for women. Dickens's encounter with Bridgman is thus a particularly provocative site for rethinking what it meant to read and write, and, on a larger scale, what it meant to be considered a human being in the mid-nineteenth century.

I. Tourism and the Problems of Consciousness and Self-Consciousness

In *The Power of Lies,* John Kucich identifies a tension between the well-established ethos of truth-telling, sincerity, and earnestness that characterized Victorian Britain, and the social prestige and evidence of multidimensionality and depth of intellect that were sometimes associated with lying and highly aware self-presentations:

> The Victorians themselves were well aware of the presence and even the desirability of theatricality in self-presentation, and characteristic Victorian debates about the tension between self-consciousness and unselfconsciousness . . . or about the proper adjustment of forthrightness and reserve, verge on an uncomfortable recognition of the relationship between the staged self and deceit.
>
> (28)

Kucich's paradigm illuminates the paradox at the heart of staging Bridgman as a tourist attraction. She is such a good site because she is supposedly the artless, unselfconscious epitome of girlhood, but she was constantly called upon to perform her literacy, which threatened to corrupt her innocence. The stakes involved in educating Bridgman were not so different from those involved in settling America: social reformers saw both as having great potential, but they also worried about tampering with those things that might be better left in their natural state.

As the suggestion in *The Boston Evening Transcript* that America could do no better than to send Laura Bridgman to the Crystal Palace shows, Samuel

Gridley Howe's success in promoting Bridgman as sort of tabula rasa also speaks to the place that America held in the British reformist imagination: America, like Bridgman, was seen as a blank canvas for experiment. Dickens was eager to find out what the British could learn from American institutions, and he visited asylums, poorhouses, and schools, in various parts of the United States. Such a tour was not unusual, partly because many of America's institutions were believed to be more progressive than their British counterparts. "In the course of my progress in the United States," wrote George Combe:

> I saw many things in a more advanced condition than similar objects were in my own country. . . . The common school system, for example, the houses of refuge, the prisons, the lunatic asylums, and the voluntary church system, are objects that in Britain are engaging a large portion of general or local attention.
>
> (I: xiii)

The reasons for which a British visitor made a tour of the U.S. were quite different from those for visiting the Continent. While the Old World offered architectural and artistic edification, the appeal of the New World lay in its promise of a geographical and social blank slate, which invited innovation and experiment. In the British reformist imagination, America was free from the traditions that encumbered Britain, and could thus build any kind of institution based on any kind of principle. As Jane Louise Mesick notes in her survey of early nineteenth-century British travelers in America, "the diseased, whether the affliction were physical, mental, or moral" represented "a kind of vast experiment station" which could not fail to be of interest to philanthropically inclined visitors (108). Tourists like Fanny Trollope, Harriet Martineau, and George Combe set the precedent for Dickens's visit by making their American tours a survey of institutions as diverse as slave plantations and common schools.

Many visitors were bold enough to suggest improvements to these institutions. Famously deaf herself, Martineau remarked that America, with its burgeoning school systems and institutions for the disabled, would be the nation most suited to the experiment of educating a deaf and blind child. Her reasoning was twofold: on the one hand, she felt that America's democratic values would facilitate the education of the disabled, while on the other hand, the nation's open-mindedness would allow for the unobstructed scientific observation of the minds of the deaf and blind (3: 197–99). At the same time, the U.S. valued both social and technological progress. In the British imagination, America was a blank landscape: both geographically and morally, it awaited construction. Part of what made Bridgman such a good tourist attraction was her ability to combine American notions of social progress with moral uplift.

In the burgeoning tourist industry of the nineteenth century, Bridgman was clearly marked as a spectacle. She remained an authentic tourist attraction, as well as an authentic icon of white middle-class womanhood, partly because her multiple sensory disabilities seemed to make her utterly immune to the perils of self-consciousness, even to the point where she was supposedly unaware of her enormous celebrity. Bridgman thus seems to resolve the double bind that Jonathan Culler has identified in the tourist attraction. "To be truly satisfying," argues Culler, this attraction "needs to be certified, marked as authentic"; at the same time, any spectacle that needs to be marked as authentic automatically seems the less so (204). Bridgman's supposed lack of self-awareness solves this paradox to some degree. Her blindness makes her a particularly authentic spectacle for Dickens: he feels that the sight of the deaf and blind girl reading and writing is no performance, for she cannot see those who are watching her. Halfway through his account of Bridgman, Dickens claims that she remained "quite unconscious of the presence of visitors" for some time, thus allowing him to observe her without any affectation (40). Bridgman's "face," which is "radiant with intelligence and pleasure," bespeaks her "gentle, tender, guileless, and grateful" nature (40). Her lack of awareness seems to offer Dickens unmediated access to her consciousness.

Although Dickens finds this unselfconsciousness appealing, he also finds it disquieting. As he enters the Perkins Institute for the Blind, he notices the faces of the inmates and reflects:

> It is strange to watch the faces of the blind, and see how free they are from all concealment of what is passing in their thoughts; observing which, a man with eyes may blush to contemplate the mask he wears. Allowing for one shade of anxious expression which is never absent from their countenances, and the like of which we may readily detect in our own faces if we try to feel our way in the dark, every idea, as it rises within them, is expressed with the lightning's speed, and nature's truth. If the company at a rout, or drawing-room at court, could only for one time be as unconscious of the eyes upon them as blind men and women are, what secrets would come out, and what a worker of hypocrisy this sight, the loss of which we so much pity, would appear to be!   (39–40)

The faces of the blind are a compelling spectacle for Dickens, offering a rare opportunity on his tour of America—during which he was constantly ogled by journalists and curious passers-by—for him to look without being looked at. Utterly self-conscious himself, Dickens finds himself drawn to the idea that all could be unmasked. In Bridgman, this fantasy of transparency sits uneasily with the imperative to become literate: paradoxically, her feminine artlessness requires a strict education to be brought out.

II. A Sentimental Education

Laura Bridgman's story sits at the heart of Victorian anxieties about language and what constitutes a human being. As Christine Ferguson has recently noted, Darwin's influential assertion that language is the sine non qua of human identity was part of a fraught debate about what exactly counted as language. "Just as some philologists debated the limits of English, charting its history and contemplating which words it should retain or reject," writes Ferguson, "biologists and anthropologists such as Darwin and Lubbock discussed the boundaries of language itself, speculating on its origins and the kind of activities (gesture, grunting, monosyllabic utterance) and users (animals, savages, deaf-mutes) it might include" (21). Of course, as the example of Laura Bridgman, which predates Darwin by twenty years, and the longer span of Deaf history show, these debates had begun long before Darwin's assertion. In his influential work on Deaf history, Harlan Lane shows how a long history of oralism (the privileging of spoken language over sign, often based on the incorrect assumption that sign language is concrete and cannot express abstract thought) damaged Deaf language and culture. Howe, an inveterate reformer, was one of the main proponents of oralism, for he associated oral language with progress:

> Tribes emerging from a condition like that of the brutes, use perhaps only audible cries, and visible signs; but all people, as they rise out of savagedom and pass through barbarism, follow the instinct or disposition to express themselves by audible sounds, and begin to use arbitrary and more or less perfectly organized language, in some of its thousand forms. All come to speak, as a matter of course; and the acquisition of speech is the crowning acquisition in human development. (*Letters* 55)

He was convinced that "Laura must have this innate desire and disposition; and that, although by reason of lack of sight and hearing she could not follow it in the usual way, and imitate the sounds made by others, and so speak, she would readily adopt any substitute which should be made comprehensible to her in her dark and still abode" (*Letters* 56). Howe characterizes as an innate desire what actually took a great deal of education to bring out. He did not teach his most famous pupil to speak, but he was invested in teaching her a form of language that would be easily recognized by outsiders as English. It is not necessarily contradictory to view language as both something that humans have an innate desire and capacity for and something that requires a great deal of education to develop, but, as in the history of language debates, in accounts of Bridgman, these two views do not always sit easily together.

In Howe's account, Bridgman's story is in fact the story of how she learned to read and write. Howe's *Annual Report for 1840*—which, as I will discuss, was reprinted wholesale in numerous books and periodicals, including Dickens's *American Notes*—details her education from start to finish. As Howe saw the situation, at stake in his decision to teach her written English rather than a contemporary version of sign language was nothing less than her humanity. "There was one of two ways to be adopted," writes Howe, "either to go on to build up a language of signs," or, to "teach her the purely arbitrary language in common use," an alphabet through which "she might express her idea of the existence, and the mode and condition of existence, of anything" (*AR 1840* 25). According to Howe, sign language is limited and bestial, whereas the basic elements of English can be combined to express the almost limitless permutations of human thought. Howe therefore taught Bridgman to communicate using the manual alphabet, in which every letter had its corresponding sign. Fingerspelling out every letter of every word made communication a painstaking process, but it also made that process more transparent to a literate audience. Similarly, Howe's system of raised print—which was maintained at Perkins even after the invention of Braille (Gitter 299)—rendered his typeface just as legible to the sighted as it was to the blind. As Harlan Lane points out, the version of American Sign that was being developed as Bridgman was being educated would likely have been much easier for her to learn (288–93). The use of fingerspelling and raised print meant that, in effect, Bridgman had to learn written English in order to communicate.

In Howe's narrative, the moment when Bridgman grasps the function of the English language is the moment when she becomes human. At first, the process of teaching Bridgman to read is mechanical, and the doctor likens it to "teaching a very knowing dog a variety of tricks." But when Bridgman comes to understand the relationship between an object and its name, her countenance lights up "with a human expression": she is no longer "a dog, or parrot," but an "immortal spirit, eagerly seizing upon a new link of union with other spirits!" (*AR 1840* 26). For Howe, Bridgman's expression is only human once she understands the significance of the written word. Without the ability to communicate in English, Bridgman is dangerously close to the state of "the beasts that perish," to borrow Dickens's phrase (*AN* 42). The ability to read and write thus becomes a guarantor of Bridgman's humanity despite her disabilities.

Literacy not only made the outside world legible to Bridgman; it also made Bridgman legible to the outside world. For Howe, Bridgman's literacy proved that she had the capacity for human consciousness, though she retained her unselfconsciousness. As soon as she could read and write, but not before, Howe began to publicize Bridgman and her accomplishments in earnest (Gitter 106).[1] Bridgman performed her literacy, and thus her humanity, to rapt audiences. In particular, her ability to print unaided was taken as the final proof of the success of her education, and some privileged tourists even took away souvenirs in the form of samples of her penmanship (Freeberg 183; Gitter 121). As Combe noted on his second visit to Bridgman in 1839, one of "the most gratifying acquirement[s]" she had made since his last visit a

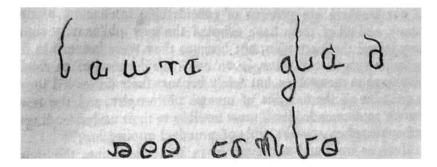

Fig. 1. A sample of Bridgman's handwriting reprinted in Combe, *Notes on the United States* (1841), 2: 206. Image Scan Olin Library, Cornell University.

year earlier was "the power of *writing a legible hand*, and expressing her thoughts upon paper." Combe watches as "she writes with a pencil in a grooved line, and makes her letters clear and distinct" (2: 207; italics original). The clarity of Bridgman's penmanship leaves little doubt as to the success of her education, while also serving as a shorthand for the worth of her character. Dickens, too, asks to see the young girl write. In compliance with his request, Bridgman signs "her name on a slip of paper, twice or thrice." He is also pleased to find her diary, "written in a fair legible square hand, and expressed in terms" which are "quite intelligible without any explanation" (50). Unlike reading or fingerspelling, Bridgman's ability to write allowed her to communicate with audiences without any mediation on the part of her teachers. Combe, like others, reprinted the sample of writing that Bridgman gave him—the provocatively phrased: "Laura glad see Combe"—in his travel writing (fig. 1). As reproducible artifacts, samples of Bridgman's writing provided proof of the success of her education even to audiences across the Atlantic. The legibility of Bridgman's hand thus becomes a means of allowing those who could not see her in person to participate in the affective spectacle of her education from the comfort of their own drawing rooms.

In the British imagination, literacy was an integral part of Bridgman's status as an emblem of America. Indeed, the "general diffusion of education," which could reach even the deaf and blind, was a source of pride for U.S. citizens and part of what many felt was distinctive about American culture (Mesick 203). Bridgman's education also befitted her position as a resident of Boston, which Dickens describes as a city of "intellectual refinement" (*AN* 35). As British travelers in the U.S. observed, in 1829, the year that Bridgman was born, there were 68 free schools in Boston alone, teaching 10, 000 children not only reading, writing, and arithmetic, but also topics as diverse as bookkeeping, political economy, and natural philosophy (Mesick 205).

Bridgman became the poster child for education in New England. In this capacity, not only was her ability to read and write at stake, but also her ability to inspire other teachers and students. In *The Common School Journal* for 1841, Howe's friend and the first secretary of education in Massachusetts, Horace Mann, communicated the "instruction and pathos" of her story to his audience of New England schoolteachers. "If able teachers, under circumstances otherwise propitious, can command such extraordinary success, notwithstanding that some of the most powerful auxiliaries of nature are wanting," writes Mann, "what might not be accomplished *under the direction of equal ability, where all the senses exist in perfection?*" (33; italics original). Mann makes the importance of Bridgman's tale to American pedagogy clear: since her circumstances are so extraordinary, she represents what is possible for the ordinary child, including those children who stood to benefit from the access to free public education that Mann spent much of his life advocating (Mary Mann 59–64). If education in America could reach even the young deaf and blind girl, the argument went, surely every child could learn to read and write.

Yet Bridgman was also seen as a more apt pupil than other children, in part because her deafness and blindness supposedly preserved her from the taint of worldly knowledge, making her completely transparent. Howe needed to prove that Bridgman had the capacity for certain forms of consciousness, but she was all the better for being completely unselfconscious. Much like little blind Muriel in Dinah Mulock Craik's 1856 bestseller *John Halifax, Gentleman*, who is too good for this world and dies before she reaches adolescence, or blind Bertha Plummer in Dickens's Christmas book *The Cricket on the Hearth* (1845), whose father preserves her childish ignorance about their poverty, there is a sense that Bridgman's blindness keeps her in the perpetual innocence of girlhood. It comes as no surprise, then, that as a full-grown deaf and blind woman Bridgman was no longer the popular tourist attraction that she had been as an attractive young girl (Gitter 229). Contemporary accounts emphasize her childish eagerness for knowledge, which often leads her to literalize words or imitate behaviors while missing their meaning. Howe, for example, tells readers that she "has been known to sit for half an hour, holding a book before her sightless eyes, and moving her lips, as she has observed seeing people do when reading" (*AN* 48). This precocious incident is taken to be a sign of Bridgman's intelligence, but the threatening potential of knowledge is completely diffused since she is not actually reading.

Rather than being threatening, her curiosity thus becomes a sign of her innocent delight in the world around her. Because her education has been hard-won, claims Mann, "She has such a love of knowledge, that the most trivial acquisition is a luxury'' (35). Supposing that Bridgman's multiple sensory disabilities have preserved her from the taint of worldliness, Mann also argues that this love of knowledge would be natural to all children ''were it not destroyed by mismanagement'' (35). This cautionary tale about the dangers of bad teaching posits Bridgman and her teachers as exemplars of the limitless possibilities of good teaching. Though ''she dwells in the voiceless silence of a desert'' while ''beneath her is a barren and unfragrant earth'' and ''above, the sky is an empty vault,'' writes Mann, Bridgman is happy (35). The less-than-subtle implication here is that able-bodied teachers and pupils would do well to accept their comparatively light burdens with the same courage and cheerfulness as Bridgman. In reprinting Howe's 1840 report on Bridgman in his journal for New England schoolteachers, Mann shored up his own educational agenda through the use of a sentimental narrative that highlighted the achievement of one individual as a means of inspiring others. The narrative structure of Bridgman's overcoming narrative presents her as a unique and isolated individual. As a genre, sentiment thus shores up the ideal of the autonomous liberal individual, effacing the interdependency of the student and her teachers.

Perhaps the one point that Bridgman is seen as reaching out to others is as a moral teacher. As Mann points out, the story of Bridgman's education was also an education for the able-bodied, who, ''touched with compassion at the privations of this interesting child,'' might go out into the world and help other children (34). This image of Bridgman as a moral teacher was widespread. Her story provided a moral uplift for working-class audiences in the U.K., where it was reprinted in periodicals such as the short-lived *Howitt's Journal of Literature and Popular Progress* and *The Youth's Magazine and Evangelical Miscellany*. In addition to inculcating morality, these periodicals also aimed to cultivate literacy in the working classes and children, so that the tale of Bridgman learning to read and write was considered especially appropriate didactic fare for working-class youth and adults learning the same skills.

Some also imagined Bridgman as a literal teacher. In addition to reprinting the annual report of the Perkins Institute of 1840, which tells the story of Bridgman's acquisition of literacy, many writers, including Dickens, reprinted the annual report of 1841, which tells the story of how she taught another deaf and blind child, Oliver Caswell, to read and write. Although Bridgman probably never taught Caswell to any great extent (Gitter 136–39), the popularity of the idea that she did suggests the importance of pedagogy to her narrative. Having already excerpted from Howe's reports on Bridgman at great length, Dickens cannot resist excerpting from the scene that shows the young girl ''interested even to agitation,'' her face ''flushed and anxious'' as she follows Caswell's progress in learning to read (52). The passages that

Dickens reprints emphasize the transparency of her emotional investment in teaching Caswell, which can be read clearly in her animated face. Howe is clear that Bridgman's emotions express themselves in "that radiant flash of intelligence" and "glow of joy" that are peculiar to her and absent in Caswell's own face (52). A widely reprinted lithograph emphasized the eager expression of Bridgman's face (fig. 2). The image shows Bridgman, book in hand, guiding Caswell's fingers over the raised print, her head turned toward her pupil and his open book as if she were sighted despite the ribbon tied around her eyes. Meanwhile, Caswell raises his face heavenward, making it clear that his fingertips, and not his eyes, are doing the reading. In this scene, literacy brings those unable to communicate verbally or visually into close intellectual and spiritual communion. Literacy also brings teacher and pupil into close physical communion, as the scene illustrates the necessity of a close seating arrangement and intertwined hands. For Bridgman, communication inevitably foregrounds the body. The pathos of this scene depends on the contrast between the weak bodies of Caswell and Bridgman, shown in the apparatus of raised print and bound eyes, and their strong spirits, shown in the beatific expression of their faces. Here, we are reminded of the tension between Dickens's interest in Bridgman's eager expression and the less interesting but still necessary apparatus of her literacy. While reminding us that literacy guarantees the humanity of Bridgman and Caswell, bringing them into close fellowship, this illustration also draws our attention to the transparency of their delight in reading and in each other, which is legible without any printed text, and perhaps more important than their literacy.

III. Reading Slave and Working Class Literacy

The scene of writing is often staged as such an affective spectacle in Dickens, bringing out the ill-fit between the imperative to become literate and the dangers that certain forms of knowledge posed to one's authenticity. For Dickensian women in particular, literacy is often a marker of one's innate gentility, no matter what the outward circumstances. Lizzie Hexam's rise to respectability includes a murderous fight over who will teach her to read, but in the end, despite the circumstances under which her education takes place, it only serves to guarantee her innate middle-class femininity. Like Little Dorrit and Little Nell, who read and write whether they are among debtors, gamblers, or people of quality, Bridgman's literacy guarantees her gentility. This idea also finds expression in *American Notes*. On a day-trip from Boston to the mills in Lowell, Massachusetts, Dickens is quick to notice the high degree of literacy among the factory girls. He anticipates that his British audience's sense of propriety will be upset by the fact that "nearly all these

Fig. 2. "Laura Bridgman Teaching Oliver Caswell." *Howitt's Journal of Literature and Popular Progress*, 41.2 (9 October 1847): 225. Image Scan Olin Library, Cornell University.

young ladies subscribe to circulating libraries,'' and that they have gone so far as to get ''up among themselves a periodical called THE LOWELL OFFERING'' (78). Yet, as a result of these improving occupations, the factory girls, like Bridgman, have ''the manners and deportment of young women: not of degraded brutes of burden'' (76–77). Literacy thus becomes a means for women to transcend class boundaries. Popular accounts of Bridgman's education overlooked her impoverished upbringing on her family's New Hampshire farm, suggesting instead that literacy helps solely her to overcome her disabilities, and not her class background. Even at the Perkins Institute, she did not have access to a large number of books beyond raised print editions of the New Testament and *Pilgrim's Progress* (*AR 1840* Appendix C). But, in the popular imagination, to teach Bridgman to read and write was to teach her to become like any young lady, British or American, who spent her afternoons composing letters to friends or reading triple-decker novels.

Bridgman's literacy thus enables her to approximate the social position of an able-bodied young woman. Despite the fact that he is visiting an institution, Dickens describes his meeting with her in domestic terms. As Mary Klages argues in her work on blindness and disability in nineteenth-century American culture, the novelist's portrait of Bridgman, as ''she sits happily ensconced in her parlor,'' is a portrait of ''the heroine of a sentimental novel who has been rescued from imprisonment and restored to the bosom of home and family'' (127). Yet, if the schoolroom Dickens finds her in is not quite a parlor, and the company of the doctor, teachers, and other pupils not quite that of a loving family, one thing she does have in common with other girls of thirteen are her schoolbooks and diary. Her domestic space is literally built by books, for Dickens finds her ''seated in a little enclosure made by school-desks and forms, writing her daily journal'' with ''her writing book'' sitting ''on the desk she leaned upon'' (40). Here, Dickens finds Bridgman surrounded by the books that mediate her relationship to him and to the outside world. This question of mediation becomes important in considering Bridgman's literacy. Dickens finds immense satisfaction in just watching Bridgman's face, which is ''radiant with intelligence and pleasure'' (40). Borrowing from the vocabulary of phrenology, he also finds that her intellectual capacity and development are ''beautifully expressed'' in the ''graceful outline'' and ''broad open brow'' of her head (40). The joy of watching Bridgman engaged in ''animated communication'' with her teacher is enough for Dickens to see that she is a ''gentle, tender, guileless, grateful hearted being'' (40). Here, what Bridgman is communicating is not nearly as important as the animated face that communicates it. There is a tension between the supposedly unmediated access to an unselfconscious being that the pleasure of simply watching Bridgman's face offers Dickens, and the mediated acts of literacy that prove her humanity but offer at best an imperfect access to her consciousness.

The notion that literacy mediates Bridgman's humanity is borne out in contemporary discourses on working-class literacy in Britain, and on slave literacy in America. Before she learns to read and write, Bridgman's status as a human is liminal. As such, she seems to evoke a profound ambivalence about literacy that resonates throughout Dickens's oeuvre and Victorian culture more generally. Thomas Carlyle's famous characterization of the Chartists as "dumb creatures" in agony, "unable to speak what is in them" is particularly provocative in this context (155); for Carlyle, rhetoric is always untrustworthy, and the unspoken agony of the Chartists, like Bridgman's expressive countenance, seems to communicate much more than they could ever write. At the same time, Carlyle's claim links articulacy and humanity; if the British working classes are metaphorically dumb, they are also less than human. Literacy thus raises one to humanity. George Eliot explores this idea in *Adam Bede* (1859), where she imagines Bartle Massey's turn-of-the-century schoolroom as the scene of such a transformation. As the laborers attempt to read simple sentences, "It was almost as if three rough animals were making humble efforts to learn how they might become human" (235). Yet, Massey's observation sits uneasily with Eliot's ongoing celebration of a kind of sympathy beyond words, and we feel for these "full grown children" without knowing what they have to say (235).

The disparity between such manly bodies and childish minds is echoed in Dickens's own work. Most provocatively, in *Great Expectations*, blindness becomes an apt metaphor for the pathos of learning to write, as Pip, with Joe Gargery by his side, begins "in a purblind groping way, to read, write, and cipher, on the very smallest scale" (45). In *American Notes*, Dickens draws a similar parallel between the signatures on treaties made with "the poor Indians," whose skill in manual labor does not translate to skill with a pen and paper. "I could not but think—as I looked at these feeble and tremulous productions of hands which could draw the longest arrow to the head in a stout elk-horn bow, or split a bead or feather with a rifle-ball," writes Dickens, "of Crabbe's musings over the Parish Register, and the irregular scratches made with a pen, by men who would plough a lengthy furrow straight from end to end" (160). This thought raises the question of how necessary literacy is at all to one's manliness, if not one's humanity. The accomplishment of a good hand pales in comparison to the ability to plow a furrow straight from end to end for Dickens and Crabbe, and literacy comes to seem a rather ambiguous achievement for these men. Although reading and writing seem to be more appropriate accomplishments for a young lady than a working-class man, Bridgman nevertheless evokes a profound ambivalence about literacy as a rather inauthentic means of communication.

This ambivalence about the place of literacy in nineteenth-century discourse is perhaps most clearly expressed in mid-century bans on slave literacy.[2]

Howe was a dedicated abolitionist as well as an educational reformist (Lane 286), so it is perhaps not surprising that both Bridgman's narrative and slave narratives of the 1840s are structured around the struggle to become literate. Henry Louis Gates, Jr. notes that slave narratives almost always included "a record of the barriers raised against slave literacy and the overwhelming difficulties encountered in learning to read and write" (Introduction to *Classic Slave Narratives* 1–2). Gates argues that, "The slave, by definition, possessed at most a liminal status within the human community. To read and to write was to transgress this nebulous realm of liminality" (*Signifying Monkey* 128). Gates's influential discussion of the trope of the talking book—a motif common to slave narratives in which the slave, having heard the Bible read aloud, holds the book to his ear and is dismayed to find that it will not speak to him—is particularly provocative when read next to Bridgman's tactile experience of literature. In both instances, the usual visual mode of reading fails to accommodate the abilities of the reader. The question then becomes what counts as reading: whereas Bridgman's understanding of the manual alphabet and raised print confirmed her literacy and thus her humanity, other modes of reading, when performed by a black person, did not constitute literacy. Stephen Best's recent account of another American celebrity of the midcentury, Tom Wiggins, better known as Blind Tom, a former slave and gifted musician who, though blind, and, as Christopher Krentz emphasizes, cognitively disabled (Krentz 553), could read the perforated rolls of sheet music for a pianola, is particularly interesting in this respect. Because Blind Tom was not considered human, his ability to read music was not considered a form of literacy. Instead, he was mechanized and staged as the "human phonograph" (Best 44). While Bridgman, as an able-minded and attractive white girl could be recuperated as fully human despite her multiple physical disabilities, in other cases the role of literacy in securing one's humanity was much more tenuous.

These social and moral issues were often found side by side in the popular press: given the historical connection between Quakerism and abolitionism, it is not surprising that, in the 9 October 1847 issue of *Howitt's Journal of Literature and Popular Progress*, the Quaker Howitt family reported both on Bridgman and on the progress of a subscription taken up to support Frederick Douglass, who was then lecturing in England. In Douglass's autobiography, which had gone through no less than three British editions within two years of its publication in London 1844, the desire to read becomes a gauge of the author's humanity, much in the same way that Bridgman's thirst for knowledge proves her humanity. Douglass describes his treatment under his harshest master, Mr. Covey, as a breaking not only of his body, but of his mind: "My natural elasticity was crushed, my intellect languished, the disposition to read departed," writes Douglass. Not the dark night of the soul but "the

dark night of slavery'' closes in on him, and the end result is ''a man transformed into a brute!'' (105). Although Bridgman's whiteness in some ways
already secures her humanity, the stakes involved in her learning to read and
write English become even clearer when one considers the relationship between humanity and literacy in slave narratives that are contemporary with
the height of Bridgman's popularity. It is worthwhile to note that while
Douglass, of course, wrote his own narrative, for the most part hearing and
sighted white men wrote about Bridgman. Yet, in each case, the texts go to
great lengths to assert the subject's literacy as the ultimate proof of his or
her humanity. The texts about Bridgman and Douglass frame the spectacle
of the subject writing with the testimony of witnesses who swear that the
slave or deaf and blind girl did in fact write unaided.

Indeed, Bridgman's success was sometimes used as proof that almost anyone could, and should, become literate. In his defense of William Freeman,
a black man with cognitive disabilities who stood trial for murder at Auburn,
New York, in July of 1846, attorney William H. Seward made the connection
between Bridgman's educability and the educability of slaves clear. ''The
color of the prisoner's skin and the form of his features,'' claimed Seward,
''are not impressed upon the spiritual, immortal mind which works beneath''
(3). If, despite her physical disabilities, ''tenderness unexampled, and skill
and assiduity unparalleled'' could open ''avenues to the mind of the benighted
Laura Bridgman,'' and develop ''it into a perfect and complete human spirit''
(8), Seward argues that there is no human mind that could not be reached.
Although Seward suggests that corporeal characteristics are not significant
in determining intelligence, the rhetoric of literacy often operates through
somatic metaphors.

In rereading Howe's account of teaching Bridgman to read and write, the
extent to which the scene of Bridgman learning to read is racialized becomes
apparent. Howe goes so far as to compare ''her progress in the acquisition
of language'' to the successive steps supposed to have been ''taken by savages
in the formation of their language'' (*AR 1840* 36). In this context, the repeated
motifs of the darkness of ignorance and the light of knowledge become ra-
cially significant. Not only is darkness a metaphor for ignorance, but Bridgman's whiteness also becomes one of the key reasons she must be saved
from darkness. Dickens makes a subtle but persistent connection between
Bridgman's whiteness and her worthiness as an object of charity. She appears
before him, ''built up as it were, in a marble cell, impervious to any ray of
light, or particle of sound; with her poor white hand peeping through a chink
in the wall, beckoning to some good man for help, that an Immortal soul
might be awakened'' (40). Howe, too, emphasizes Bridgman's white femininity. Before she caught scarlet fever, he writes, she was ''a very sprightly and
pretty infant, with bright blue eyes'' (*AR 1840* 23). Her eyes, ''inflamed''

and "superated" with scarlet fever (*AR 1840* 24), had long been gone by the time Howe met her, but he still emphasizes their blueness as a means of shoring up her whiteness. In fact, what remains of her eyes is covered by a green ribbon tied around her head. Despite the scarlet fever that damaged her eyes and ears, and likely left other visible marks, Bridgman's body becomes a blank surface in its pure whiteness. If the lengthy narrative of her acquisition of language brings her into close proximity with contemporary slave narratives that carefully delineate the process by which a black man or woman learns to read and write, the blank whiteness of her body distances her from the marked body of the slave. Whereas Bridgman is metaphorically freed from her "marble cell" when she learns to read and write, the illiterate slave remains imprisoned.

Dickens's travel writing brings Bridgman's body and the body of the slave side by side. Even though Dickens was campaigning for an international copyright law during his American tour, he cuts and pastes Howe's 1840 and 1841 annual reports, and parts of Theodore D. Weld's 1839 pamphlet "American Slavery As It Is," directly into his manuscript. The manuscript shows that Dickens began by copying out Howe's pamphlet in longhand and interspersing his own comments, but ended by pasting it directly into the manuscript with a note to the printer to set the text.[3] Giving particular attention to the passages on slavery, Amanda Claybaugh argues that reprinting these texts proved to be a "powerful technique of defamiliarization" for Dickens (79), one which allowed Southern readers to see what their newspapers looked like through foreign eyes. But Dickens's reprinting and reformulation of the material on Bridgman familiarizes rather than defamiliarizes, forming a transatlantic community of readers bound by sentiment who learn to recognize Bridgman's humanity by reading along with her. Howe meant for his report to be widely circulated, and although Dickens's reprinting gave him the most press, it was also reprinted in periodicals as diverse as *The Prisoner's Friend* and *The Mother's Monthly Magazine*, and such reprinting was not unusual or unwarranted in the nineteenth century, especially in journalism. Yet the fact that Dickens so obviously borrowed materials from these two sources invites comparison, allowing one to draw broader conclusions about the role of reprinting and recirculating such materials in transatlantic social reform debates. It is worthwhile to note that these excerpts shaped not only public opinion, but also the way in which the highly staged bodies of Bridgman and the mutilated slaves described in Weld were received. In these texts that Dickens excerpted, the body shapes and is shaped by transatlantic social debates.

Dickens's juxtaposition of these two physical and textual bodies makes readily apparent the extent to which certain corporeal characteristics are coded as morally relevant. In nineteenth-century rhetoric, both blackness and physical disabilities such as blindness or deafness become metaphors for ignorance. In these terms, the darkness of ignorance has the potential to deface and disfigure the fairer countenance of knowledge. While visiting Richmond, Virginia, Dickens compares "the darkness—not of skin, but of mind—which meets the stranger's eye at every turn" to a "brutalizing and blotting out of all the fairer characters traced by Nature's hand" (154). He imagines slavery as disabling not only for the enslaved but also for the white people who live in slave states, and he goes upon his way "with a grateful heart" that he "was not doomed to live where slavery was" and had never had his "senses blunted to its wrongs and horrors in a slave-rocked cradle" (154). Dickens figures sympathy in terms of sensory experience, a rhetorical move that resonates with his earlier visit to Bridgman. Indeed, he ends that visit by asking readers to open up their senses as a means of moral improvement: "Ye who have eyes and see not, and have ears and hear not; ye who are as the hypocrites of sad countenances, and disfigure your faces that ye may seem unto men fast; learn healthy cheerfulness, and mild contentment, from the deaf, and dumb, and blind!" (53). Dickens's suggestion that the deaf and blind could teach the able-bodied to see and hear underscores the notion of Bridgman's narrative as a lesson in moral literacy: in effect, she was teaching readers to become more human.

At stake in Bridgman's acquisition of literacy, then, was nothing less than the boundaries of the human. As a young deaf and blind girl who needed to be rescued from a liminal human status by being taught to read and write, Bridgman exemplifies a profound ambivalence about the nature of literacy in Dickens's work and in Victorian culture more broadly speaking. For the British tourist to be able to interpret American culture, was, in a manner of speaking, a matter of becoming culturally literate. To Dickens, Bridgman symbolized the affective possibilities of democracy in America. Throughout the nineteenth century, the expansion of education was a means of determining who was able to articulate his or her humanity. British and American audiences alike read Bridgman's tale as an uplifting narrative about the triumph of the human spirit over adversity, which was perhaps more keenly expressed in her eager and intelligent countenance than in anything she ever fingerspelled or wrote. But the story was also about her gentility as a middle-class white woman. A voyeuristic appreciation, on the part of the travelers who visited her in Boston and the armchair travelers who read about her alike, was part of the spectacle of this attractive young white girl, seated in her parlor, book and diary in hand. Bridgman's education of the public was an education in sentiment, which depended on the exclusion of the working classes and of slaves among others in order to shore up the young girl's status as an icon of white middle-class womanhood. For Dickens and for the Victorian public at large, Bridgman crystallized a tension between the corrupting and humanizing potentials of literacy. The sentimental presentation of Bridgman allowed Dickens and his audience to negotiate this tension, collapsing the larger cultural concerns at stake in her education into a singular portrait of an individual overcoming what were supposedly her personal challenges rather than larger social issues. For a public moved by the affective spectacle of a deaf and blind girl reading and writing, to learn to read Laura Bridgman's situation through the lens of sentiment was to learn to read rightly.

NOTES

Special thanks to Josephine McDonagh, Toni Jaudon, Shirley Samuels, and Nick Soodik for their help in the early stages of this work, to James Eli Adams for his helpful criticism of several drafts of this paper, and to Jennifer Esmail and the editors and an anonymous reviewer at *Dickens Studies Annual* for their help in bringing it all together. My especial thanks to John Meriton for allowing me to consult the manuscript of *American Notes*.

1. Exhibiting the accomplishments of deaf and blind students was not uncommon. Howe had exhibited the accomplishments of his blind pupils in order to procure funding for his school before Bridgman was among them. For an account of exhibitions of deaf pupils in the eighteenth and nineteenth centuries, see Lane 34–38.

2. For further information on laws against slave literacy, see Williams and Cornelius.

3. The manuscript for *American Notes* (F.47.A.13–14) is held in the John Forster Collection at the Victoria and Albert Museum. For a detailed account of the changes Dickens made in his manuscript regarding slavery, Brattin, '' 'A Mockery So Gross and Monstrous': Slavery in Dickens's Manuscript of American Notes for General Circulation,'' *Dickens Quarterly* 20.3 (2003): 153–65.

WORKS CITED

Anon. ''Our Country and the London Fair.'' *Boston Daily Evening Transcript* XXII.6422 (14 June 1851): 2.

Best, Stephen. *The Fugitive's Properties: Law and the Poetics of Transmission*. Chicago: U of Chicago P, 2004.

Brattin, Joel J. '' 'A Mockery So Gross and Monstrous': Slavery in Dickens's Manuscript of *American Notes for General Circulation*.'' *Dickens Quarterly* 20.3 (2003): 153–65.

Carlyle, Thomas. *Selected Writings*. Ed. Alan Shelston. New York: Penguin, 1971.

Claybaugh, Amanda. *The Novel of Purpose: Literature and Social Reform in the Anglo-American World*. Ithaca, NY: Cornell UP, 2006.

Combe, George. *Notes on the United States of North America During a Phrenological Visit in 1838–9–40*. 3 vols. Edinburgh: Maclachlan Stewart, 1841.

Cornelius, Janet Duitsman. *"When I Can Read My Title Clear": Literacy, Slavery, and Religion in the Antebellum South*. Columbia: U of South Carolina P, 1991.

Culler, Jonathan. "Semiotics of Tourism." *American Journal of Semiotics* 1.1–2 (1981): 127–40.

Dickens, Charles. *American Notes: For General Circulation*. Penguin Classics. Ed. Patricia Ingham. London: Penguin, 2000.

———. *American Notes for General Circulation*. F.47.A.13–14. John Forster Collection, Victoria and Albert Museum, London.

———. *The Christmas Books: "A Christmas Carol," "The Chimes," "The Cricket on the Hearth."* Ed. Michael Slater. New York: Penguin, 1994.

———. *Great Expectations*. Ed. Margaret Cardwell. New York: Oxford UP, 1993.

———. *Little Dorrit*. Ed. Helen Small and Harvey Peter Sucksmith. New York: Oxford UP, 1999.

———. *The Old Curiosity Shop*. Ed. Elizabeth M. Brennan. New York: Oxford UP, 1998.

———. *Our Mutual Friend*. Ed. Michael Cotsell. New York: Oxford UP, 1998.

———. *A Tale of Two Cities*. Ed. George Woodcock. New York: Penguin, 1989.

Douglass, Frederick. *Narrative of the Life of Frederick Douglass*. Ed. Houston A. Baker. New York: Penguin, 1982.

Eliot, George. *Adam Bede*. Ed. Stephen Gill. New York: Penguin, 1985.

Farnham, Mrs. E. W. "Laura Bridgman." *The Prisoner's Friend* November 1848: 105–11.

Ferguson, Christine. *Language, Science and Popular Fiction in the Victorian Fin-de-Siècle: The Brutal Tongue*. Burlington, VT: Ashgate, 2005.

Freeberg, Ernest. *The Education of Laura Bridgman: The First Deaf and Blind Person to Learn Language*. Cambridge, MA: Harvard UP, 2001.

Gates Jr., Henry Louis. Introduction. *The Classic Slave Narratives*. New York: Signet, 2002.

———. *The Signifying Monkey*. New York: Oxford UP, 1988.

Gitter, Elisabeth. *The Imprisoned Guest: Samuel Howe and Laura Bridgman, the Original Deaf-Blind Girl*. New York: Farrar, 2001.

Holmes Stoddard, Martha. *Fictions of Affliction: Physical Disability in Victorian Culture*. Ann Arbor: U of Michigan P, 2004.

Howe, Samuel Gridley. *Annual Report for 1840*. Boston: Perkins Institute for the Blind, 1841.

———. *Letters and Journals of Samuel Gridley Howe*. Ed. Laura E. Richards. Vol. 2. Boston: Dana Estes, 1909.

Howitt, Mary. "Laura Bridgman." *Howitt's Journal of Literature and Popular Progress* 41.2 (9 October 1847): 226–28.

Klages, Mary. *Woeful Afflictions: Disability and Sentimentality in Victorian America*. Philadelphia: U of Pennsylvania P, 1999.

Krentz, Christopher. "A 'Vacant Receptacle'? Blind Tom, Cognitive Difference, and Pedagogy." *PMLA* (March 2005): 552–57.

Kucich, John. *The Power of Lies: Transgression in Victorian Fiction*. Ithaca, NY: Cornell UP, 1994.

Lane, Harlan L. *When the Mind Hears: A History of the Deaf*. Pelican Books. London: Penguin, 1988.

Mann, Horace. "Laura Bridgman." *The Common School Journal* (1 February 1841): 33–50.

Mann, Mary. *Life of Horace Mann by His Wife*. Boston: Walker, Fuller, 1865.

Martineau, Harriet. *Society in America*. 3 vols. London: Saunders and Otley, 1837.

Mesick, Jane Louise. *The English Traveller in America, 1785–1835*. Columbia UP, 1922.

Rodas, Julia Miele. "Tiny Tim, Blind Bertha, and the Resistance of Miss Mowcher: Charles Dickens and the Uses of Disability." *Dickens Studies Annual* 34 (2004): 51–97.

Seward, William Henry. *Argument of William H. Seward, in Defence of William Freeman, on His Trial for Murder, at Auburn, July 21st and 22d, 1846*. E441.M46 v. 72 no. 11. Samuel J. May Anti-Slavery Collection, Cornell University, Ithaca, NY.

Trollope, Frances Milton. *Domestic Manners of the Americans*. Ed. Pamela Neville-Sington. New York: Penguin, 1997.

Weld, Theodore. *American Slavery as It Is; Testimony of a Thousand Witnesses*. New York: American Anti-Slavery Society, 1839.

Williams, Heather Andrea. *Self-Taught: African American Education in Slavery and Freedom*. Chapel Hill: U of North Carolina P, 2005.

The Youth's Magazine and Evangelical Miscellany. ''Some Account of Laura Bridgman.'' London: Hamilton, Adams. 4.7 (July 1841): 233–37.

The Youth's Magazine and Evangelical Miscellany. ''Some Account of Laura Bridgman (*concluded*).'' London: Hamilton, Adams. 4.8 (August 1841): 265–69.

Dombey and Son and the "Parlour on Wheels"

Michael Klotz

Dombey and Son *is a narrative concerned with the preservation and maintenance of domestic space, from the redecoration of the Dombey mansion and the subsequent estate sale on the premises, to the threatened dispersal of the items in the Wooden Midshipman and the ultimate securing of the shop as a refuge for Rob Toodle, Captain Cuttle, and Florence Dombey. I argue that the novel reflects a broader cultural concern with the ways that the nascent industry of interior decoration imperiled the cherished ideal of the home as a fixed and unchanging refuge. The expansion of the railway in the 1840s is an important context for understanding this effect, since the railway was a visible sign of the mobility of possessions and facilitated the distribution of domestic goods throughout the country. I suggest that the railway emblematizes an anxiety about the stability of the domestic interior. This essay concludes with a rereading of the well-known "take the housetops off" passage in chapter 47, proposing that the perspective is that of a passenger on the railway.*

A particular panic is twice raised in *Dombey and Son*, as characters searching for a house in London discover that the residence they are looking for has disappeared into the confusion of traffic, commerce, noise, and construction that comprises the urban cityscape. In chapter 15, with Paul Dombey ill, Susan Nipper and Walter Gay rush to Staggs's Gardens in search of Mrs. Toodle, Paul's former wet nurse. Although they try to explain to the coachman where the neighborhood is located, they have great difficulty in finding it, and at first it seems as though they are simply lost. But after a bit of futile journeying the narrator lets the reader in on the real difficulty of their trip:

> There was no such place as Staggs's Gardens. It had vanished from the earth. Where the old rotten summer-houses once had stood, palaces now reared their heads, and granite columns of gigantic girth opened a vista to the railway world beyond. The miserable waste ground, where the refuse-matter had been heaped of yore, was swallowed up and gone; and in its frowsy stead were tiers of warehouses, crammed with rich goods and costly merchandise. The old by-streets now swarmed with passengers and vehicles of every kind; the new streets that had stopped disheartened in the mud and wagon-ruts, formed towns within themselves, originating wholesome comforts and conveniences belonging to themselves, and never tried nor thought of until they sprung into existence. . . . The carcasses of houses, and beginnings of new thoroughfares, had started off upon the line at steam's own speed, and shot away into the country in a monster train.   (244–45)

This moment of locational bewilderment can be properly understood in conjunction with a related instance later in the novel. In chapter 28, Florence Dombey is returning from visiting her brother Paul at boarding school, and is traveling with Susan Nipper toward the Dombey mansion in London. Riding along, they discuss their sense of relief at the prospect of arriving home. Florence reflects that she finds "greater peace within" the Dombey mansion than outside of it, since it is "better and easier to keep her secret shut up there, among the tall dark walls"; and Susan confides that she will be "glad to go through the old rooms" (441). As Florence and Susan turn onto their street, however, they undergo a confusion similar to what Susan and Walter experienced when looking for the Toodles in Staggs's Gardens. Susan exclaims "Where's our house!" and Florence repeats her question (441). They each have trouble spotting the Dombey mansion behind the bustle of work that accompanies its redecoration:

> There was a labyrinth of scaffolding raised all round the house, from the basement to the roof. Loads of bricks and stones, and heaps of mortar, and piles of wood, blocked up half the width and length of the broad street at their side. Ladders were raised against the walls; labourers were climbing up and down; men were at work upon the stages of the scaffolding; painters and decorators were busy inside; great rolls of ornamental paper were being delivered from a cart at the door; an upholsterer's wagon also stopped the way. . . . Inside and outside alike: bricklayers, painters, carpenters, masons: hammer, hod, brush, pickaxe, saw, and trowel: all at work together, in full chorus!   (441–42)

In placing these narrative clips side by side, my intention is to consider their resonance as a starting point for rereading the novel. Walter Gay and Florence

Dombey, who by the end of *Dombey and Son* are married and have established a secure and stable home (no small feat in the novel, or in Dickens's fiction in general), are in turn subjected to what might be thought of as a cautionary spectacle of a problem inherent to domesticity. Directing the coachman in a vain search for the Toodles' house, Walter finds in Staggs's Gardens that houses have been "knocked down" to allow the extension of the railway. It is impossible to characterize this as an entirely negative change. In place of "old rotten" houses there now stands a modern railway station with adjoining warehouses "crammed" with merchandise ready for distribution to the marketplace. There is a certain appeal in this image of efficient capitalism. But the narrator is evidently aware of what this alteration means for the men, women, and children living in the neighborhood. The railway has brought attractive merchandise into the area, but it has also meant that local families must vacate it.[1] The imaginative vocabulary employed in presenting this event to the reader is, as we shall see, significant: "carcasses of houses" are "shot away into the country in a monster train." Edifices have been transformed from fixed and certain refuges into a mobile component of this new modernity. The result is a travesty of domesticity: "[c]rowds of people and mountains of goods," produce "a fermentation in the place that was always in action," with the "very houses. . . . disposed to pack up and take trips" (245).

Although Florence's returning trip to the Dombey mansion in chapter 28 is cast in an entirely different tenor with regard to class status and financial security, the scene similarly presents an imperative of capitalist progress. Renovating and redecorating the Dombey mansion to reflect its owner's hearty financial health seems as natural as modernizing the transportation infrastructure in a country with the economic vitality of England. Before his marriage to Edith, Dombey's renovation includes the installation of gas lighting, the addition of new "hangings and soft carpets," and the adornment of the walls and floors with representations of "roses" (462, 540). Dombey not only introduces new chairs, tables, curtains, and bibelots in place of familiar ones, but he makes the house a thoroughfare for the march of the unfamiliar sphere of work: laborers climbing, painters and decorators "busy inside," bricklayers, carpenters, and masons in a "full chorus" of activity. The familiar house is obscured behind a "labyrinth" of scaffolding: renovation and redecoration has a maze-like effect, turning a nondescript edifice into an inscrutable spectacle. The building appears as an extension of Dombey's counting house. But whereas Dombey's business affairs are conducted in a calculated and orderly fashion, applying the ethos of improvement and progress at home creates chaos. The capitalist aura of this work is frighteningly inimical to the set of domestic values that Florence embodies and seeks to transmit. A vision of home that is secure, still, and stable has been overtaken by the reminder that in the working world one cannot escape the ceaseless rearranging of things and passing of objects from one hand to another. The forces of speculation, risk, and disaster have followed Dombey home.

The impact of waking market life on the nineteenth-century domestic dream has been considered at length by Walter Benjamin, Richard Sennett, Jürgen Habermas, and others. More recently, scholarship by Elizabeth Langland, Monica Cohen, Karen Chase, and Michael Levenson has recovered cultural suppositions and justifications that allow contemporary readers and scholars to bring to bear a more accurately nuanced picture of the ways that domestic privacy was articulated through the experience of the alienated capitalist individual. An important aspect of Victorian domesticity, however, that has not been adequately addressed by scholars, is the way that the burgeoning industry of interior decoration that came into being in England in the 1840s and 1850s facilitated the interest in interior space. It was through a shared language of color, texture, style, and craftsmanship that men and women pursued the business of arranging their homes. The collage of texts that remain with us offer a starting point for approximating the influence of decorative cogitation on the shared internal sense of home. Design manuals such as Shirley Hibberd's *Rustic Adornments for Homes of Taste* (1856), Isabella Beeton's *Book of Household Management* (1861), and Charles Eastlake's extremely popular *Hints on Household Taste* (1868) provided the impetus for British subjects to think seriously about how to properly adorn their houses. Marketing the necessity of domestic possessions to consumers infused a commercial longing into the striving for the domestic ideal. At any time there would be some carpet that was faded, sofa that was ragged, chair that was out of style—one more thing that might be done. Always there was something more to purchase.

Numerous authors documented their decorative attention to their homes, and Dickens's correspondence tells us something about his perspective. When the Dickens family had the drawing room of their Devonshire Terrace home redecorated, they were away on the continent, but Dickens superintended the changes from abroad. In a letter on April 14, 1845, Dickens writes to his friend Thomas Mitton specifying paper for the drawing room (''the paper must be blue and gold or purple and gold—to agree with the furniture and curtains''), and colors for the ceiling, hall, and staircase (*Letters* 4: 297–98). Dickens was similarly hands-on in the arrangement of a cottage that he rented for his parents in Alphington, where they stayed from March 1839 until November or December 1842. Dickens traveled to Alphington to undertake the furnishing of the rooms himself, and his letters to his wife, Kate, record his satisfaction with his decorative work.[2] Dickens goes so far as to offer an inventory to his wife of the pieces that he installed in each chamber: ''six painted in imitation of rosewood chairs, a Pembroke table, a round dining-table, a kidderminster carpet, and some second-hand red curtains'' in the worst sitting room; "six better chairs, a second-hand sofa table, a couch, white muslin curtains, and a second hand brussels carpet" in the best sitting room; "a tent bedstead with best bedding and white dimity furniture" in the best bedroom; "a French bed and mattress" in the second best bedroom; and "necessaries, the crockery and glass, the stair-carpet, and the floorcloth" in the kitchen (*Letters* 1: 522). To Forster, Dickens recalls the special attention that he gave to the furnishing of his parents' drawing room—"calling over the articles in requisition and checking off the prices as the upholsterer exhibited the goods"—and to his wife he confides that he has been "most attentive all day" to the upholsterer's daughter "in the hope of keeping down the small account" (*Letters* 1: 520, 523). In a postscript to a later letter to his wife on November 8, 1844, Dickens instructs her: "Keep things in their places. I cannot bear to picture them otherwise" (*Letters* 4: 216). This addendum to a letter that otherwise includes no mention of domestic affairs reflects Dickens's psychological investment in the fixed character of the house.

Stillness, security, and certainty were qualities associated with the domestic sphere, and decorative goods had an important position in the perception of the Victorian home as a safe and private space, sequestered from the anxieties of the marketplace. As a scene of exorbitant ornamentation, overflowing with vases, pictures, bibelots, overstuffed sofas, and a garish profusion of fabric in various forms, the typical drawing room, according to Thad Logan, "focus[ed] attention on the security and enclosure of domestic space" (140). Jenni Calder has similarly observed that the "solidity of Victorian furnishing" suggests "a need for the home to represent that security in every way possible" (99). However, this process was complicated by the mental labor required to reimagine furniture and possessions, to separate out the numerous emotional, psychological, and familial meanings ingrained in the things of the home. This activity has typically been understood in the context of commodity culture, as a fight to preserve personal significance in the face of the abstraction of objects and the alienation of individuals. In *The Arcades Project* Walter Benjamin writes that the collector is faced with the "Sisyphean" task of "divesting things" of their "commodity character" (9). Similarly, Wolfgang Schivelbusch refers to the latent mechanized trace in commodities as the "memory of industrial objects." He points to various mid-nineteenth-century design attempts to conceal the evidence of the machine past still visible in domestic wares: for instance, covering hard metal frames and compressed springs with thick cushions, padded layers, and other frills (123).

Recent scholarship by Elaine Freedgood, however, has argued convincingly that Victorian culture was marked by a reordering, recategorizing, and renaming of goods for sale. Events such as the Great Exhibition of 1851—in which items were exhibited along with a detailed explanation regarding the processes used to manufacture them—gradually helped forge the modern perception of commodities. The commodification of the world, the passing of mere objects into the strangely distant realm of the commodity, is described by Freedgood as a transition from "thing culture" to "commodity culture." One characteristic of this regime change was the evacuation of the meanings inscribed in possessions, and their reinscription in the impersonal grammar of the marketplace. "Ideas swarmed in the many and various things of that world: the processes of commodification—abstraction, alienation, and specularization—were achieved slowly rather than suddenly, unevenly rather than consistently or finally" (Freedgood 142). The Victorian home played a privileged role in this process. As Talia Schaffer has noted, many of the ornaments and adornments that filled the interior of homes were clearly *not* commodities: they were handmade rather than manufactured, had no discernible usefulness, and were sold using the bartering system of the bazaar. Schaffer writes that the "domestic handicraft craze" was at its peak between 1840 and 1870, and the items produced included "wax fruit under glass, beaded bags, embroidered slippers, seaweed collages, shell-encrusted boxes, wool-work cushions, painted china, woven workbaskets, scrap screens, and satin pincushions" (223). The amount of time, attention, and industry invested in producing these handicrafts is indicative of the view of the home as a container of things, and yet a space quite different from a storefront, warehouse, or street-side stall. An important edict of the gospel of Victorian domesticity was that the interior of the home should be certain and stable, and that the possessions within should be vitalized with energy. Each thing should carry with it a vibrancy distinct from the sales pitch or the shop-window allure, one that is rather individual, authentic, and durable. Reading *Dombey and Son*, we are again and again made aware of the tension between the way property functions outside and within the home. The narrative is structured by attempts to navigate these concerns, and, in so doing, to discover a proper home for Florence Dombey. From the 1840s, when the spread of the railway enabled the easy distribution of merchandise throughout the country, until the end of the century domestic values were often articulated through the language of interior arrangement. Putting together a beautiful home meant consulting decoration manuals, considering the decorative choices of neighbors and friends, and—if one had the means to do so—hiring an interior decorator.

In terms of sheer commerce, the Victorian house would not have developed as it did without a national railway to distribute decorative objects.[3] The modern rail age began during the third decade of the nineteenth century, and the opening of the Liverpool and Manchester Railway on September 15, 1830 is often cited as its inception. For the first time service included "a reserved track, public traffic facilities, provisions for passengers, and mechanical power" (Gourvish 57). The railway, however, was just getting established during the thirties, and it was not until the next decade that a national network was truly in place. In 1839 there were only one hundred miles of railway track available in England, but by 1852 there were six thousand six hundred miles of track ready for travel (Freeman 1). The rapid spread of the railway in the 1840s coincided with significant innovations in the production of aesthetic goods. The combination of the removal of excise taxes on glass and paper and the public appetite for aesthetic design meant that the 1840s were a period of significant industrial expansion. Records for the sale and production of domestic goods during this period are hard to come by, but the information on the production of wallpaper is perhaps representative: "In 1834, British wallpaper manufacturers recorded an output of 1.2 million pieces; by 1851, they were producing 5.5 million; in 1860, 19 million, and in 1874, 32 million" (Cohen 36).

Beyond this practical economic impact, the railway was relevant to the conception of the Victorian home because the railway carriage was itself a site of aesthetic display and ornamentation. In associating railway travel with domestic comfort, railway owners sought to lessen the anxieties associated with travel: the disconcerting speed, with all of the attendant bumps, vibrations, and abrupt starts and stops; the fear of injury, maiming, or death resulting from an accident; and, finally, the role that the railway played in several well-publicized crimes, including John Tawell's trip to Paddington Station after committing a murder in Slough in 1845, and a murder committed by Franz Muller aboard the North London Railway in 1864. Railway operators sought to counter these fears by making the railway compartment feel like the interior of a home. Riders could read, eat, or converse in familiarly snug circumstances, surrounded by objects that suggested the security of the domestic bower. Historian Michael Freeman has described the Victorian railway compartment as a veritable "parlour on wheels," a ready-made home in motion (84). In the first-class railway carriage (and in second-class carriages from the 1850s and on), passengers rode "comfortably ensconced in their cozy and luxurious train carriages with velvet seats and wood-paneled walls" (Wosk 5). "Each first-class compartment was distinguished by full-height partitions, and seats formed by a padded backrest and cushioned seat. There was cloth upholstery pulled tight over a base, usually stuffed with horsehair, but sometimes hay, and secured with buttons to give a quilted effect" (Simmons and Biddle 154). Amenities of the railway carriage included "railway luncheon baskets, railway rugs and foot warmers," aspects of design that afforded the rider with the comfortable feeling of being at home (Freeman 84).

During the remainder of the century, a number of innovations were introduced, from steam heating (on the Midland in 1874), to dining cars (on the Great Northern in 1879), and gas lighting (on the Metropolitan and Great Eastern Railways in 1876–78) (Perkin 106). According to C. Hamilton Ellis, the most elaborate railway carriage was one designed by Richard Mansell and introduced on the South Eastern Railway in 1851. The decoration included "windows . . . furnished with white Lutestring," a floor "fitted with a rich velvet pile Carpet," a "State Chair with carved fronts in Maple and partly gilt representing the Rose, Shamrock, and Thistle. . . . with its back surmounted by richly carved ornaments supporting the Crown and Cushion richly gilt," "two couches with carved scroll fronts. . . . spring stuffed and covered with a silk Damask," and a "Table of fine Maple wood with Marqueterie Inlaid." The interior was "covered with damask in shades of Amber, White and Drab, decorated ornamental silk tufts, handsome Gimp and Silk and Stout Silk cord," and ornamented with "Draperies of Amber and White Satin. . . . trimmed with cord, gimp and fringe of silk" (48). With railway carriages such as Mansell's, little luxury was lost for those traveling on iron rails.

The interpenetration of the mid-Victorian vision of home and the experience of railway travel is also discernible in visual culture of the period. Julie Wosk notes that "in paintings as well as in newspaper and magazine illustrations after 1850, the interiors of railroad carriages became a new pictorial arena for intimate vignettes, a miniature stage" where passengers are pictured "sadly parting, conversing, and even courting" (65). Augustus Egg's *The Travelling Companions* (1862) depicts two women traveling on the railway, one asleep and the other reading a novel, as if at home.[4] Abraham Solomon's *First Class—The Return* (1855) similarly provides an example of how the railway compartment functioned as an intimate private space (fig. 1). The sumptuous golden upholstery of the seat and the seemingly overflowing fabric of the room (from the clothing of the riders, to the curtains, the cloth on the side, and the blanket in the foreground) highlight the richly tactile experience of early train travel. The naval officer's attention is evidently divided—as he converses with the father, he routinely observes the daughter staring intently at him. The scene resonates as more than a chance, and easily forgotten, encounter. In place of a suitor's meeting in a comfortable parlor at home, the officer in *First Class—The Return* flatters the father and incites the interest of the daughter within the confines of the railway carriage. The adornment of the compartment materially connects it with the drawing room: similar emotional, imaginative, and social experiences unfolded in each.

*

Many of the commentaries on *Dombey and Son* in the last two decades have addressed the significance of the railway, and these accounts tend to interpret it as in some way emblematic of industry, mechanization, technology, or

Fig. 1. Abraham Solomon. *First Class—The Return*, 1855. Reproduced by permission of the National Railway Museum/Science and Society Picture Library.

trauma.[5] While the railway might suggest these quite different cultural valences, *Dombey and Son* primarily draws on the association between the railway and everyday domestic life; the narrative works through cultural problems surrounding the distribution, purchase, and installation of possessions within the home. Decorating the interior of the Dombey house is comparable to the aestheticization of the railway compartment: each decorative act aims to mask latent anxieties, in the case of the Dombey house Florence's profound sadness and Edith's masochistic resentment. But the tragedy of the novel is that home is supposed to be a privileged realm, and while there is a kind of candor in the decoration of the railway compartment the redecoration of the Dombey house is a conspicuous act of emotional denial. In the superintendence of his mansion, Dombey aims to proclaim his power—to show what money can do—without suggesting anything about his personal taste or private character; the design of the interior substitutes impersonal opulence for comfort and genuine feeling. Dombey wants his home to function as a testament to his potency and status, as though no one actually lived there. But strangely, his interior in fact undergoes an extraordinarily tempestuous change during the course of *Dombey and Son*. At the beginning of the novel, the Dombey mansion is sparsely furnished and cold. Dombey, the "specimen of a frozen gentleman,'' aims to save money in heating the grand house, and the family abode appears like a wilderness: the "black, cold rooms" seem "to be in mourning, like the inmates of the house" (67, 74). The bookcase "repudiate[s] all familiarities," dusty urns in each corner "preach desolation and decay," and the chimney glass, which reflects the image of its master, "seem[s] fraught with melancholy meditations" (67). Although Florence attempts to bring warmth to the mansion at several points in the novel, by rearranging the furniture in a way that she hopes her father will like and by introducing objects she expects will be pleasing to him, all of these efforts are ignored. These authentic, personal efforts at transforming the home are forbidden.

For the single-minded, self-determined Dombey, it is not much of a surprise that his mansion becomes an extension of his business. The upheaval of objects in the Dombey house and the intrusion of workers are so many fingerprints of the financial world that he is unable to escape. More curious is the way that an ostensible place of business, Sol Gills's shop, also known as the Wooden Midshipman, functions as a surrogate home for so many characters in the novel. Captain Cuttle escapes from the house he shares with the dominating Mrs. MacStinger—a woman who threateningly demands the right to know whether "an Englishwoman's house [is] her castle or not"— and moves to the Wooden Midshipman; Rob, the son of Mr. and Mrs. Toodle, lives there for a time, helping Captain Cuttle while Sol Gills is abroad searching for Walter; and, later in the novel, Sol's shop becomes a refuge for Florence Dombey when she is cast out of her father's mansion (138). After Dombey strikes Florence and banishes her at the end of chapter 47, the home that Florence turns to for comfort, the place where she can hide from her father's wrath, is of a very peculiar kind. The Wooden Midshipman appears to be a place of business—it is a store "[j]ust round the corner" from the "rich East India House"—where various items necessary for sea voyages can be purchased (46). But in fact nothing there is ever sold. Filled to the brim with goods on display, yet without any customers, funds exchanged, or bills of sale, the Wooden Midshipman becomes a home for Walter Gay, Sol Gills, and later Captain Cuttle at the same time that it is a storefront visible to those passing by in a hackney coach.

Readers of Dickens can readily situate the Wooden Midshipman in a series of novelistic attempts to carve out an imaginative space where the world of work is not morally polluting. The Cheeryble brothers' office in *Nicholas Nickleby* (1838–39) is an early example, and a later very well known instance can be found in *Great Expectations* (1860–61), where Wemmick's castle is set against that place of careful perjury, obsessive handwashing, and useless begging—the law office where Wemmick works with Jaggers. In *Dombey and Son*, Dickens takes this idea even further, since Walter, Sol Gills, and (in the second half of the novel) Captain Cuttle and Florence Dombey have literally nowhere else to retreat to, no other home to which to retire. Outside Sol Gills's store the Wooden Midshipman points to a place that is both domestic and mercantile, where wares have neither use-value nor exchange-value but instead play an integral, but difficult to define, part in the atmosphere.

The defunct shop has been transformed into a makeshift home, yet nothing has been altered inside: the Wooden Midshipman is opened for business every day and the displays inside are carefully preserved. The packed space of the store is only dusted and polished, but otherwise the stock in Sol's shop sits unaltered during the course of the novel. Forgotten by consumers, though, the contents of the house have an enduring sentimental importance for its residents. When we are first introduced to Walter at the home/shop of Sol in chapter 4, they are engrossed in a conversation in which Sol futilely warns Walter against the influence of the things within their nautical interior. "It's natural enough," Sol explains to his nephew, that he should dream of working on a ship in the future, having grown up in the shop "with all these familiar things" (53). But Sol sets out to convince Walter to forget the stories that the arrangement of the house has awakened. In doing so, Sol appeals to Walter's penchant for narrativizing objects, by imagining a tale that takes the bottle of Madeira they have been drinking as its protagonist: " 'Think of this wine for instance,' said old Sol, 'which has been to the East Indies and back, I'm not able to say how often, and has been once around the world. Think of the pitch-dark nights, the roaring winds, the rolling seas. . . . Think what a straining and creaking of timbers and masts: what a whistling and howling of the gale through ropes and rigging" (53–54). In fact, the story of the Madeira that Sol invents to alert Walter to the dangers of the sea only sparks his adventurous impulse, and by the end of his tale Walter's "kindling eye and heightened colour" remind Sol of something that the "encircling mist had hitherto shut out" (55). Unlike Dombey, whose house is as "blank. . . . inside as outside," Walter's interior imagination reads the home as a collection of objects imbued with narratives, an arrangement of things whose placement is significant and that potentially have much to tell (34).

It is difficult to interpret Sol Gills's nautical wares as anything more than decorative, since "none but the initiated" could have "guessed [their] use," and the consumer public is uniformly uninterested. The narrator provides the impression that the goods in the Wooden Midshipman have not been "placed" up for sale so much as installed, in a physical sense, as a part of the interior: "[J]ammed" into cases, "fitted" into narrow corners, "fenced up" behind cushions, and "screwed" into angles (47). Everything about this display is designed to make customers hesitant to disturb their arrangement, lest they get things out of place. But while the objects are imbued with

considerable psychological and sentimental value, the question of their management and arrangement is entirely elided. This storehouse containing nautical detritus provides a strangely ideal home for Florence, where ornament is
free from the taint of the marketplace and at the same time there is no question
of which objects will be brought into the home or how they will be maintained,
arranged, or cared for. Put simply, the Wooden Midshipman is an imaginative
solution to the problem of producing a home: Sol, Walter, Captain Cuttle, and
others are bound together by these possessions, united to pursue extraordinary
measures to preserve the interior. And yet these efforts have nothing to do
with acquisition or accumulation. It is literally impossible to put a price on
the contents of Sol's shop because they are no longer marketable and no one
can guess their use. They cannot be understood within the system of economic
exchange that exists outside of the shop because they are part of an earlier,
forgotten market. These objects can only have meaning given to them: they
bring no narrative history with them. There is no way that they can be con-
strued in terms of monetary value or class status. Because of the strangely
uncategorizeable, uncountable contents of the house, the process of preserving
family property for Uncle Sol and Walter cannot fall prey to avaricious
motives. The "thing-ness" of these objects forestalls the misappropriation of
their meaning.

A potential crisis for the Wooden Midshipman, however, appears in the
form of Mr. Brogley, the used-furniture dealer, in whose shop furnishings
are carelessly stacked and separated. In chapter 9, Walter returns home to
find Mr. Brogley occupying his uncle's house. In recompense for an old,
unpaid bill, the furniture dealer has taken possession of the shop. He threatens
to seize the things that have been carefully preserved and place them among
the amalgam of repossessed objects in his shop. Around the corner from the
Wooden Midshipman, the used-furniture dealer's store contains a pile of
domestic objects that are eternally in the process of being sold, bought, or
looked at:

> Dozens of chairs hooked on to washing-stands, which with difficulty poised
> themselves on the shoulders of sideboards, which in their turn stood upon the
> wrong side of dining-tables, gymnastic with their legs upward on the tops of
> other dining-tables, were among its most reasonable arrangements. A banquet
> array of dish-covers, wine-glasses, and decanters was generally to be seen,
> spread forth upon the bosom of a four post bedstead, for the entertainment of
> such genial company as half-a-dozen pokers, and a hall lamp. A set of window
> curtains with no windows belonging to them, would be seen gracefully draping
> a barricade of chests and drawers, loaded with little jars from chemists' shops;
> while a homeless hearth rug severed from its natural companion the fireside,
> braved the shrewd east wind in its adversity.   (134)

The anatomy of Brogley's shop points to the strangeness of things wrenched from their rightful positions, arranged without any thought of their real purpose or former function. A shop filled with furniture for the home, everything in Brogley's store is nonetheless "exhibited in the most uncomfortable aspect" (134). Items that could be thoughtfully arranged to suit the needs of a family are here simply piled in a heap. "Chairs" are attached to washing-stands, which are now "poised" on "side-boards"; "dish-covers, wine-glasses, and decanters" are spread out on a repossessed "four post bedstead"; "window curtains" have been draped over a "barricade of chests and drawers." Every thing is out of place. Anxiety about the seizure of possessions is overlaid with intense discontent at the thought of a home pulled apart. The most disconcerting part of this scene is not that the goods have been repossessed, but that they have been denied their natural function at home. These possessions have been forced into a role that is at odds with their true identity. Most jarring among these displacements is the "homeless hearth rug," a powerful emblem of middle-class Victorian comfort. It has been pulled from "its natural companion the fireside" and carelessly added to the general assortment of goods.

Walter and his uncle eventually manage to avert Brogley's repossession, but only after they appeal to Dombey to borrow the sum remaining on the bond owed by Walter's father. It is, fittingly, Little Paul, the intended young capitalist in training, who convinces Dombey to go through with the transaction. Although Paul is unable to find domestic comfort during his own life (the narrator tells us suggestively that he "had taken life unfurnished, and the upholsterer was never coming"), the boy manages to persuade his father to lend money to Sol and Walter to preserve the home that later serves as a sanctuary for his sister (171). The neglected storefront of the Wooden Midshipman is a truly idiosyncratic, Dickensian place of enduring, sentimental remembering, set apart from the ceaseless change and unfeeling transformation of Florence's nominal home.

It is reflective of Dickens's conception of the inescapable pathology of trade, exchange, and profit, that while the Wooden Midshipman witnesses Walter and Florence reunited, engaged, and married, the Dombey house is destroyed by the threat that they avoid. The collapse of the Dombey and Son firm at the end of the novel requires that every part of Dombey's life be appraised and repossessed, and an estate sale is ordered to dispose of his possessions. This sale of family property is held on the premises (as was often the case in the nineteenth century), and in preparing for the Dombey auction, objects are misused and misarranged in precisely the way that they are neglected in Brogley's shop. The spectacle of the estate sale is dismaying as much because of the purposeless disarray it occasions as because of the financial ruin that it records. Gentlemen with "pens and ink" "sit upon

pieces of furniture never made to be sat upon, and eat bread and cheese from
the public-house on other pieces of furniture never made to be eaten on, and
seem to have a delight in appropriating precious articles to strange uses''
(897). Unlike the Wooden Midshipman, where goods with little consumer
value have incalculable sentimental and nostalgic capital, things in the Dombey mansion are readily put to ''strange uses.'' Without a story of their own,
these things can be reordered as easily as one takes an item from the shelf.
But unlike a warehouse, in which there is a system for positioning goods and
a protocol for taking them down and replacing them, the possessions are
treated neglectfully and carelessly. ''[M]attresses and bedding appear in the
dining-room; the glass and china get into the conservatory; the great dinner
service is set out in heaps on the long divan in the large drawing-room; and
the stair-wires, made into fasces, decorate the marble chimney-pieces'' (897).
Taking apart the house strangely juxtaposes formality of endeavor—items
carefully inventoried, precisely described, and presented in a procession before the bidders—with the disorder, scarcely held beneath the surface, of a
home torn to pieces. The fiction of domestic stability is no longer convincing
for visitors, and in viewing the house overturned it is difficult to imagine that
it formerly had any special purpose or value beyond what the highest bidder
was willing to pay. The capacity for estrangement—both from owner and
from proper place—evident in these possessions indicates their inability to
constitute a home.

*

A visible emblem of security, safety, and nostalgic remembering in Sol Gills's
shop, domestic possessions are by contrast a marker of the ceaseless getting
and spending, superficiality, and financial and emotional insecurity in the
Dombey home. The Wooden Midshipman denies the strictures of separate
spheres ideology by reimagining a failed business as an idyllic home, representing a compromise between the ethos of collective endeavor and the incalculable profit of genuine care and affection. Unlike this store turned into a
home, the Dombey mansion is only further poisoned by efforts to bring it up
to speed with its proprietor's commercial status.

  Dombey and Son is written as a series of motorized moments in which the
interior of a house is set in motion with a jerking start. The crashing fall that
follows plagues observers who never know when the ride will begin or when
the journey is at its end. As readers we are led to cherish the firm, undisturbed
ground of the Wooden Midshipman precisely because it does not feel the
tremors of the surrounding commercial world. It offers a calming answer to
the anxieties in Victorian culture surrounding the articulation of interior

space. Not only is the presence of the railway crucial to understanding the way that domesticity functions in the novel, but the fragmented reflections between the railway and the domestic sphere illuminate a passage that has puzzled commentators. The counter-imagining of the railway and the Victorian home in *Dombey and Son* seems to me the proper context for understanding the famous passage in chapter 47, in which the narrator imagines what it would be like to "take the house-tops off" (702).

> Oh for a good spirit who would take the house-tops off, with a more potent and benignant hand than the lame demon in the tale, and show a Christian people what dark shapes issue from amidst their homes, to swell the retinue of the Destroying Angel as he moves forth among them! For only one night's view of the pale phantoms rising from the scenes of our too-long neglect; and, from the thick and sullen air where Vice and Fever propagate together, raining the tremendous social retributions which are ever pouring down, and ever coming thicker!   (702)

There have been a number of suggestions of how to interpret the "take the house-tops off" section; however, critics of the novel have been unable to find an explanation that seems to fit. Although the passage could suggest the point of view of a subject looking down from heaven, this appears unlikely since bricks, mortar, and tar would not impede that kind of sight in the first place. Dickens and his Christian readers shared the assumption that their acts of vice were always being observed regardless of the roof over their heads. In her insightful reading in *Vanishing Points: Dickens, Narrative, and the Subject of Omniscience*, Audrey Jaffe points out that the perspective imagined could be the panoptic viewpoint enjoyed by the reader of omniscient narration. Yet Jaffe notes that this type of looking, again, is neither aided nor impeded by architectural changes (79–80). "Tak[ing] the house-tops off" exposes domestic space to the kind of mortal gaze that it could not expect and improves a divine perspective that is needless of assistance.

But perhaps the perspective here is in fact that of a passenger on a railway, of the type depicted later in the century by Gustave Doré in his etching *Over London by Rail* (1872). An earlier scene in *Dombey and Son* provides encouragement for this view. When Dombey and Joey Bagstock visit Leamington in chapter 20 they travel using the railway, and without anything to read the reticent Dombey "looks out of his carriage window" during the trip (312). As he looks down on "jagged walls and falling houses," he sees "through the battered roofs and broken windows, wretched rooms . . . where want and fever hide themselves in many wretched shapes, while smoke, and crowded gables, and distorted chimneys, and deformity of brick and mortar penning up deformity of mind and body, choke the murky distance" (312). In through the windows and un-patched roofs of the houses that he passes,

Dombey sees lives marked by forms of deprivation, disease, and misery that he has never known. Viewing domestic life in this way appears very much like the privileged view of the interior that the narrator imagines in the "house-tops" passage. It allows passengers to look in from above on the domestic circumstances of anonymous townspeople, and it provides a special kind of access since it is unexpected—quite different from a planned visit by a neighbor, friend, or family member—and unobserved.

There is further evidence for this idea in the fact that Dombey's view from the railway compartment into the homes that he passes is described in language that parallels that of the "house-tops" passage. As the narrator imagines seeing "thick and sullen air where Vice and Fever propagate together," we are shown Dombey looking down on homes "where want and fever hide themselves in many wretched shapes" (702, 312). In the "house-tops" passage the narrator yearns for a chance to linger and look down for longer rather than to continue to move along. He desires the opportunity to pause and observe a hidden, yet familiar, portion of life for an unknown family. But Dombey is eager to continue on his trip and suffers no regret about neglecting to improve what he has witnessed. Considering the "house-tops" passage in the context of the railway refocuses it as a problem of mediated distance. The passage gestures to the everyday moments in which we are offered access to a private spectacle of misery and have to make a choice: to stop, investigate, and inquire how to help, or look away and continue on our journey.

In *Dombey and Son*, railway expansion necessitates the disruption of Staggs's Gardens, the razing of houses, the relocation of families such as the Toodles; but, at the same time, this amalgam of construction, relocation, and adaptation provides an opportunity for reflecting on what home can offer and what it in fact brings. Fittingly, when the fallen Dombey eventually recognizes, at the end of the novel, the value of the daughter to whom he has been callous and neglectful, there is time left for him to repair his relationship with Florence but not to make a home with her. Dombey, now happily reconciled to his daughter, appears in the final chapter out of doors on a "sea-beach," where he strolls with Florence, Walter, and their two children (947). This improbable family reunion, significantly, does not require the reader to imagine a house that could accommodate both Dombey and Florence, sidestepping one of the central problems of the novel. Ultimately, the bankruptcy of Dombey and Son, like the auction of the contents of the family house, ensures that both institutions have met their final end. As Dombey's employee, Mr. Morfin, informs Harriet Carker: "the House has fallen, never to be built up any more" (882).

NOTES

1. The introduction of the railway system had a real impact on the distribution of Londoners. One estimate is that four major railway building projects in London between 1856 and 1897 displaced between 4,000 and 5,000 people (Freeman and Aldcroft 5).

2. It is fair to note that John Dickens could not be trusted with money, and this is one reason why Dickens would have been reluctant to give him funds to furnish the cottage himself. On several occasions Johns Dickens forged Charles's name on a bill to borrow money and this later came to Dickens's attention. For more on this, see Ackroyd, *Dickens* 314, 324.

3. It is significant that the London & Birmingham Railway, the model for the railway line described in *Dombey and Son*, not only contributed to the alteration of the London cityscape but was also a pioneer in the efficient circulation of domestic wares. Prior to 1842 a map of the railway in England shows a number of short, privately owned, unconnected lines, making the shipping of objects from factory to warehouse, and from one depot to the next, unnecessarily cumbersome. Simmons and Biddle outline some of these problems. "Some companies would not accept the carriages of 'foreign' railways on their own lines . . . even when there was agreement on the through transit of 'foreign' wagons, there were disputes over the division of receipts between companies as there were no generally accepted mileage tables giving distances between stations. Some companies carried freight in their own wagons, others employed carriers on contract" (412). In response to the inefficiency of the system, the chairman of the London & Birmingham Railway, George Carr Glyn, arranged a meeting with the representatives of nine other railway companies on January 2, 1842. The conference resulted in the creation of the Railway Clearing House, which transformed railway transportation from a segmented, haphazard system into an efficient collective effort. Among the innovations of the Railway Clearing House was the establishment in 1847 of the first General Classification of Goods (sorting shipments of merchandise into five separate classes) and the recommendation of standard freight rates for the transportation of merchandise (Simmons and Biddle 413).

4. The railway compartment became a site for reading that rivaled the home during the 1840s, and publishers scurried to meet the public demand. In 1848 W. H. Smith secured the exclusive right to sell novels at Euston station, and the success of this stall quickly led the business to expand into a franchise (Schivelbusch 65). A year earlier the publishers Simm and Macintyre had opened their *Parlour Library*, a monthly series of one-shilling titles for sale on train platforms (Freeman 88). And in 1849, Routledge followed them into the market, cashing in on the craze for "railway literature" with the *Railway Library*.

5. For instance, see chapter 1 of Daly; chapter 2 of Sicher; and Baumgarten 65–89.

WORKS CITED

Ackroyd, Peter. *Dickens*. London: Sinclair-Stevenson, 1990.

Baumgarten, Murray. "Railway/Reading/Time: *Dombey and Son* and the Industrial World" *Dickens Studies Annual* 19 (1990) 65–89.

Beeton, Isabella. *Book of Household Management*. London, 1861.

Benjamin, Walter. *The Arcades Project*. Ed. Rolf Tiedemann. Trans. Howard Eiland and Kevin McLaughlin. Cambridge, MA: Belknap-Harvard UP, 1999.

Calder, Jenni. *The Victorian Home*. London: B. T. Batsford, 1977.

Chase, Karen and Michael Levenson. *The Spectacle of Intimacy*. Princeton, NJ: Princeton UP, 2000.

Cohen, Deborah. *Household Gods: The British and Their Possessions*. New Haven: Yale UP, 2006.

Cohen, Monica. *Professional Domesticity in the Victorian Novel: Women, Work, and Home*. Cambridge: Cambridge UP, 1998.

Daly, Nicholas. *Literature, Technology, and Modernity, 1860–2000*. Cambridge: Cambridge UP, 2004.

Dickens, Charles. *Dombey and Son*. Hammondsworth: Penguin, 2002.

———. *Great Expectations*. Hammondsworth: Penguin, 1965.

———. *Nicholas Nickleby*. Hammondsworth: Penguin, 1999.

———. *The Letters of Charles Dickens*. Volume 1: Ed. Madeline House and Graham Storey. Oxford: Clarendon, 1965. Volume 4: Ed. Madeline House, Graham Storey, and Kathleen Tillotson. Oxford: Clarendon, 1977.

Eastlake, Charles. *Hints on Household Taste*. 1868. New York: Dover, 1969.

Ellis, C. Hamilton. *Railway Carriages in the British Isles from 1830 to 1914*. London: George Allen & Unwin, 1965.

Freedgood, Elaine. *The Ideas in Things: Fugitive Meaning in the Victorian Novel*. Chicago: U of Chicago P, 2006.

Freeman, Michael. *Railways and the Victorian Imagination*. New Haven: Yale UP, 1999.

Freeman, Michael, and Derek H. Aldcroft, eds. *Transport in Victorian Britain*. Manchester: Manchester UP, 1988.

Gideon, Siegfried. *Mechanization Takes Command*. New York: Norton, 1969.

Gourvish, T. R. "Railways 1830–70: The Formative Years." *Transport in Victorian Britain*. Ed. Michael Freeman and Derek H. Aldcroft. Manchester: Manchester UP, 1988.

Habermas, Jürgen. *The Structural Transformation of the Public Sphere*. Trans. Thomas Burger. Cambridge, MA: MIT Press, 1989.

Hibberd, Shirley. *Rustic Adornments for Homes of Taste*. London, 1856.

Jaffe, Audrey. *Vanishing Points: Dickens, Narrative, and the Subject of Omniscience*. Berkeley: U of California P, 1991.

Langland, Elizabeth. *Nobody's Angels: Middle-Class Women and Domestic Ideology in Victorian Culture*. Ithaca, NY: Cornell UP, 1995.

Logan, Thad. *The Victorian Parlour*. Cambridge: Cambridge UP, 2001.

Perkin, Harold. *The Age of the Railway*. London: Panther Books, 1970.

Schaffer, Talia. ''Craft, Authorial Anxiety, and 'The Cranford Papers.' '' *Victorian Periodicals Review* 38.2 (Summer 2005): 221–39.

Schivelbusch, Wolfgang. *The Railway Journey: The Annihilation of Space and Time.* Berkeley: U of California P, 1986.

Sennett, Richard. *The Fall of Public Man.* New York: Knopf, 1977.

Sicher, Efraim. *Rereading the City, Rereading Dickens: Representation, the Novel, and Urban Realism.* New York: AMS, 2003.

Simmons, Jack, and Gordon Biddle. *The Oxford Companion to British Railway History.* Oxford: Oxford UP, 1997.

Wosk, Julie. *Breaking Frame: Technology and the Visual Arts in the Nineteenth Century.* New Brunswick, NJ: Rutgers UP, 1992.

Dickens, Collins, and the Influence of the Arctic

John Kofron

This essay examines the links between the Victorian fascination with Arctic exploration and three Dickens and Collins texts that were inspired by it. Using their collaboration on The Frozen Deep *as a lens through which to view their later novels, I trace the play's roots to Dickens's reliance on John Franklin's* Narrative of a Journey to the Shores of the Polar Sea *in his 1854 series of* Household Words *articles, "The Lost Arctic Voyagers," and follow the imagery that repeats from exploration narrative to periodical article to play. Then, moving forward, I examine* The Frozen Deep's *Arctic-inspired themes and motifs in Dickens's and Collins's later solo works,* A Tale of Two Cities *and* No Name, *finding that while each author incorporated the Arctic aesthetic into his novel, it resonates in Dickens's novel as an image of sublime sacrifice, and in Collins's as sublime defeat. This contrast seems to reveal both the culture's complicated response to Arctic exploration and the essential features of each writer's novelistic modus operandi.*

For a few nights in January 1857, in the gaslit schoolroom of Dickens's Tavistock House, which had been converted into a theater for the occasion, Charles Dickens and Wilkie Collins starred in performances of *The Frozen Deep*, a three-act play attributed to Collins, about a failed Arctic expedition. It was extremely well received, earning enthusiastic newspaper reviews and command performances before Queen Victoria, despite what Robert Louis Brannan calls "the negligible artistic merits of the play" (5). Dickens and

---

Collins played shipwrecked sailors marooned on the ice with the remnants of their crew and waiting out the polar winter in a drafty hut. Onstage,[1] icicles sprouted from chinks in the walls and snow fell through a gap in the ceiling while the characters described the scene as "pinching cold" and "below zero indoors" (119–20).[1] A door at the back of the room, center stage, opened on steadily falling snow and "a bleak polar prospect" (119). Against this desolate backdrop, the two authors performed in the melodrama of revenge and redemption that they had written for Dickens's Twelfth Night theatricals, but the play was a success because they were acting out a larger drama as well.

At the time of *The Frozen Deep* performances, Victorians were spellbound by the Arctic. Burke's theory of the sublime had combined with the mid-nineteenth century's steady stream of polar exploration narratives to create an image of the Arctic that embedded itself in the public imagination, as Francis Spufford details in *I May Be Some Time: Ice and the English Imagination*. Many of the era's most famous explorers, men like Parry, Ross, Franklin, and McClintock, wrote memoirs of their Arctic travels. These travel narratives were extremely popular, and they inspired fictional accounts and visual representations, like the Arctic diorama that dazzled visitors to Vauxhall gardens in the summer of 1852.[2] Francis Spufford describes how the culture became so preoccupied with ice and exploration that even the explorers began to imagine themselves engaged in an idealized encounter with the sublime.

A survey of nineteenth-century British novels reveals the extent to which Arctic exploration permeated the culture. Mary Shelley's *Frankenstein* (1818) is narrated from an Arctic expedition, and Charlotte Brontë's *Jane Eyre* (1847) opens with Jane reading an account of Arctic bird life in *Bewick's Birds*. In *The Mill on the Floss* (1860), George Eliot compares Maggie's new feelings toward Mrs. Stelling to those of Arctic explorers, "as to haggard men among the icebergs the mere presence of an ordinary comrade stirs the deep fountains of affection" (159). Dickens refers to the North Pole, where "wandering Esquimaux or civilized man" (231) would have verified Pip's supposed debt to Pumblechook in *Great Expectations* (1860–61), and Conrad's Marlow refers to the Arctic as "one of those particularly inviting" (5) blank spaces on the map in *Heart of Darkness* (1899). Each of these writers taps into their period's fascination with Arctic exploration, exploiting its aesthetic to create topical and thematic resonance. This widespread literary use of Arctic imagery helps explain the popularity of *The Frozen Deep*. The play's conceit, tropes, and imagery all proceed from the aesthetics of Arctic exploration that were in circulation at the time and would have had special significance with its original audience.

So, having written their own roles as polar explorers,[3] Dickens and Collins were acting out the larger, romantic vision of Arctic exploration that gripped the English imagination in the middle of the nineteenth century, and the experience lingered with each of them long after their performances in the play. Both authors incorporated aspects of *The Frozen Deep* into later novels that seem to have little to do with the Arctic: *A Tale of Two Cities* (1859) and *No Name* (1862). Like their contemporaries, Dickens and Collins subtly employed the Arctic exploration aesthetic to connect their novels with the culture's Arctic obsession, but they imagined the endeavor in very different ways. While Dickens was attracted to Arctic exploration as a moral struggle (resulting in a moral victory), it appealed to Collins as an image of quest and defeat. This difference reveals both the culture's complicated response to polar exploration and essential features of each writer's modus operandi.

Dickens and Collins wrote *The Frozen Deep* in direct response to the Franklin controversy, during "the period in which Victorian awareness of the Arctic was at its most intense—and at its grimmest" (Loomis 100). Sir John Franklin had set out in May 1845 on an expedition in search of the Northwest Passage. He was a veteran Arctic explorer, as were many of his officers and crew. His two steel-plated ships, the *Erebus* and the *Terror*, had also seen previous Arctic duty. They were equipped with propellers and locomotive engines to supplement their sails and were amply provisioned with fuel and food. The expedition was to travel in luxury (each ship held a full library and musical instruments for the crew's entertainment, as well as silver, cut glass, and fine china for dining), and their success was eagerly anticipated. The ships were last sighted in July 1845, by a whaling ship in Lancaster Sound. In 1847, the British Admiralty launched a fruitless search for Franklin and his men. In 1849, it offered a £10,000 reward for conclusive evidence of the expedition's fate. Years passed, and the British public grew anxious: "Franklin, his two ships, and his 128 men had utterly disappeared into that strange, cold world that had begun to haunt their imaginations" (Loomis 106).

Dr. John Rae of the Hudson Bay Company claimed the Admiralty's reward in 1854. In the course of his surveying work, Rae had heard from his Inuit contacts about a group of explorers who had died on the ice four winters earlier. He related this story in his report to the Secretary of the Admiralty and supported his claims with expedition relics that he had purchased from the Inuit; the Admiralty made Rae's report public in *The Times*. According to the Rae report, the *Erebus* and the *Terror* had become stuck in the ice, forcing the men to abandon ship. Inuit hunters had seen a small party of the expedition dragging a sledge across the ice. The explorers had communicated their story to the Inuit and bought a seal from them. Later in the spring, Inuit hunters discovered the remains of the expedition's camp, where some bodies were buried, others lay dead in their tents, some were found under a boat, and some were scattered on the ground. Rae horrified the public by adding, "From the mutilated state of many of the corpses and the contents of the pots it is evident that our wretched countrymen had been driven to the last resource—cannibalism—as a means of prolonging their existence'' (*The Times* Oct. 23, 1854).

Accounts of British sailors forced to the extremity of eating their companions' corpses were well known at the time, but the allegations of cannibalism in connection with Franklin and polar exploration deeply disturbed the Victorian reading public. Franklin embodied the idealized image of Arctic exploration that existed in the public imagination. He was a national hero who had fought alongside Lord Nelson at Trafalgar and represented the dignity of the British fleet. His popular *Narrative of a Journey to the Shores of the Polar Sea in the Years 1819–1822* had predisposed Victorian readers to gain inspiration from accounts of the long marches and staggering privations of Arctic exploration; that the explorers should succumb to their hunger was virtually inconceivable. Dr. Rae was a remarkable Arctic explorer in his own right, but his conclusions were unacceptable to most readers.

Lady Jane Franklin vehemently objected to Rae's allegations and their consequent stain on her husband's image. She was the living image of the sailor's wife peering hopefully out to sea from her widow's walk, though she had publicly worn mourning clothes for years. Through her worldwide appeals for help in finding her husband, she became a symbol of hope and feminine resilience. She had raised money to fund earlier rescue attempts, and she would later raise the funds for McClintock's expedition to clear her husband's name. Charles Dickens admired Lady Franklin's loyalty and fortitude and was in communication with her as he wrote his own defense of her husband.

In "The Lost Arctic Voyagers," a series of front-page *Household Words* articles published in December 1854, Dickens concedes the deaths of the Franklin party but refutes Rae's inference of cannibalism, writing that "close analogy, and the mass of experience are decidedly against the reception of any such statement" (361). The "close analogy" that Dickens proposes is to Franklin's *Narrative of a Journey to the Shores of the Polar Sea*. He supports his claims by appealing to his readers' familiarity with the literature of Arctic exploration, and it is in these articles that Dickens begins to cultivate the aesthetic of those narratives.

He begins by discrediting Rae's Inuit testimony, disparaging it as second-hand information from less than credible sources. He characterizes the Inuit as "savages" and writes, "we believe every savage to be in his heart covetous, treacherous, and cruel" (362). Dickens adds that he does not believe in the idea of the noble savage, that the Inuit had reasons to lie, and that they could have murdered Franklin and his men themselves. He elaborates on the issue of second-hand information by noting that it was "given at second-hand through an interpreter; and he was, in all probability, imperfectly acquainted with the language he translated to the white man'' (361). Citing Franklin's book in support of this last claim, Dickens refers to Franklin's own experience of the dialects spoken in the Arctic, and his interpreters' difficulty understanding the people they encountered. If this was the case with Franklin, he argues, it was likely the case with Rae's interpreters.

He continues the analogy between Franklin's book and Rae's report throughout "The Lost Arctic Voyagers," praising Franklin's narrative as "one of the most explicit and enthralling in the whole literature of Voyage and Travel" (363). He repeatedly quotes Franklin's descriptions of starvation and long marches on his earlier expedition, the men forced to eat their own shoes but never touching the nearby bodies. If Franklin and his men resisted the temptation then, Dickens argues, they were not likely to have succumbed to the temptation subsequently.

Significantly, there is one cannibal mentioned in Franklin's *Narrative*. Dickens cites Michel, an Iroquois hunter turned cannibal, as an illustration of the Arctic explorers' loathing for the act. During the long march from the Arctic Sea to Fort Enterprise, Michel had remained strong, as his fellow survivors grew more and more emaciated. When Michel was discovered to be murdering and eating his comrades, Sir John Richardson shot him through the head, as Dickens writes, "to the infinite joy of all the generations of readers who will honour him in his admirable narrative of that transaction" (364–65). Dickens concludes the article by comparing Michel's actions to Richardson's description[4] of him in the narrative, and emphasizing that the difference between the cannibal and the other explorers was the cannibal's lack of education, discipline, and religion. As men who possessed these qualities, the explorers, Dickens claims were impervious to the temptations of hunger.

The next week's installment tests "the Esquimaux kettle-stories by some of the most trying and famous cases of hunger and exposure on record" (365). In this article, Dickens retells several famous shipwreck stories, some resulting in cannibalism and some not, and again concludes that the source of cannibalism is the lack of education, discipline, and religion. He describes the undisciplined men aboard *The Peggy* who drew lots to determine which of them would be murdered and eaten, and he describes the drunken cannibalism of men on other ships. He maintains that to the lower classes, as well as to the undisciplined, the experience of privation "is much more maddening at sea than on shore" (391). Dickens claims that they become delusional at sea and begin hearing voices, among other symptoms; there are no examples of this type of behavior in Franklin's narrative because Franklin's men were educated, disciplined Christians. Dickens concludes, "the foremost question is—not the nature of the extremity; but, the nature of the men" (392).

Most of the third installment of "The Lost Arctic Voyagers" is given over to Dr. Rae's point-by-point reply to Dickens's arguments. Rae stands by his report, defending the character of the Inuit people and the credibility of his interpreter. Like Dickens, Rae supports his case by citing Franklin's *Narrative of a Journey to the Shores of the Polar Sea*, and bolsters it with reference to his own substantial Arctic experience. That both novelist and Arctic explorer support their arguments with accounts lifted from published exploration narratives makes perfect sense considering the subject of their dispute, but that they would lean so heavily on those accounts in the pages of a mainstream weekly magazine is a testament to the popular familiarity with Arctic exploration narratives at the time.

Three years later, Dickens still had "The Lost Arctic Voyagers" on his mind when he hired his friend Wilkie Collins to write a story of self-sacrificing Arctic heroism for his annual Twelfth Night theatricals. Franklin is named in the play's prologue, which sets the action in the Arctic, "Where Parry conquer'd and Franklin died" (97). *The Frozen Deep* is riddled with references to the expedition and continues the themes from the earlier *Household Words* articles. Lillian Nayder writes, "Indeed, Dickens conceived of the melodrama as a defense of the national honor; it was to safeguard the values embodied by Sir John Franklin and his lost band of Arctic explorers" (60).

The Frozen Deep opens in a country house where the female relatives of the members of a lost Arctic expedition have been living together for three years, waiting like Lady Franklin for their men's return. Mrs. Steventon, Rose Ebsworth, and Lucy Crayford express their concerns about a secret worry that torments Clara Burnham and about her prophesying Scottish nurse's troubling influence over her. Clara reveals her secret fear at the end of the first act. She explains that the spurned and brokenhearted Richard Wardour (played by Dickens) has sworn revenge on her betrothed, though ignorant of his identity, and that the two men had shipped out on the same polar expedition.

Nurse Esther claims that her "second sight" shows the explorers in terrible danger, especially Clara's fiancé, Frank Aldersley (played by Collins). She prophesizes to Clara: "Doos the Sight show me Frank? Aye! And anither beside Frank. I see the lamb I' the grasp o' the lion. I see your bonnie bird alone wi' the hawk. I see you and all around you crying bluid! The stain is on you! Oh my bairn, my bairn, the stain o' that bluid is on you!" (116). The curtain falls with Clara weeping on Lucy's breast.

The second act moves the action to the expedition's Arctic camp. The men of the *Sea Mew* and the *Wanderer* are marooned on the polar ice and running out of supplies. John Want, their cook, has no food to prepare (as his name suggests) and is reduced to pounding bones for soup. The men choose members for a last-ditch rescue mission by drawing lots from Want's empty cooking pot. The suspense builds as Wardour discovers that Aldersley is Clara's fiancé, and the act ends with the villainous Wardour joining Aldersley in the rescue attempt and leading him off into the icy wastes—a clear echo of the murderous Iroquois hunter from Franklin's *Narrative*.

In act 3, the women have traveled to the Newfoundland coast to meet their rescued men. The entire expedition has been accounted for except Wardour and Aldersley, when a disheveled Wardour enters the room alone, seemingly confirming his villainy. But, going outside again, he comes back holding Aldersley, who has survived. The exhausted Wardour describes carrying Aldersley across the ice and tells of hearing voices debating whether he should kill this rival. Wardour, after revealing that his final decision was to save Frank for the woman they both love, dies in the play's final tableau, having sacrificed his life for Clara's happiness.

The Frozen Deep is essentially an adaptation of Dickens's "Lost Arctic Voyagers" articles into melodramatic form. As we have observed, Franklin is named in the play's prologue, and the image of two ships stuck in the ice makes it clear that the play alludes to the expedition. The women wait together for news of their men, like Lady Franklin, who waited for news of her husband, and like the British public awaiting news of the Franklin expedition. Nurse Esther's misleading second-sight represents the speculations fueled by Franklin's disappearance, as well as Rae's secondhand information.

References to hunger and cannibalistic allusions run throughout the play as well. The cook, John Want, is a comedic figure, and the vehicle for many of the implicit references to the Franklin controversy. John Want's comedic allusions to the tropes of cannibalism (like the drawing of lots and empty cooking pots) sucks the power from its imagery, and the story that he tells about overcoming sea sickness reinforces Dickens's belief in the civilizing power of discipline: "never you give in to your stomach," Want says, "and your stomach will end in giving in to you" (123).

The sum of these themes would make *The Frozen Deep* appear to be Dickens's work, but its authorship has always been credited to Collins. According to Brannan, Collins wrote the script "to meet the requirements of a notion suggested by Dickens and of an amateur cast selected by Dickens" (5). He explains that Dickens's "notion" was Wardour's regeneration through self-sacrifice, set on the Arctic wastes where Franklin had died, as well as the character of the Scottish housekeeper. Collins worked these ideas into a plot of his own construction and submitted it to Dickens for revisions, but Brannan credits the plot to Collins, built around Dickens's imagery. The early focus on the women waiting at home, which is so suggestive of Lady Franklin, the rivalry plot, and Wardour's long march at the end all seem to be Collins's creation. This last element is a trope of Arctic exploration narratives. The explorers were often forced to leave their boats, and large portions of the narratives detail the resulting marches. Spufford writes, "the march-till-you-drop plots of the polar narratives, while dramatic, were not easy to mount onstage'' (179). Collins addresses the issue neatly by keeping it off-stage.

Wardour's actions in the march-till-you-drop plot reinforce Dickens's belief in the morality of Franklin's men and of Arctic explorers in general. Over the course of his long march, Wardour battles with himself over whether or not to kill Aldersley. His decision in the end to sacrifice his own life redeems the otherwise villainous character and illustrates the sacrifice Dickens imagined of Franklin and his men. Rather than stain the image of the British navy, Dickens imagines the explorers as disciplined and honorable to the end. Diana Arbin Ben-Merre characterizes the play as a Dickensian insistence that ''despite temptation, the white man in the Arctic will triumph morally'' (212).

Two years later, in his preface to *A Tale of Two Cities*, Dickens wrote, ''When I was acting, with my children and friends, in Mr. Wilkie Collins's drama of The Frozen Deep, I first conceived the main idea of this story'' (397). The idea of the self-sacrificing hero is found in ''The Lost Arctic Voyagers,'' becomes Richard Wardour in the *The Frozen Deep*, and then Sydney Carton in *A Tale of Two Cities*. The self-sacrificing Englishman transmigrates from article to play to novel, the Arctic connection becoming subtler as the successive characters' moral foundations become stronger.

Richard Wardour and Sydney Carton are both withdrawn individuals, negatively viewed by those around them. Both characters are unsuccessful lovers who, in their moments of defeat, make dramatic promises to the women they adore, and each ultimately lays down his own life for the life of his rival. Both characters transform into unlikely heroes, but while Richard Wardour's transformation comes from resisting the temptation to kill, Sydney Carton is never regarded as a villain. A morally improved adaptation of the Wardour character, he is ''recalled to life'' by resolving to die for others, as Wardour is morally improved as he is adapted from Michel, Franklin's wolfish Iroquois cannibal.

When Richard Wardour is introduced in act II of *The Frozen Deep*, he is the only member of the lost expedition who seems content in the Arctic isolation. His bitterness makes the frozen waste seem like a refuge, as he explains in a conversation with his rival:

> Wardour: You may think it horrible—I like it.
> Aldersley: Like it! Good Heavens! Why?
> Wardour: (Seating himself in a corner) Because there are no women here.
>
> (126)

Sydney Carton has a similar conversation with his rival early in *A Tale of Two Cities*, but in Carton Dickens has removed the motivation for his character's bitterness, leaving only a vague melancholy. Carton describes his attitude toward civilization this way: "As to me, the greatest desire I have, is to forget that I belong to it. It has no good in it for me—except wine like this—nor I for it" (87).

Both versions of the character have their defenders—friends who see the inner virtue beneath the bitterness or dissipation, and this role of defending a noble man to his critics is much like Dickens's role as Franklin's defender in the "Lost Arctic Voyagers." Each character is defended to his rival, and these defenses function in both cases to foreshadow the character's transformation at the story's end. Lieutenant Crayford tells Aldersley, "He is not a naturally sullen man. Under all his outward defects there beats a generous heart. You are prejudiced against Richard Wardour from not knowing enough of him" (125). Lucie Manette tells Charles Darnay, "My husband, it is so. I fear he is not to be reclaimed; there is scarcely a hope that anything in his character or fortunes is reparable now. But, I am sure that he is capable of good things, gentle things, even magnanimous things" (217). Wardour's "generous heart" and Carton's "magnanimous things" spring to life at the end of each work, redeeming both characters.

The most striking difference between Wardour and Carton lies in the nature of their promises. Wardour vows a bitter revenge when rejected by Clara, setting himself up as a villain for the bulk of the play so that his sacrifice at the end comes as a complete surprise. Wardour says, "The time may come when I shall forgive *you* . . . but the man who has robbed me of you shall rue the day when you and he first met" (113). Sydney Carton's promise uses almost the same language, but to a very different purpose:

> The time will come, the time will not be long in coming, when new ties will be formed about you—ties that will bind you yet more tenderly and strongly to the home you so adorn—the dearest ties that will ever grace and gladden you. O Miss Manette, when the little picture of a happy father's face looks up in yours, when you see your own bright beauty springing up anew at your feet, think now and then that there is a man who would give his life, to keep a life you love beside you!   (159)

Carton's vow is almost inexplicable except in contrast with Wardour's. While Wardour's decision to sacrifice himself comes from an inner struggle between good and evil as a result of his Arctic privations, Carton's inner virtue is constant (if buried under his dissipation) throughout *A Tale of Two Cities*. Again, Dickens's characters become more idealized and self-sacrificing with each transformation, drawing closer to his image of Arctic explorers as the connection becomes less explicit.

Both Wardour and Carton take dramatic walks near the ends of their lives. The distinction between constancy and temptation in their characters is most evident in these final walks. As he lies dying at the end of act III, Wardour recounts his conflict over whether to kill or rescue Aldersley. He describes the voices tempting him over the course of his icy walk. He is the lower-class delusional extracted from ''The Lost Arctic Voyagers,'' but somehow overcomes himself and does not kill. In Sydney Carton's famous walk before consummating his vow, his resolve only deepens. Carton's dissipated life finds purpose in sacrifice and he never falters, repeating his allusion to John 11:25, ''I am the resurrection and the life'' (327). Wardour's dangerous, low-class delusion is transformed into Carton's Christian resolve, and though not an Arctic explorer, Carton *is* a self-sacrificing Englishman who dies for a noble cause.

The influence of *The Frozen Deep* did not end with Sydney Carton and the guillotine. Two years after the publication of *A Tale of Two Cities*, Wilkie Collins incorporated aspects of *The Frozen Deep* into *No Name*. This use serves as a counterpoint to Dickens's approach, and is as revealing of his attitude toward Arctic exploration and his novelist's technique as Dickens's use of it is of his own.

No Name tells the story of Magdalen Vanstone, who loses her family fortune through a legal technicality and swears that she will regain it by whatever means necessary. This single-minded determination to revenge bears a strong resemblance to Richard Wardour's in *The Frozen Deep* and, metaphorically, to the determination of polar explorers in general. In Collins's *No Name*, Magdalen exploits her innate acting ability to perform three counterfeit roles in three failed attempts at recovering her family fortune. It is the last of these schemes that draws specifically on *The Frozen Deep*. Posing as her former maid Louisa, Magdalen goes to work at St. Crux, Admiral Bartram's country estate where she hopes to find a document known as ''the secret trust'' that may hold the key to her fortune. Magdalen spends most of her time at St. Crux watching and waiting. Lengthy waiting, as the twentieth-century nature-writer Barry Lopez suggests, seems associated with polar exploration: ''To travel in the Arctic is to wait'' (357).

The Admiral and his servant, Mazey, are two former sailors who bring to mind the camaraderie of the Arctic explorers in *The Frozen Deep*. The elderly seamen make frequent allusions to polar exploration in their dialogue and in their descriptions of St. Crux's banquet hall, which Philip Allingham details in an article on the Victorian Web.[5] Old Mazey, as the novel's chief spokesman for things Arctic, is a sailor without a ship, as John Want is a cook without food, and his comic incongruity deflates the otherwise powerful Franklin allusions as Want's deflates his allusions to cannibalism. Mazey describes the hall in words that echo Want's voice in *The Frozen Deep*: ''The floor's mortal cold, and the damp sticks to the place like cockroaches to a collier [a coal ship]. His honour the admiral calls it the Arctic Passage. I've got my name for it too. I call it, Freeze-your-Bones''(630). The banquet hall is a vast and inexplicably cold room that connects St. Crux's two wings. Magdalen's exploration of the house hinges on her exploration of Freeze-your-Bones, and her last hope of achieving her revenge depends on crossing "the Arctic Passage" to steal the secret trust. This chilly room leads to the sickness that kills Admiral Bartram as the Arctic Passage killed Franklin, and it nearly causes the death of Magdalen, who becomes gravely ill. As Allingham explains, "Upon the verge of the truth, the Secret Trust actually in her hands, she is again frustrated—this time by old Mazey. Like Franklin and his party, she is brought to a halt within clear sight of her goal."

Yet, despite all of this suffering, Collins keeps his Arctic references light. While Dickens envisions Arctic exploration as a moral triumph, it gets a wink and a nod from Collins. Magdalen's eventual failure is foreshadowed by the first casual mention of the Northwest Passage in *No Name*, when Captain Wragge sends word that the friends searching for Magdalen "will as soon find the North-West Passage" (184) as find her. Finding a sea route along North America's northern coast is referred to as an impossibility here, and Collins maintains his sardonic tone toward the endeavor throughout the novel. He goes on to use the Northwest Passage as a pun in the St. Crux section of the novel, effectively mocking Franklin though Magdalen's parallel adventures, and the resonance is darkly humorous.

The suspense in both *No Name* and *The Frozen Deep* hinges on revenge plots. We learn early in each work of the vengeance driving Magdalen Vanstone and Richard Wardour and the pressure builds as we follow their schemes. Like Wardour, Magdalen becomes feverishly delusional; like Dickens's lower-class seamen and like Wardour, she abandons her revenge plot in the process. Both characters undergo deathbed redemptions, but unlike Wardour, Magdalen recovers. Captain Kirk, whose ship is aptly named *The Deliverance*, aids Magdalen's recovery. This is a deliverance that Wardour and Franklin never had, but it is also a salvation that Magdalen is not responsible for herself. Unlike Carton, who makes a sublime sacrifice, Magdalen experiences a sublime defeat. The quest and defeat motif is another feature of Arctic exploration narratives, but a very different one than Dickens emphasizes, and while Dickens transforms the specifics of these narratives into a form that only faintly echoes his Arctic sources, Collins keeps the echoes specific and right on the surface.

These details are among the hallmarks of their writing styles. Dickens wrote on broad, moral themes, and his later social novels attacked broad issues like poverty and injustice. Collins wrote on very specific issues, like inheritance law reform in *No Name*. His later novels attacked such specific topics that Bradford Booth describes the later Collins as a "propaganda novelist" (134).

Yet these two novels, *A Tale of Two Cities* and *No Name*, draw their inspiration from the same source, and the ways that these two authors adopt the Arctic exploration motifs to reinforce themes in their novels reveal the complicated public perception of the Arctic endeavor. Far from being a homogenous idealization, Victorians imagined Arctic exploration in starkly contrasting ways, which, while hidden in the authors' staging of *The Frozen Deep*, are revealed in their later uses of the Arctic aesthetic. Like Carton, Dickens's heroes often undergo a moral transformation, in keeping with his romantic image of the Arctic explorers. Like Magdalen, Collins's rebellious heroes are generally contained by his conventional endings; their aspirations, like those of the Arctic explorers, end in defeat. When the two authors stood onstage together at Tavistock House, seeming to embody the Victorian ideal of Arctic exploration, they were in fact embodying conflicting ideals.

Some of this is a function of the different interests of the two novelists, but the age difference may also account for the different ways Dickens and Collins used the Arctic aesthetic in their work. Dickens, the older writer, was a child of the early part of the century and was inspired by Parry's and Franklin's narratives. He wanted to believe in civilized man overcoming the awesome coldness of inhospitable nature. But the controversy over the Franklin expedition changed things. Collins, Dickens's junior by twelve years, had his formative impressions of Arctic exploration in Franklin's last voyage. He could joke in his work about the disparity between the dream of Arctic exploration and the reality.

NOTES

1. This set description is based on the text of *The Frozen Deep*, a photograph of the Tavistock House schoolroom that appeared in *The Dickensian* 22 (1926), and Nathaniel Powell's sketch of the stage, in *The Dickensian* 56 (1960).
2. See Potter for an examination of Victorian visual representations of the Arctic.
3. While *The Frozen Deep* was originally attributed to Collins, it has long been considered a collaboration. As Robert Louis Brannan writes, ''Dickens' part in the genesis of the idea and of the script and Dickens' contributions as manager and actor make the 1857 version of 'The Frozen Deep' at least as much Dickens' work as Collins' ''(5). Also see Nayder and Trodd for analyses of the Dickens/ Collins collaborative relationship.
4. Franklin included extracts from his fellow officers' journals in his narrative, and this section is in Richardson's words (395–406).
5. Allingham gives credit to Professor Peter Caracciolo for first suggesting that in *No Name* Collins is alluding to the Franklin Expedition when describing the ''Freeze-your-Bones'' passage of St. Crux.

WORKS CITED

Allingham, Philip V. "Wilkie Collins's *No Name* (1862): Charles Dickens, Sheridan's *The Rivals*, and the Lost Franklin Expedition." The Victorian Web. http://victorianweb. org/authors/collins/1.html. February 1, 2006.

Ben-Merre, Diana Arbin. "Conrad's Marlow and Britain's Franklin: Redoubling the Narrative in Heart of Darkness." *Conradiana* 34 (2002): 211–28.

Booth, Bradford A. "Wilkie Collins and the Art of Fiction." *Nineteenth Century Fiction* 6 (1951–1952): 131–43.

Brannan, Robert Louis. Introduction. *Under the Management of Mr. Charles Dickens: His Production of "The Frozen Deep."* Ithaca, NY: Cornell UP, 1966. 1–92.

Brontë, Charlotte. *Jane Eyre: An Authoritative Text, Contexts, Criticism.* Ed. Richard J. Dunn. New York: Norton, 2001.

Collins, Wilkie. "The Frozen Deep." *Under the Management of Mr. Charles Dickens.* Ed. Robert Louis Brannan. Ithaca, NY: Cornell UP, 1966. 93–160.

———. *No Name.* Ed. Virginia Blain. Oxford: Oxford UP, 1998.

Conrad, Joseph. *Heart of Darkness.* New York: Dover, 1990.

Dickens, Charles. *Great Expectations.* Ed. Charlotte Mitchell. London: Penguin, 1996.

———. "The Lost Arctic Voyagers." *Household Words*, 2 December 1854: 361–65.

———. "The Lost Arctic Voyagers." *Household Words*, 9 December 1854: 385–93.

———. "The Lost Arctic Voyagers." *Household Words*, 23 December 1854: 433–36.

———. "The Lost Arctic Voyagers." *Household Words*, 30 December 1854: 457–59.

———. *A Tale of Two Cities.* Ed. Richard Maxwell. London: Penguin, 2003.

Eliot, George. *The Mill on the Floss: An Authoritative Text, Backgrounds and Contemporary Reactions, Criticism.* Ed. Carol T. Christ. New York: Norton, 1994.

Franklin, John. *Narrative of a Journey to the Polar Sea in the Years 1818–1822.* New York: Cosimo, 2005.

Kirwan, L. P. *A History of Polar Exploration.* New York: Norton, 1960.

Loomis, Chauncey C. "The Arctic Sublime." *Nature and the Victorian Imagination.* Ed. U. C. Knoepflmacher and G. B. Tennyson. Berkeley: U of California P, 1977.

Lopez, Barry. *Arctic Dreams.* New York: Simon and Schuster, 1986.

Nayder, Lillian. *Unequal Partners: Charles Dickens, Wilkie Collins, and Victorian Authorship.* Ithaca, NY: Cornell UP, 2002.

Potter, Russell. *Arctic Spectacles: The Frozen North in Visual Culture, 1818–1875.* Seattle: U of Washington P; Montréal: McGill-Queen's UP, 2007.

Rae, John. "Report to the Secretary of the Admiralty." *The Times (London).* 23 October 1854: 7.

Spufford, Francis. *I May Be Some Time: Ice and the English Imagination.* New York: St. Martin's, 1997.

"Tavistock House." *The Dickensian* 22 (1926): 48–50.

"Tavistock House Theatricals." *The Dickensian* 56 (1960): 158–59.

Trodd, Anthea. "Collaborating in Open Boats: Dickens, Collins, Franklin, and Bligh." *Victorian Studies* 42 (2000): 201–26.

Darkness, Light, and Various Shades of Gray: The Prison and the Outside World in Charles Dickens's *A Tale of Two Cities*[1]

Jan Alber

This essay deals with the psychological and narrative effects of the prison experience in Charles Dickens's A Tale of Two Cities *(1859). More specifically, by analyzing the imprisonment of Dr. Manette and Charles Darnay, I show that the Bastille and the prison of La Force serve as the novel's most important focal points at which the reciprocal connections between the narrative's binary oppositions are negotiated and restructured. The novel as a whole and its color symbolism in particular accentuate the dynamic relationship between dichotomies by merging the prisons' darkness with the brightness of the free world. Dickens's* Tale *thus demonstrates that, albeit to various different degrees, everyone in society oscillates between poles. And, surprisingly, sometimes prisoners can teach the free world something it has forgotten about, namely how to achieve a sense of decency, community, and respect for others.*

1.

As many critics have shown, and indeed as the novel's opening suggests, Charles Dickens's *A Tale of Two Cities*, which was published in 31 installments during the course of the year 1859, is structured around a number of dichotomies:

Dickens Studies Annual, Volume 40, Copyright © 2009 by AMS Press, Inc. All rights reserved.

It was the *best* of times, it was the *worst* of times, it was the age of *wisdom*, it was the age of *foolishness*, it was the epoch of *belief*, it was the epoch of *incredulity*, it was the season of *Light*, it was the season of *Darkness*, it was the spring of *hope*, it was the winter of *despair*, we had *everything* before us, we had *nothing* before us, we were all going direct to *Heaven*, we were all going direct *the other way*—in short, the period was so far like the present period, that some of its noisiest authorities insisted on its being received, for good or for evil, in the superlative degree of comparison only.

(5; my emphasis)

Stange adds that a "notion of reciprocity between private and public, England and France, past and present, imposes a pattern of parallelism on Dickens's novel" (385). Other mutual connections in the novel concern poles like stasis and kinesis, solitude and community, stable (or coherent) selves and the erasure of identities, decency and cruelty, and so forth. However, the significance of the prison institution with regard to the dialectical relationship between these dichotomies has been neglected by Dickens critics.[2] In this essay, I show that the prisons in this novel actually serve as the most important focal points at which the reciprocal connections between the narrative's binary oppositions are negotiated and then restructured.[3]

At first glance, the novel associates the prison with darkness, hopelessness, stasis, solitude, cruelty, the erasure of identities, and death.[4] The outside world, on the other hand, is linked with light, hope, kinesis, community, friendship, decency, stable identities, and, quite generally, life. Yet, upon closer inspection, the novel deconstructs the dichotomies around which it is structured by positing a homological structure between the prison and the outside world. In Stephen Greenblatt's terminology, one may describe the connection between the prison and the outside world in Dickens's *Tale* in terms of "extended borrowings, collective exchanges, and mutual enchantments" (7). The novel merges the prison's darkness with the brightness of the outside world, thus presenting us with various shades of gray. More specifically, many segments of the world outside the prison are shown to be prison-like correlates of constraint (e.g., Manette's room at the Defarges and also Tellson's bank) or metaphorical prisons (e.g., revolutionary France is represented as a prison, and Sydney Carton is metaphorically imprisoned by his individualism in so far as it correlates with loneliness and a lack of interaction), while the prison of La Force is represented as a matrix of spiritual rebirth and the only space in revolutionary France where true friendship is possible.

I will first look at the way in which the novel narrates the imprisonment of Dr. Manette and then move on to the confinement of Charles Darnay. My ultimate goal is to show that the prisons in *A Tale of Two Cities* renegotiate the narrative's dichotomies.

2.

Dr. Manette is one of the many victims of Charles Darnay's father and the marquis's twin brother, who are aristocratic tyrants: they are both Evrémondes and after Charles's father had died, the uncle inherited the title Marquis St. Evrémonde. Manette was unjustly imprisoned in the Bastille for eighteen years because he knew that Charles's father, the marquis, had allowed his brother to rape a "common" woman and kill her brother (333–40). More specifically, Manette was imprisoned because he wrote "privately to the Minister" about "the knowledge that [he] possessed" (342). After his release, Manette lives in the house of the Defarges, two major plotters of the French Revolution, and is then taken to England by his daughter Lucie and Mr. Lorry.

We first "see" Manette's cell during the storming of the Bastille toward the end of the novel's second book. Before this event, we get to know the ex-inmate Manette in a "dim and dark" (41) room above the wine shop of the Defarges. Even though Manette's prison experience is only rendered retrospectively and by means of external focalization, the novel's authorial narrator manages to represent the Bastille as a powerful tool for erasing the prisoner's identity and his status as a human being.[5]

When Mr. Lorry and Lucie visit the freed Manette in his room, Mr. Lorry asks the formerly "buried man" Manette, "I hope you care to be recalled to life?" Manette then answers "I can't say" (53). This conversation associates the prison with a tomb,[6] and this connotation might imply that Manette has experienced some sort of death that correlates with the loss of his former identity. Nevertheless, Manette got so used to the stasis and solitude of prison life that he continues to live in a state of quasi-voluntary self-confinement. From this perspective, one might associate the static world of the prison with a womb that makes prisoners dependent.[7] The ex-inmate wishes to be locked up in his room because, as Defarge puts it, "he has lived so long, locked up, that he would be frightened—rave—tear himself to pieces—die—come to I know not what harm—if his door was left open" (39). In other words, Manette would not be able to cope with his freedom any longer and therefore has to be imprisoned by Defarge.

It is worth noting that Defarge is not at all interested in Manette as a person but only as a victim of the ancien régime with special knowledge of the marquis. Furthermore, Defarge becomes Manette's turnkey and continues to imprison him because he intends to use Manette for his purposes later on. Defarge thus objectifies the former prisoner in a manner that is rather similar to the objectification Manette experienced in prison.[8] We learn more about Manette's objectification in the Bastille as the novel continues, but it is worth noting that already at this point, the prison and the outside world begin to merge.

The objectification Manette experienced in prison is conveyed as follows: When Defarge asks the former prisoner for his name, Manette answers: "One Hundred and Five, North Tower" (44). In the Bastille, Manette has lost his former identity. And even though he was freed, the ex-inmate still considers himself to be nothing but an insignificant number.[9] Manette no longer fully exists as a person, and even appears to have become indistinguishable from his clothes: "He, and his old canvas frock, and his loose stockings, and all his poor tatters of clothes, had, in a long seclusion from direct light and air, faded down to such a dull uniformity of parchment-yellow, that it would have been hard to say which was which" (43). This image illustrates that the prison has turned Manette into an object devoid of human features. Manette's body is described as being "withered and worn," and when he puts up his hand to shield his eyes from the incoming light, "the very bones . . . seemed transparent" (43). His voice appears to be similar to that of a ghost: "it was like the last feeble echo of a sound made long ago"; "it was like a voice underground" (42). According to Gross, such ghostliness suggests some kind of "death in life to which men are reduced by imprisonment, psychological or actual" (188).

Moreover, the prisoner appears to have "lost the habit of associating place with sound" (*TTC* 43). This should come as no surprise because, as I have shown elsewhere (Alber, "Bodies Behind Bars"), the complete lack of sensory stimulation with which solitary confinement in dark cells correlates frequently results in disorientation and sometimes even drives prison inmates to the verge of madness. Fear has presumably transformed Manette into a "docile" body used to complying with orders. We learn that "in the submissive way of one long accustomed to obey under coercion, he ate and drank what they gave him to eat and drink" (51).

At one point, Miss Pross tells Mr. Lorry that Manette probably does not want to talk about his former imprisonment because he is afraid of it. In this passage, we also learn that Manette's former identity was erased in prison and that he continuously returns to his prison cell during the night:

> He is afraid of the whole subject. . . . It's plain enough, I should think, why he may be. It's a dreadful remembrance. *Besides that, his loss of himself grew out of it. Not knowing how he lost himself, or how he recovered himself, he may never feel certain of not losing himself again.* . . . Sometimes, he gets up in the dead of the night, and will be heard, by us overhead there, walking up and down, walking up and down, in his room. Ladybird has learnt to know then that his mind is walking up and down, walking up and down, in his old prison. She hurries to him, and they go on together, walking up and down, walking up and down, until he is composed. But he never says a word of the true reason of his restlessness, to her, and she finds it best not to hint at it to him. In silence they go walking up and down together, walking up and down together, till her love and company have brought him to himself.   (101–02; my emphasis)

Later on, when his daughter marries Darnay and Manette finds out that Lucie's husband is the nephew of the evil marquis, Manette relapses into the shoemaking he learned in prison. Thus, "the bench was turned toward the light, as it had been when he [Lorry] had seen the shoemaker at his work before [i.e., at the wine shop], and his head was bent down, and he was very busy" (202). That is to say, like the Dorrits in Dickens's *Little Dorrit* (1855–57), Manette has internalized the prison and does not manage to over-come it.[10] The formerly imprisoned doctor remains tied to its static world even after his release.

Up until now, the narrator of the *Tale* has primarily conveyed the horrors of the prison through dialogue and description of Manette's body. More specifically, the narrator concentrates on the representation of Manette's state of mind through exterior details such as his appearance (43), his bodily consti-tution (43), the tone of his voice (42), his facial expressions (51), and his disconcerting actions (43, 51, 98, 202). Even though the internalization of the prison is primarily rendered in retrospect and through external focaliza-tion, the depiction of Manette is a plausible portrait of a human being who is severely damaged after the experience of imprisonment.

Later on, the novel's narrator begins to elucidate the marks on Manette's body and mind by finally showing us Manette's cell during the storming of the Bastille. He describes the solitary prison cell as follows:

> There was a small, heavily grated, unglazed window high in the wall, with a stone screen before it, so that *the sky could be only seen by stooping low and looking up*. There was a small chimney, heavily barred across, a few feet within. *There was a heap of old feathery wood ashes on the hearth.* There was a stool, and table, and a straw bed. There were four blackened walls, and a rusted iron ring in one of them.   (227; my emphasis)

This dreary image provides the context for Manette's state after his release. We can now "see" that the Bastille was a cruel institution in which inmates were exposed to austerity, solitude, monotony, and darkness. To begin with, since the inmate presumably tried to look at the sky quite frequently, the position of the window must have had rather severe effects on his body. On a symbolic level, the distance between the small gap and the prisoner might additionally connote the absence of hope in this prison scenario. Furthermore, the "heap of old feathery wood ashes on the hearth" might symbolize Manet-te's former identity which the prison managed to erase. The monotony of prison life is here also conveyed through the anaphoric use of "there was."

However, the narrator of Dickens's novel does not only allude to the horrors of the prison through external details; rather, he also allows us to get proper inside views. At one point, the narrator moves to a quasi-close-up of Manette's face, and argues that it is difficult to learn something about the prisoner's mind by studying his external features: "No human intelligence could have read the mysteries of his mind, in the scared blank wonder of his face. Whether he knew what had happened, whether he recollected what they had said to him, whether he knew that he was free, were questions which no sagacity could have solved" (51). The narrator seems to know that it is easier to understand the mysteries of the prisoner's mind from an internal (as opposed to an external) perspective.

Hence, in the novel's second book, the narrator allows Manette to present his own internally focalized account of the prison. We learn more about what the prison did to Manette when he presents Lucie with a report of "his old condition" (197) and tells her that in the Bastille, he imagined two daughters. One version of Lucie was "perfectly forgetful of me—rather, altogether ignorant of me, and unconscious of me" (196). The other version was sympathetic but of course unable to free him from his cell: the ex-prisoner argues that the second Lucie would take him "out to show me that the home of her married life was full of her loving remembrance of her lost father. My picture was in her room, and I was in her prayers. Her life was active, cheerful, useful; but my poor history pervaded it all" (197).

This account and our knowledge of the existence of two versions of Lucie allow us to elaborate on the effects of imprisonment. The Bastille has turned Manette into some sort of split personality. The prison has created two selves[11] which he does not manage to reconcile, namely, an imprisoned and hopeless self on the one hand, and a hopeful self (which ultimately does not manage to set him free), on the other. And these two selves seem to have fed into Manette's vision of two Lucies. Furthermore, Manette's account allows us to expand upon what happens to Manette when he requests his shoemaking tools. At this stage, his hopeful self is erased, and he is entirely dominated by his hopeless prison self.

The novel's third book continues to depict the prison from an internal perspective and presents us with Manette's testimony (331–45). To begin with, Manette notes that he was continuously policed by agents of the prison, and that he was only in a position to work "at stolen intervals, under every difficulty." We also learn that he had "slowly and laboriously made a place of concealment for it [his testimony]," namely "the wall of the chimney" (331). Furthermore, we are told that after a weary decade in prison, Manette's senses began to wither away ("my reason will not long remain unimpaired" [331]), and he argues that "[h]ope has quite departed from [his] breast" [331]) in the Bastille, which he calls his "living grave" (344). This document illustrates that the prison can gain complete control over the prisoner and his mind. The prison does not only correlate with the incarceration of Manette's body; it also gains access to and power over the prisoner's thoughts and feelings by policing its inmates.

As we have seen, the narrator represents the prison as a powerful tool for erasing the prisoner's former identity. I will demonstrate now the way in which Manette's identity is wiped out again outside prison when the revolutionaries begin to redefine and reinterpret his role in society. This redefinition of Manette's identity constitutes a further instance of how the prison and its agenda ''infect'' the outside world.

When the men and women from the workers' quarter of Faubourg St.-Antoine storm the Bastille, they come across a memoir concerning the cruelties of the St. Evrémonde family written by Manette. In this document, Manette denounces all Evrémondes: ''I, Alexandre Manette, unhappy prisoner, do this last night of the year 1767, in my unbearable agony, denounce to the times when all these things shall be answered for. I denounce them to Heaven and to earth'' (344). Furthermore, when the marquis is killed, his nephew Charles Darnay inherits his title. The Defarges then manage to lure Darnay to France with a letter from Gabelle, a former servant of the St. Evrémonde family. As an aristocrat, Darnay is sent to the prison of La Force. Later on, he is released owing to Manette's intervention. Darnay thus profits from the fact that Manette's imprisonment under the ancien régime has entitled him to a privileged position. At this stage, the revolutionaries turn Manette into a celebrity. His long years of hopeless misery allow him to experience a social rebirth under the Reign of Terror and to save his accused son-in-law: ''His high personal popularity, and the clearness of his answers made a great impression; . . . as he showed that the Accused was his first friend on his release from his long imprisonment; . . . the Jury and the populace became one'' (295).

However, Madame Defarge's hatred of the aristocracy causes Darnay to be sent before the tribunal again, which this time consigns him to ''the black prison of the Conciergerie'' (360) and sentences him to be guillotined. The second condemnation is ironically based on the document written by Manette in prison, and the connection between this document and the condemnation causes Manette to return to the mode of consciousness that possessed him in the Bastille. Manette's testimony was, of course, only an attempt to express the thoughts and feelings he had at that time (and they have obviously changed). Nevertheless, the revolutionaries gain power over this document as well as Manette's identity by redefining the meanings of both. The revolutionaries manage to transform the meaning of Manette's account and condemn Darnay to death by making the testimony say something that Manette no longer subscribes to. After all, his thoughts about the Evrémondes primarily concerned the marquis and his twin brother rather than Charles Darnay. As Cockshut has shown (46), the cruelty of the revolutionaries renders the supposed utility of Manette's suffering pointless, and leads to his entire disillusionment.[12] When Manette then requests his shoemaking tools, we know that he will remain tied to the prison until he dies. He shrinks "into the exact figure that Defarge had had in keeping" (356). Once again his identity is erased, and at this stage, revolutionary France becomes Manette's metaphorical prison or living grave.

As I have shown, the novel associates the prison with darkness, hopelessness, stasis, solitude, cruelty, the erasure of identities, and death. However, the prison also transcends its boundaries because its agenda and associations continue to exist in the free world. Even outside prison, Manette lives as a prisoner in a prison-like room (with Defarge as his turnkey), and later on, the violent revolutionaries "undo" Manette's regained identity again. Ultimately, revolutionary France becomes for him a figurative prison where he would have to spend the rest of his life in static solitude.

Another example of a prison-like setting in the novel is Tellson's Bank. To begin with, we learn that the bank in London is as dark as a prison: "Tellson's wanted no light" (55). Its interior is described in terms of a "dismal twilight" which is caused by the "iron bars" before the dingy windows and "the heavy shadow of Temple Bar" (56).[13] Second, in a manner that is clearly reminiscent of the way in which Manette has internalized the prison, Mr. Lorry has interiorized the "daily routine of his employment" (26). The narrator tells us that "the bank was almost always with him" (17), and, later on, Mr. Lorry even explicitly states: "I have no feelings; I am a mere machine. . . . Feelings! I have no time for them, no chance of them. I pass my whole life . . . in turning an immense pecuniary Mangle" (25–26). In a sense, Mr. Lorry is imprisoned by his job, which objectifies him by reducing him to some sort of "it" or machine. And this erasure of human features is rather similar to the objectification Manette experienced in the Bastille.

In the following section, I will analyze the imprisonment of Charles Darnay and show that the novel represents the walls between the prison and the free world as being even more permeable. More specifically, it is not only the case that the prison and its associations seep into the world outside prison; it is also the case that the free world and its connotations seep into the prison. The prisons of the ancien régime and the prisons of the revolution obviously have important differences, in particular with regard to the inmates' social status. However, it is worth noting that both the old regime and the revolutionaries use the prison as a political tool to control the inmates' selves, and to eradicate undesired identities. Both the Bastille and the prison of La Force confine innocent individuals (like Manette and Darnay) who are considered to be a threat to the political order: Manette was imprisoned because he knew of a crime that had been committed by the marquis's brother, and Darnay is incarcerated merely because he is an aristocrat. Neither Manette nor Darnay is guilty of any crime. On the contrary, they are both well-meaning and law-abiding citizens.

3.

After his first conviction, the aristocrat Charles Darnay is incarcerated at the prison of La Force, which is described as "a gloomy prison, dark and filthy, and with a horrible smell of foul sleep in it" (265). Darnay is separated from the rest of the prison community and led "into a solitary cell. It struck cold and damp, but was not dark" (267). As in the case of Manette, the narrator uses an internally focalized account to familiarize us with the effects of the prison cell on Charles Darnay. More specifically, the initial shock upon arrival in prison causes Darnay to experience an identity crisis similar to the one Manette had experienced in the Bastille.

At first, Darnay begins to walk to and fro in his almost empty cell, counting its measurements: "Five paces by four and a half, five paces by four and a half, five paces by four and a half" (267). His thoughts then descend into a confused interior monologue in which bits and pieces of his tenuously retained identity "toss . . . and roll . . . upwards from the depths of his mind" (267). The repetitions in his interior monologue may suggest that he desperately tries to stick to his former identity but nevertheless begins to give in to the psychological pressure of the prison: "Let us ride on again, for God's sake, through the illuminated villages with the people all awake! **** He made shoes, he made shoes, he made shoes. **** Five paces by four and a half" (267). Indeed, as Lloyd has shown, the prison's solitary cell comes close to reducing Darnay to an "it" like Manette: "removed from any immediate human contact in his cell, Darnay is thrown upon his intelligence, which begins to disintegrate, and his heart, which momentarily is distracted from Lucie Manette's influence" (168n.8).

At first glance, the prison is again reminiscent of a tomb that leads to some kind of inner, psychological, or social, death. The narrator even explicitly mentions that the inmates "were changed by the *death* they had died in coming here" (*TTC* 265; my emphasis). However, when Charles arrives at the prison of La Force, he is also struck by the other inmates' strange dignity:

> In the instinctive association of prisoners with shameful crime and disgrace, the new comer recoiled from this company. But, the crowning unreality of his long unreal ride, was, their all at once rising to receive him, *with every refinement of manner known to the time*, and *with all the engaging graces and courtesies of life*. So strangely clouded were these refinements by the prison manners and gloom, so spectral did they become in the inappropriate squalor and misery through which they were seen, that Charles Darnay seemed to stand in a company of the dead. *Ghosts* all! . . . 'In the name of the assembled companions of misfortune,' said a gentleman of *courtly appearance and address*, coming forward, 'I have the honour of giving you welcome to La Force, and of condoling with you on the calamity that has brought you among us. May it soon terminate happily!' (265; my emphasis)

Before Darnay leaves these prisoners and is sent to solitary confinement, they express their "hope" that he will not be "in secret," and give him "good wishes and encouragement" (266). These kind prisoners, who are presumably all aristocrats or other representatives of the old regime, are significant because they occupy an important place between the enormous metaphorical prison of France and Darnay's solitary cells—first at La Force and then in the Conciergerie where he is replaced by the self-sacrificing Sydney Carton.

Most critics who deal with the prisons in the novel (e.g., Collins and Grass) have overlooked the significance of this small community of benevolent prisoners at the prison of La Force. These decent prisoners are diametrically opposed to both France, which is dominated by public violence, and the individualist Carton, who retreats into privacy and dies a noble death. In contrast to the prisoners at La Force, both the revolutionaries and Carton do not really achieve a decent sense of community. More specifically, the revolutionaries strive for power, justice, and liberation but exercise violence, tyranny, and injustice, while the selfless Carton achieves a triumphant redemption but has to accept his own erasure.

In this context, it is perhaps worth noting that in prison, Carton dictates a letter to Darnay that begins as follows: "If you remember . . . the words that passed between us, long ago [he refers to the moment when he told Lucie that he would give his life to keep a life she loves beside her], you will readily comprehend this when you see it. You do remember them, I know. It is not in your nature to forget them" (365). Hence, the meaning of Carton's love crucially depends on Lucie's correct interpretation. Like Manette, Carton thus potentially loses control over his identity and the meaning of his benevolent actions. Carton's letter is paralleled by Darnay's story about an anonymous prisoner in the Tower of London who hid some personal writing under the (almost undecipherable) sign "D.I.G.," which turned out to be the imperative "dig!" Darnay's story continues as follows:

'The floor was examined very carefully under the inscription, and, in the earth beneath a stone, or tile, or some fragment of paving, were found the ashes of a paper, mingled with the ashes of a small leathern case or bag. What the unknown prisoner had written will never be read, but he had written something, and hidden it away to keep it from the gaoler.'   (105)

The writings by this unknown prisoner and Carton's letter are similar insofar as they both allude to the possibility that identity may not necessarily be preserved in the memories of others (Lloyd 155–56).

Carton's prophetic vision at the end, which he notably does not share with anyone, in fact constitutes the one and only "correct" (but potentially unknown) version of himself and his true intentions: "In the case of Carton's internalized grammar at the close, his repeated stress on private vision is delivered in first-person rather than second, inner-directed, unperformed, unconfirmed" (Stewart 170), that is, without any results in the world of the novel. Furthermore, Carton's vision is a counterfactual thought experiment rather than something he actually says. The narrator introduces Carton's vision as follows: "If he had given any utterance to this, and they were prophetic, they would have been these" (389). In other words, Carton does not speak and he does not utter a prophetic vision. For me, this "vision" is rather like a hidden potentiality that is never realized. And if one wants to see Carton's "vision" as a vision at all, one has to note that it is private and intimate, and not shared with anyone.

The novel repeatedly suggests that Carton is metaphorically imprisoned by his individualism and his hesitant interactions with others. For example, Carton frequently stresses that he does not belong to "this terrestrial scheme." He puts it as follows: "As to me, the greatest desire I have is to forget that I belong to it. It has no good in it for me—except wine like this—nor I for it" (87). A page later, Carton accentuates that he is not really interested in other people: "I care for no man on earth, and no man on earth cares for me" (89). Mr. Stryver additionally points out that Carton's utterances are either ironic or completely unimportant: "I know you don't mean half you say; and if you meant it at all, it would be of no importance" (145). The narrator also informs us that Carton refuses to interact with others to talk about his personal problems. More specifically, we learn that his "pillow was wet with wasted tears" (95), but he refuses to talk about his feelings. Later on, the narrator describes him as a "man of good abilities, and good emotions, incapable of their directed exercise, incapable of his own help and his own happiness" (95). Interestingly, at some point, Mr. Lorry even thinks that Carton looks like a prisoner: "Taking note of the wasted air which clouded the naturally handsome features, and having the expression of prisoners' faces fresh in his mind, he [Lorry] was strongly reminded of that expression" (322). It is worth noting that Carton occasionally tries to break out of his metaphorical prison,[14] but he remains relatively isolated until the end of the novel.

The prison of La Force, a space that has to be located between the power-driven revolutionaries and the individualist Carton, is represented as the only space in France where relationships, friendship, and dignity are truly possible. Both the metaphorical incarceration in the world (as in the case of revolutionary France) and in the self (as in the case of Carton) render human relations and friendship impossible. In this sense, the revolution and Carton's private sacrifice are merged at the end of the novel. From a certain perspective, the revolutionaries do too much, while Carton does too little. The aristocratic prisoners of La Force, on the other hand, are safely isolated from the aggression of revolutionary France, and in contrast to the lonely Carton, they form intense relationships that are unparalleled in the outside world. The description of these prisoners as "ghosts" (265) or "apparitions" (266) might even have a positive connotation and suggest that they are weightless spirits—and as such free from prosaic concerns. These aristocratic prisoners do something which the power-driven revolutionaries do not achieve and Carton's actions only occasionally allude to: like a family, they express respect for and share an interest in others. The novel demonstrates that our intuitive associations are reversed when one of the prisoners tells Darnay that "it would be an impertinence elsewhere, but it is not so here, to ask your name and condition" (266).

Dickens sometimes uses positive prison images in his novels. For example, *Little Dorrit* contains a number of positive metaphors of imprisonment. At some point we learn that even though the debtor William Dorrit clearly suffers in the Marshalsea, he simultaneously experiences this prison in terms of a place of "refuge" (74) that protects him from the world outside: "Crushed at first by his imprisonment, he had soon found a dull relief in it. He was under lock and key; but the lock and key that kept him in, kept numbers of his troubles out" (73). In contrast to his brother Frederick, who is lost in "the labyrinthian world" (219) outside, William knows that he is "safe within the walls" (223). The prison is here represented as a peaceful and safe place amidst the hurly-burly of life. It is also worth noting that once Amy Dorrit, the little Dorrit of the novel's title, is released, she begins to miss the Marshalsea and longs for its security and protection. And when she visits the imprisoned Arthur Clennam, the prison even evokes the association with a womb or a protecting mother: "the Marshalsea walls, during a portion of every day, again embraced her in their shadows as their child" (766).

Since Dickens only rarely presents us with such positive prison images, one has to pay particular attention to the instances in which he uses them. The prison community at the prison of La Force clearly falsifies Gross's argument that "in *A Tale of Two Cities* other people are primarily a threat and source of danger" (189). It is rather the case that the novel idealizes this family-like community of aristocrats and presents it as an alternative to the violent macrocosm of revolutionary France, where the attempt to achieve absolute liberation leads to nothing but senseless massacres and the erasure of identities. And Carton's behavior is also problematic because he decides to erase his own identity. By contrast, the aristocratic prisoners at La Force neither seek to dominate the self-construction of others (which is what the revolutionaries do), nor do they withdraw from interaction into a state of private intimacy (which is what the individualist Carton typically does). From this perspective, the prison at La Force may even be seen as a matrix of spiritual rebirth because it reawakens an interest in the identity of others.

4.

The prisons in *A Tale of Two Cities* serve as important focal points at which the novel's dichotomies are redefined and redeployed. At first, the novel represents the Bastille as a violent tool for gaining power over Manette's identity. In a second step, we learn that the prison does not only enter the minds of its inmates. Rather, the prison-like settings or correlates of constraint in the novel (like Manette's room above the wine shop of the Defarges or Tellson's bank) demonstrate that the prison transcends its borders and "infects" the world outside. Other forms of metaphorical imprisonment can be found in the novel as well. First, revolutionary France is represented as a metaphorical prison which is ruled by violence, hatred, and cruelty, and erases various identities. Second, the self-sacrificing individualist Carton is confined insofar as he decides to live in a state of figurative solitary confinement up until the end of the novel and then decides to withdraw from the world. Both the revolutionaries and Carton are emotionally restrained or "imprisoned" because they do not manage to achieve a sense of community or friendship.

Interestingly, the outside world and its associations also enter the prison. More specifically, the prison of La Force is represented as the only space in revolutionary France where true friendship is possible. The novel idealizes the community of benevolent aristocratic prisoners at La Force as an alternative to both the revolutionaries' violence and Carton's inward retreat and selfless death. In the words of Martha Grace Duncan, "incarceration imposes an isolation from the world, but those who share this isolation see themselves as forming relationships of an emotional power unequaled in the world outside" (15). Although this is not always the case, Dickens's novel clearly argues in favor of community, decency, and friendship, and from this perspective, the prison "family" at La Force contrasts with both the self-sacrificing Carton and the violent revolutionaries who erase identities.

The novel might even argue that kindness and generosity presuppose limitations or restrictions. In other words, compassion can only exist in small segments or units of society and not in pure individualists like Carton or people like the revolutionaries who try to change society in its totality. The prison community of La Force can even be said to merge with Dickens's concept of the home. As Frances Armstrong has shown, Dickens frequently celebrates home as a source of inexplicable power or "a place of individual self-expression as well as a means of engaging with the world" (2).[15] Interestingly, certain types of imprisonment in Dickens's fiction—like the prison of La Force or the Marshalsea debtors' prison in *Little Dorrit*—bear interesting resemblances to Dickens's notion of the home that are worth being explored.

A Tale of Two Cities uses a scale of different shades of gray—ranging from ashen to leaden—to underline the way in which the prison and the outside world (as well as their respective associations and connotations) are merged. The brightness of the free world (e.g., in "the sun rose bright, placid, beautiful" [18]) is located at one end of this scale, while the darkness of the prison (e.g., the "gloomy vaults" of the Bastille where "the light of day had never shone" [227]) is to be found at the other end. Between these poles, one can locate Manette's (only slightly brighter) prison-like "dim and dark" room above the wine shop of the Defarges to which "such a scanty portion of light was admitted . . . that it was difficult, on first coming in, to see anything" (41). The "dismal twilight" (56) of Tellson's bank, the "dismal prison twilight" (265) of La Force, and Darnay's solitary cell, which is "cold and damp, but . . . *not dark*" (267; my emphasis), have to be located between the two extremes as well. One also has to place Sydney Carton between these two poles because at one point, the narrator tells us that "the cloud of caring for nothing, which overshadowed him with such a fatal darkness, was very rarely pierced by the light within him" (155). It is also worth noting that imprisonment seems to affect prisoners and their keepers in a very similar manner. On the one hand, we learn that Marie-Antoinette's face has turned to "grey" after "eight weary months of imprisoned widowhood and misery" (283), but, on the other hand, we are also told that the heads of "prison officers" may turn "grey" (225). Finally, we are informed that even workers whose job is not related to the prison at all may also work "till [they are] grey at it" (318).

A Tale of Two Cities does not claim that the world is only organized around a simple structure of dichotomies. Rather, the novel as a whole and its color symbolism in particular accentuate the dynamic relationship between binary oppositions by merging the prison's darkness with the brightness of the free world. Dickens's *Tale* thus demonstrates that, albeit to various different degrees, everyone in society continuously oscillates between poles like hopelessness and hope, life and death, decency and cruelty, the construction of stable (or coherent) identities and the lack thereof. And, quite surprisingly, sometimes prisoners, of all people, can teach the free world something it has forgotten about, namely how to achieve a decent sense of community and respect for others.[16]

NOTES

1. I am grateful to Katharina Böhm for her invaluable comments on an earlier draft of this essay. This article develops some material present in my book *Narrating*

the Prison. In the book I trace out a different, complementary argument. I would like to thank Cambria Press for permission to partly reuse this material.

2. The novel has primarily been analyzed with regard to the portrayal of the French Revolution. See, for example, Goldberg, Baumgarten, Craig, Timko, Hobsbawm, Lamb, Daleski, and Rosen. For an analysis of how Dickens's experiences in the Eastern State Penitentiary in Philadelphia influenced the prisons of *A Tale of Two Cities*, see DePuy, and for two earlier discussions of the prisons in the novel, see Cockshut and Collins.

3. For more on how nineteenth-century authors use the prison as a discursive icon to negotiate the moral, sexual, social, and national structure of Victorian Britain, see the essays in Alber and Lauterbach.

4. Even though this may seem counterintuitive, stasis and cruelty can coexist. For example, the nexus of stasis, monotony, and boredom with which solitary confinement correlates can indeed be quite cruel and brutal. For instance, Dickens puts his attitude toward the ''separate'' system in Pennsylvania as follows: ''The system here, is rigid, strict, and hopeless solitary confinement. I believe it in its effects, to be cruel and wrong. . . . I hold this slow and daily tampering with the mysteries of the brain, to be immeasurably worse than any torture of the body. . . . My firm conviction is that, independent of the mental anguish it occasions—an anguish so acute and tremendous, that all imagination of it must fall far short of the reality—it wears the mind into a morbid state, which renders it unfit for the rough contact and busy action of the world. It is my fixed opinion that those who have undergone this punishment, MUST pass into society again morally unhealthy and diseased'' (Dickens, ''Philadelphia'' 99–109).

5. In *The Self and the Cell*, Grass looks at the *Tale* as an example of what he calls the general ''failure of omniscience'' (137; see also 109, 118) to narrate the prisoner's private self, i.e., the fundamental psychological meanings of the cell. However, ''omniscient'' narrators do not per se *fail* to tell us what the prison means to its inmates. As I will show, the authorial narrator of the *Tale* frequently operates like a camera eye and has a tendency to visualize the inmates' internal states by concentrating on external details. On the other hand, the narrator of Dickens's novel also uses internal focalization in order to elucidate the psychological problems related to the prison. In *The Self and the Cell*, Grass ignores interior monologues, free indirect discourse, and psychonarration, which can be (and usually are) used by authorial (or ''omniscient'') narrators to familiarize readers with a prisoner's internal processes.

6. Originally Dickens wanted to call the novel *Buried Alive* (Gross 187).

7. As I will show, this metaphor of imprisonment (PRISON IS WOMB) does not only describe the prison in terms of negative features like dependency (or infantilization); it may also imply the possibility of being (spiritually) reborn.

8. As Cockshut has shown (45), Lucie's discourse is at one point ''contaminated'' by Defarge's objectifying attitude toward the former prisoner. More specifically, in the following conversation, she begins to objectify her father like Defarge does: '' 'I am afraid of *it*', she answered, shuddering. 'Of *it*? What?' 'I mean of him. Of *my father*' '' (40; my emphasis).

9. Imprisonment always correlates with the objectification of inmates, and the prison number usually plays an important role with regard to the transformation of human beings into files and statistics. For instance, Michael Ignatieff describes the reception of a convict at Pentonville Prison as follows: "The final act in the ritual of initiation [i.e., the induction process] was the issue of his prison number. He was no longer George Withers, but HF 4736" (6–7).

10. For example, at a fashionable high society dinner organized by the Merdles in Rome, William Dorrit, a former inmate of the Marshalsea debtors' prison, loses his wits and slips back into his role as the "Father of the Marshalsea" (*LD* 621).

11. The term "self" here refers to the concept of the "private self," i.e., the way in which the prisoner himself perceives and constructs his identity (Frey 46–55).

12. In this context, it is perhaps worth noting that Defarge's violent destruction of the furniture in Manette's cell (228) is not only a desperate attempt to get "a clear definition of the mystery called Manette," as Lloyd has it (159); rather, this outbreak of physical violence foreshadows and parallels the psychological violence with which the revolutionaries gain control over Manette and his testimony. Generally speaking, the purpose of the various types of violence in the novel is to control people and their identities.

13. The bank in Paris is also prison-like insofar as it is "shut off from the street by a high wall and a strong gate" (268).

14. For instance, he tells Lucie that he is in love with her (158), and at one point, he also requests Darnay's friendship (214). Furthermore, Carton helps a mother to carry her child across a muddy street (326), and before his execution, he befriends a young seamstress (368–69, 387–89). I would like to thank Stanley Friedman for pointing these passages out to me.

15. On the other hand, Armstrong also points out that Dickens did never advocate an essentialist concept of home because he "was aware that if home is an answer it is not a place where questioning ends" (2).

16. Lord George Gordon in Dickens's *Barnaby Rudge* (1841) is another example of a benevolent prisoner. In the final chapter of the novel, Gordon dies as a Newgate inmate, and the narrator tells us the following about him: "He had his mourners. The prisoners bemoaned his loss, and missed him; for though his means were not large, his charity was great, and in bestowing alms among them he considered the necessities of all alike, and knew no distinction of sect or creed. There are wise men in the highways of the world who may learn something, even from this poor crazy lord who died in Newgate" (629).

WORKS CITED

Alber, Jan. "Bodies behind Bars: The Disciplining of the Prisoner's Body in British and American Prison Movies." *In the Grip of the Law. Prisons, Trials and the Space Between.* Ed. Monika Fludernik and Greta Olson. Frankfurt: Lang, 2004. 241–69.

————. *Narrating the Prison: Role and Representation in Charles Dickens' Novels, Twentieth-Century Fiction, and Film.* Youngstown, NY: Cambria Press, 2007.

Alber, Jan, and Frank Lauterbach, ed. *Stones of Law, Bricks of Shame: Narrating Imprisonment in the Victorian Age.* U of Toronto P, 2009.

Armstrong, Frances. *Dickens and the Concept of Home.* Ann Arbor: UMI Research Press, 1990.

Baumgarten, Murray. "Writing the Revolution." *Dickens Studies Annual* 12 (1983): 161–76.

Caramagno, Thomas Carmelo. "The Dickens Revival at the Bijou: Critical Reassessment, Film Theory and Popular Culture." *New Orleans Review* 15 (1988): 88–96.

Cockshut, A. O. J. "Prison Experiences in Dickens's Novels." *Readings on Charles Dickens.* Ed. Clarice Swisher. San Diego, CA: Greenhaven Press, 1998. 40–49.

Collins, Philip. *Dickens and Crime.* Ed. L. Radzinowicz. London and New York: Macmillan and St. Martin's Press, 1962. Cambridge Studies in Criminology 17.

Craig, David. "The Crowd in Dickens." *The Changing World of Charles Dickens.* Ed. Robert Giddings. London: Vision and Barnes and Noble, 1983. 75–90.

Daleski, H. M. "Imagining Revolution: The Eye of History and of Fiction." *The Journal of Narrative Technique* 18.1 (1988): 61–72.

DePuy, Harry. "American Prisons and *A Tale of Two Cities.*" *Cahiers Victoriens et Edouardiens* 25 (1987): 39–48.

Dickens, Charles. *Barnaby Rudge: A Tale of the Riots of 'Eighty.* Introduction by Kathleen Tillotson. London: Oxford UP, 1954.

————. *Little Dorrit.* Ed. Stephen Wall and Helen Small. London: Penguin, 1998.

————. "Philadelphia, and Its Solitary Prison." *American Notes and Pictures from Italy.* London: Oxford UP, 1957. 97–111.

————. *A Tale of Two Cities.* Ed. Richard Maxwell. London: Penguin, 2000.

Duncan, Martha Grace. *Romantic Outlaws, Beloved Prisons: The Unconscious Meanings of Crime and Punishment.* New York: New York UP, 1996.

Forster, John. "Review of *A Tale of Two Cities* [1859]." *Dickens: The Critical Heritage.* Ed. Philip Collins. London: Routledge, 1971. 424–26.

Frey, Hans-Peter. *Stigma und Identität. Eine empirische Untersuchung zur Genese und Änderung krimineller Identität bei Jugendlichen.* Weinheim: Beltz, 1983.

Goldberg, Michael. *Carlyle and Dickens.* Athens: U of Georgia P, 1972.

Grass, Sean Christopher. *The Self in the Cell: Narrating the Victorian Prisoner.* New York: Routledge, 2003.

Greenblatt, Stephen. *Shakespearean Negotiations: The Circulation of Social Energy in Renaissance England.* Berkeley: U of California P, 1988.

Gross, John. "A Tale of Two Cities." *Dickens and the Twentieth Century.* Ed. John Gross and Gabriel Pearson. London: Routledge, 1962. 187–97.

Hobsbawm, E. J. *Echoes of the Marseillaise: Two Centuries Look Back on the French Revolution.* London: Verso, 1990.

Ignatieff, Michael. *A Just Measure of Pain: The Penitentiary in the Industrial Revolution, 1750–1850.* London: Macmillan, 1978.

Lamb, John B. "Domesticating History: Revolution and Moral Management in *A Tale of Two Cities.*" *Dickens Studies Annual* 25 (1996): 227–43.

Lloyd, Tom. "Language, Love and Identity: *A Tale of Two Cities.*" *The Dickensian* 88 (1992): 154–70.

Maxwell, Richard. "Introduction." *A Tale of Two Cities.* Ed. Richard Maxwell. London: Penguin, 2000. ix–xxxiii.

Rosen, David. "*A Tale of Two Cities*: Theology of Revolution." *Dickens Studies Annual* 27 (1998): 171–85.

Stange, G. Robert. "Dickens and the Fiery Past: *A Tale of Two Cities* Reconsidered." *English Journal* 46.7 (1957): 381–90.

Stewart Garrett. "Leaving History: Dickens, Gance, Blanchot." *Yale Journal of Criticism* 2.2 (1989): 145–90.

Timko, Michael. "Splendid Impressions and Picturesque Means: Dickens, Carlyle, and *The French Revolution.*" *Dickens Studies Annual* 12 (1983): 177–95.

The Illustrations for *Great Expectations* in *Harper's Weekly* (1860–61) and in the Illustrated Library Edition (1862)— "Reading by the Light of Illustration"

Philip V. Allingham

Although a number of critics have stated that Great Expectations *was published in its initial form without illustration both serially in* All the Year Round *and in its initial volume edition (Chapman and Hall, 1861), the first American edition (which one may argue is the first edition by virtue of the publication date of the first installment) was illustrated by John McLenan, whose 40 plates were dropped into the letterpress of the* Harper's Weekly *American serialization of the novel. Not until the 1862 Chapman and Hall Library Edition of the novel were British readers able to read this novel by what a* Harper's *advertisement terms "the light of illustration," and even then the program that Marcus Stone provided for the English volume was slight in comparison: eight full-page woodcuts. In these narrative-pictorial sequences, Stone interprets the novel as Pip's "Pilgrim's Progress" as, boy and then man, he appears in every illustration, while Magwitch does not appear at all. In contrast, in his 40 plates of varying dimensions McLenan provides salient background details, offers symbols for lack of self-insight and illumination in various scenes, and describes every significant character, including Pumblechook, Mrs. Pocket, and Trabb's Boy, in a panoramic treatment. A comparison of a selection of Stone's with McLenan's plates demonstrates not merely these artists' differences in*

Dickens Studies Annual, Volume 40, Copyright © 2009 by AMS Press, Inc. All rights reserved.

*style and approach, but also their very different (one may say, "transat-
lantic") readings of the novel itself.*

> . . . it has been, at least until recently, an article
> of faith that Dickens ruled his illustrators with
> a heavy hand, using them merely as vehicles to
> translate his own visual conceptions into
> graphic images.
>
> —Michael Steig, *Dickens and Phiz* (ix)

We know now, if we did not know before Michael Steig's publication of
Dickens and Phiz in 1978 and Jane Rabb Cohen's *Charles Dickens and His
Original Illustrators* two years later, that Dickens and his visual artists were
collaborators, sometimes working as almost a Box-and-Cox pair (most famously, as "Boz" and "Phiz," as Hablot Knight Browne usually signed his
steels) and sometimes as a team (as in the illustration of all but the first of
The Christmas Books). The standard belief about the illustrations of his works
issued during Dickens's lifetime is articulated by Cohen:

> Dickens exerted unprecedented authority over everything but the actual execu-
> tion of the illustrations to his works. With few exceptions, he selected and
> entitled (often ironically) the subjects, provided the proofs or précis, and sug-
> gested captions, models, and details. He usually inspected not only the final
> drawings, but the preliminary sketches as well, which he rarely returned without
> ideas for improvement.   (5)

We should be guarded in our acceptance of the above generalizations because
of the phrase "With few exceptions," and the words "usually" and "rarely."
Perhaps stretching the truth a little, Thomas Hatton, in *The Nonesuch Dickens
Prospectus* (1937), asserted that "every one of these illustrations [included
in the original Nonesuch Edition] was made under the supervision of the
author himself, often from his own suggestions" (125). For example, Hatton,
like Arthur Waugh in the same "Prospectus," seems to have assumed that
Dickens approved or "passed" (Waugh 10) the short visual program that one
of the foremost illustrators of the sixties, Frederick Walker, provided for the
Illustrated Library Edition of *Hard Times* in 1863, even though we have no
evidence of Dickens's having formally expressed an imprimatur in "written
approbation" (Waugh 9). Then, too, much as Dickens disliked the older
notion of the author's being the artist's subordinate, sometimes, as Cohen
implies by her qualifiers, he had no choice but to accept a different relationship, particularly in terms of his "authorized" American editions.

Again, we have come to view the question of Dickens's relationship with
his various illustrators as connected intimately with the monthly publication
of "parts," each accompanied by two separate pages of illustration. "The

presence of plates in the cheap monthly (or, less often, weekly) issues attracted the widest possible audience; the increased number of readers attracted more advertisers; and the additional profits absorbed the extra graphic costs'' (Cohen 4). During the period of Victoria's reign, indeed, right up to the eve of the First World War, British and American readers seem to have regarded illustration as a value-added feature of printed material generally, and to have been attracted to works illustrated by well-known graphic artists, from Robert Seymour in the 1830s to Sir John Tenniel in the 1870s to Harry Furniss at the end of the century. The name of a well-known artist, like that of an established writer, seems to have functioned for periodical publications as a virtual guarantee of quality entertainment in a mixed-media format.

In an article published some six years before his magisterial pronouncements on the subject in *Dickens and Phiz*, Michael Steig makes distinctions that established a special class of illustrated fiction, namely that between a story that was accompanied in its *initial* publication by illustrations (such as the *Harper's Weekly* serialization of *Great Expectations* in 1860–61) and a work that was *not* initially accompanied by any form of illustration (as, for example, *Hard Times* in *Household Words*, 1854), there may be a third type that is clearly the result of collaboration between writer and illustrator (such as *Martin Chuzzlewit*, 1843–44). Further, regardless of whether it was the result of authorial and artistic collaboration or not, Steig concludes that ''To read an illustrated novel as though it had no illustrations is to distort it, to read it as though it were more like the unillustrated, twentieth-century novel than it actually was'' (119). Steig, however, would have us confer no special status or authority upon plates that the publisher inserted into a novel without the author's active collaboration. Readers could reasonably construe as possibly distorting interpolations any plates added after the author's death—for example, Rafaello Busoni's illustrations for the Grosset and Dunlap edition of *A Tale of Two Cities* (New York: Illustrated Junior Library, 1948).

What, then, would Steig have made of a novel that was originally published simultaneously and serially in two different journals, one illustrated, one not, and then after initial publication was reissued in two different illustrated volumes, but only one with plates that were the result of a loose collaboration between the original author and the visual artist? Such a novel is *Great Expectations*, a true anomaly in the Dickens canon with respect to its place in the subgenre of what Richard Maxwell has termed ''The Victorian Illustrated Book.'' Not limiting his discussion to volume publications, Maxwell acknowledges as one of the nineteenth century's ''outstanding innovations'' (xxiii) the type of illustrated magazine exemplified in Britain by *The Graphic* and in America by *Harper's Weekly*, for this approach made possible ''new ways of conceiving and displaying relations between image and word, as well as new kinds of collaboration between artists and writers'' (xxiii). We therefore cannot automatically disqualify the version of *Great Expectations* that appeared in *Harper's* as a "book." However, whereas extant evidence, letters treating of specific and detailed instructions about five plates, indicates that Dickens chose and orchestrated the scenes to be illustrated for *Martin Chuzzlewit* twenty years earlier, we have no evidence of Dickens's directing either the American illustrator John McLenan or English illustrator Marcus Stone in their choice and treatment of subjects in the New York weekly's serialization or the Library Edition of 1862. In fact, we have no indication that Dickens was even *aware* of the McLenan illustrations that appeared week by week alongside his text, and guided the initial American reception of the novel.

Another authority on the nineteenth-century illustrated novel, Robert L. Patten, seems concerned not with the issue of artistic collaboration, but rather with the interaction or mutual informing of text and image. Patten contends that pictures in a narrative text enlighten, embellish, and even make illustrious the words on the page. He cautions us that "Illustrations are not mimetic. They are not the text pictured" (91). With Victorian illustration in particular, he notes that two effects are likely: the illustrations may either follow the letterpress faithfully, supporting and explaining it, or work against it, contradicting and subverting the authority of the text by offering a visual interpretation not wholly supported by a careful reading of the text. For the most part, for example, one may "read" Browne's illustrations as authorized visual adjuncts to Dickens's letterpress in the nine novels on which the pair worked from *The Posthumous Papers of the Pickwick Club* (1836) to *A Tale of Two Cities* (1859), with Browne, one of the letterpress's first readers, realizing in a second medium the characters, settings, and situations invented by Dickens and rendering these accessible to nearly all readers, regardless of their experiences, education, class, or even mother tongue. One may certainly speak of Browne's plates as constituting a narrative-pictorial sequence, in contrast to the short programs of Fred Walker for *Hard Times* and Marcus Stone for *Great Expectations*, for example, which hold up to our notice particular moments in the letterpress and which may in themselves represent semi-autonomous works of art, but which do not attempt to convey a sense of the movement and characters of the entire story in the secondary medium that does, after all, focus on discrete and isolated textual moments.

According to such critics as Patten, the discussion of a book's illustrations should focus on the artistic *objects* rather than on the *process* that created them, so that *Great Expectations* should more properly be regarded as an illustrated book because it was visualized through cuts by John McLenan inserted into Dickens's text for the *Harper's Weekly* serialization. Edgar Rosenberg has indicated that the serial version run in that highly illustrated weekly magazine constitutes the first illustrated edition of the novel (399), although other critics remain equivocal on this point, preferring to regard the 1862 Chapman and Hall Library Edition as "the first illustrated *Great Expectations*" (Lester 179).[1] Since the serialization in *All the Year Round* fell back into tandem with that in *Harper's* owing to problems with the transatlantic shipping of the proof-sheets for the tenth installment (scheduled for American publication on 26 January 1861), which serialization, if either, constitutes the first edition of the novel remains moot: "The journals ended in a dead heat on August 3, 1861" (Rosenberg 399).

Dickens must have chosen Harper Brothers in New York as his American serial publishers back in 1859 for *A Tale of Two Cities* because, having achieved a high circulation for its periodicals "largely by the use of English serials" (Mott 128), this company would pay handsomely for Dickens's advance sheets or proofs from *All the Year Round*. From its inaugural number in June 1850, *Harper's Weekly* had been associated with such English writers as Charles Lever and Dickens, whose "Child's Dream of a Star" appeared in that number. *Harper's* contracted veteran American book and serial illustrator John McLenan (1827–65) once again to provide abundant pictorial accompaniment for the multicolumned text of *Great Expectations* that ran in *Harper's Weekly*—a week ahead of its British counterpart in *All the Year Round* until the ninth weekly part. If one cannot accept this serial as a first edition, then the single-volume version of *Great Expectations,* issued by T. B. Peterson of Philadelphia in 1861, must be regarded as the first illustrated edition, and possibly the first volume edition (see note A in appendix 2 regarding the two forms of this edition). This slight volume, now a rarity, contains McLenan's 34 full-size plates, but unfortunately not the six small-scale headnote vignettes of the original *Harper's Weekly* illustrations.

The story of the transatlantic visualization of *Great Expectations* begins a year prior to the writing of the novel, when the 47-year-old Dickens, mindful perhaps of a new style of illustration that was emerging to meet the demand being created by such illustrated magazines as *Once a Week* and distressed at Browne's dilatory manner in delivering his two plates for each of the monthly serial numbers of *A Tale of Two Cities*, severed his quarter-century connection with Phiz. There was general surprise when, the year after the unillustrated serial run of the novel in *All the Year Round*, Chapman and Hall's single-volume edition of *Great Expectations* contained a small series of staid plates by one of the newest "New Men" of the sixties, Marcus Stone, rather than a vast array of lively caricatures by Phiz. Dickens and his publishers called upon Marcus Stone, son of Dickens's old friend and occasional illustrator Frank Stone, to provide a brief series of plates in the new "Sixties" style for Chapman and Hall's 1862 one-volume Library Edition of *Great Expectations*, and later 40 wood engravings for *Our Mutual Friend* (1864) and the frontispiece for the Cheap Edition of *A Tale of Two Cities*

(1864), commissions of "the kind that might previously have gone to Browne" (Cohen 204).

Apparently without consulting their renowned author, Dickens's American licensee, Harper and Brothers, enlisted John McLenan to provide a series of 40 detailed illustrations for the weekly numbers of *Great Expectations*, just as he had for the serial run of *A Tale of Two Cities* the year before. Not all installments are as "Splendidly Illustrated" as advertised in every number (e.g., 13 April 1861, p. 229) since events of the opening phase of the American Civil War (although, pictured somewhat romantically and without the gruesome scenes later associated with it) sometimes crowded out the delightful fictional characters and events of the novel. Nevertheless, with a large-scale national literary weekly journal to illustrate, on pages measuring 27 cm by 40 cm, John McLenan was able to present the American periodical's readers with a more ample pictorial narrative than Marcus Stone in the later Chapman and Hall illustrated volume (second) edition (with standard pages of 12.7 cm by 17.6 cm). As was the case with his visual realizations of *A Tale of Two Cities* throughout 1859, the serialization which appeared in *Harper's Weekly* (unlike that published in Dickens's own *All the Year Round*) truly enabled those Americans who were subscribers to read the new novel "by the light of Mr. McLenan's admirable illustrations" (*Harper's* 1860, 740). Possibly as a consequence of its having run Dickens's new novel with such an effective program of illustration, by the close of 1861 *Harper's* achieved a circulation of 120,000, as opposed to the average American weekly's circulation of only 2,400 copies (Mott 10).

The phrase "by the light of . . . illustrations" is tantalizing in its implications, for one cannot resolve whether the advertisement is implying that attempting to read a text devoid of illustration such as that currently appearing in *All the Year Round* will leave the reader "in the dark," to put the matter in Patten's terms, about the setting and characters, or simply that a reading of any text uninformed by illustration is necessarily a less complete reading (to reiterate Michael Steig's perspective). Whereas Stone's plates are infrequent and hardly constitute detailed realizations of the letterpress, McLenan's reify forty textual moments, often in considerable detail, at an average of one for approximately every eight pages of letterpress even in the single-volume edition.

McLenan, although just 33 at the time he worked on the series for *Great Expectations*, was a seasoned commercial illustrator who was regarded as "The American Phiz" for both the quality and quantity of his illustrations of such works as Dickens's *A Tale of Two Cities* in *Harper's Weekly* (7 May–3 December 1859). In terms reminiscent of Italian Renaissance artist Cimabue's discovery of young Giotto tending sheep, Sinclair Hamilton describes the start of McLenan's 14-year career in book illustration:

Discovered by DeWitt C. Hitchcock working in a pork-packing establishment in Cincinnati and making drawings on the tops of barrels, McLenan became one of the most prolific of our [American] early illustrators. . . . He was also well known as a comic draftsman. His work will bear comparison with the best of his time.   (180)

Before undertaking the illustration of *The Woman in White, A Tale,* and *Great Expectations* for Harper, McLenan already had enjoyed a certain vogue among 18 other leading New York publishers, notably Charles Scribner and D. Appleton. He was but one of a number of prominent American illustrators who worked sporadically for *Harper's* chief rival for the New York readership, *Frank Leslie's Illustrated Newspaper,* which was launched on 15 December 1855 (Mott 453). As Leigh Dillard has observed,

> *Harper's Weekly* had been initiated by the New York publishing house in the 1850s as a visually rich experience balancing text and image, and designed to appeal to America's new urban readership. In its weekly coverage of current affairs and its serial publication of contemporary American and British fiction *Harper's* asserts the continuation of a time-oriented and time-regulated urban society.

McLenan's relationship with Harper began in 1856, and by 1859 he appears to have become a frequent contributor to *Harper's Weekly,* as well as other New York periodicals. Having undoubtedly pleased both the editors and readers of *Harper's Weekly* with his *Great Expectations* illustrations, McLenan was commissioned by that same periodical to illustrate Bulwer-Lytton's *A Strange Story,* beginning 10 August 1861, the proofs once again being supplied by *All the Year Round.* Although neither a deliberate emulator of "Phiz" nor a consistently innovative illustrator, McLenan was certainly as prolific an illustrator in mid-nineteenth-century New York as Phiz was in London; and of course neither Phiz nor McLenan, whose training had been practical and technical, worked in the somewhat academic, professional, and naturalistic style of the Sixties School to which Marcus Stone belonged. With McLenan as with Phiz, the illustration is often close to cartoon or caricature, with each artist often employing humorous distortions and comic postures to characterize villainous, whimsical, low, and minor actors on the great stage of a novel. McLenan's style, however, suggests a transition from the earlier caricature of Cruikshank to the more realistic, substantial, and focused illustration of Fred Walker, George du Maurier, and the other "New Men" of the sixties. McLenan, working rapidly with proofs furnished by Harper's for *A Tale of Two Cities, Great Expectations, The Woman in White,* and *A Strange Story* developed a pictorial style well suited to the American readership's appreciation of Dickens's visual imagination and abundance of description.

Another unique feature of this serialized "first American edition" of the novel was the half-page image of the writer—"Charles Dickens, Esq.—[From a Late Photograph.]''—(fig. 7) that preceded the first installment but appeared on the same page as that installment (740) in the 24 November 1860 edition of *Harper's Weekly*. Crowding the last of the biographical sketch-*cum*-advertisement into the right margin in a 2.5 cm column, the periodical juxtaposes this portrait against text to emphasize Dickens's authorial status. Every bit as much as the mention of McLenan's name under that of Dickens in each headnote, the portrait seems to have been intended to be a guarantee of quality to the American reading public in that it confers his immense authority as both writer and entertainer upon the serially-printed novel, which opens on the same page. As Richard L. Stein notes of a similar but much earlier Dickens portrait (June 1839) by Daniel Maclise that appeared in the final installment of Chapman and Hall's *Nicholas Nickleby*, this 1860 magisterial image in *Harper's*, with crowded print in its right margin, is a visual "guarantor of identity, as if visuality has replaced the uncertainty of a mere name, mere words, with a self both recognizable and authentic" (167). According to Frank Luther Mott, Charles Dickens was the most popular author in America (160); by 1860 in America the name "Dickens" itself was certainly a hallmark, so that the inclusion of this 20 cm high by 15 cm wide portrait of the artist seated at a table, with an emphatic left index finger pointing downward to the brief biography and the opening columns of *Great Expectations*, seems intended to reassure consumers that this is the genuine article, the latest "master-piece" (740) from the pen of the reigning monarch of the British novel. Curiously, the T. B. Peterson edition's title page describes the author as "Boz," relating the work of the mature writer to that of the anecdotal humorist of 25 years earlier (see note B in appendix 2). The new serialized novel, *Harper's* assures us, appears by "special arrangement" (740) with the novelist himself, once again implying some special bond being forged between a privileged reader (referred to as a "subscriber") and a leading contemporary (one might almost say "iconic") author on this page:

> By a special arrangement with Mr. Dickens, the proof-sheets of *All the Year Round* are dispatched to the publishers of *Harper's Weekly* some time before they are published in England, and thus the readers of this journal enjoy the benefit of every thing that appears in Mr. Dickens's periodical a fortnight or more before the regular copies reach this country. The new novel, "Great Expectations," has, we are told, aroused great expectation on the other side [of the Atlantic]. Our subscribers will have the advantage of reading by the light of Mr. McLenan's admirable illustrations.   (740)

To emphasize the quality of the visual complement for the letterpress, *Harper's* has boldfaced "**Splendidly Illustrated by John McLenan**" in the headnote, Dickens's name immediately above being in block capitals. Probably owing to the conventional layout of the T. B. Peterson single-volume edition of 1861, with page dimensions of 13.7 cm by 21.8 cm, only the 34 full-size plates were reproduced, mounted on separate pages (but with a specific page in the volume referenced as the textual source for each illustration) rather than dropped into the letterpress near the moment realized, as in the magazine serial, which thus afforded a more immediate, effective, and fuller visual complement to Dickens's narrative than either the American or British volume-edition. The unique feature of the 1861 volume is the frontispiece, signed "H. L. S.," and therefore not by McLenan, and probably by the Philadelphia-born house illustrator for Harper, Henry Louis Stephens (1824–82), whom Sinclair Hamilton credits with 17 major illustrated works, including American editions of W. M. Thackeray's *Vanity Fair* (New York: Frank J. Thompson, 1859–60) and Charles Reade's *Very Hard Cash* (New York: Harper, 1864: 18 plates). In contrast, Hamilton credits McLenan with 56 major illustrated works, including a great many travelogues, the *Harper's* serialization of *A Tale of Two Cities* (1859: 64 plates), and both Wilkie Collins's *The Woman in White* (*Harper's*, 1860: 74 plates) and *No Name* (*Harper's*, 1863: 63 plates). Hamilton, however, does not mention McLenan's having illustrated Bulwer-Lytton's *A Strange Story* for *Harper's Weekly*, and has perhaps also missed some of his work for that and other American periodicals.

Typically, as we may see in both his illustrations for *A Tale* and *Great Expectations*, for *Harper's* John McLenan produced two very different types of plates to accompany the serial text of the new Dickens novel, of which he may well have been among the first readers on the American continent: roughly square designs of 10–12 cm occupying two columns (often in the bottom right section of a page) and small rectangular designs of approximately 5.5 cm wide (in other words, the width of a single column on the four-column page) by 8.5 cm high, often in the bottom left quadrant. The presence of so many smaller illustrations embedded in the serial text, combined with an absence of any illustration in five installments (the 24th, 25th, 26th, 32nd, and 34th), undermines the advertised illustrative "splendour" which appears at the head of each installment (e.g., 13 April 1861, p. 229).

While his full-size illustrations for *Great Expectations* represent an advance over plates of similar dimensions for *A Tale of Two Cities*, McLenan's headnote "vignettes" or "miniatures" are in some cases more imaginative (the running coffin, fig. 1) and in others more evocative (the bird on a ledge in front the latticework of the Marquis's window, fig. 2, and the fountain in his village, fig. 3) than the majority of the half-dozen headnote vignettes in the American serial version of *Great Expectations*. Whereas each installment for the *Harper's A Tale of Two Cities* serial has such a vignette, only six were utilized in its serialization of *Great Expectations,* again perhaps owing to a shortage of column inches resulting from visual coverage of the Civil

War. The headnote vignette with which McLenan leads off the series is equal to his best scenic work in *A Tale of Two Cities*, the atmospheric miniature of the gibbet on the marshes (fig. 4), and the artist well conveys the bristling energy of the despotic Mrs. Joe in the miniature (fig. 5) for the 15 December 1860 installment. Such vignettes function effectively to whet the reader's appetite for reading the text, compelling the reader to attend carefully to the letterpress to find the moment anticipated. Because McLenan's illustrations for *Great Expectations* increasingly reflect his growing understanding of Dickens's characters and situations, it is unfortunate that so few of these vignettes occur in the *Harper's* numbers for *Great Expectations.*

Although he had not been able to read the entire text beforehand (an advantage from which Stone's plates undoubtedly benefited, along with the artist's having access to Dickens's expert knowledge of the text and advice about suitable subjects for illustration), McLenan has provided a graphing of a part-by-part reading that shows his perception of significant textual details and his growing awareness of the natures of the various characters. McLenan has not merely offered pictures in juxtaposition to action, but fleshed out the characters and their situations, offering a coherent reading of the British text for American readers. Unlike other serial readers on either side of the Atlantic, however, McLenan would not have been able to compare his interpretations of the text with those of other readers until *after* he had submitted his plates to Harper and Brothers—and, of course, unlike Marcus Stone, he would have been unable to compare his impressions of the letterpress with those of the author.

In the first number of the American serialization of *Great Expectations* (24 November 1860), John McLenan has deftly juxtaposed the single Joe/ Pip plate (bottom left, fig. 9) and Magwitch/Pip plates (top center, fig. 8, and bottom right, fig. 10), as if to invite the *Harper's* reader to compare and contrast Pip's relationships with these surrogate fathers. On the facing page (verso, fig. 7) is the presiding genius of the story and the ''father'' of all the characters, but he looks slightly off-left (to behind the viewer, as it were) rather than at the fruits of his imagination in text and images inspired by that text.

All three plates involving Pip and his surrogate fathers, Joe and Magwitch, occur on page 741 (figs. 8, 9, and 10), whether by design or accident inviting the reader to see one relationship in terms of the other. McLenan transforms Dickens's first-person narrative by having us view the scene from the stance of a third-person observer. The solid ruled outside plate (Magwitch and Pip on the Marshes, fig. 10) operates in opposition to the domestic interior of the Joe/Pip plate (fig. 9)—Mrs. Joe is absent in the latter (although Joe's nervousness implies her presence), and in fig. 10 Magwitch too looks nervously about (perhaps for Compeyson or the pursuing soldiers). The backgrounds as well as the costuming of the men are in sharp contrast (outdoors vs. indoors, thistles and tombstones vs. hearthside ease, convict rags and leg-iron vs. bourgeois waistcoat and trousers), whereas the costume and features of Pip (standing with Magwitch in fig. 10, but sitting with Magwitch and Joe in figs. 8 and 9) provides visual continuity between the three. To the journal's middle-class American readers, whether in the Slave or Free States, the disheveled figure of the runaway convict might even have suggested that anxiety-producing, significant other, the fugitive slave.[2]

By virtue of his savage appearance, East London dialect, and association with the natural world of the marshes and dykes and with the supernatural, the terrifying, nightmarish ghost of the gibbeted pirate, Magwitch is as alien to the restricted milieu of Pip's village as the madwoman in the attic, Edward Rochester's first wife, the Creole Bertha, is to the stable, ordered, daytime world of Thornfield in *Jane Eyre*. Sympathetic readers on both sides of the Atlantic must have interpreted both Magwitch and Joe as victims, Magwitch of the capitalistic class system (as exemplified by Compeyson) and Joe of the domestic abuser, Pip's sister, whose violence is, to some extent, the result of her extreme dissatisfaction with her social status as derived from her husband's business, whose laboring status is confirmed only a few times in McLenan's series (figs. 18 and 19) but not emphasized. McLenan has transformed Joe into a respectably-dressed small-businessman (as in fig. 16), and therefore a solid member of the middle class and representative of domesticity and civilization, as opposed to Magwitch, the criminal whose misdeeds exclude him from such society and have left him without employment or home. This transformation of the rough-hewn Hercules of Dickens's letterpress into a complacent bourgeois figure must have created a problem of credibility for *Harper's* readers when in chapter 14 the surly journeyman Orlick and his master, "like two giants," go at one another and Joe triumphs.

As opposed to his virtuosity in exploiting the visual possibilities of large-scale magazine serialization, juxtaposing such scenes as Mrs. Joe's scouring Pip (fig. 5, upper left, p. 789) with Joe's sitting companionably with him by the fire (lower right, p. 789), McLenan's style in many other drawings seems markedly old-fashioned, strongly reminiscent of the caricatures of such earlier British illustrators as Hogarth, Gillray, Cruikshank, and Browne. In contrast to the American serialization, Dickens's practice in *Household Words* and *All the Year Round* was to omit illustrations. The pulp paper and scale of both weekly magazines were unsuitable for illustrations, and omitting these kept costs down.

In 1859, Dickens had experimented with simultaneous weekly and monthly publication of *A Tale of Two Cities*. The unillustrated weekly parts ran in *All the Year Round*, while the monthly numbers were illustrated by Phiz in the manner of previous novels. This experiment in publishing in two different formats, however, proved a financial failure, probably because readers were not prepared to wait a month when each week brought forth a new installment. Moreover, resenting Phiz's apparent dilatoriness and evidently believing that the *TTC* plates revealed a want of invention, Dickens felt he should not revisit the practice of dual modes of part-publication in the serialization of *Great Expectations*. However, the situation in America was quite different: indeed, Dickens's *A Tale of Two Cities* had already run fully illustrated in *Harper's Weekly*. With its four-columned octavo pages the weekly illustrated magazine seems to have used copious illustration by McLenan as a value-added feature. In the American periodical, the visual element often predominates over the letterpress because the plates often straddle two (of the four) six centimeter columns of extremely fine print, the illustrations' captions appearing in capitals and also spanning two columns.

Marcus Clayton Stone (1840–1921) was the second son of Dickens's old friend, the self-taught Frank Stone, fellow Shakespeare Society member, neighbor at Tavistock Square, and occasional illustrator. After the latter's early death from heart-failure in November 1859, Marcus virtually became Dickens's adopted son, staying a month each year at Gad's Hill near Rochester, with the novelist's family. Since Dickens, wishing to advance Marcus's artistic career after his father's death, was instrumental in arranging lucrative commissions from Chapman and Hall, including the entire series of plates for his last complete novel, *Our Mutual Friend*, published between May 1864 and November 1865, one would naturally assume that a close working relationship existed in 1862 between the 22-year-old artist and the 50-year-old novelist. However, after the writer's displeasure with Phiz over the illustrations for the monthly numbers of *A Tale of Two Cities*, Dickens had become somewhat ambivalent about the role of illustration in his works. Nevertheless, he permitted young Stone to choose his own subjects in providing the "supplementary scenes" (Cohen 204) for the Library Edition volumes of *American Notes, Pictures from Italy, A Child's History of England*, and—most importantly because this would be its first appearance in illustrated volume form—*Great Expectations*: "These assignments, like the frontispiece Stone was commissioned to do for the Cheap Edition of *A Tale of Two Cities* in 1864, were the kind that might previously have gone to Browne. Dickens, though Stone worked independently of him, must have liked the results" (Cohen 204).

What little supervision Dickens exercised over the artist is difficult to gauge from the letters between the two that survive. J. A. Hammerton remarks of Stone's drawings for Dickens's last complete novel, *Our Mutual Friend*: "we are at once conscious of an enormous advance in their artistic quality and the disappearance of the old hearty humor of Phiz and Cruikshank" (19). Unfortunately, his eight plates for *Great Expectations* are not generally up to that standard since they have neither humor, nor sense of place, nor yet again much dramatic energy. At his best, Marcus Stone is a naturalist and realist, capable of portraying characters convincingly in the round, but he seems to have incapable of the narrative inventiveness and comic verve that character-ize Phiz's best work with Dickens, in *Martin Chuzzlewit, David Copperfield*, and *Bleak House*. Cohen speculates that Dickens, having discharged Browne after *A Tale of Two Cities*, chose the younger Stone as his next illustrator because Stone, unaffiliated either stylistically or emotionally with the old school of Cruikshank and Browne, would produce illustrations that would have a thoroughly contemporary, "Sixties" look, with the qualities which now seemed to suit the author "in his life as in his work" (Cohen 204): solidity, economy, lack of sentimentality, and a clear focus upon characters rather than upon properties and details in the backdrop.

Stone provided a mere eight plates rather than the cavalcade of caricatures so often delivered by Phiz, for Chapman and Hall's November 1862 "New and Cheap" single-volume edition *Great Expectations* (*Letters* 10: 122), ad-vertised in the *Athenaeum* for November 1, plates used again in the Library edition published in December 1864:

1. "Pip waits on Miss Havisham." *Front.*, ch. 8, p. 81 in the Nonesuch Edition, rpt. 2005 (fig.12);
2. "Old Orlick among the Cinders." Ch. 15, p. xiv in the Nonesuch Edition, rpt. 2005 (fig. 13);
3. "Taking Leave of Joe." Ch. 35, p. 145 in the Nonesuch Edition, rpt. 2005;
4. "Lecturing on Capital." Ch. 22, p. 179 in the Nonesuch Edition, rpt. 2005;
5. "A Rubber at Miss Havisham's." Ch. 29, p. 239 in the Nonesuch Edition, rpt. 2005 (fig. 20);
6. " 'Don't Go Home.' " Ch. 44, p. 359 in the Nonesuch Edition, rpt. 2005;
7. "On the Marshes, by the Lime-kiln." Ch. 52, p. 415 in the Nonesuch Edition, rpt. 2005;
8. "With Estella after All." Ch. 59, p. 475 in the Nonesuch Edition, rpt. 2005 (fig. 22).

If we regard these woodcuts, which are included in the Clarendon edition of the novel, edited by Margaret Cardwell (1993) and the 2005 reprinting of the 1937 Nonesuch Edition of Dickens, as constituting something of a narrative sequence in themselves (despite the considerable discontinuity), we may clas-sify Stone's vision of the novel as Pip's "Pilgrim's Progress," since, as boy and then as man, he appears in every illustration, while Joe, Miss Havisham, and Estella each appear twice, and Herbert Pocket and Orlick each appear once. Whereas only a few of Stone's eight plates are artistically satisfying, and "On the Marshes, by the Lime-kiln" is an utter failure in terms of realizing an important moment in the letterpress, the overall quality of McLenan's 40 illustrations, even of the six headnote vignettes (e.g., figs. 4, 5, and 6), is generally good, especially considering the time pressure under which the American periodical illustrator had to work in contrast to the leisurely pace that volume publication permitted Marcus Stone. In particular, John McLenan shows himself far more adept at exploiting the possibilities of the woodcut for atmospheric backgrounds and dramatically contrasting light and shadow. In contrast to Stone's brief and uneven series, McLenan's 40 plates of varying dimensions describe every significant character, including Pumblechook, Mrs. Pocket, and Trabb's Boy, visually elaborating a number of themes and exemplifying various genres found in the novel: the Gothic, the mystery, and the bildungsroman. Both Stone and McLenan, however, avoided illustrating the scenes related to the novel of manners features of the story, which has been much better dealt with by such later illustrators as F. A. Fraser in the Household Edition and Charles Green in the Gadshill Edition. Although McLenan's plates, created as it were ''on the fly,'' are not a thoroughly coherent and minutely planned pictorial program or ''the text pictured'' (Patten 91), they nevertheless employ varying pictorial styles to tell much of the story contained in the letterpress, and would certainly have facilitated the reading of the serial text, serving as signposts and reminders as well as crystallizing important scenes for readers not having the entire text of the novel before them.

Although available space will not permit a complete comparison of the two illustrators' treatments of Dickens's novel, a detailed consideration of several of those in McLenan's series reveals a tendency not merely to render the characters as contemporary but sometimes even as American by virtue of their costuming and backdrops. Moreover, McLenan's style, with its sense of character comedy and a diversity in setting and mood generally lacking in Stone's, ranges from somber realism (e.g., representations of Pip) to cartoonish ebullience (e.g., Orlick in fig. 17). Specifically, if we contrast Stone's ''Pip Waits on Miss Havisham'' (fig. 12) with its equivalent in *Harper's* (p. 804, 22 December 1860, fig. 14) and Stone's final illustration and greatest achievement in the series, ''With Estella after All'' (fig. 22) with McLenan's rendering of the closing scene (fig. 23), we can see these artists' very different, ''transatlantic'' readings of the novel. The final pictures in each series produce different effects, for Stone's splendid ''With Estella after All'' seems to resolve simultaneously the matters of the Pip-Estella romance and these characters' futures, whereas McLenan's equivalent, ''I Saw the Shadow of No Parting from Her,'' is oddly unsettling, as if the illustrator has seized upon the caption's and letterpress's implicit lack of closure as the governing principle of his last contribution. As the culmination of a long series, however, this illustration leaves the reader contemplating an uncertain future for the characters, for, despite their maturity and middle-class respectability, we cannot judge from the text or plate whether Pip and Estella will be happy.

Of Marcus Stone's woodcuts, only two present Miss Havisham ("'Pip Waits on Miss Havisham'' and ''A Rubber at Miss Havisham's''), whereas all depict Pip's journey from childhood to maturity, indicating that the bildungsroman aspect of the novel was uppermost in the British illustrator's mind. Of John McLenan's 34 full-size plates reprinted in the T. B. Peterson single-volume edition, four depict Miss Havisham in her boudoir (facing pages 48, 64, 70, and 204; see figs. 14, 15, and 16), one shows her candle in hand in a corridor (facing page 176), and one depicts her ablaze in the dining-room (facing page 224, fig. 21). Thus, Miss Havisham is featured prominently in five of McLenan's plates while, for example, Magwitch occurs in five, Joe in seven, and Pip in 29. Significantly, Stone has chosen to demote Magwitch in importance by not depicting Pip's alternate father figure at all.

Despite their pronounced differences in style and in interpreting Dickens's letterpress for different readerships, John McLenan and Marcus Stone, the former a caricaturist of the old school, the latter one of the newest New Men of the Sixties, share a single intention: to complement Dickens's narrative with images that he gives in so many words (such as the climactic meeting in the ruined garden), or that he merely suggests, and images made up of details that are largely invented. Illumination, announced by *Harper's* as the intention underlying McLenan's series, is also a subtheme in Stone's plates. Stone's original frontispiece (fig. 12) deals with artificial illumination both literally (the candles replacing the light of day) and figuratively (as neither Pip nor Miss Havisham herself sees the great lady for what she has become either physically or psychologically). A woman who has not seen the light of day or the light of self-awareness before Pip was born has made of herself a fairy princess caught in a spell in which the passage of time is arrested. As in an artificial world like that of the casino, day is not distinguished from night in this room, so that (at least in Miss Havisham's mind) time stands still. Influenced in part by the distorting light of the candles and partly by the aura of wealth and power guiding him out of the path of true perception, Pip fails to see either her advancing age or her mental aberration. The room, apparently so full of light in Stone's representation of it, contains dense shadows, darkly shaded areas that betoken the secrets and mysteries surrounding Miss Havisham. Here, as in ''Old Orlick Among the Cinders'' (fig. 13), we can identify ourselves with the figure of Pip because Stone has depicted him as a spectator, although each picture's perspective is established as belonging to a detached viewer who regards Pip as he in turn looks at Miss Havisham in the frontispiece and Joe and Orlick in the forge scene. Pip, as storyteller, as observer and recorder of events, is once again dwarfed by the other actors in the scene in the latter woodcut, but here his expression is critical rather than adoring. Although neither illustration contains as much detail as the Browne and Cruickshank steels that adorn the earlier Dickens novels, each contains a significant object with thematic associations: the former plate includes Miss Havisham's disregarded timepiece (to the right of her left elbow), and the latter plate shows a vise, suggestive of Pip's position in the argument that has erupted between Joe, Mrs. Joe, and Orlick over the protagonist's taking time off.

The relatively benign mutual scrutiny of Pip and Herbert in "Lecturing on Capital" continues the motif of the activity allied to illumination: observation or surveillance (found in Stone's first, second, third, fourth, fifth, and sixth plates). In "A Rubber at Miss Havisham's" (fig. 20), this mutual scrutinizing of one another becomes intensified as each player attempts to detect what cards lie in the others' hands. Gradually, as in the letterpress, a mood of watchful suspicion appropriate to the veins of the Gothic and mystery genres contained in *Great Expectations* is established in the accompanying illustrations, all of which are set at night.

In illuminating the text of Dickens's second great pseudo-autobiographical novel of development, each artist has attempted to both engage and enlighten the reader, interpreting and commenting upon the original story by providing a visual analogue, the story as they visualized it. In the process, each artist sometimes created pictures which convey meaning independent of the text that inspired them, pictures like Stone's "Pip Waits on Miss Havisham" (fig. 12) and McLenan's "It's a great cake. A bride-cake. Mine!" (fig. 15)—pictures that at their best are works of art rather than mere illustrations that rely for their meanings upon a text in another medium.

In "Pip Waits on Miss Havisham" in contradiction to the letterpress, Marcus Stone depicts Miss Havisham as youthful and attractive. Commanding in presence, she is lit by candelabra, enthroned as it were before her humble supplicant, the blacksmith's boy. Cloth cap in hand, Pip slightly bends at the knees, before the large-eyed, imperious aristocrat with the elaborately arranged blonde hair and bare-shouldered, voluminous wedding dress (apparently no worse for many years of wear), her mirror just disappearing off the right-hand margin. Contrast this glowing image from Pip's memory with the despondent, introverted, somewhat elderly, and angular bride in front of her mirror given us by McLenan (in figs. 14 and 16), who has here reflected the letterpress more accurately.

As we turn page 48 in the 1861 Philadelphia volume we encounter the vignetted illustration " 'Who is it?' said the lady at the table. 'Pip, ma'am.'—Page 49" (fig. 14) before we actually find the same moment in the letterpress. Whereas Stone had filled the frame with a youthful, enchanting fairy godmother, McLenan has set his crone in the midst of her furnishings and belongings. As in the text, open trunks (left and right) covered with clothing frame the scene, and an inward-gazing Miss Havisham in an attitude of despondency, hand supporting her head, sits before an oval mirror that has four candelabra attached. Faithful to his text in proof, the illustrator has included such details as the white shoe on the dressing table (Pip indicates that he can see the other white shoe on her foot, which McLenan conceals beneath her skirts). Although neither artist has depicted the faded flowers, the watch and chain are evident just to the right of Miss Havisham's left elbow in Stone's version, important symbols of her rejection of the passage of time. An interesting (if minor) detail which varies in the two renditions of the scene is Pip's hat: in Stone's plate (fig. 12), it is a cloth cap such as was worn by the British working class, whereas in McLenan's plate it is a brimmed felt hat, which the American artist supplied from his own experience and period.

This tendency to bring in the American milieu is nowhere more evident than in his depiction of the blacksmith's journeyman "old" Orlick as a Western villain in a high-crowned, wide-brimmed "Western" hat in fig. 17, " 'Hulloa!' he growled; 'Where are you two going?'—Page 86," in which Biddy wears a decidedly 1860s American "poke-bonnet" similar to that worn by Estella in the final *Harper's* plate. At least McLenan has given his villain gaiters rather than cowboy boots, but the eyes in particular betray a style more geared toward caricature than realism, despite the wealth of detail incorporated into each scene such as the pollarded willow, swamp grass, and cattails here. Stone's fallen Orlick, in the foreground (left) of "Old Orlick Among the Cinders" (fig. 13, which serves as the frontispiece for the new Nonesuch Edition), is far more plausible and decidedly younger than McLenan's figure, rendering him a more suitable "double" psychologically for Pip, who also appears in working-class garb in the two Stone plates that precede his coming into his expectations. McLenan's figure lacks the dynamic nature of Stone's rebellious journeyman, looking more like a waxworks dummy of a Western desperado than a living entity representative of the tradition of the melodramatic lower-class villain, epitomized somewhat later by Dick Dead-Eye in Gilbert and Sullivan's *H. M. S. Pinafore*. Regarding Joe as an American artisan of the entrepreneurial, "owner-operator" class, McLenan has chosen to depict him as mild-mannered, moderately plump, beardless, and clad in respectably bourgeois attire. Only in the 8 December and 9 February installments (figs. 18 and 19) does McLenan specifically depict Joe as a blacksmith, with jacket removed and sleeves rolled back to reveal brawny forearms which could not possibly fit under the jacket sleeves of the other plates in which he appears. In the first of these two illustrations McLenan minimizes Joe's bulk by making the soldiers taller and having Joe stoop over his anvil, his large arms and hands looking somewhat incongruous. Stone, on the other hand, consistently depicts Joe as a blonde, bearded, Nordic giant presiding over his forge and menacing Orlick, restraining the power in his mighty arms by a supreme act of self-control (see fig.13).

Moreover, whereas Stone's renditions of Pip (in "Pip Waits on Miss Havisham" and "Old Orlick Among the Cinders") interpret him as a "laboring boy," McLenan consistently depicts young Pip in thoroughly respectable, American middle-class costume. For example, in "Oh, Un-cle Pum-ble-chook! This *Is* Kind!" (1 Dec. 1860, p. 765), Pip is wearing a shirt with a broad collar, a short jacket with large buttons, matching trousers, and shoes (rather than working-class boots), his garb seeming consistent with Mrs. Joe's hooped skirt, bonnet, and shoulder-covering. Pip, however, appears in less formal attire in McLenan's hearthside plates such as the headnote vignette for 15 December (fig. 5), which reveals a perfectly white shirt and collar and suspenders. In this chapter headnote vignette, Mrs. Joe vigorously assists Pip in washing prior to his making his social debut at Satis House, where (through the agency of Uncle Pumblechook) Miss Havisham has invited him to "play." Despite a skeletal forearm, Mrs. Joe's form seems to be bursting out of her pinned apron, as if reflecting her envy of Pip's having been summoned to the village's social Olympus, whose presiding deity is also female. Dillard notes that McLenan herein effectively transforms the first-person narrative of Dickens's text to an objective or dramatic rendering that communicates directly Pip's vividly remembered feelings and experience by rough, almost hasty lines and deep, irregular cross-hatching in the figures, the washstand, and the bowl. McLenan has subordinated the background by merely lightly sketching in the surroundings, keeping the eye well forward in this kinetic miniature. Pip is once again passive and rigid in his more formal attire when he visits Satis House in " 'Who is it?' said the lady at the table. 'Pip, ma'am.' " (fig. 14).

Again, whereas the American artist has depicted the jewels that the letter-press twice mentions, these are not present in Stone's plate, which nevertheless glimmers by the light of four powerful candles in contrast to the faint glare of the four tapers in McLenan's. Without unnecessarily dwelling upon such minutiae, we may simply note that the overall effect of the American periodical illustration is awkward and stilted, although technically accurate in many respects other than costume, whereas that of the English illustration is dramatic and powerful because Stone has reduced the scene to its essentials, and placed the contrasting figures in close proximity, balancing the difference in their heights by placing three candles above Pip and creating a sense of the numinous that the American plate entirely lacks. Haloed, cherubic Pip basks in the luminous presence of the great lady.

Miss Havisham remains a static, almost blind figure in McLenan's " 'It's a great cake. A bride-cake. Mine!'—Page 63" and " 'Which I meantersay, Pip.'—Page 70" (figs. 15 and 16), both of which are nevertheless accurate in the details of each scene, the dining room and the boudoir. However, McLenan's Pip, ward of a middle-class businessman as the American artist conceived of Joe, is too well dressed for the mere laboring boy of Dickens's text, and one wonders about the lighting for the latter scene, since the windows are covered but the candles above Estella are unlit. Interestingly, in all three Havisham plates, mirrors are central features, though none of these mirrors actually *reflects* anything. These "blind" mirrors may imply the psychological blindness of Miss Havisham to her true condition; in David Lean's 1946 film, Miss Havisham is, as Regina Barreca notes, "framed next to mirrors in a number of scenes, making visual the way the spinster wishes to multiply her image through Estella" (41). However, McLenan's mirrors return no image, suggesting, like the dried-up brewery of the letterpress, the sterility of Satis House, which accords well with the static, rigid depiction of the figures, rotund Joe furnishing in his darkly clad amplitude a sharp contrast to Miss Havisham's severe whiteness, stark thinness, and pronounced angularity. In Joe's figure, McLenan suggests the enjoyment of many a substantial meal, the fruits of his virtuous labors, and the evidence of the efficacy of the American Protestant work-ethic, while Stone's is less the broadcloth-garbed bourgeoisie and more the blond, muscular giant of the laboring class, although both interpretations are certainly possible in Dickens's letterpress.

Nevertheless, as Stein points out, even the most faithful illustrations—that is, those which attempt to realize as much as possible the textual moment to be illuminated—are reconstructed "from the perspective of a second medium and a second imagination" (171). For the most part, ironically (given the close relationship between Stone and the author), it is McLenan rather than Stone who allows himself to be more closely guided by the letterpress as he attempts to incorporate most of the details that Dickens has provided. In contrast, despite the solidity of his figures and his placing them more effectively in a three-dimensional setting, Stone's style veers deliberately away from literal realism toward the creation of an appropriate mood or atmosphere, as we have seen in "Pip Waits on Miss Havisham."

The desiccated old woman who serves as a chronometer for the mature Pip, Herbert, and Estella in Stone's "A Rubber at Miss Havisham's" (fig. 20) is still not quite the fairytale crone who becomes her own candle in McLenan's plate opposite page 224 in the Peterson edition (bottom, p. 286, *Harper's*, 4 May 1861, fig. 21), but in Stone's narrative-pictorial sequence we have the distinct sense that she has aged and shrunk considerably since Pip first encountered her. Although she is still associated in Stone's plate with lighted tapers, our view of Miss Havisham is blocked by the youthful figure of Estella, who is now the real power over Pip. As the smoke billows (right) and flames engulf her skirts in McLenan's plate, we are still struck by the awkward rigidity of the figures: Miss Havisham's look of horror is utterly convincing, but her waist is not. In contrast, real bodies seem to have sat as the originals for all of Stone's plates, which convey a pronounced tendency toward realistic portraiture: "Stone worked from models, and his naturalistic portrayals of characters suited the academic tastes of the times" (Cohen 204). Perhaps nowhere else in his series of plates for *Great Expecta-*tions is Stone's departure from what Cohen terms the outmoded "Hogarth-Cruikshank-Browne tradition" (204) of the steel etching more evident and effective than in his last, with the mature Pip and Estella in the ruined garden at Satis House.

Stone's "With Estella After All" contrasts with McLenan's " 'I saw the shadow of no parting from her.'—Page 266," although both illustrate the following passage: "I took her hand in mine, and we went out of the ruined place; and as the mists had risen long ago when I first left the forge, so the evening mists were rising now, and in all the broad expanse of tranquil light they showed to me, I saw the shadow of no parting from her. THE END" (ch. 59, T. B. Peterson, p. 266).

Since Dickens's interest is psychological here, he offers very few external points of description to aid his illustrators, who thus have had to improvise with and select from what little background the author has provided: the rising moon (given prominence by McLenan), the garden bench, the remnants of the mansion's foundations, a gate in the fence, old ivy growing on low mounds, and the silvery mist enveloping all. The contrast between McLenan's and Stone's treatments of this highly significant textual moment is telling: in the former, the static, pillar-like pair stand as in a *tableau vivant*, posed against and framed by a theatrical backdrop of wall, ivy, and rising moon, looking at the viewer as actors on stage might regard the audience. The young middle-class couple is respectably, even soberly clad, and they clutch one another's hands, as if to resist any further blocks to their relationship. In contrast to their thinness and woodenness, Stone's couple fills the space with their ample, vital presences: a bearded, handsome, undeniably mature Pip has removed his silk hat (indicative of his success in the struggle to remain a member of the rising middle class) in perhaps a courteous gesture, or as a sign of reverence, and a still most fetching Estella gently supports herself on Pip's left arm with both hands, thoroughly committing herself to his love and protection. Their heads together (rather than unemotionally apart, as in McLenan's somewhat dour depiction), they seem to confide in one another, communing rather than speaking, utterly absorbed in one another. Pip has removed his hat, as if in the presence of the sacred; Stone has thereby reduced his height and humanized the slightly bowed head. While the textually accu-rate McLenan has clothed his couple in the same, dark-hued broadcloth, Stone has Pip in black but Estella in a lighter hue, as if to imply the complementary nature of their relationship and experiences since last having seen one another, and perhaps to suggest that there is a wedding in the offing, despite Estella's remark that they will live "friends apart."

The five stars shining above the reunited lovers in Stone's plate seem less intended to suggest the twilight setting than to imply the providential nature of their meeting again, in the ruined garden, across time and space reunited "after all." Eleven years before, Stone's Pip was a slender, beardless youth when last seen reading the monitory note in "Don't Go Home." However, in this final illustration Pip and Estella are substantial figures, respectable, middle-class Victorians seemingly approaching their mid-thirties. Pip's beard and general bulk (besides heavy outer garments suitable for a chilly December evening on the Thames Marshes) suggest at least a physical maturity; however, his hair bears no hint of grey, and is precisely the same as in "A Rubber at Miss Havisham's" (the sixth plate in Stone's series). Estella clings to Pip's arm and gloved left hand with her hands. The background only barely suggests the ruined garden's vegetation, and a patch of grass in the paving (bottom center) is all we are given of the rank ground and the decayed garden-walk. As opposed to Phiz's now-unfashionable steel etchings, last seen in the monthly parts of Dickens's *A Tale of Two Cities* (1859), young Marcus Stone's plates, executed only three years later, are printed in typical sixties style from woodblocks,[3] a form that prohibits the detailism of the earlier Victorian style of illustration, but is fully capable of suggesting a mood or atmosphere, as in Fred Walker's renowned theatrical poster for Wilkie Collins's *The Woman in White,* designed for the Olympic's October 1871 production of Collins's dramatic adaptation of the novel. Walker's later use of stars to suggest the role of destiny in the picture may, in fact, be derived from Stone's here.

The mood of Stone's final illustration is certainly suitable to a scene played out under the gathering shadows of a December twilight. Ironically, having given up "that poor dream" of marrying Estella, Pip visits "the site of the old house that evening, alone, for her sake" after an absence of over a decade. It is still "before dark" when he enters the precincts of Satis House, of which all that is left is the garden wall (depicted two-dimensionally by McLenan in the T. B. Peterson edition, but not represented by Stone). Stone suggests the evening mist by the use of cross-hatching behind the figures in the garden walk (implied by the light stones barely sketched in at their feet). The text makes clear that this is the first time either Pip or Estella has visited the "poor old place," so that their coincidental meeting seems an act of Providence, whose emblems, in Stone's illustrations, are the five stars in the murky sky above the lovers' heads. That moonlight illuminates the scene is implied by the light behind Pip (left) and the moonlight's throwing a chiaroscuro over Estella's coat and skirts (right). In McLenan's plate, the half-obscured moon similarly throws half of Pip's leaner, clean-shaven face into shadow. Stone evokes the essential feeling of the moment when, the interview apparently ended, they rise from the bench and Pip bends over her. Perhaps she is already remarking, "And will continue friends apart." Instead of Pip's taking her hand in his in preparation to leave "the ruined place," she takes his left in both of hers, seeking support and comfort from a man of whose gentleness she can be sure. Stone, then, wishes us to regard Estella as changed, as softened by time and suffering, and ready to return Pip's love at last. In fig. 22, Stone, like Dickens, would have us see "no shadow of another parting" (the reading of the 1862 Library edition). In McLenan's illustration (fig. 23), the line from Estella's head moves upward diagonally to Pip's head, which, being higher because he is wearing his hat, carries the eye upward to the rising moon.

Both McLenan's and Stone's plates are renderings of precisely the same textual moment, but what we see today, almost a century and a half later, are the differences. These are, in part, the products of the very different pictorial styles of the illustrators, McLenan's being early- and Stone's mid-Victorian. But some of the difference must lie in the personal and social contexts of their readings of Dickens.

What is interesting is what the illustrators have chosen *not* to represent, for the remnants of Satis House, emblematic of the past and of upper-class privilege divorced from labor, appear in neither Stone's nor McLenan's final plates. Rather, the green world (not a mere patch of rank ground) and night sky frame the characters, making them each picture's focus and detaching them from any trace of the traumatic edifice. The presence of the moon in McLenan's work and the stars in Stone's defines the scene as constructed in time, at the end of day. The green space as represented in McLenan's final illustration by new growth—ivy covering the old wall and low trees—beneath the moon, on the other hand, perhaps implies a regaining of the Eden that Pip loses at the end of the first stage of his "Expectations" at the close of chapter 19. Both pictorial sequences depict at this point Joe in blacksmith's clothing, as if the artists wish to emphasize the social stratum that Pip is renouncing in becoming a London "gentleman" in order to win Estella. At the conclusion of each pictorial sequence, from the noise, stench, and criminal associations of the metropolis, we retreat with Pip and Estella, renewed and reunited in the green world. Aside from the fragment of wall that serves as a theatrical backdrop in McLenan's plate, there is no analogue for the negative aspects of the past in either illustration, so that both artists have chosen to situate their male and female leads in a space physically divorced from London and from the past.

McLenan has shaped his Estella and Pip as a pyramid and a column respectively, forms, which convey stability, with associations to a more grounded and cultured history than either character has in fact experienced. McLenan's space is, as already noted, strangely two-dimensional compared to Stone's, its frozen figures waiting, aloof yet contiguous, mutually supportive yet independent and apart. Through their pose and form McLenan conveys an uneasy sense of the future, perhaps of events beyond the boundary of the text (as if, although Pip sees "the shadow of no parting from her," that parting may still come, unanticipated).

The energy, intellect, and spirit of the British middle class, exemplified by the noble heads of Stone's Pip and Estella in his final plate, are the forces upon which the commercial and political stability of the Empire depends. Rising above their laboring-class origins and turbid past, Pip and Estella, as envisaged by Stone, as possessing a mutual confidence in each other and an affection for one another that contrast with the static stoicism of McLenan's younger, more slender figures, for in Stone's plate the couple's future together seems assured. Pip and Estella are at last about to become a married couple, the reader would like to think, united by matrimony, as well as by a shared past and shared values based on loyalty, duty, and perseverance. However, every reading—especially every illustrator's reading—of a text amounts to an appropriation of a text, and therefore inevitably a distortion. In order to convey the inner truth of the text, the imaginative illustrator adds to or subtracts in rendering a narrative moment pictorially. The illustrator may be faithful to the superficialities of the text and yet fail to convey its spirit, underlying meaning, or inner truth. Against these criteria, one may regard Stone's two best plates and McLenan's whole series as inviting and interesting but perhaps distorted and distorting readings animated by the differing spirits of the early sixties on either side of the Atlantic.

The final illustration in McLenan's series, that of Pip and Estella providentially reunited in the ruined garden of Satis House, is so surprisingly without emotion that it fails to communicate any indication of mutual comfort or devotion. Pip stands detached in body, thought, and feeling, looking at us (as if on stage) rather than at Estella.

We see McLenan at his best in an earlier scene, that depicting Miss Havisham's immolation, one of the most exciting textual moments in the story. Here, as Leigh Dillard has noted, the illustrator has abandoned patient attention to detail (the inclusion of minute details to create verisimilitude) in favor of impressionism: the artist has rendered Pip as a mere black statue while he shows Miss Havisham as dynamic, expressive, and terrified. He captures Miss Havisham in a moment of violent, frenzied motion; Pip, in contrast, is immobile, as if unable to assist, powerless, inanimate.

Despite such instances of visual experimentation and dynamic action arrested, we may ultimately regard McLenan as a traditional illustrator most at home with caricature and visual humor. McLenan has failed to offer a psychological reading of either of these focal characters at the of the novel's moment of closure. In fact, in this final visual adaptation or translation of Dickens's letterpress he fails to engage the reader-viewer because he has not imbued his image of the middle-aged lovers with the guarded optimism and sense of wonder at the workings of Providence that readers on both sides of the Atlantic would have detected in the narrative voice.

Nevertheless, working under considerable time constraints, with proofs sent from England needing to be reset in the multicolumned format of *Harper's Weekly*, John McLenan has provided a comprehensive and uniformly competent visual reading of Dickens's fragmented text. Of his 40 illustrations, some are much stronger than others, and none should be pronounced a complete failure in terms of effect, composition, or realization. Marcus Stone's series in contrast, especially considering the comparatively leisurely pace at which he was able to work, with adequate time to reflect upon his reading and even consult the novelist, is uneven and frequently disappointing, perhaps because Stone viewed his task as the creation of independent works of art rather than as visual complements to the letterpress, and perhaps because of his lack of familiarity with the artistic medium. His best studies (the first four plates and the last) involve large-scale figures in moments of strong emotion and in evocative poses. These strengths become more evident in Stone's narrative-pictorial sequences for *Our Mutual Friend*.

Unfortunately, *Great Expectations* was among the last works that McLenan illustrated. Because he died just four years later, at the age of 38, he missed the opportunity to meet Charles Dickens on his 1867 American reading tour, an opportunity enjoyed by Sol Eytinge (1833–1905), illustrator of Ticknor and Fields's new, six-volume Diamond edition of CD's works:

> The memorial which appeared in the May [1865] number of *Yankee Notions* called [John McLenan] "one of the best draughtsmen America has ever produced" and said of him: "Equally at home in caricature and in sketches from the life, with a quick perception of the ridiculous and a fine appreciation of the picturesque, he soon took his place among the illustrators of our current literature, second to none."   (qtd. in Hamilton xli)

CHAPTER XIV.

THE HONEST TRADESMAN.

TO the eyes of Mr. Jere-
miah Cruncher, sitting
on his stool in Fleet Street,
with his grisly urchin beside
him, a vast number and va-

Fig. 1. John McLenan. *A Tale of Two Cities*, book 2, ch. 14: uncaptioned headnote vignette (animated coffin pursuing young Jerry in the youth's imagination). *Harper's Weekly* 30 July 1859: 485. 4.5 cm wide by 6.1 cm high.

BOOK II.
THE GOLDEN THREAD.

CHAPTER IX.
THE GORGON'S HEAD.

IT was a heavy mass of building, that chateau of Monsieur the Marquis, with a large stone court-yard before it, and two stone sweeps of staircase meeting in a stone terrace before the principal door. A stony business

Fig. 2. John McLenan. *A Tale of Two Cities,* book 2, ch. 9: uncaptioned headnote vignette ("on the weather-beaten sill of the great window of the bedchamber of Monsieur the Marquis, one little bird sang with all its might"). *Harper's Weekly* 9 July 1859: 437. 7.3 cm high by 4.5 cm wide.

THERE had been
earlier drinking
than usual in the
wine shop of Mon-
sieur Defarge.   As
early as six o'clock

Fig. 3. John McLenan. *A Tale of Two Cities,* book 2, ch. 15: uncaptioned headnote vignette (the poisoned fountain in the marquis's village). *Harper's Weekly* 6 Aug. 1859: 508. 7.6 cm high by 4.5 cm wide.

GREAT EXPECTATIONS.

A NOVEL.

By CHARLES DICKENS.

Splendidly Illustrated by John McLenan.

☞ Printed from the Manuscript and early Proof-sheets purchased from the Author by the Proprietors of "Harper's Weekly."

CHAPTER I.

Fig. 4. John McLenan. *Great Expectations,* book 1, ch. 1: uncaptioned head-note vignette (the gibbet on the marshes). *Harper's Weekly* 24 Nov. 1860: 740. 9.5 cm high by 6 cm wide.

GREAT EXPECTATIONS.

A NOVEL.

By CHARLES DICKENS.

Splendidly Illustrated by John McLenan.

☞ Printed from the Manuscript and
early Proof-sheets purchased from the
Author by the Proprietors of "Harper's
Weekly."

CHAPTER VI.

Fig. 5. John McLenan. *Great Expectations,* book 1, ch. 6: uncaptioned head-note vignette (Mrs. Joe scrubbing Pip). *Harper's Weekly* 15 Dec. 1860: 789. 9.6 cm high by 6 cm wide.

Fig. 6. John McLenan. *Great Expectations,* book 1, ch. 17: uncaptioned head-note vignette (Jaggers, Pip, Joe, and Whopsle at the Three Jolly Bargemen). *Harper's Weekly* 9 Feb. 1861: 85. 11.5 cm high by 6 cm wide.

Fig. 7. Artist unnamed. ''Charles Dickens, Esq.—[From a Late Photograph.].'' *Harper's Weekly* 24 Nov. 1860: 740. Plate 20 cm high by 15 cm wide.

HARPER'S WEEKLY.

"YOU YOUNG DOG!" SAID THE MAN, LICKING HIS LIPS AT ME, "WHAT FAT CHEEKS YOU HA'
GOT!"

Fig. 8. John McLenan. *Great Expectations*, installment 1, plate 2: " 'You
young dog!' said the man, licking his lips at me, 'What fat cheeks you ha'
got!' " *Harper's Weekly* 24 Nov. 1860: 741. 10 cm high by 12 cm wide.
Reproduced in the T. B. Peterson edition as plate 3 (first in the list of illustrations): " 'You young dog!'' said the man, licking his lips at me, ''What fat
cheeks you ha' got!'—Page 22.'' Philadelphia, 1861, facing p. 22.

"PIP, OLD CHAP! YOU'LL DO YOURSELF A MISCHIEF. IT'LL STICK SOMEWHERE. YOU CAN'T HAVE CHAWED IT, PIP."

Fig. 9. John McLenan. *Great Expectations*, installment 1, plate 3: "Pip, old chap! You'll do yourself a mischief. It'll stick somewhere. You can't have chawed it, Pip." *Harper's Weekly* 24 Nov. 1860, 741. 11.5 cm high by 12 cm wide. Reproduced in the T. B. Peterson edition as plate 4 (second in the list of illustrations): " 'Pip, old chap! You'll do yourself a mischief. It'll stick somewhere. You can't have chawed it, Pip.'—Page 25." Philadelphia, 1861, facing p. 24.

"YOU'RE NOT A FALSE IMP? YOU BROUGHT NO ONE WITH YOU?"

Fig. 10. John McLenan. *Great Expectations*, installment 1, plate 4: "You're not a false imp? You brought no one with you?" *Harper's Weekly* 24 Nov. 1860: 741. 11.6 cm high by 11.7 cm wide. Reproduced in the T. B. Peterson edition as plate 5 (third in the list of illustrations): " 'You're not a false imp? You brought no one with you?'—Page 29." Philadelphia, 1861, facing p. 28.

DECEMBER 1, 1860.]

"BUT HE WAS DOWN ON THE RANK WET GRASS, FILING AT HIS IRON
LIKE A MADMAN."

Fig. 11. John McLenan. *Great Expectations*, installment 2, plate 8: "But he was down on the rank wet grass, filing at his iron like a madman." *Harper's Weekly* 1 Dec. 1860: 765. 12 cm high by 8.9 cm wide. Reproduced in the T. B. Peterson edition as plate 6 (fourth in the list of illustrations): " 'But he was down on the rank wet grass, filing at his iron like a madman.'—Page 30." Philadelphia, 1861, facing p. 30.

PIP WAITS ON MISS HAVISHAM.

Fig. 12. Marcus Stone. *Great Expectations*, ch. 8: "Pip Waits on Miss Havis-ham." The Library Edition. London: Chapman and Hall, 1862. Wood engraving 13.3 cm high by 8.8 cm wide.

OLD ORLICK AMONG THE CINDERS.

Fig. 13. Marcus Stone. *Great Expectations*, ch. 15: "Old Orlick among the Cinders." The Library Edition. London: Chapman and Hall, 1862. Wood engraving 13.1 cm high by 8.8 cm wide.

"WHO IS IT?" SAID THE LADY AT THE TABLE. "PIP, MA'AM.'

Fig. 14. John McLenan. *Great Expectations*, installment 5, plate 11: " 'Who is it?' said the lady at the table. 'Pip, Ma'am.' " *Harper's Weekly* 22 Dec. 1860: 804. 11.4 cm high by 11.8 cm wide. Reproduced in the T. B. Peterson edition as plate 10 (eighth in the list of illustrations): " 'Who is it?' said the lady at the table. 'Pip, Ma'am.'—Page 49." Philadelphia, 1861, facing p. 48.

Fig. 15. John McLenan. *Great Expectations*, installment 7, plate 13: "It's a great cake. A bride-cake. Mine!" *Harper's Weekly* 5 Jan. 1861, 5. 11.4 cm high by 11.8 cm wide. Reproduced in the T. B. Peterson edition as plate 11 (tenth in the list of illustrations): " 'It's a great cake. A bride-cake. Mine!'—Page 63." Philadelphia, 1861, facing p. 64.

"WHICH I MEANTERSAY, PIP."

Fig. 16. John McLenan. *Great Expectations*, installment 8, plate 14: "Which I meantersay, Pip." *Harper's Weekly* 12 Jan. 1861: 21 (center). 11.3 cm high by 11.3 cm wide. Reproduced in the T. B. Peterson edition as plate 12 (eleventh in the list of illustrations): " 'Which I meantersay, Pip.'—Page 70.'' Philadelphia, 1861, facing p. 70.

"HULLOA!" HE GROWLED; "WHERE ARE YOU TWO GOING?"

Fig. 17. John McLenan. *Great Expectations*, installment 10, plate 16: " 'Hul-loa!' he growled; 'Where are you two going?' " *Harper's Weekly* 2 Feb. 1861: 69. 11.8 cm high by 11.9 cm wide. Reproduced in the T. B. Peterson edition as plate 13 (twelfth in the list of illustrations): " 'Hulloa!' he growled; 'Where are you two going?'—Page 86." Philadelphia, 1861, facing p. 86.

Fig. 18. John McLenan. *Great Expectations*, installment 3, plate 8: "Then Joe began to hammer and clink, hammer and clink." *Harper's Weekly* 8 Dec. 1860: 773. 11.9 cm high by 12 cm wide. Reproduced in the T. B. Peterson edition as plate 8 (sixth in the list of illustrations): "Then Joe began to hammer and clink, hammer and clink.—Page 36." Philadelphia, 1861, facing p. 36.

"PIP'S A GENTLEMAN OF FORTUN', THEN," SAID JOE, "AND GOD BLESS HIM IN IT!"

Fig. 19. John McLenan. *Great Expectations*, installment 18, plate 18: "Pip's a gentleman of fortune, then," said Joe, "and God bless him in it!" *Harper's Weekly* 9 Feb. 1861: 85. 11.8 cm high by 11.9 cm wide. Reproduced in the T. B. Peterson edition as plate 14 (thirteenth in the list of illustrations): " 'Pip's a gentleman of fortune, then,' said Joe, 'and God bless him in it!'—Page 93." Philadelphia, 1861, facing p. 92.

A RUBBER AT MISS HAVISHAM'S.

Fig. 20. Marcus Stone. *Great Expectations*, ch. 29: "A Rubber at Miss Havisham's." The Library Edition. London: Chapman and Hall, 1862. Wood engraving 13.4 cm high by 9 cm wide.

Fig. 21. John McLenan. *Great Expectations* installment 30, plate 35: " 'I saw her running at me, shrieking, with a whirl of fire blazing all about her,' etc." *Harper's Weekly* 22 June 1861: 398 (bottom right). 11.6 cm high by 11.5 cm wide. Reproduced in the T. B. Peterson edition as plate 29: " 'I saw her running at me, shrieking, with a whirl of fire blazing all about her,' ETC.—Page 224." Philadelphia, 1861, facing p. 224.

Fig. 22. Marcus Stone. *Great Expectations*, ch. 59: ''With Estella after All.''
The Library Edition. London: Chapman and Hall, 1862. Wood engraving
13.1 cm high by 8.9 cm wide.

Fig. 23. John McLenan. *Great Expectations*, installment 38, plate 40: ''I saw the shadow of no parting from her.'' *Harper's Weekly* 3 Aug. 1861: 494. 11.4 cm high by 11.5 cm wide. Reproduced in the T. B. Peterson edition as plate 34: '' 'I saw the shadow of no parting from her.'—Page 266.'' Philadelphia, 1861, facing p. 266.

Appendix One

McLenan's Plates in the Harper's Serial *(24 November 1860–3 August 1861) and the T. B. Peterson (Philadelphia, 1861) Volume Edition*

1. Installment 1, plate 1: 24 Nov. 1860: No title or caption, "Chapter I." underneath [scene: the gibbet on the marshes]. Bottom right, p. 740 (9.5 cm high by 6 cm wide) for the end of ch. 1, p. 741. This and the remaining five headnote vignettes were not reproduced in the T. B. Peterson edition of 1861.
2. Installment 1, plate 2, 24 Nov. 1860: " 'You young dog!' said the man, licking his lips at me, 'What fat cheeks you ha' got!' " [Pip, left, and Magwitch, right, in the churchyard]. Top middle, p. 741 (10 cm high by 12 cm wide) for ch. 1, p. 740 (plate 1 in Peterson, facing p. 22, references "Page 22").
3. Installment 1, plate 3, 24 Nov. 1860: "Pip, old chap! You'll do yourself a mischief. It'll stick somewhere. You can't have chawed it, Pip." [Pip, left, and Joe, right, seated before the hearth in the parlor of the forge]. Bottom left, p. 741 (11.5 cm high by 12 cm wide) for ch. 2, p. 742 (plate 2 in Peterson, facing p. 28, references "Page 25").
4. Installment 1, plate 4, 24 Nov. 1860: "You're not a false imp? You brought no one with you?" [Pip, left, and Magwitch, right, on the marshes]. Bottom right, p. 741 (11.6 cm high by 11.7 cm wide) for ch. 2, p. 742 (plate 3 in Peterson, facing p. 22, references "Page 29").
5. Installment 2, plate 5, 1 Dec. 1860: "But he was down on the rank wet grass, filing at his iron like a madman." [Magwitch alone on the marshes, attempting to remove his manacle]. Top left, p. 765 (12 cm high by 8.9 cm wide) for ch. 3, p. 765 (plate 4 in Peterson, facing p. 22, references "Page 29").
6. Installment 2, plate 6, 1 Dec. 1860: "Oh, Un-cle Pum-ble-chook! This *is* kind!" [Pumblechook, right, Pip, center, and Mrs. Joe, left, at the entrance to the Gargery cottage]. Bottom right, p. 765 (11.6 cm high by 12 cm wide) for ch. 4, p. 765 (plate 5 in Peterson, facing p. 32, references "Page 32").
7. Installment 3, plate 7, 8 Dec. 1860: No title or caption [scene: three soldiers, carrying torches, are leading Magwitch, center, away in chains]. Top left, p. 773, for ch. 5, p. 774. This and the other uncaptioned chapter headnote vignettes were not reproduced in the T. B. Peterson single-volume edition.
8. Installment 3, plate 8, 8 Dec. 1860: "Then Joe began to hammer and clink, hammer and clink." [Sergeant, left, Joe at the anvil, center, and three soldiers, right]. Bottom, p. 773 (11.9 cm high by 12 cm wide) for ch. 5 (plate 6 in Peterson, facing p. 36, references "Page 36").

9. Installment 4, plate 9, 15 Dec. 1860: No title or caption [scene: Mrs. Joe roughly washes and dries Pip's face in preparation for Pip's first visit to Satis House at the end of ch. 7]. Top, p. 789 (9.2 cm high by 5.9 cm wide) for ch. 7. This and the other uncaptioned chapter headnote vignettes were not reproduced in the T. B. Peterson single-volume edition.

10. Installment 4, plate 10, 15 Dec. 1860: "At such times as your sister is on the ram-page, Pip." [Pip, left, and Joe, right, in the parlor, before the fire]. Bottom, p. 789 (11.3 cm high by 8.9 cm wide) for ch. 7 (plate 7 in Peterson, facing p. 44, references "Page 44").

11. Installment 5, plate 11, 22 Dec. 1860: " 'Who is it?' said the lady at the table. 'Pip, Ma'am.' " [Pip, left, and Miss Havisham, right, in her boudoir at Satis House]. Bottom, p. 804 (11.4 cm high by 11.8 cm wide) for ch. 8 (plate 8 in Peterson, facing p. 48, references "Page 49").

12. Installment 6, plate 12, 29 Dec. 1860: "Leave this lad to me, Ma'am; leave this lad to me." [Pumblechook, right, Mrs. Joe, center, and Pip, left, in front of the hearth in the Gargerys' parlor]. Middle, p. 821, vol. 4 (11.2 cm high by 11.3 cm wide) for ch. 9 (listed as plate 9 in Peterson, to face p. 53 and referenced to "Page 53," but used as the frontispiece in the volume inspected).

13. Installment 7, plate 13, 5 Jan. 1861: "It's a great cake. A bride-cake. Mine!" [Pip and Miss Havisham, center, in the dining room at Satis House]. Bottom, p. 5, vol. 5 (11.1 cm high by 8.9 cm wide) for ch. 10, continued (plate 10 in Peterson, facing p. 64, references "Page 63").

14. Installment 8, plate 14, 12 Jan. 1861: "Which I meantersay, Pip." [right, Estella, center, Miss Havisham and Pip, right, Joe, in Miss Havisham's boudoir at Satis House]. Middle, p. 21 (11.3 cm high by 11.3 cm wide) for ch. 11 (plate 11 in Peterson, facing p. 70, references "Page 70").

15. Note: the Jan. 19 (i.e., ninth) installment was not illustrated, and no installment appeared in the Jan. 26 issue of *Harper's*.

    Installment 10, plate 15, 2 Feb. 1861: No title or caption [scene: Pip and Biddy sitting on a bank in the Marshes]. Top left, p. 69 (10 cm high by 5.6 cm wide). This and the other uncaptioned chapter headnote vignettes were not reproduced in the T. B. Peterson single-volume edition.

16. Installment 10, plate 16, 2 Feb. 1861: "Hulloa!" he growled; "Where are you two going?" [Orlick, Pip, and Biddy]. Bottom right, p. 69. (11.6 cm high by 11.9 cm wide) for ch. 16, p. 70 (plate 12 in Peterson, facing p. 86, references "Page 86").

17. Installment 11, plate 17, 9 Feb. 1861: No title or caption [scene: Saturday night at the Three Jolly Bargemen: Pip, Joe, Jaggers, and Wopsle]." Bottom left, p. 85 (11.5 cm high by 5.8 cm wide). Not reproduced in the Peterson edition.

18. Installment 11, plate 18, 9 Feb. 1861: "Pip's a gentleman of fortune, then," said Joe, "and God bless him in it!" [Pip, Joe, Biddy, and Mrs. Joe in the parlor of the forge]. Bottom right, p. 85 (11.4 cm high by 11.5 cm wide) for ch. 17, bottom of p. 86 (plate 13 in Peterson, facing p. 92, references "Page 93").

19. Installment 12, plate 19, 16 Feb. 1861: No title or caption [scene: Pip and Joe on the marshes]. Bottom left, p. 101 (8.5 cm high by 11.5. cm wide) for ch. 18, bottom of p. 101. Not reproduced in the Peterson edition.

20. Installment 12, plate 20, 16 Feb. 1861: "And may I—May I—?" [Pip, left, and Pumblechook, right, in the Barnwell parlor (sic)]. Bottom right, p. 101 (12 cm high by 12 cm wide) for ch. 18, bottom of p. 102 (plate 14 in Peterson, facing p. 98, references "Page 98").

21. Installment 13, plate 21, 23 Feb. 1861: "You infernal scoundrel, how dare you tell me that?" [Pip, Jaggers, Mike, and Wemmick]. Bottom right, p. 117 (11.4 cm high by 11.5 cm wide) for ch. 19, bottom of p. 118 (plate 15 in Peterson, facing p. 104, references "Page 105").

22. Installment 14, plate 22, 2 Mar. 1861: "I hope your Mama is quite well?" [Pip and Mrs. Pocket in the garden at Hammersmith, with two nursemaids and children in the background]. Bottom middle, p. 133 (11.6 cm high by 11.7 cm wide) for ch. 21, bottom of p. 134 (plate 16 in Peterson, facing p. 114, references "Page 114").

23. Installment 15, plate 23, 9 Mar. 1861: "This chap murdered his master." [Pip and Wemmick in Jaggers's office]. Bottom right, p. 149 (11.5 cm high by 11.5 cm wide) for ch. 23, bottom of p. 150 (plate 17 in Peterson, facing p. 120, references "Page 121").

24. Installment 16, plate 24, 16 Mar. 1861: "Molly, let them see both your wrists. Show them. Come!" [Pip, Herbert, Jaggers, Drummle, and Molly at the dinner table in Jaggers's Gerard Street rooms]. Bottom middle, p. 173 (11.6 cm high by 11.8 cm wide) for the end of ch. 25, bottom of p. 174 (plate 18 in Peterson, facing p. 130, references "Page 129").

25. Installment 17, plate 25, 23 Mar. 1861: "Pip, how are you, Pip?" [Pip and Joe, center, with Pip's servant, "The Avenging Phantom," left, in Pip's rooms]. Bottom right, p. 181 (11.3 cm high by 11.5 cm wide) for ch. 26, bottom-left of p. 181 (listed as plate 19 in Peterson, to face p. 131, referencing "Page 131," but used as the title-page illustration instead).

26. Installment 18, plate 26, 30 Mar. 1861: " 'We walked round the garden twice or thrice more,' etc." [center: Pip, foreground, and Estella, behind, in the garden at Satis House]. Bottom right, p. 205 (11.6 cm high by 11.8 cm wide) for ch. 28, p. 206 (plate 20 in Peterson, facing p. 140, references "Page 141").

27. Installment 19, plate 27, 6 Apr. 1861: "Hold me! I'm so frightened!" [Trabb's boy, left, two members of the populace, center, and Pip, right,

in the village high street, outside the post-office]. Bottom right, p. 213 (12 cm high by 11.7 cm wide) for ch. 29, p. 213 (plate 21 in Peterson, facing p. 144, references "Page 145").

28. Installment 20, plate 28, 13 Apr. 1861: "If I say yes, may I kiss the cheek again?" [Estella, center, and Pip, right, in the coaching inn, upstairs]. Bottom right, p. 229 (11.5 cm high by 11.6 cm wide) for ch. 32, middle of p. 230 (plate 22 in Peterson, facing p. 156, references "Page 95" [a typographical error]).

29. Installment 21, plate 29, 20 Apr. 1861: "Dear Joe, how are you?" [Joe, Pip, and the undertaker's men]. Bottom center, p. 253 (11.6 cm high by 11.5 cm wide) for the end of ch. 34, p. 254 (plate 23 in Peterson, facing p. 162, references "Page 162").

30. Installment 22, plate 30, 27 Apr. 1861: "The responsible duty of making the toast was delegated to the Aged." [the Aged P., Wemmick's father, at the hearth, Walworth Castle]. Bottom right, p. 269 (11.5 cm high by 11.4 cm wide) for the end of ch. 36, p. 270 (plate 24 in Peterson, facing p. 172, references "Page 171").

31. Installment 23, plate 31, 4 May 1861: " 'She carried a bare candle in her hand,' etc." [Miss Havisham in the passageway at Satis House]. Center, p. 286 (11.2 cm high by 11.5 cm high) for ch. 37, p. 286 (plate 25 in Peterson, facing p. 176, references "Page 176").

32. Note: neither the 19 Jan. nor the 11, 18, and 25 May (i.e., the twenty-fourth through twenty-sixth) installments were illustrated, perhaps because *Harper's* was providing extensive pictorial coverage of the Civil War, depicting camps, fortresses, and battles—e.g., "Camp Curtin, Near Harrisburg, Pennsylvania, a Rendezvous of the Pennsylvania Volunteers.—[Sketched by Jasper Green, Esq.]" on p. 301 takes up three of the four columns, the fourth being the start of chapter 38 of *Great Expectations*. A Civil War scene also occupies the space that might have been devoted to McLenan illustrations on p. 318.

Installment 27, plate 32, 1 June 1861: "All done, all gone!" [Pip, left; Miss Havisham and Estella, right, in Miss Havisham's boudoir at Satis House]. Bottom right, p. 350 (11.5 cm high by 11.5 cm wide) for ch. 43, bottom of the last column on p. 351 (plate 26 in Peterson, facing p. 204, references "Page 205").

33. Installment 28, plate 33, 8 June 1861: " 'Look here,' said Herbert." [Pip, left; Herbert and Clara Barley, right, in the cottage at Mill Bank Pond]. Center, p. 366 (11.5 cm high by 11.5 cm wide) set in ch. 44, but illustrating ch. 45, p. 367 (plate 27 in Peterson, facing p. 210, references "Page 211").

34. Installment 29, plate 34, 15 June 1861: " 'Let me sit listening as I would, with dread,' etc." [Pip, center, in his rooms at The Temple]. Bottom

right, p. 350 (12 cm high by 11.5 cm wide) for the opening of ch. 46, p. 382 (plate 28 in Peterson, facing p. 214, references "Page 214").

35. Installment 30, plate 35, 22 June 1861: " 'I saw her running at me, shrieking, with a whirl of fire blazing all about her,' etc." [Pip, standing right, in his double-caped great coat; Miss Havisham, left, in the dining room of Satis House]. Bottom right, p. 398 (11.6 cm high by 11.5 cm wide) for ch. 48, p. 399 (plate 29 in Peterson, facing p. 224, references "Page 224").

36. Installment 31, plate 36, 29 June 1861: " 'Know him!' repeated the landlord. 'Ever since he was no height at all.' " [Pip, sitting left of center; the landlord of the inn, standing right]. Middle, p. 414 (11.4 cm high by 11.5 cm wide) for the end of ch. 51, p. 415 (plate 30 in Peterson, facing p. 232, references "Page 233").

37. Note: chapters 54 and 55, published on 20 July 1861, were not illustrated.

    Installment 36, plate 37, 13 July 1861: "He was taken on board, and instantly manacled at the wrists and ankles." [Magwitch, center]. Middle, p. 446 (11.5 cm wide by 11.4 cm high) for ch. 53, p. 447 (plate 31 in Peterson, facing p. 246, references "Page 246").

38. Installment 37, plate 38, 27 July 1861: " 'The placid look at the white ceiling came back, and passed away, and his head dropped quietly on his breast.'—See preceding Chapter." Top, p. 478, above the start of ch. 56, but referring to the death of Magwitch in prison in ch. 55 (11.4 cm high by 11.5 cm wide) for ch. 55, p. 447 (plate 32 in Peterson, facing p. 254, references "Page 254").

39. Installment 37, plate 39, 27 July 1861: " 'Joe now sat down to his great work,' etc." Bottom, p. 479, referring to the writing of a letter by Joe, center, in ch. 57 (11.4 cm high by 11.5 cm wide) for ch. 57, p. 479 (plate 33 in Peterson, facing p. 256, references "Page 256").

40. Installment 38, plate 40, 3 Aug. 1861: "I saw the shadow of no parting from her." Middle, p. 494, referring to the closing lines of the novel on p. 495 (11.4 cm high by 11.5 cm wide) for ch. 58, p. 495 (plate 34 in Peterson, facing p. 266, references "Page 266").

Appendix Two

Notes on the McLenan Plates and the Harper's Weekly *Text*

Note A: Edgar Rosenberg states that there were actually *two* American first (volume) editions of the novel:

> ... two editions published by the reprint house of T. B. Peterson & Brothers, Philadelphia, who had bought the rights from Harper: a one-volume edition

based on *Harper's Weekly* and issued in wrappers, which sold for a staggering twenty-five cents—the first paperback of *Great Expectations*—and a slightly later hardcover, priced at $1.50, featuring McLenan's illustrations from *Harper's*.   (423)

Note B: The title page of the first American volume edition, published by T. B. Peterson in 1861 is unusual in that it uses the Dickens pseudonym (''Boz''), which he ceased to use in his British publications in the 1840s. In fact, Dickens last used the pen-name ''Boz'' for the transitional picaresque novel *Martin Chuzzl*ewit (1843–44); in his next volume work (*A Christmas Carol*) and in subsequent works he did not use the nickname on either wrappers or title pages. The first full-length Dickens novel not described as written by ''Boz'' on the title page and wrapper was *Dombey and Son* (1846), ''with illustrations by H. K. Browne'' rather than ''Phiz.''

The 1861 American volume's title page mentions ''thirty-four illustrations from original designs by John McLenan,'' and indicates that its double-columned text (the format used by *All the Year Round* in Britain) has been ''printed from the manuscript and early proof-sheets purchased from the author, for which Charles Dickens has been paid in cash, the sum of one thousand pounds sterling.''

NOTES

1. Alan S. Watts speculates that Dickens chose not to bring out *Great Expectations* in his customary illustrated monthly parts because he ''no longer felt the need for illustrations'' (8)—if this were so, in 1862 he would not have approached Marcus Stone to illustrate the Library Edition. However, a number of critics have stated that the novel first appeared as an unillustrated serial, and immediately afterward in an unadorned triple-decker issued by Chapman and Hall in 1861. Mistakenly, Harry Furniss (1905) states that the 1862 Illustrated Library Edition of the novel was ''the first time that the novel had been illustrated'' (qtd. in Cordery 34). Arthur Waugh (1937)—doubtless speaking from a strictly British publishing perspective—contends that ''The first edition, without illustrations, appeared in August 1861'' (44).

   Such inaccuracies may be ascribed to the fact that John McLenan's series of 40 plates in *Harper's Weekly: A Journal of Civilization*, vols. 4: 740 through 5: 495 (for 24 November 1860 through 3 August 1861) was not subsequently reproduced in its entirety in either American or British editions (see note B, above). As Edgar Rosenberg notes in the Norton Critical Edition of the novel (1999), although the first installment appeared on Saturday, 24 November 1860, in *Harper's Weekly*, that same installment did not appear in Dickens's own weekly, *All the Year Round*, until the following Saturday (1 December 1860). The American periodical remained a week in advance of the British until 26 January 1861, when (owing to the long passage on the transatlantic route, which prevented the publishers from getting the advance proof-sheets to the illustrator) Harper and Company decided not to run the tenth installment (chapters 15 and 16). Until this point, the American version, illustrated by John McLenan (spelled ''M'Lenan'' for his work on Bulwer-Lytton's *A Strange Story* on 10 August 1861 in *Harper's*), was certainly ''the first edition'' of the novel.

2. Images of fugitive slaves appear in a variety of formats, ranging from abolitionist tracts to posters offering rewards for recapturing plantation escapees, throughout the Colonial period and into the antebellum era. Although slave-finders on horseback, usually accompanied by a pack of hounds, are shown pursuing the fugitives, images of ''A Slave Hunt'' may focus on the naturalistically depicted, ragged figure in flight—for example, ''Chasing a Fugitive Slave, 1840s'' (1877), ''Adult male slave escaping through woods, slavecatchers in pursuit'' (c. 1872), and ''Escaped adult male slave hiding out in woods, huddling next to fire'' (c. 1872). Whereas in eighteenth-century depictions the escapee tends to be a stock figure caught in the act of running and distinguished by his African skirt, headdress, and spear or walking stick, in nineteenth-century American depictions the fugitives wear European clothing (albeit often in a state of disrepair as a consequence of the pursuit). In one of the British abolitionists' most powerful images, Josiah Wedgewood's cameo with the caption above ''Am I Not A Man And A Brother,'' the recumbent, scantily clad Black is in chains.

Closer to the time at which McLenan illustrated *Great Expectations* we see a similarly sympathetic image of slaves, ''Escaping Slavery, U.S. South, 1850s,'' from *The Suppressed Book About Slavery!* (prepared in 1857, but not published until 1864 in New York). In this response to the Fugitive Slave Act of 1850, which authorized slave-catchers to apprehend fugitive slaves, a young Black family, fleeing a posse on horseback, are about to be halted in their flight to freedom by a river, a scene which immediately elicits a sense of apprehension on their behalf in the viewer. In McLenan's image of Magwitch as an escaped convict (1 Dec. 1860, p. 765, fig. 11), surrounded by rank vegetation instead of the cemetery, a disheveled figure, blackened by mud from the marshes, squats on the ground in the semi-darkness, his clothes mere rags, as he files away at a leg-iron (not clearly depicted). American readers would likely have made the connection between the image of the escaped convict here, his long file replacing the spear or walking stick of eighteenth-century posters and his bandana head-covering replacing the traditional African hat, and the images of escaped slaves that had been very much a part of antebellum popular and abolitionist literature.

3. Stone is working not merely in the new sixties style, but with the new print-medium technology of the woodblock, which would develop the process of photographic transfer of the design to the woodblock by the time that Dickens's last collaborative illustrator, Luke Fildes, was working on the images to accompany *The Mystery of Edwin Drood* (1870). When he received his first Chapman and Hall commissions, Marcus Stone knew little about the techniques necessary for using the woodcut to its most artistic effect, but he obviously had learned much about these techniques by the time he illustrated *Our Mutual Friend* just three years later.

WORKS CITED

Barreca, Regina. "David Lean's *Great Expectations.*" *Dickens on Screen.* Ed. John Glavin. Cambridge: Cambridge UP, 2003. 39–44.

Bussoni, Rafaello, illus. Charles Dickens's *A Tale of Two Cities.* Ed. Grosset and Dunlap. New York: Illustrated Junior Library, 1948.

"Charles Dickens, Esq.—[From a Late Photograph.]." *Harper's Weekly: A Journal of Civilization* 24 November 1860, 740.

"Charles Dickens." *Harper's Weekly: A Journal of Civilization* 24 November 1860, 740.

"Chasing a Fugitive Slave, 1840s." *The Atlantic Slave Trade and Slave Life in the Americas: A Visual Record.* Ed. Jerome S. Handler and Michael L. Tuite, Jr. Virginia Foundation for the Humanities, 2006. Updated 18 April 2007. Accessed 18 April 2007. Original caption: "A Slave Hunt." Edmund Ollier. *Cassell's History of the United States.* London, 1874–77. 3: 91. <http://hitchcock.itc.virginia.edu/Slavery/details.php?categorynum=16&categoryName=Physical%H20Punishment,%20Rebellion,%20Running%20Away&theRecord=9&recordCount=84>.

Cheadle, Brian. "The Late Novels: *Great Expectations* and *Our Mutual Friend.*" *The Cambridge Companion to Charles Dickens.* Ed. John O. Jordan. Cambridge: Cambridge UP, 2001. 78–91.

Cohen, Jane Rabb. "Marcus Stone." *Charles Dickens and His Original Illustrators.* Columbus: Ohio State UP, 1980. 203–28.

Cordery, Gareth. *An Edwardian's View of Dickens and His Illustrators: Harry Furniss's "A Sketch of Boz."* Greensboro: U of North Carolina P, 2005.

Davis, Paul. *Charles Dickens A to Z: The Essential Reference to His Life and Work.* New York: Facts on File, 1998.

Dickens, Charles. *Great Expectations. Harper's Weekly: A Journal of Civilization.* Illus. John McLenan. Vol. 4: 740 through 5: 495 (24 November 1860–3 August 1861).

———. ("Boz."). *Great Expectations.* With 34 illustrations from original designs by John McLenan. Philadelphia: T. B. Peterson (by agreement with Harper and Bros., New York), 1861.

———. *Great Expectations* and *Hard Times.* Illus. Marcus Stone, Fred Walker, and A. B. Houghton. London: Duckworth, Overlook, and Worth, 2005. Facsimile of the 1937 Nonesuch Edition. [Stone's illustrations appear on pp. xiv, 81, 145, 179, 239, 359, 415, and 475; they are reproduced from the 1862 Library Edition published by Chapman and Hall.]

———. *The Letters of Charles Dickens.* Ed. Graham Storey. Oxford: Clarendon, 1997, vol. 9 (1859–1861); 1998, vol. 10 (1862–1864). The Pilgrim Edition.

———. *A Tale of Two Cities.* Ed. George Woodcock. Illus. Hablot Knight Browne. Harmondsworth: Penguin, 1970.

Dillard, Leigh G. "A Transatlantic Vision: Drawing *Great Expectations* in its American Context." Paper presented at the Tenth Annual Dickens Society of America Symposium, Springfield Technical Community College. Session Three, "Sound and Sight.'' Springfield Technical Community College, Springfield, MA: 15 October 2005.

"Escaping Slavery, U.S. South, 1850s.'' *The Atlantic Slave Trade and Slave Life in the Americas: A Visual Record*. Ed. Jerome S. Handler and Michael L. Tuite, Jr. Virginia Foundation for the Humanities, 2006. Updated 18 April 2007. Accessed 18 April 2007. Original caption: "Running Away.'' *The Suppressed Book about Slavery!* Prepared for publication in 1857 (New York, 1864), facing p. 336. <http://hitchcock.itc.virginia.edu/Slavery/details.php?categorynum=16&category Name=Physical%20Punishment,%20Rebellion,%20Running%20Away&theRecord=52&recordCount=84>.

Greenblatt, Harmon. "David Lean Production.'' *The Dickens Magazine* ser. 1, issue 5 (2001): 8–9.

Hamilton, Sinclair. Foreword. Frank Weitenkampf. *Early American Book and Wood Engravers 1670–1870*. Vol. 1, Main Catalogue. Princeton: Princeton UP, 1968.

Hammerton, J. A. *The Dickens Picture-Book*. London: Educational Book [1910]. The Charles Dickens Library 17.

Hatton, Thomas. "A Bibliographical List of the Original Illustrations to the Works of Charles Dickens Being Those Made under His Supervision.'' "Prospectus: The Nonesuch Dickens.'' *Retrospectus and Prospectus: The Nonesuch Dickens*. London: Bloomsbury, 1937, rpt. 2003. 55–78, 123–28.

Lacey, Barbara E. "Visual Images of Blacks in Early American Imprints.'' *William and Mary Quarterly* 3rd ser., 53: 1 (January 1996): 137–80. Accessed 18 April 2007. <http://www.jstor.org/view/00435597/di976425/97p0609p/0>.

Lester, Valerie Browne. *Phiz: The Man Who Drew Dickens*. London: Chatto and Windus, 2004.

Maxwell, Richard. Introduction. *The Victorian Illustrated Book*. Charlottesville: UP of Virginia, 2002. xxi–xxx.

McLenan, John, illus. *Great Expectations* (the first American edition). By Charles Dickens. *Harper's Weekly*, 4: 740 through 5: 495 (24 November 1860–3 August 1861). See also the single-volume edition issued by T. B. Peterson and Company, Philadelphia, 1861, for 34 of the 40 original illustrations mounted on separate pages rather than dropped into the text, as in the magazine.

———. illus. *A Tale of Two Cities* (the first American edition). By Charles Dickens. *Harper's Weekly*, 3: 289 through 4: 781 (7 May–3 December 1859).

Mott, Frank Luther. *A History of American Magazines, Vol. 2: 1850–1865*. 1938. Cambridge: Belknap-Harvard UP, 1957.

Patten, Robert L. "Serial Illustration and Storytelling in *David Copperfield*.'' *The Victorian Illustrated Book*. Ed. Richard Maxwell. Charlottesville: UP of Virginia, 2002. 91–128.

Rosenberg, Edgar, ed. "Launching *Great Expectations*.'' *Great Expectations*. By Charles Dickens. New York: Norton, 1999. 389–423.

Schlicke, Paul, ed. *Oxford Reader's Companion to Dickens*. Oxford: Oxford UP, 1999.

Staples, Leslie C. "*Great Expectations* Realised.'' *Dickensian* 43 (1947): 79–81.

Steig, Michael. *Dickens and Phiz*. Bloomington: Indiana UP, 1978.

———. "*Martin Chuzzlewit's* Progress by Dickens and Phiz.'' *Dickens Studies Annual* 2 (1972): 119–49.

Stein, Richard L. ''Dickens and Illustration.'' *The Cambridge Companion to Charles Dickens*. Ed. John O. Jordan. Cambridge: Cambridge UP, 2001. 167–88.

Stone, Marcus, illus. *Great Expectations*. By Charles Dickens. Ed. Margaret Cardwell. Oxford: Clarendon, 1993. 505–12.

Walker, Frederick. ''*The Woman in White* Poster'' (1871). Reproduced in Catherine Peters. *The King of the Inventors: A Life of Wilkie Collins*. London: Minerva, 1991. Fig. 13. See also '' 'The Woman in White' by Fred Walker.'' The Victorian Web. <http://www.victorianweb.org/art/illustration/walker/8.html>. Accessed 5 February 2009.

Watt, Alan S. ''Why Wasn't *Great Expectations* Illustrated?'' *The Dickens Magazine* series 1, issue 2. Haslemere, UK: Euromed Communications, 2001: 8–9.

Waugh, Arthur. ''Charles Dickens and His Illustrators.'' *Retrospectus and Prospectus: The Nonesuch Dickens*. London: Bloomsbury, 1937, rpt. 2003. 6–52.

Weitenkampf, Frank. *Early American Book and Wood Engravers 1670–1870*. Vol. 1, Main Catalogue. Princeton, NJ: Princeton UP, 1968.

Dolls and Imaginative Agency in Bradford, Pardoe, and Dickens

Victoria Ford Smith

This essay argues that fiction written for both adults and children in the nineteenth century recognizes that dolls can perform work that is much more complicated—and sometimes more subversive—than imagined by Victorians who upheld the toys as training wheels for motherhood. Doll narratives written for children, in particular Clara Bradford's Ethel's Adventures in the Doll Country *(1880) and Julia Pardoe's* Lady Arabella, or, The Adventures of a Doll *(1856), as well as adult literature, in particular Charles Dickens's* Our Mutual Friend *(1864–65), illustrate how authors use distortions of size and animation to subvert or sustain relationships between the poor and the privileged, the weak and the powerful, the small and the enormous. Such texts demonstrate not only that the doll and the agency it generates can be employed to interrogate and manipulate social hierarchies but also that fantasies of subversion registered through the miniature and the gigantic had imaginative currency powerful enough to cross the boundaries of genre.*

In *Queen Victoria's Dolls* (1894), Frances H. Low provides detailed descriptions of a selection of the queen's 132 dolls, mostly replicas of opera stars and court ladies, 32 of which the fledgling sovercign dressed herself.[1] Much of Low's commentary describes the queen's doll collection as evidence of her future dedication to motherhood and wifedom; for example, she concludes her text by describing the dolls as "the charming playthings which

---

Dickens Studies Annual, Volume 40, Copyright © 2009 by AMS Press, Inc. All rights reserved.

made happy the childhood of her who is endeared to her subjects as *a good wife, a good mother*'' and—lastly, almost an afterthought—''a wise and exemplary ruler'' (introduction, emphasis added). These words mark Low as part of a tradition that reads a girl's interaction with her dolls as evidence of her future feminine sensibilities, dictating that a young girl attentive to her doll develops a lasting maternal instinct while the girl disinterested in such play will, one day, be characterized by ''lack of feeling'' (Boehn 174). This tradition relies on a very limited definition of doll play, in which the doll is either what Ina Schäbert calls ''the ladylike, passive, fragile doll that had to be handled with great care—not to be cuddled but admired,'' which fosters the passivity and reserve thought proper for a young lady, or the coddled and cared-for doll that provides a simulation of domesticity, ''a joyous labour to a little girl second only to nursing a live baby'' (Schäbert 122; Low introduction).

But perhaps Low is suspicious of such easy definitions, for before she launches into a saccharine account of dainty dress trimming and impossibly small handkerchiefs, she takes a moment to depict Victoria interacting with her dolls in a manner decidedly different:

> [I]f the picture of any little girl amongst her dolls is one that attracts us; if we delight to discover premonitions of unfolded individuality and winged fancies that will presently bear fruit, how much more absorbing and interesting does this study become when that little player is a child-Princess who is at once a child like any other, and yet at the same time how unlike! A little being, as yet unweighted with a crown, yet set apart and shadowed by sovereignty. We remember the duties and responsibilities awaiting her, the momentous ''yea'' and ''nay'' that will some day have to be pronounced by those soft young lips; and then is it any wonder that we turn and watch her among her Liliputian subjects, stitching, devising, cutting, and measuring infinitesimal garments, with a feeling that is something deeper than that which is usually aroused by a child's play? (introduction)

Here, the princess hovers over her playthings with needle and scissors. The slightly malevolent tone of the words ''devising'' and ''cutting'' and the unsettling contrast between Victoria's ''soft young lips'' and the import of the ''momentous'' words they will pronounce to her future subjects suggest less the early impulses of domesticity and more fantasies of control, manipulation, and even violence. The illustrations by Alan Wright that accompany Low's words only underscore this tension; for example, an illustration of Victoria's doll-box shows some dolls balanced precariously on its edge, some stuffed headfirst in the box (see fig. 1). Low attributes the ''something deeper'' of the princess's doll play to the unique position of an almost-queen. However, I will argue that fiction written for both adults and children in the Victorian period recognizes that dolls, whether dressed by Victoria or by

Fig. 1. Alan Wright. "The Doll's Home." Illustration for *Queen Victoria's Dolls* (1894). By Frances H. Low.

girls in less exalted positions, can perform work that is much more compli-cated—and sometimes more subversive—than thought possible by those who look upon them as training wheels for motherhood. In what follows, I will examine a number of texts: first, a selection of doll narratives written for children—in particular, Clara Bradford's *Ethel's Adventures in the Doll Coun-try* (1880) and Julia Pardoe's *Lady Arabella, or, The Adventures of a Doll* (1856)—and, subsequently, Charles Dickens's *Our Mutual Friend* (1864–65), paying attention to how these authors use distortions of size and animation to subvert or sustain relationships between the poor and the privileged, the weak and the powerful, the small and the enormous.[2] Such texts, I will argue, demonstrate how the doll and the imaginative agency it generates can be employed to interrogate and manipulate social hierarchies. In particular, Dickens, in his representation of Jenny Wren, incorporates strategies of violence present in Bradford's text and strategies of class subversion present in Pardoe's.[3]

I. Heartless Bodies

To begin this discussion, we must shut Victoria's nursery door and consider another little girl among her dolls: Ethel, the title character of Bradford's *Ethel's Adventures in the Doll Country*. While royal authority is not in Ethel's future, she has no qualms about holding court over her dolls with an aggression that exceeds the vaguely menacing threat of young Victoria's scissors. Ethel's narrative opens as she searches the house for a missing doll, explaining to her nurse, "You know I scolded her well the morning she was found standing by the hall door—besides that, we [Ethel and her brothers] tried her by court-martial" (2). Later in the story, as Ethel's doll recounts the injuries done to her by her mistress, the reader will hear an account of this court-martial from the doll's point of view. Ethel's brothers "try" the doll and sentence her to be hanged. "I was hoisted up and down from the ceiling," sobs the doll. "I kicked, and screamed, but all in vain! those boys exulted over my downfall! But worse than all . . . my mistress, my once dear little mistress, laughed at each fresh insult" (175). Throughout the narrative, the reader is introduced to a number of dolls that have similarly suffered under Ethel's unforgiving hand, including a set of dilapidated baby dolls, one of which wears a bandage around her head to hide "an ugly crack, and the loss of one eye," and a broken-legged Robinson Crusoe doll (83).

Bradford's story is an extreme example among a great number of doll narratives written for children in the nineteenth century. Few girl heroines are as violent and unforgiving as Ethel, who punishes her dolls in an often irrational and nearly always unjust manner. But it is productive to consider how this violence operates in opposition to the expected dynamic between girl and doll. Like Low's depiction of Victoria above, Bradford's characterization of Ethel at play among her dolls disallows or at least problematizes reading dolls as stand-ins for future children or equating doll play with domestic education.[4] In fact, while Ethel fills many roles in relation to her favorite doll—entertainer, puppet-master, teacher—she pointedly does not identify herself as its mother. When its automated voice cries "Pa-pa—Ma-ma," Ethel muses, "I wonder if she means you and my papa, mamma, when she calls out; or is she asking for her own parents?" (126). For Ethel, dolls are not objects to coddle and nurse but instead opportunities for violence. They are what Sharon Marcus would call "beautifully dressed objects to admire or humiliate," toys that "inspire fantasies of omnipotence and subjection" (149). Marcus is part of a new critical perspective on the doll that examines doll play like Ethel's, dismissing the doll's association with female acculturation and instead understanding it as a site of female agency. Dolls, in this perspective, are inviting because they are what Hans Bellmer calls "heartless bodies," toys of "infinite malleability" (qtd. in Schäbert 127–28). This agency is enabled not only by the doll's replication of the human—an aspect of doll play discussed at length by Marcus, who approaches dolls as opportunities for young girls to inflict pleasure or pain on representations of the female—but also by the power dynamic activated by the incongruity of size between human and doll. As Steven Millhauser argues, the miniature (and, I would add, particularly the miniature replica of the human form) "invites possession," the ability to claim an object, to hold it in the palm of one's hand (130).[5] The miniature world of the doll, as Schäbert notes, "exerts a soothing influence on the observer. One imagines oneself in the position of control" (129). Thus, when Ethel's doll tries to run away, Ethel reaffirms her authority by boxing its ears and stringing it from the ceiling. When her violent actions are challenged later in the narrative, she insists that "the doll was *mine*, and I could do as I liked" (175, emphasis added).

However, if Ethel's treatment of her dolls provides a model of the way power relations can be registered through size—the tyranny of the gigantic over the miniature—this model is provided only to be radically reversed when Ethel follows her Robinson Crusoe doll to Toy Land and Doll Country, where a series of distortions of size allow the long-abused dolls to exact their revenge.[6] In the alternative world of Ethel's dolls, the malicious young girl is unable to establish any claim on her surroundings, which shift in size and perspective in a manner she cannot understand. At times, Ethel seems to have shrunk; when she first enters Toy Land, for example, she can rest her head against the stalk of a flower, and everyday objects suddenly seem out of proportion: "[S]he saw in the distance a tall gate, or it might be a stile, but that it was higher than stiles generally are in this world" (10). And yet the illustrations by T. Pym that accompany the text often depict Ethel as towering over her dolls, even in Doll Country (see figs. 2 and 3). These strange shifts of perspective are matched by the landscape, which often seems to move along without Ethel. Sometimes this is pleasant, as when a richly decorated Christmas tree, which seems to stretch for miles, passes her by while she is standing still—"How obliging," remarks Ethel, "*I* cannot walk around it, so it walks past me instead" (28). At other times, it is decidedly unpleasant and disconcerting, as when a leering birch rod multiplies itself and stretches before the frightened Ethel. "[T]he road must have been a telescope road,

Fig. 2. T. Pym. Ethel leaning against a flower in Toy Land. Illustration for
Ethel's Adventures in the Doll Country (1880). By Clara Bradford. Cotsen
Children's Library. Princeton University Library.

and been gradually shutting itself up,'' writes Bradford, ''for Ethel was certain
she had not moved, so the road and the rods must have been drawing themselves in'' (13).[7] Ethel, simultaneously shrinking and growing, moving and
standing still, is now at the mercy of the world that surrounds her—a position
quite different than the authority she enjoyed over her dolls, who people a
minute world that corresponds perfectly to her intentions.

The confusing landscape and Ethel's inability to govern the world around
her are the first clues that the order of authority has been inverted, for soon
Ethel encounters an array of creatures that abuse her as she abused her dolls.
Jumping Jacks flail their legs at her, threatening to kick her, while monkeys

THE INJURED FAVOURITE.——*Page* 116.

Fig. 3. T. Pym. ''The Injured Favorite.'' Ethel towering over her dolls in Doll Country. Illustration for *Ethel's Adventures in the Doll Country* (1880). By Clara Bradford. Cotsen Children's Library. Princeton University Library.

ask her for peanuts, only to pelt her with the shells (13–14, 18–20). Throughout her travels, Ethel is pursued and menaced by personified birch rods, each
"with two greenish sort of eyes like a cat's, a huge mouth, and little feet and
hands" (10–11). These are the guardians of the dolls, and they shrink, grow,
and even multiply themselves while persistently threatening Ethel by waving
in the air and winking in her direction.[8] The language the rods employ to
express their pleasure over the prospect of punishing her often refigures her,
the human girl, as the doll. Apparently, in the Doll Country, the punishment
must fit the crime. For example, they threaten to break her limbs: "*I* am the
means of making little folk beautiful," boasts a birch rod. "[A] few applica-
tions of me prove beneficial in many cases, for removing cross faces and
pouting lips" (23). This threat is particularly resonant in the Doll Country,
where Ethel is surrounded by the toys she discarded because they are missing
limbs or eyes. The rods also scold Ethel into silence, replicating the doll-girl
relationship of the speaking and the silent, the active and the passive. "[Y]ou
ought to allow other people to think for you," warns one rod (22); "think
what you please, but don't put your thoughts into words," it cautions later
(42). And, of course, the rods magnify themselves until Ethel is miniature
and helpless. As Ethel flies through the air with an exquisite fairy doll, for
example, the rod is close behind, growing taller and taller. "They will become
giant birch-rods soon," says Ethel, "and when I return to the ground they
will be miles and miles too tall to see a little girl like me." "We always see
little girls," replies the rod, "however insignificant they may be" (40).

Ethel incorporates a theme characteristic of most doll narratives, even those
less violent: how the doll can be deployed to configure and reconfigure power
relationships. *Ethel* represents both how the stronger can use this dynamic to
their advantage—here, how Ethel soothes her violent spirit by punishing her
dolls—and how that dynamic can be subverted by the less powerful through
the imaginative agency that surrounds the doll—here, the subverted authority
in the topsy-turvy world of the Doll County. Yet Bradford's text does not
address the power relationship that most consistently surrounds the doll in
both fictional and nonfictional accounts—that of class. It seems only natural
that doll narratives would address class distinctions, for as Schäbert notes,
the purchase and adornment of luxury fashion dolls was an opportunity to
display goods and a testament to the owner's wealth and class (122). The
myriad of innovations in doll production in the nineteenth century—the introduction of ball-joints for realistic movement of limbs; the use of flax, silk, or
human hair for doll wigs; the invention of the speaking doll and the walking
doll—only underscored the toy's ability to express class privilege (Boehn
154–55). The little girl who cuddled a bran-filled doll with molded hair was
painfully reminded of her position by the little girl who fussed over a wax
doll with enamel eyes and real hair that walks and says "Mama" when

squeezed. The social advantages and disadvantages made apparent through the body of the doll found their way into the miniature economies represented in children's doll narratives, in which girls often negotiate class positions, struggling for social superiority by comparing dolls.[9] But dolls could become part of an economy in a much more practical manner, as I will show in the next section.

II. Miniature Economies

It is late, and yet as we pass through the streets of London we find that the upper windows of an old school building are illuminated. Here, the Children's Happy Evenings Association has organized an evening of entertainment for local poor children. Inside, a circle of children listen to fairy tales, a troop of little boys march in formation and wrestle, and, in a quieter classroom, a collection of young girls is allowed, for a few moments, to play with finely dressed wax dolls. Leslie Hope Cornford describes the scene in her book *London Pride and London Shame* (1910): "The little people with the dolls are all seated at desks, each with a doll, whose dress so gloriously outshines her own. Some are dressing or undressing them; others are merely sitting perfectly still, nursing the waxen lady; rapt, sober, wholly content" (93–94). Cornford praises the Association, explaining that these evenings of recreation allow poor children to, "for a while, forget the cruel wilderness of street and court and alley into which they were born" and instead enjoy "some of the light and happiness of another condition of life," maintaining that the "ladies and gentlemen who give their time to the children do so for love; and the children know it" (95, 92).

Yet Pamela Horn, who quotes this anecdote in her study of Victorian town children, seems correct when she reads the "rapt" faces of the little girls holding expensive dolls not as a sign of contentment but instead as evidence of "a dumb awareness of social deficiency" (163). I would push Horn's argument even further and maintain that this awareness is the product of the nature of the doll, for these well-to-do young ladies are lending poorer children exact replicas of themselves—offering, in miniature, the privileged world these lower-class "little people" will most likely never inhabit—and then swiftly taking it away. This class dynamic is only underscored by the fact that dollmakers would often cut these luxury dolls' clothes, shoes, and hats—even their tiny parasols—from the same fabric as their owners' wardrobes, using a young patron's hair to create doll wigs of the same texture and hue (Schäbert 123). The doll, therefore, becomes an object through which social privilege is represented and reinforced. It is both a marker and maker of class distinctions. As Schäbert notes, these young girls, in fashioning luxury dolls after their own appearance, could say, "Look, this is the shade of my hair, this is the quality of my lace. This is my clone" (123).

The doll could encapsulate, in a striking and material way, the negotiations between social classes, and it is this capacity of the doll that attracted authors of children's literature in the early and mid-nineteenth century, who wrote for children's moral instruction as well as for their entertainment.[10] Doll narrators or doll characters in this literature are often employed to encourage charity and selflessness while warning against materialism or greed. For example, in Jane M. Besset's *Memoirs of a Doll, Written by Herself: A New Year's Gift* (1854), an adaptation of a French tale by Louise D'Aulnay, Henrietta, an upper-class little girl, recognizes the difference between her own position and that of the impoverished family begging at her door when she compares the half-clothed children to her doll, Violet. The doll herself observes,

> I was asleep in [Henrietta's] arms, but this did not prevent my noticing the way in which she contemplated their clothes, all in rags, and I felt, at the same time, that her dear little hand was stroking my merino wool stockings which she had knitted. No doubt she said to herself, "Violet, my doll, as has nice warm stockings, fur shoes, in fact every thing she does *not* want; but these poor children are almost barefoot."   (24)

It is the striking difference between the luxurious circumstances of the doll, an inanimate representation of the human, and the true hardships of the poor woman and her children that provides the moral momentum of the narrative. Henrietta, at her mother's suggestion, auctions off her doll and donates the money she earns to the beggar family. In other stories, a high-end fashion doll, designed for and sold to the elite, suffers a series of disappointments and mishaps until it finds itself the plaything of a poor (but usually virtuous) little girl. For example, in *Victoria-Bess: The Ups and Downs of a Doll's Life* (1879), written by Mrs. Castle Smith under the pseudonym Brenda, the title-doll is remorseful and reflective, remembering with scorn her arrogance and snobbishness:

> I was contented enough when fashionably dressed ladies and gentlemen and children stopped to admire me—*their* homage was all very well; but I remember (oh, with how much shame and sorrow now!) how contemptuous and proud I used to feel when occasionally little dirty children, with pale faces and shabby clothes, wandered up to the window, and stared at me through the glass with mouths and eyes wide open, completely awed and wonderstruck by my marvellous beauty.   (17)

Predictably, by the end of the tale, Victoria-Bess belongs to these same pale-faced children. She concludes her story with a lesson in charity, imploring her readers "never to throw us dolls away into the dust-bin" but instead to "send us . . . to an Hospital for Sick Children, where in spite of broken noses, and cracked heads, and faded garments, we shall be received and warmly welcomed" (77). The tattered and damaged doll, it seems, is the appropriate plaything for the poor. Indeed, many of these doll narratives, while calling for sympathy for the lower classes, end with a recognition and reinforcement of the social structures the doll represents. The doll may have traveled from rich to poor, but the rich little girl maintains her advantage, most likely smoothing the luxurious hair of a new doll while her impoverished counterpart nurses the discarded and decidedly less desirable toy.

However, while doll narratives are replete with examples of the doll as signifier of privilege and wealth, many of these narratives simultaneously make possible, through the doll, a challenge to or subversion of class distinctions. Sometimes such subversion is achieved through violence, in a manner similar to that found in Low's account of Victoria or Bradford's image of Ethel dangling her Pa-Ma doll on a string. In Pardoe's *Lady Arabella*, for instance, Lady Breezeby asks the servant Lenox to take Arabella, the expensive doll of her daughter, Miss Tantrum, to a baby-linen shop, and have it dressed in a robe "of real French cambric, richly embroidered, and edged with Valenciennes lace" and a cap to match—to adorn the doll, as Arabella herself boasts, so that "no infant princess of the blood-royal was ever more carefully attired" (24–25). But the circle of working-class women in the shop handle the doll roughly, recognizing that here, in the absence of Miss Tantrum and her mother, is the perfect place to express disgust for the material excess of the aristocracy. Arabella is shocked when she discovers that her claims to privilege are undermined by the disadvantage of size:

> I was handed from one to another in the rudest manner in the world. . . . [T]he mirth at last came to an end, but not before every particle of bran in my body shook with indignation. The length of my legs was particularly condemned; and one black-eyed, curly-headed girl, who had turned and twisted me about until I was becoming perfectly giddy, actually had the audacity to propose that they should be cut off at the knees.   (24)

Arabella becomes the object of the manipulative and even violent fantasies of this small circle of women, who bend the doll's limbs to and fro and threaten to cut off her legs. These fantasies of control are made possible not only by the doll's replication of the human—which allows Lenox and her servants, and perhaps the reader of *Lady Arabella*, to imagine a correspondence between the abuse of Arabella and an imagined abuse of Miss Tantrum or her extravagant, morally corrupt, spendthrift mother—but also by the nature of the miniature, which allows the circle of women to possess and manipulate the body of the socially superior doll. While Arabella finds the physical discomfort of her trip to the baby-linen shop extraordinarily unsettling, it is not the discrepancy of size brought into relief by the doll that offers the most ripe opportunity for social subversion but instead the very practical matter of payment. Lenox manages to profit from her errand to dress the newly purchased Arabella, for while the bill for the gown and cap amounts to thirteen pounds five shillings, the proprietor of the shop charges fourteen pounds to Lady Breezeby's account and hands the change over to Lenox, who calls this payment "my percentage" (25). Lenox then uses this money to travel to the lodgings of a male friend of another servant to deliver a clandestine message. The doll, while most likely dressed in fabrics far more splendid than those of Lenox's dress, circulates and accrues value for the working class in a sort of sub-economy operating below the notice of the Breezebys.

Later in the narrative, this economy surfaces once again when Lady Breezeby runs off to Paris with a lover, leaving Lord Breezeby and Miss Tantrum behind in London. Marshal, a lady "evidently deep in the secrets of the family" and most likely a former servant, visits the household, ostensibly to support them in their distress (39). Learning that the family is leaving for Paris in the morning, Marshal offers to take some of their possessions off their hands to aid the move, thieving small objects and baubles into her box, among them Arabella. When the doll is unpacked in Marshal's much humbler home, she is swiftly divested of her expensive robe and cap and dressed in "an ill-made frock of common print," renamed Amelia Ann, and given to Marshal's young daughter, Jane (50). Jane punishes Arabella, now Amelia Ann, in a manner that would make Ethel proud, abusing her new doll whenever her raging mother, who suffers from "occasional fits of fury," punishes the children of the household (51). The aggression and revenge enabled by the doll empower young Jane, but it is the robe and cap, folded neatly and sold, that empower her mother. While Pardoe does not detail how Marshal plans to spend the profits, the reader can assume that the money will be spent on one of the many parties the family hosts, in which valets and ladies' maids mimic the excesses of their employers, displaying, according to Arabella, "all the arrogance and vanity of their superiors, without any of the refinement which helps to make such vices endurable" (51).

The clothing of the luxury doll may not allow the deceitful Marshal to swap social status with the Breezebys, then, but it does allow her to collapse or, in a way, erase class distinctions. Marshal's entertainments, where valets parade as lords, recall a lesson the doll has learned earlier in the narrative:

> I was astonished to find how very little difference there was in point of fact between [the ladies in the baby-linen shop] and the young ladies of the doll shop where I first came into being; except, indeed, that while my new acquaintance lounged idly in their chairs, and talked of Sir Harry and Lord William, the Botanical Gardens, and the French play, my former companions had busily

plied their fingers as they whispered together about Mr. Smith the stationer, and Sergeant Sabretach of the Blues, the Cremorre Gardens, the Adelphi, and Astley's.   (30)

Arabella has recognized here something like universal human nature. The doll has become a vanishing point where all class distinctions disappear; it matters little whether the doll is Arabella, flaunting Valenciennes lace and French cambric, or Amelia Ann, in an "ill-made frock of common print." Beneath both is the same bran-filled leather body.

III. Dreaming in Miniature

Arabella is painfully aware of the simple body beneath her expensive robes. She recalls frequently that her maker has mistakenly filled her with damp bran, a circumstance that causes her much distress. Her complaints are echoed in the refrain of Jenny Wren, the self-described "person of the house, dolls' dressmaker and manufacturer of ornamental pincushions and penwipers" in Dickens's novel *Our Mutual Friend*—a character who regularly complains of her bad back and queer legs (233). Dickens introduced Jenny Wren in 1864, between the appearance of Arabella in 1856 and Ethel in 1880, and while she is but a minor player in the novel, an examination of her character reveals that she employs, in collusion with her dolls, strategies of miniaturization similar to those used by Bradford and Pardoe in their children's stories: the violent agency described by the former and the economic agency described by the latter. In other words, Dickens, like Pardoe before him and Bradford after him, understands the doll as an object of imaginative power around which social structures can pivot. The doll's passivity once again becomes a means of its owner's expression of decisive action and even aggression.

However, this assertion would at first appear unlucky for the character of Jenny Wren, who appears in the novel much like a large doll. She is first introduced in the text as "a child—a dwarf—a doll—something" (222). Descriptions of Jenny suggest that, as Hilary M. Schor notes, "neither the narrator nor any other character is sure what to call Jenny Wren" (199), but it is this last characterization—"a doll"—that recurs throughout the novel.[11] The characters that surround Jenny, Schor argues, constantly move her about, name her, and misidentify her (200); they manipulate her age, maturity, and social position much like a young girl would manipulate the dress and demeanor of her dolls. Her small form is crowned with an abundance of golden hair, which Mrs. Potterson, the owner of the Six Jolly Fellowship Porters, exclaims is "enough to make wigs for all the dolls in the world" (438).

Lizzie Hexam enjoys "playfully smoothing" this "bright long fair hair" much as a girl would arrange the hair of her dolls (233). When Charley Hexam and his schoolmaster, Bradley Headstone, visit Jenny, her abode is described in terms of the miniature that strangely seem to suggest a dollhouse. The door opens "promptly . . . with a spring and a click," and Jenny is seated "on a little low old-fashioned arm-chair, which had a kind of little working bench before it" (222). Eugene Wrayburn, meanwhile, insists on calling her father "Mr. Dolls." "Child, or woman?" asks Mrs. Potterson upon encountering Jenny for the first time. "Child in years," answers Mr. Riah, "woman in self-reliance and trial" (439).

As Mrs. Potterson suggests here, Jenny has had much more to overcome than her small size. Her occupation as a seamstress of sorts marks her as part of a tradition of seamstress characters in Victorian literature—a tradition that focused on the power dynamic between affluent patron and pitiable needle-woman. Literary and visual representations of the seamstress, as Lynn Alexander argues, were meant to encourage upper and middle classes to sympathize with the working class in general and move for reform and were therefore romanticized, the needlewoman usually being characterized as "a young woman, often displaced from the middle class, struggling alone, often in an attic room" (18).[12] For example, Richard Redgrave and Ann Blunden both are known for their paintings that depict the sentimental figure of the lone seamstress, plying her needle late into the night. As Alexander points out, these characters, while appealing, were beset with many of the same mental and physical burdens of factory workers—including long hours, mea-ger pay, extreme tedium, constant vulnerability to poverty or starvation, and high incidence of disease, in particular consumption. Dickens's Jenny Wren, who appears more than a decade later than most of the examples cited by Alexander, nonetheless takes part in the tradition of needlewomen represented in Victorian texts and illustrations, and, like such characters, she is over-worked and sickly. She claims she is "poorly paid" and "often so pressed for time," and she is crooked and small, with a bad back and "queer" legs (223). She states that her dressmaking business requires long hours—"I had a doll married, last week, and was obliged to work all night," she says—and she is unappreciated by her clients, who "never keep to the same fashions a month" (223). The narrator laments Jenny's occupation in a manner that recalls the sympathy and sentimentality prevalent in the discourse of social awareness that surrounded the seamstress in the nineteenth century: "Poor dolls' dressmaker! How often so dragged down by hands that should have raised her up; how often so misdirected when losing her way on the eternal road, and asking guidance! Poor, poor little dolls' dressmaker!" (243).

Yet Jenny Wren is a *dolls'* dressmaker. Unlike her seamstress predecessors in literature, such as Mary Barton and Kate Nickleby, Jenny spends weary hours not piecing together gowns for well-to-do ladies but rather designing miniature ensembles for fashion dolls. Critics such as Henry James may have found her occupation unusual and perhaps even farfetched—merely one of Dickens's quirks[13]—but it is this odd career that lends Jenny her imaginative agency, firstly because it recalls the history of dolls' dressmakers, a profession far more noble than James supposed. As Max von Boehn explains in his history of dolls and puppets, dolls were used from the 1300s through the early nineteenth century to display the latest fashions to both royal courts and upper-class customers, particularly in France but in time across the Continent and throughout England (136). Mary Hillier similarly notes that the fashion doll, particularly the French *mannequin* or *poupée modèle*, was ''from very early times the servant of fashion and its ambassadress abroad'' (43). The popularity of the fashion doll, which was often life-sized and fitted with ready-to-wear clothes, waned in the nineteenth century, and its function of advertising the latest trends in dress and coif were fulfilled instead by hand-colored fashion plates, which were easier to circulate (Hillier 47). However, Dickens's decision to characterize Jenny Wren as a dolls' dressmaker marks her as a descendant of those who designed ensembles for fashion dolls—models sent to circulate among the elite and the royal. She is a makeshift equivalent of the royal milliner, mimicking with her rags and scraps the powerful role of trendsetter. Indeed, the faded power of Jenny's profession seems to be recognized in the text by Wrayburn, who refers to her as the ''Court Dressmaker'' (532).[14]

The reader is never granted a detailed description of Jenny's designs, and her influence will certainly never reach the court. But Jenny's approach to her process of design and manufacture proves far more powerful than the intimation that Jenny is part of this trendsetting tradition. She is pointedly interested not in puffed sleeves and fitted corsets but instead in the power dynamic suggested in the relationship between dressmaker and model. Rather than remaining the passive object understood and labeled by those larger than her, Jenny turns the relationship between doll and owner—between person-made-small and the larger world—on its head. Jenny and her creations can act as sites from which the order of the social world, despite its grand scale, can be manipulated or reversed, at least in the imagination; such transformations are achieved when Jenny triangulates her relationships to those who would understand her stature, both social and physical, in undesirable ways through her dolls, projecting doll-like passivity onto the upper class patrons she serves. Jenny acts in cooperation with her creations, directing the doll's transformative potential toward the social hierarchy that has defined her as a working-class woman. The dynamic is illustrated powerfully in Jenny's conversation with her friend Mr. Riah about her methods of dolls' dress design:

"There's a Drawing Room, or a grand day in the park, or a Show, or a Fête, or what you like. Very well. I squeeze among the crowd, and I look about me. When I see a great lady very suitable for my business, I say, 'You'll do, my dear!' and I take particular notice of her, and run home and cut her out and baste her. Then another day, I come scudding back again to try on, and then I take particular notice of her again. Sometimes she plainly seems to say, 'How that little creature is staring!' and sometimes likes it and sometimes don't. . . . At the time I am only saying to myself, 'I must hollow out a bit here; I must slope away there;' and I am making a perfect slave of her, with making her try on my doll's dress. . . . I dare say they think I am wondering and admiring with all my eyes and heart, but they little think they're only working for my dolls!"

(436)

This passage recalls the historical position of the dolls' dressmaker, who imagines her dolls as "servants of fashion" much as Jenny imagines these women as slaves. Her profession as a dolls' dressmaker and her methods of research and design enable her to transform the ladies she observes in lit parlor windows into passive models for her millinery.[15] The reader shares in Jenny's fantasy, in which the only words these women utter originate in Jenny's brain and the movements they make are put to Jenny's service. Just as the helpless and mute doll, according to Marcus, became an object on which Victorian girls projected their will, Jenny projects her own social desires onto unsuspecting upper-class ladies by transforming them into the dolls that, when complete, will appear as perfect imitations of their dress and demeanor. In claiming the "great" ladies as subservient to the demands of her trade, Jenny is reversing the relationship between the seamstress and her patron as it is commonly understood. This reversal is particularly important in the use of the word "slaves," a word that not only connotes total submission but also echoes Jenny's earlier description of her work as a seamstress: "Slave, slave slave, from morning to night" (241).[16]

While the dialectic of passivity and agency embodied in the object of the doll is important in the social transformations Jenny performs, the doll's size—and Jenny's own smallness—also figure in the subordination of upper-class party-goers to working-class Jenny. The discrepancy of size between Jenny's dolls—which, if Jenny followed Victorian doll-making conventions, were most likely between seventeen and twenty inches tall (Schäbert 128)—and the great ladies who inspire their fashions is particularly important in that it allows Jenny, quite literally, to possess minute but perfect doubles of those ladies who would otherwise scoff at her from their carriage windows—those ladies who are, in a physical sense, so much larger than she is. In possessing the women she forces to "try on" her dolls' clothes, Jenny controls them. For example, Jenny explains that she not only observed the form of Lady Belinda as a possible model for her designs but also mentally moved her about in an almost violent manner: "And I made her try on—oh!

and take pains about it too—before she got seated'' (436). And when Jenny shows her dolls to Mr. Riah in finished form behind the glass of a toy store, they seem arranged in arrested action to please their observers: ''a dazzling semicircle of dolls in all the colours of the rainbow, who were dressed for presentation at court, for going to balls, for going out driving, for going out on horseback, for going out walking, for going to get married, for going to help other dolls to get married, for all the gay events of life'' (435). Jenny is literally ''toying'' with grand ladies, and, as Susan Stewart notes, using the miniature to toy with something is ''to manipulate it, to try it out within sets of contexts'' (56). In this case, Jenny toys with these ladies to reverse her social context, to ''try out'' the role of social mover in spite of her size and standing.

The control Jenny exerts through her dolls seems to spiral outward and influence other elements of the animate world. When she is interrogating Bradley Headstone regarding his feelings for her friend Lizzie, for instance, Jenny mediates her questions through a doll she calls ''Mrs. Truth, The Honourable. Full Dressed'' (342):

> ''I stand the Honourable Mrs. T. on my bench in this corner against the wall, where her blue eyes can shine upon you,'' pursued Miss Wren, doing so, and making two little dabs at him in the air with her needle, as if she pricked him with it in his own eyes; ''and I defy you to tell me, with Mrs. T. for a witness, what you have come here for.''
>
> ''To see Hexam's sister.''
>
> ''You don't say so!'' retorted Miss Wren, hitching her chin.
>
> . . .
>
> ''For her own sake,'' repeated Bradley, warming, ''and for her brother's, and as a perfectly disinterested person.''
>
> ''Really, Mrs. T.,'' remarked the dressmaker, ''since it comes to this, we must positively turn you with your face to the wall.''   (Dickens 342–43)

If Jenny cannot elicit the truth from Headstone regarding his designs on Lizzie Hexam by subjecting him to the unblinking gaze of ''the Honourable Mrs. T.,'' she is able to use the doll as an object to assert her keen perception regarding Headstone's intentions. Headstone grows increasingly angry and uncomfortable in this scene, and it is only the entrance of Lizzie herself that ends Jenny's assault. The influence Jenny is able to exert through her dolls is limited in this scene and could possibly be attributed to her peculiarity, but other moments in the text attest to the nearly prophetic nature of her dolls. For example, Jenny suggests to Riah that the clergyman doll she fashions after her father's funeral is not only an imitation of life but also an object that is prophetic of life's events, perhaps even controlling them. A marriage performed by the doll clergyman will be replicated in real life, not vice versa: ''If you don't see . . . three at the altar in Bond Street, in a jiffy,'' sing-songs

Jenny, "my name's Jack Robinson!" (734). Jenny's matrimonial prediction is fulfilled when Eugene Wrayburn and Lizzie marry two chapters later. In fact, as Helena Michie notes, it is Jenny, whose trade requires the skill of piecing together the seemingly small and insignificant, that makes the marriage possible. "Her knowledge that desire grows out of parts," writes Michie, "allows her to articulate for Eugene the word 'wife,' lost to him in the confusion and fragmentation of his mind" (210). In scenes such as these, the reader is led to suspect that the control Jenny exerts over her dolls and the universe they inhabit is not limited to fantasy.

Dickens does not fail to add a sinister note to the sense of control afforded by the dolls. For example, as Jenny and Mr. Riah stand before the colorful display of her handiwork, Jenny comments, "That's Lady Belinda hanging up by the waist, much too near the gaslight for a wax one, with her toes turned in" (436). The waxen figure of Belinda melting in the shop window calls forth associations of voodoo—suggestions strengthened by Jenny's habit of furtively "making two little dabs . . . in the air" with her sewing needle when displeased with her visitors, a gesture the narrator understands as figuratively pricking out their eyes (342). The sadistic side of Jenny's doll-making revealed in scenes such as this one resonates with the long history of the doll, an object that was thought to possess what Boehn calls "image magic." Boehn cites a tradition of dolls created as objects "made in order to gain power over those they represent"—in many cases a malignant power. "Image magic proper," writes Boehn, "necessitates the making of a figure of the man whose hurt is secretly sought; this figure is pierced with holes, lacerated, and burned, on the assumption that all that is done to it is transferred to the living original" (Boehn 58–59). While many of the instances of voodoo or image magic that doll historians describe are historically distant from Dickens's Jenny Wren, these scholars consistently acknowledge that the doll is an object that has remained evocative through the nineteenth century and beyond, inspiring fantasies of vicarious violence and revenge.[17] Boehn notes that "the belief in the power of image magic had a remarkably tenacious life," spanning the East and West and many centuries, and Hillier notes that the practice of fashioning small wax figures to burn or punish remains an active ritual in the twentieth century (Boehn 60, Hillier 29).

Jenny's pin-pricking gestures and her dark comment on the melting Lady Belinda are accompanied by a number of moments in the text in which Jenny's doll-making recalls image magic or voodoo, suggesting an intimate relationship between her craft and what Michie calls her "powerful fantasies of revenge" (200). For example, when Jenny discovers "Fascination" Fledgeby severely beaten by Alfred Lammle, she uses the delicacy and dexterity she has developed in working as a seamstress not to alleviate his misery but rather to punish him in a manner that positions Jenny as witch doctor tormenter and Fledgeby as both voodoo doll and, in Boehn's words, "living original": "The busy little dressmaker quickly snipped [Fledgeby's] shirt away, and laid bare the results of as furious and sound a thrashing as even Mr. Fledgeby merited. 'You may well smart, young man!' exclaimed Miss Jenny. And stealthily rubbed her little hands behind him, and poked a few exultant pokes with her two forefingers over the crown of his head" (723). Commissioned by Fledgeby to bandage his wounds, Jenny "repaired to the kitchen, scissors in hand, found the brown paper and found the vinegar, and skillfully cut out and steeped six large plasters" (724). The dolls' dressmaker's scissors, which she uses to shape designs for her replicas of London ladies, here quickly fashion Fledgeby's bandages, which will be used not as a means to control Fledgeby, as her dolls imaginatively control lady socialites, but instead to punish him. Before applying the plasters to Fledgeby's raw back, Jenny finds the pepper-box on the chimney-piece, and "sprinkle[s] all the plasters with a judicious hand" (724). Jenny finishes her work by dressing Fledgeby much as she would dress one of her dolls; she "got his Persian gown upon him, extinguished his eyes crookedly with his Persian cap, and helped him to his bed" (724). Jenny punishes the body of Fledgeby much as the witches and magicians in Boehn's and Hillier's research punish waxen images of their enemies. However, Jenny is practiced in imaginatively transforming those who physically and socially overpower her into dolls that can be manipulated and mastered, and therefore the mediating object of the doll is unnecessary.[18] This scene is another reversal of the relationship between seamstress and socialite; while Fledgeby is a far cry from the well-dressed ladies who would patronize nineteenth-century dressmakers, his body-turned-doll nevertheless offers Jenny a site upon which she can project the pain and ill treatment more often experienced by the working class.

Jenny's "fantasies of revenge," as well as her reversal of social relationships, rely not only on the creative deployment of her position as dolls' dressmaker and the miniaturization of those in the "larger world" but also on a corresponding sense of self-magnification; in miniaturizing upper-class ladies, Jenny is magnifying herself in relationship to them. She transforms from a shockingly small child-woman "hobbling among the wheels of the carriages and the legs of the horses" (Dickens 436) into a giant, her "eye blazing down in an act of fierce attention" (Millhauser 131) at the submissive bodies of her charges. The gigantic, contrary to the miniature, challenges any attempt of control, according to Steven Millhauser: "The gigantic continually threatens to elude us, to grow too large for possession by the eye. There is something lush, profuse, unstoppable in the very idea of the gigantic" (129). As the women Jenny observes dwindle into dolls ranged in a store window, Jenny grows; her magnification not only protects her from the objectifying gaze of "great society"—a gaze that would dismiss her as insignificant or shrink her into submission—but also offers her a sense of security in a world that otherwise seems ready to crush her. Jenny experiences this joy of looming large over a miniature universe on the roof of Pubsey & Co., where she experiences a moment of moral elevation as she gazes down from the rooftop, observing people who appear like animate dolls. For Jenny, the roof, in the words of Stewart, is "a transcendent space," a "space above" that allows her to abstract from the physical circumstances of her own body (102). While the sensation of looming enormous over a small world indeed encourages her to contemplate the ultimate space above—the yet higher and larger space of heaven—it also allows her literally to look down upon, and extend pity to, those who would, on the ground, pity *her*. "[Y]ou hear the people who are alive, crying, and working, and calling to one another down in the close dark streets," explains Jenny, "and you seem to pity them so! And such a chain has fallen from you, and such a strange good sorrowful happiness comes upon you!" (281).

The imagination and agency Jenny appropriates through miniaturization and magnification, however, is transient; the transformations made possible by manipulations of scale are not, according to Stewart, "determinative"—they cannot last (56). The sensation of "sorrowful happiness" Jenny experiences on the roof is tellingly characterized by the young woman herself as a state separate from the life below. "You feel as if you were dead," she explains (281). Eventually Jenny must, like Fledgby and Riah before her, descend to the street, where the wagon and horses' legs will once again remind her of her true size. In quiet moments of work, Jenny reveals her knowledge that her fantasies are impermanent and constantly in danger of dissolving. For example, the narrator depicts "Miss Wren . . . alone at her work, with the house-door set open for coolness . . . trolling in a small sweet voice a mournful little song which might have been the song of the doll she was dressing, bemoaning the brittleness and meltability of wax" (714). Here, Jenny not only is surrounded by the "small" and "little," words that ground her in the realm of the diminutive, but also is forced to acknowledge the "brittleness and meltability" of the world she creates.

Moments such as this arrest the flamboyant imagination so present in *Our Mutual Friend* and ground Jenny's occupation and its realities. While her imagination enslaves those who would spurn her, and while her creations enable her to transcend the social limitations written legibly on her body, these fantasies cannot withstand the pressure of the reality of her existence. The narrator gestures toward the instability of her imaginative power earlier in the novel, when even Lizzie cannot enliven Jenny's downtrodden spirits after a particularly nasty bout with her father, the drunken Mr. Dolls: "The person of the house was the person of a house full of sordid shames and cares," comments the narrator, "with an upper room in which that abased figure [Jenny's father] was infecting even the innocent sleep with sensual brutality and degradation. The dolls' dressmaker had become a quaint little shrew; of the world, worldly; of the earth, earthly'' (243). Those moments in the text, then, that are poignant in their depiction of the realities of Jenny's domestic life are also powerful in that they undermine her fantasies and connect her not only with the small—in this case "a quaint little shrew"—but also with the world outside the imagination—"the world, worldly . . . the earth, earthly.''

The ephemeral nature of her agency is nowhere more apparent than at the moment of her father's death, when "in the midst of the dolls with no specula-tion in their eyes, lay Mr. Dolls with no speculation in his" (731). The lifeless bodies of Jenny's dolls become oppressive when a great many of them "had to be gaily dressed, before that money was in the dressmaker's pocket to get mourning" (731). The imaginative transformation Jenny had achieved as she rushed between her workshop and the great halls of fashionable gentle-women—the ability to transcend her social condition and, for a moment, reverse the patron/slave relationship—has failed her. Her millinery is not a source of imaginary agency but instead a burden; finally, Jenny truly fits the image of the seamstress working late into the night, scraping together enough money for her father's funeral costs. Such conditions cause Jenny to mourn her smallness, recognizing it as a curse that is unchangeable, even by her powers of fancy. "How can I say what I might have turned out myself," muses Jenny to Mr. Riah, "but for my back having been bad and my legs so queer when I was young! . . . I had nothing to do but work, and so I worked" (732). As Schor notes, while Jenny's imagination lends her a limited agency, she never achieves narrative autonomy: "Her life story is written by the incessant and draining labor her father's drunkenness commits her to" (201).

But perhaps it is not in terms of physical transformation that we are meant to understand the role of Jenny Wren's dolls in *Our Mutual Friend*. The anxiety and doubt regarding her own agency and imagination that Jenny experiences at the moment of her father's death is matched by a moment of promise at the end of the novel: the acquaintance of Jenny with Sloppy, the gape-mouthed orphan Noddy Boffin is training in cabinet-making. In the brief episode between Sloppy and Jenny, the reader is able to detect, once again, the potential of world-making through the miniature as the logic of scale is thrown into disorder. Jenny describes Sloppy as "like the giant . . . when he came home in the land of Beanstalk" (808). This moment has the potential to dismantle again the transformative magic of the dressmaker's workshop; the sheer size of the giant Sloppy seems to threaten Jenny, who appears smaller than ever as she labors over "a full-dressed doll some two sizes larger than that young person" (808). Instead, in a moment that recuperates and revises Jenny's imaginative power, Sloppy does not immediately comprehend

Jenny as a dwarfed figure; he first perceives her full hair "in a burst of admiration"—"What a lot, and what a colour!''—and only recognizes her disability when Jenny herself points it out to him, identifying the crutch lying in her corner as her own (809). When Jenny insists on revealing the truth of her condition, admitting "with a quick flush of face and neck" that she is lame, he dismisses the fact by insisting that "it seems . . . that you hardly want [the crutch] at all'' (809, 810).

The two figures—the magnified Sloppy and the miniaturized Jenny—begin to form a partnership based on Jenny's ability to transform her collection of scraps and notions into her own dolls' universe. "I could make you a handy set of nests to lay the dolls in," offers Sloppy. "Or I could make you a handy little set of drawers, to keep your silks and threads and scraps in'' (809). Sloppy's encounter with Jenny ensures that the dream of the miniature is not in fact over—that there remains an interior world to be constructed from the baskets of scraps Jenny buys for two shillings from Pubsey & Co. Their relationship is not more fully imagined within the space of the novel, but one can envision Jenny's continued appropriation of those bits of the larger world that are considered too small or too insignificant and her continued act of refashioning those odds and ends into another world altogether—a world that lends the waste of the middle and upper classes new life and in turn lends the working-class seamstress a power she previously did not possess. Sloppy's collaboration ensures that Jenny's world can exist within the space of their relationship. While the agency she wields as part of her dolls' dressmaking trade may remain in the fictive realm, continually challenged by the poverty and marginalization that surrounds her workshop, she has discovered in Sloppy someone who does not define her in terms of "a queer little comicality" but rather as a true artisan, someone who "must have been taught a long time . . . to work so neatly . . . and with such a pretty taste" (808, 809).

Focusing on the doll has temporarily obscured issues of genre: Dickens's *Our Mutual Friend* is a novel written for an adult audience, while Bradford's *Ethel's Adventures in Doll Country* and Pardoe's *Lady Arabella* were both intended for a child audience. There are those scholars who would argue that this difference in genre matters little—that much of Dickens can be read as children's literature.[19] However, as I have demonstrated, an examination of Dickens's text alongside Bradford's and Pardoe's is interesting not because of the similar play of imagination present in all three but rather because of the structures of power and subordination this imagination—and in particular fantasies of the miniature and the gigantic—can enable. Jenny playfully pokes her needle in the air in a manner that anticipates the violent fantasies of the Doll Country, and she transforms upper-class ladies into docile dress mannequins in a manner that recalls the circle of working-class women manipulating the limbs of the vulnerable Arabella, but these similarities are not merely evidence that Dickens has appropriated an aesthetic often found in literature for children; it instead evidences the imaginative currency of fantasies of size, suggesting that strategies of subversion registered through the miniature and the gigantic are powerful enough to cross the boundaries of genre. Regardless of audience, distortions and discrepancies of size suggest, even generate, alternative narratives. Notably, as Low concludes her examination of the young Victoria's dolls, she feels compelled to provide such alternative stories. "Do you not feel with me that the little wooden figures invest their living prototypes with so personal an interest that one would gladly learn something more about their life's histories," she asks, "whether tragedy of happiness fell to their lot, and whether those eyes which have long ceased to shine were more sorrowful than smiling?" (conclusion). This impulse to examine, to look closer, to "learn something more," stages the miniature as a site where narrative possibilities multiply and expand.

NOTES

1. Low's text is accompanied by illustrations by Alan Wright. As a motivation for her text, Low cites "an article in *The Strand Magazine* a few months ago, containing an account of the dolls that Her Majesty had dressed and played with in her childhood," which "aroused an astonishing amount of attention and interest" (introduction).
2. I would like to thank Sharon Marcus, who provided me with a prepublication draft of her chapter on fashion and dolls in *Between Women*, a study that finds similar possibilities of female agency in the object of the doll. Many of the doll narratives I use here I first encountered in her work.
3. Note that I am not examining these texts in chronological order. I do not posit that Dickens was influenced by Bradford and Pardoe—an argument that would require a certain chronology of publication—but instead that the doll provided many narrative possibilities that are utilized by different authors in different ways and to particular effect in *Our Mutual Friend*.
4. The moment when Ethel joins the boys to court-martial her doll, I believe, would be seen as the ultimate failure of the doll to acculturate the young girl. The doll here encourages rather than subdues the aggression of the unruly girl and implicates her in masculine war play. In the nineteenth century, as today, passive doll play was considered feminine, while aggressive war play was considered the proper domain of the young boy. Low quotes Victor Hugo as saying "the girl who is indifferent to dolls is as abnormal as the boy who cares nothing for soldiers or ships" (introduction).
5. Many scholars recognize the desirability of the miniature. As Schäbert notes, "Victorians were fond of little people," as is evidenced in the popularity of J.

N. Paton's fairy paintings and the tiny human figures that adorned the illuminated letters of William M. Thackeray's *Vanity Fair* (128). See also Peter Ackroyd's appropriately short discussion of the miniature portrait in *Albion* (285–89).

6. These distortions of size and perspective, and basic elements of the plot of Bradford's narrative, suggest that *Ethel's Adventures in the Doll Country* is influenced in many ways by Lewis Carroll's *Alice's Adventures in Wonderland* (1865). Marcus notes that "[t]he narrative . . . is governed by the dream logic of texts like *Alice in Wonderland*," in which "events abruptly start and stop and inanimate objects come to life," but she does not explore in detail the many correspondences between *Alice* and *Ethel* (150). In both texts, for example, the culminating event is a meeting with the queen in a beautiful garden—in Ethel's case for a tea party (not attended, unfortunately, by hare or hatter) and in Alice's case for a game of croquet. Additionally, both end in a trial—in Ethel's case the testimony of her abused doll and in Alice's case the great trial over the queen's tarts. Notably, one of Ethel's dolls is named Alice. Finally, in both texts, dream-like logic can only be overcome when the protagonist wakes from a dream.

7. This is yet another correspondence with Carroll's text. Alice thinks of her own changes in size as the shutting up of a telescope. See Carroll 17.

8. It is impossible to ignore the sexual nature of the birch rods in Doll Country, although that will not be the focus of my discussion here. See Marcus 150–52.

9. An interesting reversal of this system of valuation is found in Frances Hodgson Burnett's *Racketty-Packetty House* (1907), in which a little girl, when a princess visits her nursery, hides the careworn Racketty-Packetty dollhouse and its inhabitants in the corner, showcasing her new Tidy Castle. The princess is bored of such luxuries as can be found in the dolls and furnishings of Tidy Castle and instead recognizes the value of tradition and heritage in the older dollhouse, which the little girl inherited from her grandmother.

10. For a useful history of children's literature that documents this movement, see chapter 8 in F. J. Harvey Darton's study, which discusses the Peter Paley–Felix Summerley debate, or the opposition in children's literature between didacticism and pleasure.

11. Schor argues that Jenny is a "sign of social fact" in Dickens's novel, marked and hobbled by hard labor. What is interesting about Jenny, Schor argues, is that attached to her realism are some of the most transporting fantasies in the text—fantasies that help ease her own social anxieties. Schor only briefly reads the creation and purpose of Jenny's dolls (198–200).

12. Alexander compares this to the reality of needlework in the mid-nineteenth century, which was most likely undertaken by married women, "sewing to provide a second income or to replace one lost to the illness or injuring of the male head of the household. And rather than living in a dry, romantic garret, all too often these women and their families lived in damp, often polluted, cellar dwellings" (18).

13. Henry James famously disliked *Our Mutual Friend*, writing, "It is hardly too much to say that every character here put before us is a mere bundle of eccentricities, animated by no principle of nature whatever. . . . What do we get in return for accepting Miss Jenny Wren as a possible person?" And his assault on Jenny

does not stop there. He calls her "a little monster," "deformed, unhealthy, unnatural," and insists that "she belongs to the troop of hunchbacks, imbeciles, and precocious children who have carried on the sentimental business in all Mr. Dickens's novels" (qtd. in Schor 197–98).

14. Interestingly, Low similarly refers to the young Victoria as the "Court milliner" and the "Royal dressmaker" (introduction).

15. Schor discusses this scene, arguing that Jenny "walks the streets, forcing ladies of fashion (unknowingly) to pose for her dolls, lessening her own physical discomfort by imagining them pushed about as she forces them into postures" (200). However, Schor addresses this moment in the text only briefly.

16. Often children's doll narratives use the language of slave and master to describe the relationship between little girl and doll. See, for example, the opening pages to Julia Charlotte Maitland's *The Doll and Her Friends*: "We are a race of mere dependents," explains the doll narrator, "some might even call us slaves. Unable to change our place, or move hand or foot at our own pleasure, and forced to submit to every caprice of our possessors, we cannot be said to have even a will of our own" (2).

17. The English encountered voodoo at least as early as the late eighteenth century, due to British interests in the West Indian colonies. See Richardson 172–73.

18. The collapse of victim and doll is echoed, almost comically, in a scene in which Jenny threatens to use her dolls themselves as weapons. She menaces her drunken father by saying, "Don't cry like that, or I'll throw a doll at you" (532).

19. Peter Hunt, for example, writes that Dickens's "rapidity of wit" and his "talent for exaggeration . . . made his popular writing live on the margins of children's literature, just as it does on the margins of respectable adult literature" (69).

WORKS CITED

Ackroyd, Peter. "The Miniature." *Albion: The Origins of the English Imagination*. New York: Doubleday, 2002. 285–89.

Alexander, Lynn. *Women, Work, and Representation: Needlewomen in Victorian Art and Literature*. Athens: Ohio UP, 2003.

Besset, Jane M. *Memoirs of a Doll, Written by Herself: A New Year's Gift*. Adapted from *Mémoirs d'une poupée* by Louise d'Aulnay. London: Routledge, 1854.

Boehn, Max von. *Dolls and Puppets*. Trans. Josephine Nicoll. New York: Cooper Square, 1966.

Bradford, Clara. *Ethel's Adventures in Doll-Country*. Illus. T. Pym. London: John F. Shaw, 1880.

Brenda [Mrs. Castle Smith]. *Victoria Bess: The Ups and Downs of a Doll's Life* [1879]. Illus. T. Pym. In *Victorian Doll Stories, by Brenda, Mrs. Gatty, and Frances Hodgson Burnett.* Introduction Gillian Avery. New York: Schocken, 1969. 11–77.

Burnett, Frances Hodgson. *Racketty-Packetty House,* in *Victorian Doll Stories.* 113–41.

Carroll, Lewis [Charles Dodgson]. *Alice's Adventures in Wonderland.* In *The Annotated Alice: The Definitive Edition.* Introduction and notes by Martin Gardner. New York: Norton, 2000. 2–127.

Cornford, Leslie Cope. *London Pride and London Shame.* London: P. S. King, 1910.

Cotsen Children's Library. Department of Rare Books and Special Collections. Princeton University Library.

Darton, F. J. Harvey. *Children's Books in England.* Newcastle, DE: Oak Knoll, 1999.

Dickens, Charles. *Our Mutual Friend.* Ed. Michael Cotsell. Oxford: Oxford UP, 1989.

Hillier, Mary. *Dolls and Doll-Makers.* New York: Putnam's, 1968.

Horn, Pamela. *The Victorian Town Child.* New York: New York UP, 1997.

Hunt, Peter. *An Introduction to Children's Literature.* Oxford: Oxford UP, 1994.

James, Henry. "The Limitations of Dickens." *Views and Reviews.* Boston: Bell, 1908. 153–61.

Low, Frances H. *Queen Victoria's Dolls.* Illus. Alan Wright. London: George Newnes, 1894.

Maitland, Julia Charlotte. *The Doll and Her Friends, or, Memoirs of the Lady Seraphina.* Ed. Richard Henry Horne. New York: Brentano's, 1893.

Marcus, Sharon. "Dressing Up and Dressing Down the Feminine Plaything." *Between Women: Friendship, Desire, and Marriage in Victorian England.* Princeton: Princeton UP, 2007. 111–66.

Michie, Helena. " 'Who is this in Pain?': Scarring, Disfigurement, and Female Identity in *Bleak House* and *Our Mutual Friend.*" *Novel: A Forum on Fiction* 22.2 (1989): 199–212.

Millhauser, Steven. "The Fascination of the Miniature." *Grand Street* 2 (1983): 128–35.

Pardoe, Julia. *Lady Arabella, or, The Adventures of a Doll.* Illus. George Cruikshank. London: Kerby, 1856.

Richardson, Allen. "Romantic Voodoo: Obeah and British Culture, 1797–1807." *Sacred Possessions: Vodou, Santería, Obeah, and the Caribbean.* Ed. Margarite Fernández Olmos and Lizabeth Paravisini-Gebert. New Brunswick, NJ: Rutgers UP, 1997. 171–94.

Schäbert, Ina. "Bourgeois Counter-Art: Dolls in Victorian Culture." *Journal for the Study of British Cultures* 8.2 (2001): 121–35.

Schor, Hilary. "*Our Mutual Friend* and the Daughter's Book of the Dead." *Dickens and the Daughter of the House*. Cambridge: Cambridge UP, 1999. 178–207.

Stewart, Susan. *On Longing: Narratives of the Miniature, the Gigantic, the Souvenir, the Collection*. Durham, NC: Duke UP, 1993.

"Opium Is the True Hero of the Tale": De Quincey, Dickens, and *The Mystery of Edwin Drood*

Robert Tracy

Writing about Jasper's opium dreams in The Mystery of Edwin Drood, *Dickens turned for information about the nature of the opium experience to Thomas De Quincey's* Confessions of an English Opium-Eater. *There he found descriptions of De Quincey's elaborate opium dreams, which underlie Jasper's repeatedly induced dream about a journey among great heights and depths with a doomed fellow-traveler, presumably his way of imagining in anticipation the murder of Edwin Drood. In the* Confessions *Dickens also found opium associated with the Orient and with violent death, a juxtaposition he employs in the unfinished novel. In portraying Jasper rehearsing and savoring his dream of murdering Drood, and later threatening to destroy Neville Landless by proving him to be Drood's murderer, Dickens also draws on De Quincey's essay "On Murder Considered as One of the Fine Arts," which invokes a theory of the aesthetic murder that applies to Jasper, a musician and would-be artist in crime.*

> "All opium-eaters are tainted with the infirmity of leaving works unfinished"
> —De Quincey, "Coleridge and Opium-Eating" (1845)

In the opening paragraph of *The Mystery of Edwin Drood*, Dickens lets us experience an awakening from an opium dream. A confused consciousness, at this stage without name or context, is hovering midway between *Arabian*

Nights visions induced by the drug, and the intrusive recollection of a Gothic cathedral tower. The dreamer is somehow merging images of barbaric Oriental splendor with the ancient stones of an English cathedral city, so much so that the Sultan's guards seem about to impale "a horde of Turkish robbers" on a finial at a corner of the cathedral's square tower. There are flashing scimitars. "Thrice ten thousand dancing-girls strew flowers," followed by "white elephants caparisoned in countless gorgeous colors, and infinite in numbers and attendants." But still that disturbing tower "rises in the background, *where it cannot be* [italics mine], and still no writhing figure is on the grim spike." Then the awakening opium dreamer begins to recognize that spike for what it is, the top of a bedpost. His "scattered consciousness has . . . fantastically pieced itself together" into this vision of exotica, opulence, and punishment, an epilogue to the drug-induced dream he has entertained.

As his consciousness begins to reassemble itself more conventionally, he recognizes that he is sprawled across a broken bedstead in an opium den and it is dawn. He has smoked five pipefuls since midnight, and vaguely accepts another from the woman who keeps the den and prepares the opium. She has already inhaled "much of its contents," and presumably weakened its hallucinatory potential. Her client examines her, and then the two other inhabitants of the den—a Lascar and a "Chinaman"—listening to their mutterings and reassuring himself that all three are " 'Unintelligible.' " His own visions have apparently not penetrated into theirs; they cannot have shared them or repeat anything he might have said. But he is not quite free of the drug yet. As he scrutinizes the "spasmodic shoots and darts that break out of" the opium woman's "face and limbs, like fitful lightning out of a dark sky, some contagion in them seizes upon him," and he too begins to tremble, so much so that he has to sit down "on a lean arm-chair by the hearth—placed there, perhaps, for such emergencies—and to sit in it, holding tight, until he has got the better of this unclean spirit of imitation" (7–10; ch. 1).

Dickens, we know, visited a similar opium den, escorted by two police officers, when preparing to write this chapter (Johnson 2: 1113). There he noted the clientele, the generally sordid atmosphere, the proprietress's habit of making pipes out of penny ink-bottles, and no doubt this emergency chair, suggesting that the use of opium was often succeeded by such spasmodic jerkings and tremblings. When the chapter ends "That same afternoon," the dreamer, still unnamed, becomes "a jaded traveller" before whom "the massive grey square tower of an old Cathedral rises." He hurriedly takes his place among members of the cathedral choir robing for Evensong (11; ch. 1).

Dickens's phrase, "the jaded traveller," reminds us that the opium dreamer has been on a journey much longer, much stranger, and certainly more emotionally exhausting, than the railroad and omnibus journey between London and Cloisterham, the location of the square-towered cathedral that draws on Dickens's intimate acquaintance with Rochester Cathedral. Early in the second chapter, we learn that the opium dreamer/jaded traveler is John Jasper, and that he may not have the constitution needed for the frequent use of opium. Though he reached the cathedral in time for Evensong, the verger later reports that Jasper was " 'took a little poorly' " during the service, so short of breath " 'when he came in [began to intone], that it distressed him mightily to get his notes out: which was perhaps the cause of his having a kind of fit on him after a little. His memory grew DAZED . . . and a dimness and giddiness crept over him as strange as ever I saw . . . he was very shivery.' " Jasper soon insists that he is better, but less than an hour later he alarms his nephew by looking " 'frightfully ill,' " with " 'a strange film' " coming over his eyes; he admits that he has been " 'taking opium for a pain—an agony—that sometimes overcomes me. The effects of the medicine steal over me like a blight or a cloud and pass. You see them in the act of passing' " (18; ch. 2).

Dickens invents an opium dream and its processional aftermath to introduce us to John Jasper and to his preoccupations and fantasies, which will determine his behavior in the novel we are beginning to read. The dream is literature, not clinical observation. But Dickens does draw on contemporary medical ideas about the nature of the opium experience and its after-effects, and about the nature of dreaming and of hallucination. He owned *Human Physiology* (1835 edition) by his friend Dr. John Elliotson, and *The Anatomy of Drunkenness* (1827) and *The Philosophy of Sleep* (1840 edition) by Dr. Robert Macnish (*Letters* 4: 713, 725; Stonehouse 42, 77), books that examined the phenomena of dreaming, including drug-induced dreaming. David Paroissien has persuasively argued that Dickens drew on *The Philosophy of Sleep* in *Oliver Twist* to describe Oliver's half-waking visions of Fagin with his box of jewels and Fagin and Monks outside the window (*Oliver Twist*, chs. 9, 35; Paroissien 101, 217). *Human Physiology* and *The Philosophy of Sleep* both provide Dickens with his explanation of Miss Twinkelton's "two distinct and separate phases of being" (24; ch. 3), which seems to prepare us for Jasper's dual nature: the anecdote of the Irish porter who, when drunk, "left a parcel at the wrong house, and when sober could not recollect what he had done with it; but the next time he got drunk, he recollected where he had left it, and went and recovered it" (*Philosophy of Sleep* 82; *Human Physiology* 646).

Elliotson has sections on Sleep, Dreaming, "Sleep-Waking," and Mesmerism, all of them suggestive in the context of *Edwin Drood*. He quotes Franz Joseph Gall, the founder of phrenology, on the ability of hallucinogens or illness to alter personality and behavior, in terms that suggest the effects that the use of opium combined with his obsessive love for Rosa Bud have on Jasper: "How often in intoxication, hysterical and hypochondriacal attacks, convulsions, fevers, insanity, *under violent emotions,* after long fasting, *through the effects of such poisons as opium,* hemlock, belladonna, are we not in some measure transformed into *perfectly different beings,* for instance into poets, actors, &c.?'' (Elliotson 677; italics mine). Opium, Elliotson writes, ''excites the intellect and feelings; gives headach [sic]; and renders noise intolerable'' (609). Jasper's opium dream invokes murder and lust. It is presumably the opium that makes the singing of the cathedral choir seem to him '' 'quite devilish,' '' while Edwin Drood finds it '' 'Beautiful! Quite celestial!' '' (19; ch. 2). Macnish declares that ''of all dreams, there are none which, for unlimited wildness, equal those produced by narcotics'' (*Philosophy of Sleep* 95). ''Opium acts differently on different constitutions,'' Macnish declares;

> While it disposes some to calm, it arouses others to fury. Whatever passion predominates at the time, it increases; whether it be love, or hatred, or revenge, or benevolence. Lord Kames . . . speaks of the fanatical Faquirs, who, when excited by this drug, have been known, with poisoned daggers, to assail and butcher every European whom they could overcome. . . . The Malays are strongly addicted to opium. When violently aroused by it, they sometimes perform what is called *Running-a-Muck,* which consists of rushing out in a state of phrensied excitement, heightened by fanaticism, and murdering everyone who comes in their way.   (*Anatomy of Drunkenness* 49–50)

Macnish provides Dickens with links between the use of opium and an eagerness to kill, and also with links between opium and visions of oriental splendor. He imagines the ''halo of poetic thought'' by which opium allows ''the luxurious and opulent mussulman'' to penetrate ''the veil which shades the world of fancy'' and see ''palaces and temples in the clouds; or the Paradise of Mahomet, with its houris and bowers.'' Macnish also warns that prolonged use of opium leads to visions of ''horror and disgust . . . Frightful dreams,'' and general physical and mental disintegration (*Anatomy of Drunkenness* 51–53).

But Dickens's ideas about opium and its effects come primarily from literary rather than scientific sources. Among nineteenth-century writers and artists, opium and the visions it could provide had achieved considerable prestige. Coleridge had famously taken opium before he fell asleep reading about China in *Purchas his Pilgrimes,* thereby providing method and matter for the vision that he tried to record in ''Kubla Khan.'' Elliotson even prints Coleridge's note describing that experience, and uses it as an example of how ''in a dream certain faculties occasionally display more energy than in the waking state.'' He also cites La Fontaine's producing ''admirable verses,'' Alexander the Great's planning a battle, and Condillac's solving ''difficult problems'' while dreaming (615).

Elliotson suggests that dreams are often more intense than waking experience, and quotes with approval Charles Wheatstone's statement, that in dreams we may "perform the most ruthless crime without compunction, and see what in our waking hours would cause us unmitigated grief, without the smallest feeling of sorrow" (Elliotson 621). Emotions, among them "sexual desire, terror, rage," rather than intellect usually shape dreams. "The dreams of drunkenness and under the influence of narcotics are the most extravagant" (624). Elliotson's examples suggest certain affinities between Jasper's dreaming and dreams recorded in contemporary medical literature, but there is a major difference: Jasper seems able to control the content of his favorite dream, at least until he has actually committed the murder. The dream is apparently less tractable and satisfactory afterwards, which he blames on his own inability to mix the drug as the opium woman does. Elliotson never suggests that dreams can be bespoke.

In Wilkie Collins, Dickens had a close friend who was a potential source of information about the effects of opium. A frequent user of opium in its liquid form, laudanum, and a student of its effects, Collins had recently given the drug a major role in *his* mystery novel, *The Moonstone* (1868), drawing on Elliotson's book as well as his own experience, and in reading *The Moonstone* (440–41) Dickens had already encountered Elliotson's and Macnish's drunken porter. Elliotson could have added Collins to his list of men who had produced art or solved problems while dreaming: Collins sometimes read with surprise whole chapters of a novel in progress which he had written under the influence of laudanum (Hayter 259–60).

But Collins uses opium sparingly in his fiction, and does not provide fantastic visions of the sort Jasper demanded. In *The Moonstone* the opium is a plot device: Franklin Blake, unaware that he has been given laudanum, walks in his sleep and takes the gem, intending to hide it in a safer place. Like the drunken porter, he needs a second dose to reenact his movements. Ezra Jennings, who uses laudanum to suppress emotional and physical pain, persuades Blake to try that second dose by quoting Elliotson and Macnish, and recommends that he read De Quincey's *Confessions* for reassurance: opium will do him no harm (442)! Blake does not dream; we get only a brief glimpse of Jennings's own visions:

> a dreadful night; the vengeance of yesterday's opium, pursuing me though a series of frightful dreams. At one time I was whirling through empty space with the phantoms of the dead, friends and enemies together. At another, the one beloved face which I shall never see again, rose at my bedside, hideously phosphorescent in the black darkness and grinned at me.   (*Moonstone* 447)

Of Collins's own visions we know little. He sometimes had frightening hallucinations while awake or awakening, including "a reptile of the pre-Adamic period . . . ghosts trying to push him down . . . a green woman with teeth like tusks," but "none of his nightmares seem to have been recorded" (Hayter 260–61).

Dickens himself tried laudanum, "the only thing that has done me good," in combating exhaustion, sleeplessness, and a persistent cough in March 1868, on his strenuous American reading tour (*Letters* 12: 85; CD to Mary Dickens, 29/3/68). Less than a month before his death, about when he was writing Jasper's hints about the content of his opium dreams in chapter 23, Dickens was taking laudanum again, for "a neuralgic affection of the foot" which "has caused me great pain." "Last night I got a good night's rest under the influence of Laudanum but it hangs about me very heavily today," he told Georgina Hogarth (12 May 1870), in what would be his last letter to her (*Letters* 12: 524).

Jasper is an artist with a sensitive and highly developed imagination, and his dreams reflect that. To develop them, Dickens needed something more than medical books, which hardly penetrated the world of dreams, or any hints Collins might have supplied. The fullest and most accessible account of opium, its effects, and the visions it offered that was available to Dickens was Thomas De Quincey's *Confessions of an English Opium-Eater* (1821, revised 1856). In discussing the effects of opium, Elliotson and Macnish often rely on or quote the *Confessions* and seem at time almost to accept them as recording scientific investigations, thus entitling Dickens to do the same. The *Confessions* gave him entry into the imaginative world of the opium-eater, with its fantastic glimpses of wild landscapes, vast structures, and haunting forms. De Quincey celebrates "just, subtle, and mighty opium" for the physical, mental, and moral comfort it brings, and especially for the splendid visions it supplies:

> thou buildest upon the bosom of darkness, out of the fantastic imagery of the brain, cities and temples, beyond the art of Phidias and Praxiteles—beyond the splendour of Babylon and Hekatómpylos: and 'from the anarchy of dreaming sleep,' callest into sunny light the faces of long-buried beauties . . . thou hast the keys of Paradise, oh, just, subtle, and mighty opium!   (2: 51)

But to describe a dream, drug-induced or not, is inevitably to impose a certain coherence upon it. De Quincey also came to recognize that the drug had destroyed his powers of concentration and, though he eventually claims to have abandoned its use, he is still troubled by terrifying dreams and a powerful sense of guilt.

Only Christopher Herbert and Wendy Jacobson seem to have linked De Quincey's *Confessions* to *The Mystery of Edwin Drood*, but neither of them explores the connection very fully. Dickens "deeply admired" De Quincey (Johnson 2: 1131) and owned a thirteen-volume set of his works (Stonehouse

27). When James T. Fields, De Quincey's American publisher, visited Gad's Hill in May 1869, Dickens mentioned De Quincey's works as "among certain books of which [he] liked to talk during his walks" (Fields 237–38). Fields visited Jasper's opium den with Dickens, escorted by Chief Inspector Field, the model for Inspector Bucket, and noted the haggard proprietress, her " 'Ye'll pay up according, deary, won't ye?' " refrain, and the pipe made of a penny ink-bottle (Fields 202). On 10 October, back at Gad's Hill, Dickens invited Fields to his study and read him the first chapters of *Edwin Drood* (Fields 228), which Fields was to publish in the United States.

When Dickens selected Cloisterham as the "fictitious name" (22; ch. 3) for his cathedral city, he probably recalled De Quincey's novel *Klosterheim: or, the Masque* (1832), which also features a large and mysterious Gothic building. De Quincey's presence in *The Mystery of Edwin Drood* is evident when Jasper listens to the opium woman's mutterings in that first chapter. Jasper considers his own splendid *Arabian Nights* visions to be beyond the woman's stunted imaginative capacity. " 'What visions can *she* have?' " he wonders. " 'Visions of many butchers' shops, and public-houses, and much credit? Of an increase of hideous customers, and this horrible bedstead set upright again, and this horrible court swept clean? What can she rise to, under any quantity of opium, higher than that!' " (10; ch. 1).

Jasper clearly shares De Quincey's reiterated belief that "If a man 'whose talk is of oxen' should become an Opium-eater, the probability is, that (if he is not too dull to dream at all)—he will dream about oxen" (2:12). In the "Introductory Notice" to "*Suspiria de Profundis*" ("Sighs from the Depths," 1845), the first sequel to the *Confessions*, De Quincey declares that comparatively few opium-eaters possess

> this faculty of dreaming splendidly. . . . He whose talk is of oxen, will probably dream of oxen: and the condition of human life, which yokes so vast a majority to a daily experience incompatible with much elevation of thought, oftentimes neutralizes the tone of grandeur in the reproductive faculty of dreaming, even for those whose minds are populous with solemn imagery. Habitually to dream magnificently, a man must have a constitutional determination to reverie.
>
> (15: 129–30)

Jasper considers himself to be, like De Quincey, one of those comparatively rare beings for whom "getting and spending" have not destroyed the ability to evoke visions. He is well placed, by De Quincey's standards, to develop that ability. He lives a quiet life, " 'No whirl and uproar around me, no distracting commerce or calculation, no risk, no change of place, myself devoted to the art I pursue, my business my pleasure,' " but then adds, " 'I hate it. The cramped monotony of my existence grinds me away' " (19; ch. 2). Lay Precentor at Cloisterham, he has a quasi-priestly function and a central role in the solemn processions and liturgies of the Church of England, as performed with pomp and ceremony in a vast and beautiful Gothic cathedral, a situation that feeds his visions of imperial processions which somehow involve the cathedral tower.

We eventually learn that Jasper's *Arabian Nights* visions occur as a coda to the opium dream he repeatedly invokes. They are visions of grandeur and power, extravagant but in themselves probably harmless enough, though the reference to impalement suggests their source in some sense of guilt that anticipates punishment. When Jasper returns to the opium den in chapter 23, some six months after Drood's disappearance, we hear much more about the dreams he regularly went there to experience, and why he travels so far to induce them. We have already seen the opium woman in Cloisterham, where she has come on Jasper's track, aware that in his dreams he repeatedly threatens someone named "Ned," the name by which Jasper alone habitually addresses Edwin Drood (160–62; ch. 14). On Christmas Eve she encounters Drood, and warns him that "Ned" is in danger, but he fails to understand her warning. On that visit she has followed Jasper from London, concerned about his murderous threats, but loses him when he transfers from the train to the Cloisterham omnibus (264; ch. 23).

On his return visit to the opium den, Jasper reveals what he imagines when he smokes opium. The opulent vision of Sultan, dancing girls, and elephants only comes at the end of a session with the drug. At once a triumphal march and a procession to a place of punishment, it always follows his repeated and cherished dream. That dream, programmatically induced over and over when Jasper visits the opium den for the specific purpose of dreaming precisely *that* dream, consists of a phantasmagoric journey with a fellow-traveler, culminating in an intended attack on that traveler, whose name is Ned. When we finally hear more fully about this deliberately induced dream journey, we read it both as self-indulgence—Jasper takes great pleasure in it—and as a repeated rehearsing of his wish to murder Edwin Drood, in order to gain possession of Rosa Bud, Drood's fiancée. She too figures in the dream. " 'I loved you madly,' " Jasper tells Rosa six months after Drood's disappearance. " 'In the distasteful work of the day, in the wakeful misery of the night, girded by sordid realities, or wandering through Paradises and Hells of visions in which I rushed, carrying your image in my arms, I loved you madly' " (214; ch. 19). Dickens conveys the fragmentary nature of such dreams by never letting us fully experience Jasper's dream. He reveals parts of it in chapters 1, 19, and 23, and we must connect them. Dickens's separated and partial revelation of the dream's content reminds us of the difficulty of making opium's fantastic juxtapositions cohere, as in "Kubla Khan" Coleridge admits that he cannot adequately convey his visionary glimpses of the splendors of Xanadu.

When a beginner at opium, Jasper used to sing himself into his reveries, but as he became more used to it, he also became fixed on " 'something [he was] going to do . . . ,' " he tells the opium woman, when he returns to the den after Edwin Drood's disappearance, " 'But had not quite determined to do. . . . Might or might not do.' " Given such a fixation, such an intention, he asks her,

'Should you do it in your fancy, when you were lying here doing this?'
She nods her head. 'Over and over again.'
Just like me! I did it over and over again. I have done it hundreds of thousands of times in this room.'
'It's to be hoped that it was pleasant to do, deary.'
It *was* pleasant to do!'
He says this with a savage air, and a spring or start at her . . . he sinks into his former attitude.
'It was a journey, a difficult and dangerous journey. That was the subject in my mind. A hazardous and perilous journey over abysses where a slip would be destruction. Look down, look down! You see what lies at the bottom there?' . . .
'Well; I have told you. I did it, here, hundreds and thousands of times. What do I say? I did it millions and billions of times. I did it so often, and through such vast expanses of time, that when it was really done, it seemed not worth the doing, it was done so soon.'   (258–60; ch. 23)

Under the woman's careful questioning, Jasper reveals that this repeated dream journey was always the same journey, that he " 'always took the same pleasure in harping on it.' " Eventually it was a real journey that copied the dream journey. He never tired of dreaming the same journey, never sought a change. He came to the opium den only to dream that specific journey: " 'When I could not bear my life, I came to get the relief, and I got it. It WAS one! It WAS one!' This repetition with extraordinary vehemence, and the snarl of a wolf" (260–61; ch. 23). Then the opium woman asks about the fellow-traveler. " 'To think,' he cries, 'how often fellow-traveller, and yet not know it! To think how many times he went the journey, and never saw the road!' " Only after the dream-journey had been accomplished and the repeatedly imagined deed been imagined as done could " 'the changes of colors and the great landscapes and glittering processions' " begin; " 'they couldn't begin till it was off my mind. I had no room till then for anything else.' "

With professional skill, the woman talks him through his vision to reveal its details: a journey, a fellow-traveler, some action he does not put into words, and that she knows better than to try to get him to say. But he saw himself perform that unidentified action, and now sees it again: " 'when it comes to be real at last, it is so short that it seems unreal for the first time.' " It all happens too soon. " 'This is a vision,' " he declares. " 'I shall sleep it

off. It has been too short and easy. I must have a better vision than this; this
is the poorest of all. No struggle, no consciousness of peril, no entreaty—and
yet I never saw *that* before. . . . Look what a poor, mean, miserable thing it
is! *That* must be real. It's over!' '' (261–63; ch. 23).

Jasper has cultivated and enjoyed an obsessive vision, presumably of entic-
ing Edwin Drood to accompany him on a hazardous journey over deep
abysses, and then destroying him. In a famous passage from his *Confessions*,
De Quincey recalls Coleridge describing plates in Piranesi's *Dreams*, that is,
his *Invenzioni Capric di Carceri* (1745, "Imaginary Prisons"):

> Some of them . . . represented vast Gothic halls. . . . Creeping along the sides
> of the walls, you perceived a stair-case; and upon it, groping his way upward,
> was Piranesi himself: follow the stairs a little further, and you perceive it come
> to a sudden abrupt termination, without any balustrade, and allowing no step
> onwards to him who had reached the extremity, except into the depths below.
> Whatever is to become of poor Piranesi, you suppose, at least, that his labours
> must in some way terminate here. But raise your eyes, and behold a second
> flight of stairs still higher: on which again Piranesi is perceived, but this time
> standing on the very brink of the abyss. Again elevate your eye, and a still
> more aerial flight of stairs is beheld and again is poor Piranesi busy on his
> aspiring labours: and so on, until the unfinished stairs and Piranesi both are
> lost in the upper gloom of the hall.—With the same power of endless growth
> and self-reproduction did my architecture proceed in dreams. In the early stage
> of my malady, the splendours of my dreams were indeed chiefly architectural:
> and I beheld such pomps of cities and palaces as was never yet beheld by the
> waking eye, unless in the clouds.
>
>   (De Quincey 2: 68–69; the passage is almost identical in the 1856
>   version. No plate in *Carceri* quite conforms to this description.)

Dickens had remembered this passage when, in *Bleak House*, Esther Summerson experiences a similar dream during her illness, "when I laboured up
colossal staircases, ever striving to reach the top, and ever turned . . . by some
obstruction, and labouring again" (555–56; ch. 35).

Since Jasper's journey is a hazardous one over abysses, it can hardly take
place in the gentle landscape around Cloisterham/Rochester. Macnish suggests that, "if we lie awry, or if our feet slip over the side of the bed,"—Jasper
lies across a broken bedstead when we first meet him (7; ch. 1)—"we often
imagine ourselves standing upon the brink of a fearful precipice, or falling
from its beetling summit into the abyss" (*Philosophy of Sleep* 56). My guess
is that, like Piranesi's, the journey is imagined as taking place within and
perhaps even on top of a great building, Cloisterham cathedral itself. Those
required to pass long periods in a church or other large architectural space
often evade boredom by imagining journeys among its upper reaches. A vast
Gothic cathedral, with its staircases, intricately carved stonework, galleries,
clerestory and access to the roof, offers the locale for such a journey, and for

its fatal ending. While the actual murder of Drood is likely to have been by strangulation, the cathedral is probably the site of Jasper's dream murder, and perhaps of his later capture, as the pursuit up a spiral staircase depicted in the cover design for the monthly numbers of *Edwin Drood* suggests. Jasper's interest in Durdles's keys to the cathedral and the destructive possibilities of quicklime hint that Drood's body may be concealed in the cathedral crypt or the adjacent graveyard.

Jasper's dream journey, with its depths and abysses, recalls De Quincey's description of Piranesi's *Carceri* and De Quincey's own obsessive recollections of vast buildings, dangerous staircases, and great heights. "I seemed every night to descend, not metaphorically, but literally to descend, into chasms and sunless abysses, depths below depths," De Quincey recalls; "The sense of space [was] powerfully affected. Buildings, landscapes, &c. were exhibited in proportions so vast as the bodily eye is not fitted to receive. Space swelled, and was amplified to an extent of unutterable infinity" (De Quincey 2: 66–67; quoted by Macnish, *Philosophy of Sleep* 60).

In "The English Mail-Coach" (1849), his second sequel to the *Confessions*, De Quincey introduces this opium-eater's tendency to enlarge buildings until they seem to stretch to infinity. In that essay he develops another obsessive recollection, of being drugged and riding atop a speeding mail-coach carrying the great news of Wellington's victory at Waterloo through the night:

> Two hours after midnight we reached a mighty minster. Its gates, which rose to the clouds, were closed . . . silently they moved back upon their hinges; and at a flying gallop our equipage entered the grand aisle of the cathedral. Headlong was our pace; and at every altar, in the little chapels and oratories on the right hand and left of our course, the lamps, dying or sickening, kindled anew in sympathy with the secret word that was flying past. Forty leagues we might have run in the cathedral . . . when we saw before us the aerial galleries of the organ and the choir. Every pinnacle of the fret-work, every station of advantage amongst the traceries, was crested by white-robed choristers. . . . Vast sarcophagi rose on every side, having towers and turrets that, upon the limits of the central aisle, strode forward with haughty intrusion, then ran back with mighty shadows into answering recesses.
> (16: 446–48)

Can we recognize in this both the vastness of Cloisterham Cathedral and the oppression Jasper feels while officiating there? Could it not become in his bespoke vision the vast arena where a fatal accident is to be arranged? Whatever the effects of opium on an opium-eater's apprehension of architecture, De Quincey's fantastic description has permitted Jasper to imagine Cloisterham cathedral as vast and menacing in his dream, and Dickens to make it a kind of sinister presence in his novel as in Jasper's life.

De Quincey frequently combines hallucinogens, the Orient, and murder in a thematic cluster that Dickens has carried over into *Edwin Drood*. In the

Confessions he describes recurrent nightmares about a "ferocious looking Malay," who inexplicably came to his door at Grasmere, and to whom he gave some opium. "This Malay . . . fastened afterwards upon my dreams, and brought other Malays with him worse than himself, that ran 'a-muck' at me, and led me into a world of troubles''; he glosses " 'a-muck' " as "the frantic excesses committed by Malays who have taken opium" (De Quincey 2: 57–58). In May 1818 he reports that

> The Malay has been a fearful enemy for months. I have been every night, through his means, transported into Asiatic scenes . . . if I were compelled . . . to live in China, and among Chinese manners and modes of life and scenery, I should go mad. . . . Southern Asia, in general, is the seat of awful images and associations. . . . I could sooner live with lunatics, [1856: "with vermin, with crocodiles or snakes''] . . . I brought together all creatures, birds, beasts, rep-tiles, all trees and plants, . . . and assembled them together in China or Indostan. From kindred feelings, I soon brought Egypt and her gods under the same law. I was stared at, hooted at, grinned at, chattered at, by monkeys, by paroquets, by cockatoos. I ran into pagodas: and was fixed, for centuries, at the summit, or in secret rooms; I was the idol; I was the priest; I was worshipped; I was sacrificed. I fled from the wrath of Brama through all the forests of Asia: Vishnu hated me: Seeva laid in wait for me. I came suddenly upon Isis and Osiris: I had done a deed, they said, which the ibis and the crocodile trembled at. I was buried, for a thousand years, in stone coffins, with mummies and sphynxes, in narrow chambers at the heart of eternal pyramids. I was kissed, with cancerous kisses, by crocodiles, and was laid, confounded with all unutterable slimy things, amongst reeds and Nilotic mud.
> (2: 70–71; the passage is almost identical in the 1856 version)

Macnish quotes most of this long passage in *The Philosophy of Sleep* (95–97) as an example of "the effects produced by [opium] upon the imagination during sleep," giving Dickens a scientist's endorsement for De Quincey's dramatic accounts of opium-induced hallucinations. Rosa Bud succinctly ech-oes it with her hatred of " 'Arabs, and Turks, and Fellahs . . . Pyramids . . . Tiresome old burying-grounds! Isises, and Ibises, and Cheopses . . . Belzoni . . . dragged out by the legs, half choked with bats and dust' " (31; ch. 3).

Jasper's opium dream is also a mixture of terror and guilt, invariably ending in a march to punishment. Dickens connects Jasper's opium use with his murderous intentions and with Oriental references: the Landless twins are from Ceylon, Edwin is going to Egypt. Rosa is even addicted to Turkish Delight. Tartar's unusual name recalls De Quincey's famous essay, "Revolt of the Tartars" (1837). "John Chinaman" is the opium woman's rival and appears on the cover design for serial publication that Dickens instructed Charles Collins, and later Luke Fildes to draw. On that cover, the several vignettes hinting at details of the story are all sustained in the cloud of opium fumes produced by the opium woman and "John Chinaman," puffing away and between them dreaming up the entire novel. Their presence suggests that *The Mystery of Edwin Drood* is really, after all, an opium dream, albeit with apparently fatal consequences. As De Quincey says of his *Confessions*: "Not the opium-eater, but the opium, is the true hero of the tale" (2: 74).

Aesthetic in his visions of the *Arabian Nights*, Jasper is equally so in imagining the murder he is to commit, and its setting. It is to be no sordid stabbing or clubbing, no brutal Bill Sikes murdering Nancy with a heavy club, no Jonas Chuzzlewit assaulting Montague Tigg with a stake torn from a fence, but an artist's performance, worthy of inclusion in De Quincey's two-part essay "On Murder Considered as One of the Fine Arts" (1827, 1839). De Quincey imagines a "Society of Connoisseurs in Murder" (De Quincey 6:112), aesthetes of crime who scorn ordinary murders motivated by rage or greed but admire a murder committed with style, or as an end in itself. In an 1854 "Postscript" added to "On Murder," De Quincey describes the activities of one John Williams, something of a dandy in his personal style, "And, beyond a doubt, in that perilous little branch of business which was practiced by himself he might be regarded as the most aristocratic and fastidious of artists" (20: 43). In December 1811, not far from Jasper's opium den, in a neighborhood where "Lascars, Chinese, Moors, Negroes, were met at every step" (20: 41), Williams terrified London by murdering all four members of the Marr household, one of them a sleeping infant; twelve days later he murdered Mr. and Mrs. Williamson and their servant, near neighbors of the Marrs.

Williams was brutal enough; he smashed his victims' skulls with a hammer, then cut their throats. His motive was robbery. But De Quincey celebrates him as an artist in crime, attempting not so much the perfect crime as crimes that will become notorious for deliberately exterminating entire households. De Quincey insists that such a murderer will strike and strike again. "A murderer who is such by passion and by a wolfish craving for bloodshed as a mode of unnatural luxury cannot relapse into *inertia*," he argues; "Such a man . . . comes to crave the dangers and the hairbreadth escapes of his trade, as a condiment for seasoning the insipid monotonies of daily life" (20: 55). Jasper has used his murderous dream to offset " 'the cramped monotony of my existence' " (19; ch. 2). With Drood dead, we expect he will murder again; he threatens Landless, telling Rosa Bud that he can make Landless appear responsible for Drood's disappearance. Jasper kills Landless in many suggested solutions to the novel's mystery.

Williams had planned the Marr murders carefully. He and Marr had once been friends, had sailed to India together. De Quincey considers their later rivalry for Mrs. Marr the probable motive for the murders. Careful planning, a close relationship with the victim, sexual rivalry, and a real or imaginary experience of the East, all played their part, as they do in *The Mystery of Edwin Drood*. De Quincey's sinister Malay was a "tiger-cat" (2: 57), and in the "Postscript" to "On Murder" he equates Williams's "tiger spirit" with "the murderous mind" and notes the murderer's "natural tiger character . . . the tiger's heart was masked by the most insinuating and snaky refinement" (20: 42–43). In Cloisterham Jasper is trusted and respected for his musical abilities. His murderous potential is masked, recognized only by the opium woman, who on Christmas Eve tries to warn Edwin Drood of his danger. Dickens waits until chapter 23 to show us Jasper's "savage air" as he remembers the deed he has repeatedly imagined, and his sudden "spring or start" at the opium woman as he does so, neatly endowing Jasper with Williams's "tiger spirit" and "wolfish craving for bloodshed."

Neville Landless admits to Crisparkle that he himself might have " 'a drop of what is tigerish in my blood,' " contracted somehow from the " 'inferior race' " among whom he has been brought up in Ceylon (64; ch. 7). After quarreling with Drood at Jasper's, Neville describes the encounter to Crisparkle and blames Drood for heating " 'that tigerish blood I told you of' " (80; ch. 8); Jasper has followed him and probably eavesdropped, for he echoes the phrase a few moments later, describing the quarrel to Crisparkle and adding, " 'There is something of the tiger in [Neville's] dark blood' " (80–81; ch. 8).

The Marrs' servant had been sent on an errand and so survived. When she returned and no one answered the bell, she became alarmed. As she knocked and rang, she heard someone breathing, and a furtive step inside the door. "What was the murderer's meaning in coming along the passage to the front door?" De Quincey asks;

> The meaning was this: Separately, as an individual, Mary was worth nothing at all to him. But, considered as a member of a household, she had this value, viz. that she, if caught and murdered, perfected and rounded the desolation of the house . . . The whole covey of victims was thus netted; the household ruin was thus full and orbicular.   (20: 50)

De Quincey considers that for Williams the murder was aesthetically imperfect if any member of the household survived. He risked capture by delaying his escape in order to make his deed more notorious in the annals of crime by adding a final victim. This seems farfetched, but it is De Quincey's notion of how a murderer might think if he considered murder to be a fine art. In Williams's second murder, he lingers to search the house for other victims, in the same quest for perfection.

Jasper could have contrived any of a dozen ways to kill Edwin Drood, and as his trusted kinsman had plenty of opportunity to do so. The opium-induced rehearsals of the murder are thrilling to him, an exciting pleasure that may partly have been a way of accustoming himself to the idea of killing. The imaginary murder is perhaps more important to him than its actual commission; it satisfies him aesthetically in a way that killing Drood could not.

De Quincey insists that Williams lingered at his second murder scene to find and kill a child he knew was asleep upstairs, to complete the household, but also to savor her terror and pleas for mercy. A lodger in the house saved the child, but the delay led to Williams's capture. "To an epicure in murder such as Williams," De Quincey suggests, "it would be taking away the very sting of the enjoyment if the poor child" should die "without fully apprehending the misery of the situation. . . . in a murder of pure voluptuousness, . . . where no hostile witness was to be removed, no extra booty to be gained, and no revenge to be gratified, it is clear that to hurry would be altogether to ruin." De Quincey defends himself against the charge that he is exaggerating or romanticizing Williams's "pure fiendishness" in a footnote, insisting that "except for the luxurious purpose of basking and reveling in the anguish of dying despair, he had no motive at all . . . for attempting the murder of this young girl" (20: 65). Is Jasper's tormenting Rosa while serving as her music teacher, and later beside the sundial in the Nuns' House garden, another luxurious "basking and reveling" in a terrified victim?

Jasper doesn't just want Drood dead. He wants to kill him in a certain way, and he wants his victim to know his murderer and to plead with him for his life—a feature of the dream, apparently, but not of the actual murder. " 'It has been too short and easy,' " he complains; " '. . . No struggle, no consciousness of peril, no entreaty' " (263; ch. 23). But the dream is not a very effective way of planning a crime. For Jasper, to do the deed is not enough. It must be done aesthetically, at Christmas, in or near a Christian church he hates as the scene of his dreary routine, and it must create a mystery that will long be discussed. If Drood's body had been found in Cloisterham Weir, instead of his watch and shirt-pin, he might have been considered the victim of a casual assault. Jasper wants him to be seen as the victim of determined malevolence. By arranging events in such a way that Drood seems to have been murdered by Neville Landless, Jasper would perfect his crime by making Landless a second victim, thus eliminating both of his rivals for Rosa. It is indeed murder as a fine art.

WORKS CITED

Collins, Wilkie. *The Moonstone.* Ed. J. I. M. Stewart. Harmondsworth: Penguin, 1966.

De Quincey, Thomas. *Works.* Ed. Grevel Lindop. 21 vols. London: Pickering and Chatto, 2000–03.

Dickens, Charles. *Bleak House*. Ed. Nicola Bradbury. London: Penguin, 1996.

———. *The Letters of Charles Dickens*. Vol. 4 (1844–46). Ed. Kathleen Tillotson. Oxford: Clarendon, 1977.

———. *The Letters of Charles Dickens*. Vol. 12 (1868–70). Ed. Graham Storey. Oxford: Clarendon, 2002.

———. *The Mystery of Edwin Drood*. Ed. David Paroissien. London: Penguin, 2002.

———. *Oliver Twist*. Ed. Kathleen Tillotson. Oxford: Clarendon, 1966.

Elliotson, John. *Human Physiology*. London, 1835.

Fields, James T. *Yesterdays with Authors*. Boston, 1872.

Hayter, Alethea. *Opium and the Romantic Imagination*. Berkeley: U of California P, 1968.

Herbert, Christopher. "De Quincey and Dickens." *Victorian Studies* 17:3 (March 1974): 247–63.

Jacobson, Wendy S. *The Companion to "The Mystery of Edwin Drood."* London: Allen & Unwin, 1986.

Johnson, Edgar. *Charles Dickens: His Tragedy and Triumph*. 2 vols. New York: Simon and Schuster, 1952.

Macnish, Robert. *The Anatomy of Drunkenness*. New York: Appleton, 1835.

———. *The Philosophy of Sleep*. 2nd edition. Glasgow: W. R. M'Phun, 1834.

Paroissien, David. *The Companion to Oliver Twist*. Edinburgh: Edinburgh UP, 1992.

Piranesi, Giovanni Battista. *The Prisons [Le Carceri]*. New York: Dover, 1973.

Stonehouse, J. H. *Catalogue of the Libraries of Charles Dickens and W. M. Thackeray*. London, 1935.

Intoxication, Provocation, and Derangement: Interrogating the Nature of Criminal Responsibility in *The Mystery of Edwin Drood*

Stephanie Peña-Sy

This article argues that Dickens's unfinished final novel, The Mystery of Edwin Drood *(1870), contains phantom trajectories of an unborn commentary on the triangulation of the Victorians' developing understanding of the unconscious mind, the law, and the medical/legal turf war then being fought over criminal responsibility. Contrary to legal critics' claims that Dickens's novels are backward glances at near-extinct issues of law, I argue that studying the Drood case alongside real-life court cases reveals Dickens's engagement with a current, emerging medico-legal discourse that he foresaw would change the structure of future criminal defenses. This article moots the cases a prosecutor might bring against the two most likely suspects, Neville Landless and John Jasper, and centers both their defenses on the exculpatory potential of both characters' having episodes of altered consciousness. Ultimately, I argue that Dickens is exploring the way in which a legal acknowledgement of altered states and dual personalities might produce the moral vacuum of crimes without a criminally responsible perpetrator.*

Even in its unfinished state, *The Mystery of Edwin Drood* evinces an interest in the scholarly legal discourse that Dickens more fully engages with in novels such as *The Pickwick Papers* and *Bleak House*. The undeveloped subplots surrounding two major characters—Neville Landless's studies in law and John Jasper's evidence-gathering activities toward the end of the unfinished novel—give the reader the imaginative space to conceive of the plot eventually going to court and either one of these two characters being pressed into using his newly acquired knowledge to mount a legal defense. As one critic notes, "much is hinted, much is left unsaid, and it is possible to see many different patterns" (Forsyte 24) in the novel, and for this reason, there is a rich post-*Drood* tradition of speculation. I do not intend to participate, however, in the "whodunit" back-and-forth that dominates the post-*Drood* critical conversation. Instead, this examination of some of the "many different patterns" of the Drood case will contend that in his final novel Dickens has left behind the phantom trajectories of an unborn commentary on the triangulation of the Victorians' developing understanding of the unconscious mind, the law, and the medical/legal turf war then being fought over criminal responsibility. This article will contextualize Dickens's writing against the available legal defenses of his time for the purpose of mooting the two most likely prosecutorial tracks: namely, that either Neville Landless or John Jasper is criminally responsible for the murder of Edwin Drood.

Readers of *Little Dorrit, The Pickwick Papers*, or *Bleak House* will know that Dickens's engagement with the law in his writing often comes in the form of blistering critiques of the injustice of the legal system's inefficiency. Contemporary legal intellectuals reciprocally engaged with Dickens and his fiction. James Fitzjames Stephen, a major Victorian legal thinker often referred to as the first historian of English criminal law, reviewed some of Dickens's novels and in the article "The License of Modern Novelists" accuses Dickens of "beget[ting] hasty generalisations and false conclusions" in applying his "imagination upon subjects which properly belong to the intellect" (Collins 378). Randall Craig sums up the debate between Dickens and Stephen as being over "fictional license, whether placed in service of law or literature," and its "strict adherence to 'the rule of truth' " (109). Dickens objects to "the irresponsible use of suppositional narrative . . . in the pursuit of 'truth and justice' " (111) while, inversely, Stephen objects to the "depiction of judicial institutions in fictional narratives" (112) and "the fictional misrepresentations of public institutions" (121).

In general, what many of Dickens's detractors contend is that his novels sound a forward-looking reformist tone when, in fact, "they tended toward a retrospective portrait of the law, looking backward to times when abuses had been unchecked" (Boyer 600) and, consequently,

> Dickens's treatment of nineteenth-century law has been most misleading [because] he gives no indication that the problems he depicts were the symptoms which had even then called forth reform . . . his portraits read like indictments; they were actually obituaries.   (Boyer 622)

Stephen writes in "Mr. Dickens as a Politician" that,

> Imprisonment for debt on *mesne* process was doomed, if not abolished, before he wrote *Pickwick*. The Court of Chancery was reformed before he published *Bleak House*. In his attacks on Parliament he certainly relied on his own experience, and was utterly and hopelessly wrong. (8)

Whether or not Dickens's legal arguments in the novels prior to *The Mystery of Edwin Drood* do in fact constitute elegies for Victorian legal procedure is beyond the scope of this project. I argue, however, that *The Mystery of Edwin Drood* is structured in such a way that had this novel been completed, it would have broken with the backward-looking approach the critics argue marks Dickens's use of legal discourse in fiction. In his final novel, Dickens raises issues surrounding criminal responsibility, intent, and the nature of the criminal mind that were *current* concepts in scholarly debate at the time of his writing. This unfinished novel represents Dickens's attempt to engage with emerging—rather than vestigial—legal issues. In fact, many of the issues I will argue are being set up in *The Mystery of Edwin Drood* are precisely the issues that James Fitzjames Stephen himself formally expounds and codifies in his own opus, *The Digest of Criminal Law*, several years after Dickens's death.

To begin, I must explain my methodology. I make four central assumptions. First, I assume that Edwin Drood is, in fact, dead. There is not, by any means, a critical consensus surrounding this assumption. Felix Aylmer, for example, takes inspiration from the fact that Dickens once considered entitling the novel "In Hiding" and proposes that Drood has *not*, in fact, been killed and has instead gone into hiding after surviving an attempted murder. I cast my lot with the mainstream view that Drood has been murdered and is not in hiding, however, because I find the contrary claims about Drood's fate made by Dickens's daughter, Kate Perugini, and Dickens's friend, executor, and biographer John Forster[1] more persuasive. Second, I assume that Drood's death results from a culpable homicide rather than from accident or misadventure: I do not, for example, explore the possibility that Drood had slipped and fallen into the weir on the night of his disappearance. Third, I focus on Jasper and Neville Landless as murder suspects even as I concede that the other characters in the novel are theoretically not beyond suspicion. And, fourth, I use the first meeting of Jasper, Neville Landless, and Drood in the "Daggers Drawn" chapter as the model or template for my speculations on the same three characters' actions during the second dinner party held on the night of Drood's disappearance.

My investigation focuses on two periods in legal history. The first coincides with the time leading up to the novel's narrative present, which, based on the narrative's descriptions of the railways in relation to Cloisterham (as it stands in for Rochester), is widely thought to be the 1840s. The second time period of legal history I examine coincides with the decade or so directly preceding the publication of the first monthly number of *The Mystery of Edwin Drood* in April 1870. My discussion centers on and cites from the case law generated in these two intervals with special emphasis on the cases that were decided closest to these two time periods. I refer to case law to illuminate Dickens's narrative with the confidence that his prior interest in and experience with writing on the law combined with the widespread availability of information about ongoing court cases[2] mean that Dickens would probably have been aware of the developing legal innovations to which I now call attention.

And, finally, I concentrate my legal speculations on the notion that Edwin Drood's murder was committed during an altered state of consciousness and I do not consider, for example, the legal ramifications of either Jasper's or Neville Landless's murdering Drood because of a simple case of lover's jealousy. Only the possibilities of criminal acts performed in an altered state—in the various forms offered for consideration in *The Mystery of Edwin Drood*, including those produced by pathological anger, intoxication, and addiction—are discussed in this essay. Jasper and Neville Landless are both depicted as being capable of phasing in and out of their conscious selves: Neville Landless has bursts of passionate anger he attributes to "a drop of what is tigerish in [his] blood" (90) while the Jasper under the influence of opium smoke is contrasted with the Jasper who is "quite himself" (41). Dickens also explicitly makes the point that the novel is a meditation on the ontology of doubled consciousness:

> As in some cases of drunkenness, and in others of animal magnetism, there are two states of consciousness which never clash, but each of which pursues its separate course as though it were continuous instead of broken (thus, if I hide my watch when I am drunk, I must be drunk again before I can remember where), so Miss Twinkleton has two distinct and separate phases of being.
>
> (53)

"Drunkenness," "animal magnetism," and "two states of consciousness . . . two distinct and separate phases of being" (53): this passage embodies almost all of the issues I contend are central to the criminal investigation of the events in *The Mystery of Edwin Drood*.

In Defense of Neville Landless

I begin this pseudo-moot with the finger of suspicion pointed at Neville Land-less. First, if Neville Landless had voluntarily drunk wine and had become voluntarily intoxicated, then he would have no legal defense against the charge of murder. At the time of Dickens's writing, there was a no-defense rule of intoxication and common law considered the act of becoming intoxicated as tantamount to extreme recklessness. However, after the first dinner party in the "Daggers Drawn" chapter, the reader is given an intimation that Neville Landless's angry overreaction to Edwin Drood is partially the result of drinking the tainted wine in Jasper's lodgings. In this episode, the narrative specifically mentions that the wine "seems to require much mixing and compounding" and that Jasper suspiciously "*turns his back* to mix a jug of mulled wine at the fire" (100; emphasis added). Jasper also goads the two men into drinking quickly as he "sets the example of nearly emptying his glass" (101). Soon after Neville Landless and Drood follow suit, their description indicates the wine they had consumed had been suspiciously strong:

> Edwin Drood's face has become quickly and remarkably flushed by the wine; so has the face of Neville Landless . . . [Edwin's] speech has become thick and indistinct . . . when Neville speaks, *his* speech is also thick and indistinct.
> (101; emphasis original)

In fact, Neville Landless recognizes an unusual quality to his intoxication and in his recapitulation of events during his visit with Mr. Crisparkle after his first angry, drunken outburst at Jasper's party, Neville Landless says that although "[he] ha[s] had very little indeed to drink . . . it overcame [him] in the strangest and most sudden manner" (103). Moreover, another episode in the novel shows Jasper to be no stranger to using drugged wine to facilitate his exploitation of people. During their nighttime excursion in the "A Night with Durdles" chapter, Jasper plies Durdles with tainted wine in order to steal time alone in the crypt. When he wakes Durdles from his narcotized sleep, Jasper jokes about having "suspicions that my bottle was filled with something stiffer than either of us supposed" (158). The upshot of this line of speculation is the suggestion that any violent acts committed by Neville Landless while intoxicated may have been the result of an *involuntary* intoxication.

The involuntary nature of the intoxication negatives *mens rea* and as soon as the idea of the intoxication being involuntary is introduced, the burden of proof shifts to the Crown. A landmark case addressing this issue of a difference between voluntary and involuntary intoxication had in fact been decided not long before the novel's narrative present: in *Rex v. Pearson* (1835) 2 Lew. CC 144, the court decided that "if a party be made drunk by stratagem, or the fraud of another, he is not responsible for his actions" and drunkenness could, in such cases, be taken into consideration to mitigate the accused's actions.

Dickens also makes a suggestive, if slightly fanciful, gesture at the possibility that Jasper had not only drugged but also exerted a mesmerist's ventriloquizing power over Neville Landless. In the episode at the end of the "Daggers Drawn" chapter, for example, there is a striking similarity in the phraseology of Neville Landless's and Jasper's accounts of Neville's internal state during his fight with Drood. Neville claims, "he goaded me . . . beyond the power of my endurance . . . in short, sir, . . . in the passion into which [Drood] lashed me, *I would have cut him down* if I could, and I tried to do it" (104; emphasis added), and the diction of Jasper's subsequent report of the same incident echoes Neville's: "He might have laid my dear boy [Drood] dead at my feet . . . he *would have cut him down* on my hearth" (105; emphasis added), Jasper says, prompting Mr. Crisparkle to think, "Ah . . . his [Neville's] own words" (105). It is also during the same incident that Neville Landless's words of "wretched self-reproach" about his "tigerish blood" mirrors Jasper's saying "there is something of the tiger in [Neville's] dark blood" (105). Once again, Mr. Crisparkle, who is described at one point as acting "as skillfully as a Police Expert," notices the similarity in the language of the two reports: " 'Ah!' thinks Mr. Crisparkle, 'so he said!' " (105).[3]

There is another, more overt, reference to Jasper's mesmeric influence. The narrative describes "the old horrible feeling of being compelled by [Jasper] assert[ing] its hold upon [Rosa]" from "the moment she sees him from the porch" (226), furthering the notion of Jasper as mesmerist and ventriloquist who not only severs his victims' control over their will, but also compels them to act and think according to his (Jasper's) will. That Neville Landless may have committed the murder while under Jasper's spell is a tantalizing possibility and constructing a legal defense of automatism would certainly have appealed to Dickens's well-known fascination with mesmerism. Dickens is known to have frequented demonstrations of hypnotism by John Elliotson—a professor of clinical medicine who Dickens would go on to make his family doctor—and to have later himself become an amateur "magnetiser" who "his son often saw . . . send people into a 'strange sleep' " (Ackroyd 245).

However, since the reader does not actually "witness" the conjectured second drugging scene during the dinner in the "When Shall These Three Meet Again?" chapter, it would be profitable to revisit the crime and develop another potential line of criminal defense that is set up by the narrative. That is, even if the Crown were to prove successfully that Neville Landless had committed the homicide while, at the same time, his defense were to fail to prove a diminished capacity due to intoxication or automatism on his part, the language of the narrative nevertheless leaves open the possibility that Landless could plead a defense of provocation. The prior pattern of animosity between Drood and him would make such a sequence of events highly likely.

Drood is described as purposely antagonizing Neville Landless "with a provoking yawn" (100) during their first dinner. Mr. Crisparkle notes after Drood
and Neville Landless's argument that "Mr. Neville, on that unfortunate occasion, commits himself under provocation" (120). Helena Landless reads the
animosity between Drood and her brother in a similar way: she reports the
story of the dinnertime altercation to Rosa, "dwelling with a flushed cheek
on the *provocation* her brother had received" (108; emphasis added) and,
in another conversation, defends him, saying, "he was provoked" (126)
by Drood.

Dickens's use of the concept of provocation as a criminal defense must be
historically contextualized. The courts at this time were willing to allow for
the overpowering effect of *furor brevis*. The standard especially relevant to
the 1840s—the narrative's "now"—was at the time taken by the courts to
be set by *Rex v. Thomas* (1833), which stated that the homicide:

> will be only manslaughter, provided the fatal blow is to be attributed to the
> passion of anger arising from the previous provocation. The law requires two
> things—first, that there should be the provocation; and, second, that the fatal
> blow should be clearly traced to the passion arising from that provocation.

According to *Thomas*, the act is manslaughter rather than murder as long
as the violence clearly results from the act of provocation and the criminal
act is performed before there has been "time for passion to cool." Even
more interesting is that in October 1869, just months before the first number
of *The Mystery of Edwin Drood* is published, the *Regina v. Welsh* (1869) 11
Cox CC 336 decision applied another major test to this principle of provocation. To *Thomas*'s requirements regarding the timing of the act, the 1869
courts added the question of the nature of the actions that could be taken to
constitute provocation, holding that

> not merely whether there was passion in point of fact, but whether there was
> such provocation as might naturally kindle ungovernable passion in the mind
> of any *ordinary and reasonable man*. Such provocation must be something
> serious—as a blow; and mere words, or gestures, not accompanied with any-
> thing of such a serious character, will not, in point of law, be sufficient to
> reduce the crime to manslaughter.

The *Welsh* decision in turn raises two related questions that pertain to the
novel's narrative: namely, the legal fiction of the "ordinary and reasonable
man" and Neville Landless's characterization vis-à-vis this legal fiction. Critics have cited Dickens's treatments of the fiction that "a wife is 'one' with
her husband" in *Oliver Twist* and *Hard Times*, the special bail procedure of
using strawmen in *Pickwick Papers*, and the legal fiction of corporate per-
sonhood (whereby corporations are treated as if they were individuals) in

Martin Chuzzlewit as instances of his advocacy for legal reforms to abolish the antiquated legal fictions that burdened English common law. I argue that in *The Mystery of Edwin Drood*, Dickens is similarly critiquing the legal fiction of the "ordinary and reasonable man" as it stands for an ostensibly objective standard that the jury takes to understand as referring to an ordinary member of the society which they themselves represent.

The narrative of *The Mystery of Edwin Drood* questions the usefulness of such an ill-defined normative category and pierces the veil of objectivity in its construction of the persona of Neville Landless. Foreign-bred, possessing an "un-English complexion" (Dickens 188), and "brought up among abject and servile dependents of an inferior race" (90), Neville Landless is portrayed as marginalized by Empire beyond the domestic English conception of an "ordinary and reasonable man." Dickens suggests that perhaps what to a Cloisterham resident are the "mere words, or gestures" that the *Welsh* decision dismisses as insufficient grounds for provocation may amount to justifiable provocation to one accustomed to standards formed elsewhere. It must be noted, however, that Dickens builds a polarity between the residents of Cloisterham and their view of Neville as someone alienated from the Englishness of their cathedral town only to subvert it. Dickens's description, "so silent are the streets of Cloisterham (though prone to echo on the smallest provocation)" (51), intimates that the image of a peaceful Cloisterham might be a chimera, not only in the sense that it is an illusion but also in that there might be a different, less peaceable, reality lurking beneath. The idea of the peace and order of a small English town full of living specimens of the legal fiction of the "ordinary and reasonable man" as being vulnerable to "the smallest provocation" (51) certainly calls into question the assumed conceptual distance between Neville Landless's "un-English complexion" (188) and the old Cathedral town.

Rex v. Meakin (1836) 7 C & P 817, a case decided not long before the narrative's present, introduces yet another dimension to Neville Landless's potential criminal defense. If his defense were to prove successfully that Drood had provoked him and also were to reintroduce the idea that Landless had been intoxicated at the time of his altercation with Drood, then their case would almost certainly be built upon the scenario at the core of the *Meakin* decision.

> If a man uses a *stick*, you would not infer a malicious intent so strongly against him, *if drunk*, when he made an intemperate use of it, as you would if he had used a different kind of weapon; but where a dangerous instrument is used, which, if used, must produce grievous bodily harm, drunkenness can have no effect in the consideration of the malicious intent of the party.
>
> (emphasis added)

In other words, intoxication—while not in itself a defense—would be seen as modifying intent, and the lack of inherent lethality in Neville Landless's walking-stick would form the basis of his defense as a provoked assailant. Here, however, the status of Neville Landless's walking stick in the narrative must be examined.

In "When Shall These Three Meet Again?" Neville Landless is described as spending the afternoon packing and preparing for a fortnight-long walking tour on which he plans to depart the morning after the fateful reconciliation dinner to be held at Jasper's gatehouse. The narrative describes "a heavy walking-stick" that he has purchased "in the High Street . . . at the same time and at the same place" (172) with the rest of his walking equipment. It is described as "strong in the handle for the grip of the hand, and iron-shod" (172) and, as he later tells his sister, it is made out of "iron-wood" (175). The narrative devotes a notable amount of attention to the construction and heft of this walking-stick, and Neville Landless's decision to carry it to his dinner appointment sets it up as a possible murder weapon.

First, since he plans to "start to-morrow morning" (174), he does not bring his knapsack to dinner and yet, as he "is in the act of going . . . he turns back again for his walking-stick, thinking he will carry it now" (172). Also, the reader sees Neville Landless as he "tries [the walking-stick and] *swings it*" (172; emphasis added) in his room, giving not only an early foreshadowing image of the walking-stick's potential as a weapon but also of Neville Landless's awareness of its being one. In addition, when Neville Landless meets Mr. Crisparkle in the stairway, he is told that the walking-stick is not at all appropriate for walking because it is "much too heavy, . . . *much* too heavy" (172; emphasis original) yet, despite this, he decides to carry the walking-stick to dinner that evening. Neville Landless's decision to bring the walking-stick could in this way be interpreted as his deliberately bringing a ready weapon to his meeting with Drood; this would certainly jeopardize the possible defense that the stick had been used, in a defense using the formulation of the *Meakin* decision, only "intemperately" rather than "maliciously." The Crown could easily juxtapose these facts regarding the walking-stick and the history of animosity between Neville Landless and Drood to argue that there was malice aforethought on Neville Landless's part. Even more damning is that when, on the morning after Drood's disappearance, a deputation from Cloisterham tries to take Neville Landless into custody, he resists arrest and is subdued only after "the heavy stick had descended smartly" (185) on one of his captors. The "smears [of blood] which the bright cold air had already dried" (187) onto the walking-stick are then regarded by the arresting party as suspicious and proof of Neville Landless's guilt despite the fact that the smears had almost certainly been incurred during the struggle preceding the arrest. More important than the smears, though, is the violent instinct Neville

Landless evinces in automatically using the walking-stick as a weapon—clearly, he is well-acquainted with the stick's potential to inflict bodily harm.

Ultimately, however, the dominant critical opinion is that despite the presence of any physical and circumstantial evidence against Neville Landless, the combination of motive, opportunity and the malevolence of his characterization make Jasper the most likely murderer. Refining a distinction that Carlo Fruttero and Franco Lucentini make between *Drood* readers who are "Porfirians" and those who are "Agathists," Gerhard Joseph explains that:

> Agathists claim . . . the novel's detective story intention is crystal clear from the beginning and that the conventions of that genre demand a surprise ending, i.e., an ending that swerves away from the extant work's manifest implication that it is John Jasper who has murdered Drood.   (162)

Porfirians, on the other hand, are "those who already consider *The Mystery of Edwin Drood* less a detective story than a psychological thriller" (162). To Porfirians, there is no value in pursuing an outcome different from what Dickens's plot seems to offer at its midpoint: what is "truly original" (166) in the novel is not the possibility of someone other than Jasper's being the murderer but "rather [his] character and perverse motivation" (166). The second part of this moot thus shifts from an Agathist to a Porfirian approach to the novel, and considers the circumstances surrounding Jasper's possible commission of the crime and the criminal defenses that were available to him at the time.

In Defense of John Jasper

In our speculations about the guilt of Jasper, one scenario that must be raised and can be immediately dismissed is the possibility that he is, in fact, guilty of drugging Neville Landless's mulled wine and then somehow—by suggestion or by mesmerism or animal magnetism—causing him to murder Drood. In this case, Jasper would be accused of counseling murder, a charge against which he would have no real defense. The more common view, however, is that Drood had been murdered by Jasper's own hand and that Jasper's "large black scarf of strong close-woven silk" (180) is the murder weapon. Indeed, the scene in which Jasper pauses before going into the fateful dinner with Neville Landless and Drood strikes an ominous note: Jasper "pauses for an instant in the [arched entrance of his dwelling] to pull off that great black scarf, and bring it in a loop upon his arm [and] [f]or that brief time, his face is knitted and stern" (182). In addition, Jasper's covetous attraction to Drood's fiancée is a strong motive for murder, and there are intimations of Jasper's habitually having had violence-filled opium-fueled fantasies.

The very fact that he is a habitual opium-smoker, however, raises multiple legal issues about, again, intoxication and criminal responsibility. As has already been established earlier, the Victorian courts equated voluntary intoxication with extreme recklessness and did not consider it a valid legal defense for murder. Specific aspects of Jasper's character construction open up a few alternative avenues for consideration, though, that challenge whether one can unproblematically consider his intoxication from opium use as wholly voluntary. In *Rex v. Rennie* (1825) 1 Lew CC 76, the courts created an exclusion to the general rule on intoxication, ruling that intoxication does not constitute a legal defense ''unless the derangement [intoxication] causes becomes *fixed and continued*, by the [intoxication] being *habitual* and thereby rendering the party incapable of distinguishing between right and wrong'' (emphasis added). This distinction between simple intoxication and the syndrome of ''fixed and continued'' delusion resulting from habitual intoxication is what I argue Dickens is trying to dramatize through Jasper's opium habit. If Jasper is able to prove that he is an opium addict and that he committed the murder of Drood during one of recurring paroxysms—which he explains (mendaciously) as being ''the effects of the medicine steal over [him] like a blight or a cloud, and pass'' (47)—then his defense would be able to take advantage of the *Rennie* decision's provisions on pathological intoxication. And, indeed, Rosa Budd would be able to testify to the fact that Jasper had, prior to Drood's disappearance, exhibited symptoms of just such an altered state even without the presence of a direct trigger (i.e., a dose of opium): she has been present ''when a glaze comes over [his eyes] . . . and he seems to wander away into a frightful sort of dream in which he threatens most'' (95). Mr. Tope describes witnessing a similar episode in which Jasper ''ha[d] a kind of fit on him . . . his memory grew DAZED'' before soon recovering and ''go[ing] home quite himself '' (41; emphasis original).

This avenue of defense remains open to Jasper, however, even if his friends and neighbors (the typical pool from which witnesses in an insanity trial would be chosen) had been unable to detect this altered state of opium-induced impairment and could not testify to indications of derangement or delusion. It is crucial, at this point, to remember once more that *The Mystery of Edwin Drood*'s narrative is set in the 1840s because it was in 1843 that the Victorian courts decided a landmark case that would become the turning point in the history of the insanity defense. In January 1843, Daniel McNaughton,[4] laboring under the delusion that he was at the center of a conspiracy that involved the Pope and the Tory government, assassinated Prime Minister Peel's secretary. McNaughton's victim was Edward Drummond, whose name is tantalizingly assonant with Dickens's Edwin Drood.

McNaughton's barrister secured an acquittal during the jury trial but following the public uproar that greeted the verdict, Queen Victoria asked the House of Lords to retry the case. McNaughton was eventually acquitted a second time but it was in the course of this retrial that the insanity defense became officially formulated in the McNaughton Rules.[5] After the McNaughton case, witnesses for the defense were "restrict[ed] . . . to commenting on the knowing faculties" of the defendant and the focus in the courtroom turned to "criteria defining the accused's failure to understand the nature of the crime and the difference between right and wrong" (Eigen 6).

The aspect of *Regina v. M'Naghten* (1843) 10 Cl & Fin 200 of particular relevance to this discussion of Dickens's novel is the court's consideration of the forms delusions may take.

> Persons of otherwise sound mind, might be affected by morbid delusions . . . that a person so laboring under a morbid delusion, might have a moral perception of right and wrong, but that in the case of the prisoner it was a delusion which carried him away beyond the power of his control, and left him no such perception; and that he was *not capable of exercising any control over acts which had connexion with his delusion*: that it was the nature of the disease with which the prisoner was affected, to go on gradually until it had reached a climax, when it burst forth with irresistible intensity: that a man *might go on for years quietly*, though at the same time under its influence, but would *all at once break out into the most extravagant and violent paroxysms*.
>
> (emphasis added)

The Mystery of Edwin Drood shows signs of Dickens's interest in the entirely new medico-legal discourse the McNaughton case left in its wake. Until 1800, the courts did not acknowledge the concept of occasional insanity, fearing it could never be sure if a defendant had committed the crime during a lucid interval: acquittal required evidence of a complete and utter delirium and a total loss of reason. *Rex v. Hadfield* (1800) 27 St Tr 1281 introduced the concept of a "circumscribed delirium" in which the court would entertain as grounds for acquittal a "partial derangement—'total' to be sure when the subject of the delusory fear or belief was touched upon—but absent when any other subject was invoked." In 1843, *McNaughton* built on this and introduced the possibility of, essentially, symptom-free criminal insanity. First, it introduced the idea of

> a form of insanity that featured no delirium, no delusion, indeed no confusion at all. This was not an intellectual but a moral insanity, in which the afflicted was carried away by *perverse sentiments* although conscious to some extent of what he was doing. He was suffering, quite literally, from a will out of control.
>
> (emphasis added)

Criminal responsibility, then, became a problem of volitional chaos and, significantly, the *McNaughton* decision addresses the possibility that the criminally insane person might "not [be] capable of exercising any control over acts which had connexion with his delusion." Delusion, in other words, can carry a will to action but such a will, considered devoid of understanding, is not seen as being able to exercise a choice or intent: even the elaborate preparations Jasper carried out before murdering Edwin could not be used as proof of guilt because, in essence, Jasper would be able to plead that "the delusion did it all." The post-*McNaughton* split between intention and action as well as the possibility of action in the absence of intention produced a language in which "the defendant was described as 'missing', not merely deluded" (Eigen 12): after *McNaughton*, "one finds medical witnesses citing the vagaries of consciousness, and specifically the condition of unconsciousness, in testimony that sidestepped a diagnosis of madness" (155). The fact that Jasper is not in a permanently delusional state, then, does not discount him from being considered not responsible for his criminal acts. His defense could point to his reliance on opium and conjecture that despite his having "go[ne] on for years quietly," Jasper had, in fact, been in a permanent—albeit passive—state of delusion and had been "missing" during the commission of the criminal act.

Forsyte posits a theory that takes the notion of Jasper as having periods of being "missing" even further and proposes that Dickens had intended *The Mystery of Edwin Drood* to be a groundbreaking novel about the criminal dual personality: "if Dickens had lived a few months longer," Forsyte claims, "the world would never have heard of Dr. Jekyll or Mr. Hyde" (104). To this end, Forsyte conceives of two separate personae inhabiting the "Jasper" character: one he refers to as Jasper the choirmaster and another he terms the Murderer, and describes Jasper's transition from one state to the other as being flagged by his paroxysmal fits. Forsyte is not the first to point out this fracture in Jasper's characterization, of course, as Edmund Wilson refers to Jasper's "dual consciousness" and the conflicting influences of "the bad and the good in one man" (81) in his 1941 essay, "Dickens: The Two Scrooges." E. D. H. Johnson proposes a similar duality in Jasper and reads the novel's introductory passage that weaves together the two worlds of Cloisterham and the hallucinatory Orient as emblematizing this dual nature (137).[6] What is novel about Forsyte's approach, however, is his rejection of opium as the root cause of Jasper's psychological fissure. He proposes that Dickens would not have been interested in "produc[ing] an imitation *Moonstone* [Wilkie Collins's novel]" (51) and for that reason, insists that "Jasper's special [personality shifting] fits had no connection with opium" (62). Were this the case, Dickens's plan for the novel would have engaged with yet another dimension of the legal status of the unconscious in the Victorian courts:

multiple personality. In the end, however, the legal arguments would draw from the same body of common law: all roads in this novel lead back to Mc-Naughton.

The discontinuity of Jasper's selfhood and the disconnection of that discontinuous selfhood from personal identity—and personal responsibility—echo the arguments exculpating Neville Landless. Ultimately, what Dickens's explorations of the status of a dual personality and altered consciousness before the eyes of the law reveal is a potential vacuum: not only Neville Landless's but also Jasper's responsibility could have been persuasively argued away in a Victorian court. In this way, *The Mystery of Edwin Drood* embodies the conceptual rifts arising between the law, moral philosophy, and the newly established medico-legal discourse gaining ground in the Victorian courts. The novel's summation of the dilemma comes from Mr. Sapsea, a foolish character who I would nevertheless argue speaks the truth about an emerging social reality when he says, "it is not enough that Justice should be morally certain; she must be immorally certain—legally, that is" (222).

NOTES

1. Forster claims that Dickens had told him at the outset of writing *The Mystery of Edwin Drood* that "the story . . . was to be that of the murder of a nephew by his uncle; the originality of which was to consist in the review of the murderer's career by himself at the close, when its temptations were to be dwelt upon as if, not he, the culprit, but some other man, were the tempted" (Nicoll 23). Dickens's youngest daughter publicly supported Forster's assertions in an 1906 article she wrote for *Pall Mall Magazine*; in it, she says her father "d[id] not say whether he is uncertain whether he shall save the nephew, but ha[d] evidently made up his mind that the crime is to be committed" (Nicoll 32).

2. *Until the early twentieth century,* "pamphlets known as the Old Bailey Session Papers . . . report[ed] on courtroom testimony of every trial at the Old Bailey, London's central criminal court. These trial narratives of the Old Bailey's sittings ("the sessions") were taken down in shorthand, transcribed and printed nightly, and sold on the street within days of the trial. [W]ritten for nonlawyers . . . the *OBSP* were intended for a lay audience . . . [and] today's readers can hear the contemporary language of 'nonlawyerly' London" (Eigen 4). In addition, "one can supplement the trial narrative with newspaper accounts. The *Times of London-* . . . maintained a complete index of criminal trials, and other city newspapers were likely to report the events surrounding the more unusual crimes and innovative defense strategies" (5).

3. Aylmer notes Jasper's knack for echoing other characters' words verbatim but his explanation that Jasper is able to do so because he has been eavesdropping does not, I would argue, go far enough.

4. McNaughton is the proper spelling but his name also appears as M'Naghten, M'Naughten, or McNaughten.

5. The McNaughton Rules are a set of criteria that courts use to establish legal insanity as a criminal defense. Defendants who are deemed legally insane (versus psychologically insane) according to the McNaughton Rules are given a verdict of ''not guilty by reason of insanity'' and are generally incarcerated in a mental treatment facility rather than in a prison.

6. ''The characterization of John Jasper, lay precentor of Cloisterham cathedral and opium-eater, melodious singer and strangler, anticipates Stevenson's Dr. Jekyll and Mr. Hyde, for in this schizophrenic the two selves are fully internalized, and the conflict between good and evil is traced to its ultimate source in the irreconcilable duality of human nature'' (Johnson 137).

WORKS CITED

Ackroyd, Peter. *Dickens*. London: Sinclair-Stevenson, 1990.

Aylmer, Felix. *The Drood Case*. London: Hart-Davis, 1964.

Boyer, Allen. ''The Antiquarian and the Utilitarian: Charles Dickens vs. James Fitzjames Stephen.'' *Tennessee Law Review* 56 (1989): 595–628.

Craig, Randall. ''Fictional License: The Case of *Great Expectations*.'' *Dickens Studies Annual* 35 (2005): 109–32.

Dickens, Charles. *The Mystery of Edwin Drood*. Ed. Arthur J. Cox. London: Penguin, 1985.

Eigen, Joel Peter. *Unconscious Crime: Mental Absence and Criminal Responsibility in Victorian London*. Baltimore: Johns Hopkins UP, 2003.

Forsyte, Charles. *The Decoding of Edwin Drood*. London: Victor Gollancz, 1980.

Frutteri, Carlo, and Franco Lucentini. *The D. Case: The Truth about The Mystery of Edwin Drood*. Trans. Gregory Dowling. New York: Harcourt, 1989.

Johnson, E. D. H. *Charles Dickens: An Introduction to His Novels*. New York: Random, 1969.

Joseph, Gerhard. ''Who Cares Who Killed Edwin Drood? Or, on the Whole, I'd Rather Be in Philadelphia.'' *Nineteenth-Century Literature* 51 (Sep. 1996): 161–75.

Nicoll, W. Robertson. *The Problem of Edwin Drood*. London: Hodder and Stoughton, 1912.

Smith, Grahame. *Charles Dickens: A Literary Life*. New York: St. Martin's, 1996.

Stephen, James Fitzjames. "Mr. Dickens as a Politician." *Saturday Review.* Jan. 3, 1857. 8–9.

————. "The License of Modern Novelists." *Edinburgh Review* July 1857: 366–74. Rpt. in *Dickens: The Critical Heritage.* Ed. Philip Collins. London: Routledge, 1971.

Wilson, Edmund. "Dickens: the Two Scrooges." *The Wound and the Bow: Seven Studies in Literature.* New York: Oxford UP, 1965.

CASES CITED

Rex v. Hadfield (1800), 27 St Tr 1281.

R. v. Rennie (1825), 1 Lew CC 76.

R. v. Thomas (1833), 6 C & P 353

R. v. Pearson (1835), 2 Lew CC 144.

R. v. Meakin (1836), 7 C & P 817.

R. v. M'Naghten (1843), 10 Cl & Fin 200.

R. v. Welsh (1869), 11 Cox CC 336.

Before Boz: The Juvenilia and Early Writings of Charles Dickens, 1820–1833

Robert C. Hanna

Works that constitute Dickens's juvenilia and early writings include poems ("Acrostic," "The Devil's Walk," "The Churchyard," "Lodgings to Let," and "The Bill of Fare"), plays (possibly The Stratagems of Rozanza *and definitely* O'Thello*), and nonfiction ("Private Theatricals Regulations"). Yet these works neither constitute all of Dickens's earliest surviving written output nor represent all the types of writing he undertook before the publication of his first sketch, later identified as written by Boz, in December 1833. Dickens also wrote letters, recorded accounting entries with their descriptions in Ellis and Blackmore's Cash Account Book, and transcribed his own shorthand notes of the court cases Jarman vs. Bagster, and Jarman vs. Wise.*

"Before Boz" collects and annotates Dickens's first two known letters, some sample entries from the Cash Account Book, and the full texts of what has survived among the balance of the writings identified above. Dickens's other letters through November 1833 are, of course, found in the Pilgrim Edition. "Before Boz" also includes six appendices of related texts from Tobias Smollett, Walter Dexter, Oliver Goldsmith, Eugène Scribe, Germain Delavigne, William Mickle, Thomas Moore, anonymous ballads, and Charles Dickens himself. Finally, a seventh appendix provides the texts of works falsely attributed to young Dickens by John Payne Collier.

Dickens Studies Annual, Volume 40, Copyright © 2009 by AMS Press, Inc. All rights reserved.

Although many of Charles Dickens's earliest writings do not survive, there is evidence from Robert Langton that Dickens's parents were teaching him to compose short notes as early as age eight (36). Dickens himself comments in a letter to Wilkie Collins on 6 June 1856, "I had been a writer when I was a mere Baby" (*Letters* 8: 130–31). Dickens is more explicit in his 7 September 1859 letter to Mrs. Howitt: "Do you care to know that I was a great writer at 8 years old or so—was an actor and a speaker from a baby—and worked many childish experiences and many young struggles, into Copperfield?" (*Letters* 9: 118–19).

Dickens's friend and biographer John Forster reports that Dickens "became famous in his childish circle for having written a tragedy called *Misnar, the Sultan of India*, founded (and very literally founded, no doubt) on one of the *Tales of the Genii*" (1: 10). Langton, who, after Dickens's death, located and interviewed as many persons as possible who had known Dickens as a boy, adds that "the theatrical entertainments were still kept up, all through the closing months of 1821, and the spring of 1822. In the autumn of the former year he had distinguished himself by writing a tragedy called *Misnar, the Sultan of India!* and his singing, and recitation of humorous pieces was still much admired" (59). Unfortunately, Langton does not provide his source for asserting the season and year of Dickens's composition of *Misnar*.

Dickens himself recalls another undated tragedy in his essay "Our School." The boys objected to the special privileges given to a new boy who came from a wealthy family. Dickens explains:

> A tragedy in blank verse was written on the subject—if our memory does not deceive us, by the hand that now chronicles these recollections—in which his [the new boy's] father figured as a Pirate, and was shot for a voluminous catalogue of atrocities: first imparting to his wife the secret of the cave in which his wealth was stored, and from which his only son's half-crowns now issued. Dumbledon (the boy's name) was represented as "yet unborn" when his brave father met his fate; and the despair and grief of Mrs. Dumbledon at that calamity was movingly shadowed forth as having weakened the parlour-boarder's mind. This production was received with great favor, and was twice performed with closed doors in the dining-room. But, it got wind, and was seized as libelous, and brought the unlucky poet into severe affliction. (50)

Langton also learned that Dickens and a schoolmate at Wellington House Academy composed a usually weekly newspaper for the amusement of fellow pupils. Mr. Jno. W. Bowden told Langton that he and Dickens

> occupied adjoining desks, and I remember we jointly used to issue,—written on scraps of copy-book paper—almost weekly, what we called *Our Newspaper*, lending it to read on payment of marbles, and pieces of slate pencil. This paper used to contain sundry bits of boyish fun—the following I recollect—

Lost. Out of a gentleman's waistcoat pocket, an acre of land; the finder shall be rewarded on restoring the same.

Lost. By a boy with a long red nose, and grey eyes, a very bad temper. Whoever has found the same may keep it, as the owner is better without it. (89)

Of course, these humorous notices could be the work of Dickens or Bowden, or jokes already popular while Dickens attended Wellington House Academy from 1824–26.

Dickens shared with Forster information about two of his earliest compositions: "His uncle was shaved by a very odd old barber out of Dean-street, Soho, who was never tired of reviewing the events of the last war, and especially of detecting Napoleon's mistakes, and re-arranging his whole life for him on a plan of his own. The boy wrote a description of this old barber, but never had courage to show it" (1: 22).

Again, Forster remarks, "taking for his model the description of the canon's housekeeper in *Gil Blas*, he sketched a deaf old woman who waited on them in Bayham-street, and who made delicate hashes with walnut-ketchup. As little did he dare to show this, either; though he thought it, himself, extremely clever" (1: 22). Forster is here referring to Tobias Smollett's translation of *The Adventures of Gil Blas*, first published in 1749 and readily available to young Dickens in numerous contemporary and older editions. (The full description of the canon's housekeeper is presented in Appendix A.)

Dickens's interest in the theater continued throughout his life, but most of his 1832 or 1833 play *O'Thello* is missing. Dickens also composed an "introductory prologue" to the "private theatricals" in which he acted and for which he served as stage manager on 27 April 1833.[1] In an April 1833 letter to Amelia Austin (later Amelia Fillonneau), Dickens inquired, "Will you allow me to forward you a copy of the Prologue? A very great press of business has prevented my bestowing more than a couple of hours on the whole composition; copy and all; and I therefore trust to your usual kindness to excuse the very <u>unladylike</u> manner in which it is copied" (*Letters* 1: 18).

In 1905, K. F. Yapp reported that Amelia "was wont to refer with pride to the evening when she spoke the prologue of a play. . . . Until memory failed her, the dear old lady would repeat the verses with a pretty imitation of the girlish utterance and manner which had once brought down 'the house.' The MS. of this prologue remained in Madame F.'s possession for many years, but she subsequently destroyed it, on the author expressing a very urgent desire that she should do so" (205).

Fortunately, some of Dickens's earliest writings have survived. However, they have never been collected and published in their entirety. The 1937–38 Nonesuch edition of the works of Charles Dickens did include some of Dickens's juvenilia, but with numerous textual errors that have been perpetuated ever since. This collection corrects the Nonesuch errors.

This collection also adds for the first time texts attributed to Dickens's early years, both those which may or may not be of his authorship, and those which were penned or otherwise selected by literary forger John Payne Collier and have erroneously continued to be attributed to Dickens in books and articles.

It should be noted that, aside from Dickens's first known card (Chapter I) and first known letter (Chapter II), no other correspondence has been selected for inclusion, as Dickens's annotated letters are available in the Pilgrim Edition.

Each work in this collection is preceded by a brief introduction. Spellings, capitalizations, and punctuation (including words that are underlined) are faithful to the original manuscripts. Four of the thirteen original manuscripts are lost in whole or in part. The text for the card from Dickens to Master and Miss Tribe (Chapter I) is based on Mr. John Tribe's memory. The text for *The Stratagems of Rozanza* (Chapter IV) remains only as a copy in an unidentified hand. Copying errors are pointed out and explained where they occur. The three texts for "The Bill of Fare" (Chapter XI) are based on Dickens's lost manuscript. Variations among the three texts are noted only when individual lines differ in wording, spelling, and/or capitalization. Finally, only 7 pages survive of *O'Thello* (Chapter XII).

The concluding Works Cited section directs the reader to all sources used in compiling, editing, and commenting on Charles Dickens's juvenilia and earliest writings, from 1820, when the future novelist, journalist, essayist, dramatist, and poet was age 8, through November 1833, the month before the first publication of what became known as a sketch by Boz. Accordingly, Dickens's "Private Theatricals Regulations" from 1833 (Chapter XIII) is included, while his poem "A Fable (Not a Gay One)" from 1834 and signed "Boz" is excluded.

Acknowledgments

I am pleased to announce that *The Stratagems of Rozanza* now makes its first full appearance in print, owing to the generous permission of Charles Dickens's descendants. I am deeply honored to have the cooperation of Mr. Mark Charles Dickens and the Dickens family.

Also presented for the first time are the full texts of Charles Dickens's transcriptions from his own shorthand notes taken during the legal proceedings of Jarman vs. Bagster, and Jarman vs. Wise. Both court documents appear through the courtesy of the Guildhall Library, City of London. The Guildhall Library staff were exceptionally helpful and accommodating during my numerous inspections of the original manuscripts.

The Rosenbach Museum and Library kindly granted permission for the inclusion of the text of its manuscript page for *O'Thello*, while the text of an alternative version of "The Bill of Fare" is reproduced by permission of the Huntington Library, San Marino, California. The Trustees of the National Library of Scotland have authorized the reproduction in Appendix F of lyrics to the ballad "Begone Dull Care."

I am also grateful to the Charles Dickens Museum, the Folger Shakespeare Library, Harvard University's Houghton Library, the Morgan Library, Old Dominion University's Perry Library, Oxford University's Bodleian Library, and Yale University's Beinecke Library for access to their respective holdings and publication permissions.

Bethany Lutheran College in Mankato, Minnesota, made it possible for me to assemble this entire collection from original manuscripts and surviving transcriptions, along with one photocopy of a still privately held manuscript. Specifically, I thank President Dan R. Bruss, Vice President Ronald J. Younge, and Bethany Lutheran College's Faculty Development Committee.

Duane DeVries, a member of the *Dickens Studies Annual* Editorial Advisory Board, provided suggestions for my commentary as well as formatting assistance. Stanley Friedman, one of the editors of *Dickens Studies Annual*, provided additional suggestions for my commentary and was extraordinarily patient with my ongoing series of questions. I extend my warmest thanks to both Dickens scholars for their support of my now published project.

Finally, it is with great pleasure that I acknowledge and thank my daughter, Emily Hanna, for her keen proofreading ability and her most valuable assistance in deciphering manuscript words. Emily, who is majoring in English at Doane College in Crete, Nebraska, conclusively resolved *all* remaining instances of words which might otherwise have appeared here as possible or probable readings. Needless to say, this collection would not be as complete or authoritative without her time, effort, and talent.

Contents

I.

Card from Dickens (and Also on Behalf of Fanny Dickens)

In 1883, Robert Langton, member of the Manchester Academy of Fine Arts, published *The Childhood and Youth of Charles Dickens*. This book is the result, in part, of Langton's exhaustive efforts to locate and interview individuals who knew Dickens during his boyhood and youth.

One such person was Mr. John Tribe, alderman and former mayor of Rochester. Mr. Tribe's children had been friends of Dickens and his sister Fanny in 1820 and 1821. Langton reports:

> A most interesting relic . . . is still in the possession of Mr. Ald. John Tribe. It is a card of invitation written by Charles when between eight and nine years of age. Unfortunately the card itself, an address card of his father's, has been temporarily mislaid, or it would have been re-produced here in *fac-simile*, as the earliest piece of writing of Charles Dickens known to be in existence. Mr. Tribe can, however, remember it is to this effect.

> Master and Miss Dickens will be pleased to have the company of Master and Miss Tribe to spend the Evening on . . . . . [date, &c.]   (35–36)

Dickens's father's address card with Dickens's handwritten invitation has never been located. Regardless of the accuracy of Mr. Tribe's memory regarding Dickens's wording on the card, the capitalization of the word "Evening" is surely Langton's invention, as (1) he creates and publishes how the lost card might have appeared, and (2) Mr. Tribe can scarcely have said, in telling Langton the wording of the card, "I remember that the word 'evening' was capitalized."

II.

Earliest Known Letter, Written to Owen Peregrine Thomas, When Author and Recipient Attended Wellington House Academy 1824–26

The manuscript of this letter is located in the Charles Dickens Museum, London (A704). In 1926, Walter Dexter quoted Owen Thomas's explanation that "The Leg referred to was the Legend of something, a pamphlet romance I had lent him: the Clavis was, of course, the Latin school book so named."[2] House and Storey, however, interpret "Leg" as "school slang for a lexicon" (*Letters* 1: 1). The letter was written in three columns, as presented here, when Dickens was age 12 to 14. Words which Dickens underlined are so noted.

Tom/
  I am quite
ashamed I have
not returned
your Leg but
you shall have
it by Harry to
morrow If
you would
like to purchase
my Clavis you
shall have it

at a very
reduced price
Cheaper in
comparison
than a Leg.

Yours & c
C Dickens.

PS. I suppose
all this time
you have had

a wooden
leg. I have
weighed yours
every saturday
Night.

III.

Entries in Ellis and Blackmore's Cash Account Book

Ellis and Blackmore's entire original Cash Account book is located in the Harry Elkins Widener Collection, Harvard University (HEW 2.6.5.) Walter Dexter places Dickens's employment at Ellis and Blackmore, Solicitors, located at 1 Holborn Court, Gray's Inn, London, from May 1827 through November 1828.[3] However it was not until 5 January 1828 that Dickens was assigned a turn at recording the firm's cash transactions, both dispersals (ending 16 March 1828) and receipts (ending 11 March 1828), when he was age 16.

Dickens's handwriting, although superior to that of his later adult years, is unacceptable in his capacity as a clerk. Dickens, like his fellow clerks, recorded information pertaining to numerous court cases in the Cash Account book, but it is only Dickens who records many last names in characters which leave doubt as to the actual spellings of those names.

Next, Dickens employs a set of abbreviations for legal and monetary words which, if not an early experiment in shorthand writing (for which he was later to become quite well known), is significantly different from the abbreviations used by his fellow clerks.

Although both of the above characteristics of his entries would be sufficient for Ellis and Blackmore to remove the recording of accounting entries from Dickens's responsibilities, an examination of Dickens's final entries suggests why his entries ceased specifically on 16 March. On the second-to-last page of his final entries, Dickens records, in part:

	Bush
Bush	~~Yourself~~ vs. Pearce—Wm.
H. Ellis	Thumbes vs. Hanbury
Butt	Yourself vs. Unwin

The strikethrough and correction of the unprofessional designation of Bush as "Yourself" is not in Dickens's handwriting, and, two entries later, Dickens repeats this type of error, and it remains uncorrected by anyone.

Dickens's final numerical entry is preceded by the phrase "due to me," another instance of the use of a personal pronoun in a business record.

The identities of the various employees and parties to the lawsuits in the Cash Account book would need to be determined by checking various name spellings and dates against surviving legal records in London. Working from a facsimile of the entire Cash Account book would probably prove inadequate, as ink usage and stray marks on the original pages take on an importance of their own in deciphering such a text. Some help is provided, of course, by comparing Dickens's entries to those of his fellow clerks. Even then, it is questionable whether all of Dickens's abbreviations can be identified with full confidence.

Some of the names which are commonly found throughout the book, in various handwritings, are Blackmore, Butt, Cameron, Chubb, Cooper, Ellis H. (and H. Ellis), Hodding, Hoper, Kell, Leeves, Parr, Price, Proper, Roston, and Wilmot.

The book itself is titled *Cash Account commencing 1st March 1827*, and it contains 260 pages. The entries begin on page 5 and continue through page 112, at which place Dickens's 23 pages of entries begin. Dickens records dispersals on pages 113 through 135, after which other clerks continue on pages 136 through 195, with an ending date of 8 January 1829.

Pages 196 through 240 are unused, and the recording of receipts commences on pages 241 and 242, followed by unused pages on 243 and 244. This might be another error on Dickens's part, as he commences his entries of receipts on pages 245 through 247, rather than starting on 243. Page 248 is unused, and other clerks record receipts on pages 249 through 252, with an ending date of 9 September 1828. The book's remaining pages 253 through 260 are unused.

Some of Dickens's entries read:

> parcel with citation returned for amendment
> Postman Xmas box
> Parchment
> Paid Wood for keys putting bits on stool
> Common bail
> Warrant
> Docket paper & no: rolls
> The King vs. Peacher Esq.
> Attestation of signature of Mr. Badhams articles

IV.

The Stratagems of Rozanza

The manuscript of *The Stratagems of Rozanza* is privately held, but a complete photo-copy is available in the British Library's Department of Manuscripts (RP 2695). The play is an abridged and altered version of Carlo Goldoni's 1748 comedy *La vedova scaltra*, which literally means ''The Cunning (or Crafty, or Sly) Widow.'' Notations in an unidentified hand read ''about 1828'' on page i (when Dickens was age 16) and ''Paper bears water-mark 1823'' on page iii.

As Charles Dickens is named on page 1 of the manuscript, and as the play's text also begins on the lower half of page 1, it seems rather unlikely that someone found this manuscript with the upper half of page 1 blank and available for adding a false claim that this play is associated with Dickens or anyone else.

If the manuscript is a forgery dating from 1823 through late 1833, no one during this interval had any reason for associating it with Dickens, who as yet had no pub-lished original work. If the manuscript is a forgery dating from 1834 through about 1920, it is remarkable that the forger went to the time and effort to create the manu-script and then kept its existence unknown. If the manuscript is a forgery dating from the 1920s, when the earliest located newspaper accounts of its existence were published,[4] and it was subsequently bought and sold, it is remarkable that the forger obtained unused sheets of paper with a purported watermark of 1823.

Commentary on the manuscript in an unidentified hand states that ''This book belonged to Miss Georgina Hogarth & was given by her to Mrs. Horace Pym.'' Miss Hogarth's nephew Henry Fielding Dickens asserted, however, that no such manuscript was ever part of her library.[5] Further, Mrs. Pym's son asserted that no such manuscript was ever part of his mother's library.[6]

In analyzing the manuscript, four features are noteworthy. First, although the manu-script is not in the handwriting of Dickens, his mother, his father, or his sister Fanny, the text has been demonstrably copied by someone from either another full text or parts assigned to actors and actresses. While care would be taken to copy an authentic text and not alter it, the manuscript does contain copying errors, which are so noted in this edition.

Second, while the copyist began with good penmanship, apparently to produce a family heirloom, as one continues to read the text, one readily notices that the penman-ship deteriorates in a manner expected when a copier is losing patience and is hurrying to some extent to complete the task.

The final two features strongly suggest that Dickens is associated with the text. An analysis of the spelling of words reveals that of all the words used in the play which have alternate spellings, such as neighbors/neighbours and honor/honour, every spell-ing but one is the same spelling Dickens used in his letters from 1825 through 1836 (Hanna 315–16). No one from 1825 through the 1920s had access to all of Dickens's surviving letters, in order to make a forgery using Dickens's own spelling preferences. What Christine Alexander calls ''American spellings'' (8) were not standardized as such in the 1820s; Dickens himself used them.

Finally, young Dickens was not only interested in and attended London theatrical performances, but he also adapted plays for amateur productions at home. On April 27, 1833, Dickens arranged an evening performance of *Clari, The Married Bachelor,* and *Amateurs & Actors,* with his family, his friends, and himself playing parts in each.[7] *The Stratagems of Rozanza* is adapted for a home performance with a limited availability of actors and actresses.

Specifically, Dickens would have been able to cast a play calling for twelve roles, using only eight actors. A key revision of Goldoni's play is the absence of Milord from the final scene, where Rosaura is supposed to be in the presence of all four of her suitors. This absence permits the roles of Milord/Doctor and Arlecchino/Pantalone to be combined. An examination of all characters who are together onstage, along with which characters make entrances and exits within scenes, reveals the available combinations of Monsieur/Birif and Eleanor/Foletto. While Milord/Pantalone and Arlecchino/Doctor would also work, as would Monsieur/Foletto and Eleanor/Birif, all other combinations are either impossible or unnecessarily difficult, or they negate the necessity of removing Milord from the final scene.

Corrections and notes are *[italicized within brackets]*. All other brackets are as they appear in the manuscript. All original punctuation has been retained.

THE STRATAGEMS OF ROZANZA
A VENETIAN COMEDIETTA
BY
C. J. H. DICKENS

[The first ''Z'' of ''ROZANZA'' was initially written as an ''S.'' The ''Z'' was then superimposed on the ''S,'' yet throughout the rest of the play, Goldoni's spelling ''Rosaura'' is used.]

Room at a Hotel, table with Wine and Glasses round which are seated Milord Runebif the Count di Bosconero, Don Alvaro, and Monsieur le Blan who is singing a French Air. The others join in chorus.

[Goldoni's corresponding characters are Milord Runebif, the Conte di Bosco Nero, Don Alvaro de Castiglia, and Monsieur le Blau.]

Mons. .   Long live the bottle! long live mirth!

All. .   Huzza.

Cou. .   Really our landlord has provided us with a famous spread.

Mons. .   So so, but you will allow that in the art of cooking, the Italians must yield the palm to their more fortunate neighbours.

Cou. .   True but we have French cooks.

Mons. .   Ah yes. But when arrived in Italy how soon they lose the happy art. Oh could you know how we live in Paris; it is my belief that there alone, life is capable of enjoyment.

Mil. .   You Frenchmen are so conceited that you seem to fancy there can be no other world than Paris, where as I am a good Englishman yet never mention London.

Alv. .   I cannot help smiling when I hear Paris so extoled *[sic]*. why Madrid is the Palace of the world.

Cou. .   Gentlemen, I will now address you as a true Italian. Go where you will, happiness may still be at your command so long as you have mirth in your hearts and a few ducats in your purse.

Mons. .   Well said Monsieur le Conte. Long live mirth. It is now near sun rise we must think of retiring. But first, what say you of the pretty Widow, we had the pleasure of escorting at the ball last night.

Mil. .   Very discreet and civil

Alv. .   She has a gravity of deportment that I greatly admire.

Mons. .	I am sure she is a French woman for her wit is a spark shiny as one of our Parisian Demiselles.
Cou	Signora Rosaura is a lady of most noble mien, revered and respected by all (and she adored of this heart.) aside.
Mons. .	Come gentlemen let us drink to the health of Madame Rosaura. [They fill their glasses
Alv. .	Long live Donna Rosaura.
Mil. . ⎫ Con ⎭	Long live the Signora *[Spelling alternates between "Signora/ Signiora" and "Signor/Signior" throughout the manuscript; "Signora" and "Signor" are used consistently in this edition]*

[Monsieur le Blan renews the song]

Arlecchino enters. *[Goldoni uses the same spelling]* stands listening for some time to the song. Then seats himself at the table. fills a glass of wine and when the air is concluded joins in the chorus Drinks then goes out with glasses.

Cou. .	Bravo Mr Laquet! *[lackey]* I admire your spirit.
Alv. .	Is it possible you can smile at such impudence? In Spain his reward would have been a good thrashing.
Mons. .	And in France he would make his fortune. but let us return to our subject—this Widow reigns in my heart.
Alv. .	I already sigh for her.
Cou. .	I advise you not to cherish a hope.
Mons. .	And why?
Cou	Because the lady Rosaura is inimical to love, disdainful of Men and incapable of tenderness (To me alone tender and kind.)
Mons.	Let her nature be frigid as the pole, when I, true Frenchman as I trust I am, shall come and whisper in her ear some of our pretty conceits formed to enchant the ladies. I swear to you then shall she begin to sigh and ask of me my pity.
Alv.	She would indeed be the first lady to reject the addresses of Don Alvara *[sic]* di Castiglia, men of my descent maintain the privilege of allowing the lady to supplicate.
Cou.	No not even French vivacity nor Spanish gravity, can draw from this lady either sighs or supplications I can vouch for the truth of

	what I advance, I am acquainted with her, believe me gentlemen I speak as a friend.
Mons.	During the dance I beheld her gazing on me with such fixed attention that I immediately concluded my eyes had made a lasting impression on her heart, in giving me her hand in the last Minuet she spoke so sweetly that it was a miracle I did not throw myself at her feet.
Alv. .	I make no boast of favors received from the fair sex, or the recital would quite confound you.
Cou. .	I burn with jealousy. (aside)
Mons. .	M. Pantalone [*"Pantalone de' Bisognosi" in Goldoni*] one of her acquaintance is my friend, he will not fail to introduce me.
Alv. .	The doctor her father is dependent on me; he will therefore be my guide.
Cou. .	(And it shall be my care to prevent him) aside
Mil.	Ho there! [A servant comes in with a light which Mil. takes] Friends I wish you good night. (exit)
Mons. .	Adieu Milord, we shall soon follow. I think we shall scarcely require lights.
Cou. .	Were we to peep into the Cafe, I doubt not but that we should find them all at breakfast.
Mons. .	I shall not see you again today.
Cou. .	Why are you engaged?
Mons. .	I hope to be with Madame Ros.
Cou. .	That is impossible she will receive no company. (exit)
Mons. .	How mad that poor Count is. his case appears even more desperate than ours. he may probably already enjoy those favors which we now seek.
Alv. .	Indeed then he will soon have cause to feel many a jealous pang.
Mons.	Well it will be a desperate contest. but what has le Blan to fear. Adieu mon ami. exit)
Alv. .	Jealousy thou fiend avaunt! I fear thee not. T'is for those to tremble who love, where Don Alvaro condescends to woo. (exit)

Scene the 2^d

Day. *[not in Goldoni]*

A dressing room in Rosaura's house with seats [for] Rosaura and Marionette *[same spelling for Rosaura's maid in Goldoni]* dressed as a French femme de chambre.

Ros.	Why does not my sister make her appearance?
Mar.	She is still at her toilet.
Ros.	When will she have finished adorning?
Mar.	Now do not scold the poor little thing you know it is her only hope in finding a husband.
Ros. .	Indeed then I fear it rests with me to provide her with one. I think my friend Pantalone admires her. what say you? would she have any objection to him.
Mar.	Not the least in the world, provided he would pass off as obligingly as your good gentleman did. but I fear that is not likely and that she will therefore prefer some handsome dashing young fellow.
Ros. .	Who is that now entering the vestibule? run and see.
Mar. .	T'is an English gentleman.
Ros.	I should not be surprised to find in him Milord Englais I met at the Ball last night. well show him in.

Enter Milord.

Mar.	Milord Runebif
Mil.	Madam.
Ros.	Milord, I am your servant. pray be seated
Mil	I wait till you are.
Ros.	Favor me I pray.
Mil.	Do not torment me with such ceremony. [They seat themselves]
Ros.	I hope you where *[sic]* not much fatigued last night?
Mil.	Rather so.
Ros.	Do our festivals please you?

Mil.   Much.

Ros.   Did you think there was much beauty?

Mil.   Yes some fine women.

Ros.   And who among the ladies pleased you most?

Mil.   You M'am. *[sic]*

Ros.   Oh! you jest.

Mil.   Believe me I speak from my heart.

Ros   I do not merit so flattering a distinction.

Mil.   You are so conscious of your own attractions that my humble praise is no doubt wearisome.

Ros.   Oh Milord indeed you do me wrong. (heavens! what a strange creature thank goodness here comes Marionette.)

Enter Marionette with chocolate

Mil.   Madam. [takes a cup of chocolate presents it to Rosaura]

Ros.   (What a laconic style) aside.

Mil.   Marionette are you french?

Mar.   Yes Sir (makes a curtsy.).

Mil   Serve your mistress with attention.

Mar.   I strive to do my best Milord.

[Milord puts down his cup and under it a guinea]

Mar.   (This is for me I suppose. what a guinea!) exit.

Mil.   Are you not a Widow?

Ros.   I am. but if I meet with a good offer perhaps I may . . . return . . .

Mil.   I have no intention of taking a wife

Ros.   And what are your objections?

Mil.   I am pleased with my liberty.

Ros.   And love does not molest you.

Mil. .   I love when I see an amiable woman.

Ros.   Your's *[sic]* then is but a transitory flame

Mil. .	How! am I always to love.
Ros.	Constancy is the true lover's pledge.
Mil	Constant so long as love remains and a lover whilst in the presence of the object I love.
Ros	I do not understand you.
Mil	I will explain myself. Suppose that I love you, you shall be faithful so long as I love and I will love so long as I remain in your presence probably during my stay here.
Ros. .	Then when you leave Venice I shall cease to be remembered?
Mil. .	Of what benefit could it be to you, were I to continue to love you when in Paris or returned to London, my love, would be of no avail and I should suffer without recompense.
Ros.	Then what advantage do you seek in now visiting me?
Mil	To see you and be believed by you.
Ros.	You are indeed a very discreet man.
Mil	No honorable lady would wish me otherwise.
Ros	Ha ha! You are most charming.
Mil.	I am your devoted servant.
Ros. .	But will you remain so all the time you are in Venice?
Mil. .	I think so.
Ros	(What a buffoon!)
Mil	(How she pleases me.)

Marionette returns

Mar.	Madame the Count wishes to pay his respects to you.
Ros.	Place a chair and beg the Count to enter.
Mar.	Certainly (this jealous fellow never lets any thing slip from his hand.) exit.
Mil. .	Is not this Count your lover Madam?
Ros. .	He would be.

Enter Count

Count.	I come to pay my adorations at the shrine of my divinity.

Ros. .	Good day Count be seated I pray.
Cou. .	I congratulate myself no*[w]* meeting with such good company.
Mil.	My friend you come in good time for this good lady is dying of melancholy.
Cou.	Then I fear that you are the party to blame for conversation rarely flags in the company of Signora Rosaura.
Mil.	You know my disposition Count.
Ros.	Marionette!—with your leave gentlemen. [comes to the front of the stage and whispers] tell my sister Eleanor *["Eleanora" in Goldoni]* to come and contrive to seat herself next to Milord. I wish this affair to end well. [Mar. exit]
Cou	I did not think at so early an hour to have found you thus engaged. I may at least concluded *[sic]* that you are well?
Ros.	Milord has done me the favor to take his chocolate with me this morning.
Cou	Oh yes you are so kind to all.
Ros.	Count you displease me.
Mil. .	(aside) how strange, the fellow's quite jealous)
Cou	No one can doubt that Milord possesses all the qualification requisite for an introduction to Lady Rosaura's boudoir. (ironically)
Mil.	Well I am tired.

Enter Eleanor

Ele.	And will it be allowed me also to join this good company.
Ros.	Oh yes come in Eleanor.
Mil.	Who is that lady?
Ros.	My sister.
Ele.	And your most humble servant.
Ros.	Seat yourself next to Milord.
Ele.	If he will permit me?
Mil.	You do me an honor (without looking at her)

Ele.	You are English are you not?
Mil.	Yes Miss (as before)
Ele.	Have you been long in Venice?
Mil.	Three months (as before)
Ele	Does this city please you
Mil. .	Certainly (as before)
Ele.	But Milord why do you treat me with such coolness I am Rosaura's sister.
Mil	Excuse me I am a little bewildered (this one does not please me.)
Ele	I would not disturb your thoughts but . . .
Mil	I am your servant (rises)
Ros.	Where are you going Milord.
Mil.	To walk on the parade.
Ros.	You are not displeased I hope?
Mil	Oh you may think so. I will return sometime to say Madam farewell, Count I shall see you again.
Ros	Allow me to accompany you.
Mil.	No, no I do not wish it. stay and console the poor Count who I see is dying for you. I also love you, and because I love it pleases me to see you surrounded by admirers who will do justice to your merits and applaud my choice (exit)
Ele	An interesting conversation truly sister I am infinitely obliged to you for the introduction.
Ros	You must forgive him he has an excellent heart but like all others has his peculiarities.
Cou.	Milord's heart is no doubt of the very [omitted word here?] but it would have given mine the greatest satisfaction to have kicked his Lordship out of the room. how dare such unmannerly rascals show their vulgar faces in the society of a lady and such a lady as Signora Rosaura by heavens! It makes my blood boil to see you thus bestow your favor on a beggarly stranger.
Ros.	How Sir does this in any way concern you, perhaps you consider me as already your's [sic] and subservient to your wishes pray

why do you thus dictate to me who has given you such authority. Count I love you. love you *[copying error; "love you" ends one page and is repeated at the beginning of the next page, indicating losing one's place while copying]* perhaps more than you suppose but I could never consent to such a sacrifice of my liberty. General conversation is surely allowable among all ranks of life. A lady of spirit discourses freely but with indifference with all and so I have always acted, but if I have made any distinction it has been in your favor which if you abuse I shall again look on you as one of the crowd and probably entirely banish you my house. (exit)

Ele.   Well Count there is consolation for you, let me tell you that jealousy is the scourge of poor women. My sister does well to show you a little spirit; as for me give me a jealous man and I would soon torment him to death. exit.

Cou.   Solus.) *[not in Goldoni]* How, can I tear from me this fiend that preys upon my heart devouring the very food of love on which existence hangs. Loathsomeness, distorting by its baneful aspect the very symbols of enchantment into dire forms of hatred disgust and vengeance. Jealousy, compared with thee each other passion's passionless all torment is delight. Alas! for thy poor victim. O Woman emblem of tenderness should thy gentle form have power to raise this whirlwind of the passions should it not rather as the pale moonbeam defuse o'er its votaries a soothing ray and quell the coming storm

Scene 3^{d}
The street before Rosaura's house.
The Doctor and Pantalone.

["Il Dottore" in Goldoni]

Pan.   My good friend and relation you must know that my brother Stefanelo *["Stefanello" in Goldoni]* dying without children our house would fall to decay at my death, and as I would not have it so if it can be avoided I am determined to marry.

Doc.   You are perfectly right, it is very natural you should wish for an heir.

Pan.   I'll tell you, I am advanced in life but as I was provident in my youth I hope to have something to enjoy in my old age.

Doc.   You are very right, and who would you make your partner?

Pan.   My Brother took Signora Rosaura to wife, and I am much pleased
            with her sister Eleanor.

Doc.   Nothing my dear friend could give me greater satisfaction than
            to see you my son in law and I am quite at a loss to thank you
            sufficiently for the honor you do me and my daughter.

Pan.   I'll tell you. you see she may remain in the same house and shall
            enjoy her sister's company, therefore I hope she will not refuse
            me and that I shall appear favorable in her eyes.

Doc.   If you wish I will speak to Eleanor and you may mention it to
            Rosaura, so with the joint entreaties of her sister, her father, and
            her lover I trust she will comply. I must now leave you my friend
            but I shall hope to see you again in the evening. (exeunt)

Monsieur le Blan enters and knocks at the door

Marionette (from the window)

[Mar.]   Who knocks?

Mon.   Is your mistress at home ah! Marionette!

Mar.   Monsieur le Blan!

Mon.   What you here?

Mar.   You in Venice!

Mon.   Yes here I am, but is your mistress within?

Mar   Come up, come up. then we can speak more at our ease. [shuts
            the window and opens the door

Mon.   Tis thus we make our way through life! fal lal de ra. fal lal de
            ral de re. [enters]

Scene 4th

Rosaura seated reading in her boudoir Marionette at her work.

Ros.   This is indeed a charming theory. who ever the author of this
            book may be, he has written it with the determination of pleasing
            the ladies. (reads) "It is the parent's care to provide a husband
            for his child, but she should herself choose a cicisbeo [same in
            Goldoni; "married woman's gigolo"], he is to be the lady's
            confidant and consulted by her on all occasions, the most useful

person to a good husband is his wife's cicisbeo. he relieves him of an infinitude of trouble and moderates the restless spirit of a whimsical woman." well this unknown author and I by no means concur in our opinions. I should imagine no married woman could wish to be surrounded by these ganimedes *[dandies]* who assume even more authority than the husband. The prudent woman in marrying rejects all cicisbeos *["cicisbei" in Goldoni]*, and by that means subjects herself to the whims and caprices of one alone. whilst others on the contrary seek but to multiply their chains.

Mar.	I do not wish to interrupt your reflections.
Ros.	Take your work do not mind me.
Mar.	It would be unbecoming in me to confute your opinion, or I would assure you that your author perfectly understands the general feeling of the ladies. but let us for the present drop the subject, and turn to one of more importance. my dear Mistress fate now offers you a most brilliant opportunity of profitting *[sic]* by your beauty.
Ros.	In what manner.
Mar.	There is a French chevalier who is enraptured with your charms and sighs to be admitted to your presence.
Ros.	What is his name?
Mar.	Monsieur le Blan.
Ros.	Oh I know him I danced with him at the ball last night, but he appeared the very epitome of affectation and if I recollect right he appeared quite tame.
Mar.	Oh that's nothing. he is a chevalier of good fortune high birth, young, handsome and witty neither jealous nor deceitful, suffice it to say he is a Frenchman.
Ros.	You never will conquer your national conceits.
Mar.	But here I speak the truth in fact he is in the anteroom, consciously expecting permission to enter.
Ros.	And have you dared without my knowledge to admit a perfect stranger?
Mar.	He is my country man.

Ros.   Of what consequence is it to me his being your Countryman.

Mar.   Come, come you will some day repent of this squeamishness.

Ros.   No impertinence I beg, what then . . .

Mar.   My dear Mistress I'm only joking if you do not wish him to come in . . .

[Mons le Blan from behind the scene]

[Mon.]   Marrionette *[sic]* is your Mistress asleep?

Mar.   No Sir but at present you cannot . . .

Mon.   Oh then if she be risen permit me to enter [comes in]

Mar.   What have you done?

Ros.   It is not here Sir the fashion so freely . . .

Mon.   Behold me at your feet entreating pardon for my impudence. If your heart be as kind as your person is lovely I may yet hope for forgiveness.
[he kneels]

Mar   (Bravo Monsieur le Blan)

Ros.   Rise Sir, your fault is not sufficiently heinous to demand the necessity of throwing yourself at the feet of one who claim not such humiliation.

Mon.   Ah Heavens! Your words have brought sweet consolation to this aching heart. (Marionette I have no further need of you, so you may go my sweet girl about your affairs in the dressing room.) aside to Marionette.)

Mar.   Have you any commands Mistress?

Ros.   Place two chairs.

Mar.   Certainly (you remember your little promises) aside to le Blan.)

Mon. .   Yes never doubt me.

Mar. .   What a charming fellow.

Mon.   Ah. Madame! the heavens which do every thing for the best, could not surely have formed you thus lovely to be the torment of your adorers, therefore on account of your great beauty in your pity must we put our trust.

Ros.   But I knowing that my attractions are few must not boast of my compassion.

Mon.   The humble opinion you entertain of your own merits but adds another grace. how lovely is retiring beauty! by heavens had Apelles *["Apelle" in Goldoni; 4th century B.C. Greek painter]* now to draw his Venus what a model might he find.

Ros.   Such overdreamed praise. This will degenerate into flattery.

Mon.   Believe me I would assure you from my heart to the best of my abilities as a Chevalier as a true Frenchman that you are beautiful above all that is beauteous on earth, Added to this natural loveliness I see you are perfect Mistress of all the pretty accomplishments of the toilet your head methinks now resemble the style of a sweet Flora. Pray who is your Friseur—our Marionette?

Ros.   The same.

Mon.   You find her no doubt perfectly acquainted with the Parisian fashions. But I beg pardon, an insolent hair would wander from its fair companions.

Ros   Oh tis nothing.

Mons. Pardon me it must not be allowed. by your leave I will replace it.

Ros.   I will ring for Marionette.

Mon.   No I will myself aspire to the honor of serving you. (He takes from his pocket a gold case and out of that a pair of scissors *[and]* cuts off Rosaura's stray hair then replaces them, arranges her curls then to see if it need her approbation presents her a pocket mirror, which having laid aside he takes up a bottle of essence and throws it over his hands, wipes them with his embroidered handkerchief saying a few words whilst thus employed without meeting with any interruption from Rosaura who is all astonishment at length he seats himself saying) now I think it is quite comme il faut.

Ros.   One cannot deny that you possess good taste and the very essence of gallantry.

Mons. Oh my taste, it is not for me to speak. Tis true that in Paris it is highly esteemed all the French tailors correspond with me that they may communicate their ideas, and would never venture to introduce a new fashion without seeking my advice.

Ros. .   Indeed I perceive you do not dress in the ordinary style of the day.

Mons.   Ah! do you not admire this little coat? (rises and walks about] see how this collar adorns the person. it is to its peculiar*[ity]* and that I attribute my success in the ballet which you have no doubt observed.

Ros.   (He could not have looked more ridiculous.)

Mon.   But I lose time with these trifles whilst I neglected to tell you how much you enchant me, how I live but in the light of your eyes and sigh for the continuance of your favors as the only solace to my woes.

Ros.   Sir I am at a loss to express my gratitude for the honor you do me by this flattering distinction. but I can consider you at present merely a common acquaintance.

Mon. .   On whom are *[you]* dependent are you not your own Mistress?

Ros. .   A Widow is more open to criticism than any other woman and cannot therefore be too circumspect.

Mon.   But popular opinion should have but little weight with a lady of such spirit as Madame Rosaura.

Ros.   Pardon me, disregard for public opinion in such cases; is no demonstration of a generous or independent spirit.

Mon.   Some might doubt the breath of such an assertion. but why should you any longer subject yourself to such restraint, forsake your widowhood and listen to my tale.

Ros.   But who is the hero of that tale.

Mon. .   Le Blan who adores you. I am the valiant hero who would seek to win the hand and heart of Madame Rosaura let kings and princes envy me my prize.

Ros.   Give me time to consider.

Mon. .   Take what time you please, my delight, but grant me one little token of affection on which I may exist during the interval. [approaches to take her hand]

Ros.   O Monsieur a little more prudence.

Mon. .   And will you persist in refusing so small a favor to one so soon to be your all.

Ros.	Consider you are but a stranger to me at present.
Mon.	But I adore you. I will not be refused. [Turns as before to take her hand]
Ros.	(I must put a stop to this) [aside, rises]
Mon.	And would you leave me thus the victim to despair have pity I entreat. the day may come when you will repent you of this unmerited cruelty. [affects to weep]
Ros	A little prudence and respect Sir you are too importunate.
Mon.	(kneeling) On my knees will I seek your pardon.
Ros.	(Here we are again) aside Rise! it is granted you but do not again trouble me with such weakness.
Mon.	Madam an oppression of my heart prevents my rising from the ground without the assistance of your little hand.
Ros.	There, to assist you to rise. [gives him her hand he kisses it.]
Mon	Such little robberies are pardonable in a lover are they not sweet lady?
Ros.	Ah Monsieur you are too cunning.
Mon. .	Ah! Madame you are too bewitching.
Ros.	Away I must no longer allow myself the pleasure of your company.
Mon. .	And it would be impolite to begin by disobeying therefore my soul's idol I leave you to the cogitation of your own sweet thoughts.
Ros.	I defer until some future period my reply to your proposals.
Mon.	Adieu sovereign ruler of my heart and thoughts. What beauty! what grace! Would to heaven she had been born in Paris [exit.]
Ros.	(sola) *[same in Goldoni]* Ha ha. had I indeed been born in Paris I fear my attractions would have proved too much for the poor little man's wits which appear none of the strongest.

Act the Second
Scene 1st

Rosaura's apartment.
Rosaura and her father the Doctor.

Ros.   I fear I have unconsciously offended my honored parent how
            else can I account for his so seldom visiting me

Doc.   My dear child you know that in my profession a man's time is
            not at his own disposal. he is the slave of the public. it is for them
            he refrains from rest, scarcely allowing himself the necessary
            sustenance of life. but the object of my present visit is in the first
            place, to thank you for your kind attentions to your sister Eleanor
            in allowing her so long to visit you.

Ros.   I wish to give her an opportunity of marrying.

Doc.   It is on that subject I now wish to consult you. our friend Signor
            Pantalone is much inclined to make her his wife.

Ros.   Oh. do not give her an old man.

Doc.   Why! have you not already set her the example.

Ros.   It is too true, let her therefore profit by my experience.

Doc.   Pshaw! *["Basta" in Goldoni; "Nonsense!"]* however I'll speak
            to the girl, and if she be inclined I presume you will not be the
            one to mar her good fortune.

Ros.   I should be the last to oppose your wish but do not my dear
            Father do not compel the poor girl to bestow her hand upon one
            who never can gain her affections.

Doc.   Well well we'll say no more about it. but tell me Rosaura what
            say you to marrying again.

Ros.   I should not have the slightest objection provided I meet with an
            eligible offer.

Doc.   There is a Spanish Don who is much pleased with you.

Ros.   What is his name?

Doc.   Don Alvaro di Castiglia.

Ros.   O I know him. I met him at the ball last night.

Doc.   He was very solicitous to be introduced to you, so I brought him
            with me. I know him to be an honest, well bred man, and if you
            have no other engagement, you may probably be able to turn his
            good opinion of you to some account.

Ros.   My only motive in receiving the Spanish gentleman is in acquiescence of my father's wish.

Doc.   I must now wish you good morning. I think it will be a most desirable thing for you to marry again my dear Daughter, for excuse me if I tell you. A Widow who is constantly gading [*sic*] about to balls and Masquerades does not make the most respectable figure in the world. [exit.]

Scene 2^d
Rosaura sola. *[not in Goldoni]*

Ros.   He would give me a gentle check. good old gentleman but only think of the conquests I last night achieved! I should have them recorded in letter*[s]* of gold. what could there have been in me so particularly fascinating. Milord Runebif. Monsieur le Blan. the poor Count, and here comes the grave Don to complete this interesting quartetto. *[This review of Rosaura's beaux is absent from Goldoni, as is the Italian word "quartetto"]*

[Enter Don Alvaro]

Alv.   I have the honor to salute Signora Rosaura de Bisognosi.

Ros. .   Don Alvaro di Castiglia.

Alv. .   It was by your father's earnest entreaty that I was induced to accompany him here. but I cannot now repent of my condescension since it has afforded me so agreeable an interview.

Ros.   My father has done wrong to persuade you to take so much trouble, and conduct you here merely to be annoyed by my wearisome conversation.

Alv.   You are a lady of such superior mind, that I was fully aware I should be recompensed for my trouble.

Ros.   Will you favor me by taking a seat. [they seat themselves.] What do you think of Italy Don Alvaro?

Alv.   It is a fine country tho' not to be compared with Spain.

Ros.   But what do you say to the Italians.

Alv.   They do not sufficiently appreciate their own merits. neither do they maintain a proper dignity of deportment.

Ros.   You would not have them proud or knightly

Alv.   I should wish to see them graver in their manners, and less seen in public.

Ros.   But it is the custom of our country.

Alv   Softly. I do not include you in my remark. You do not resemble an Italian, the other night you astonished me. whereso[e']er you moved respect and veneration seized on all around, you bore the escort semblance of a Spanish Donna, and notwithstanding the universally acknowledged superiority of our females over all other nations, at that moment you appeared to my eyes still more lovely.

Ros.   Such uncommonness from the lips of Don Alvaro may well inspire that Self Respect of which you hold us so deficient.

Alv.   It is not my wish long to intrude upon your leisure. How goes the day?

Ros   Tis nearly twelve o'clock.

Alv.   What says our infallible? [takes out his watch.] This is a fine piece of English workmanship.

Ros   But they are manufactured in Spain likewise, am I not right?

Alv.   Possibly! but in Spain there are few who work.

Ros.   Indeed then how do the poor subsist?

Alv.   Madam, there are no poor in Spain.

Ros.   (Oh that is capital).

Alv.   [whilst looking at the hour lets fall his watch upon the ground.] Va al Diavolo [same in Goldoni; "Go to the devil."] [gives it a kick and tosses it to the front of the stage].

Ros.   What have you done? a watch of such value!

Alv.   That which has lain at my feet, is no longer worthy for my hands to touch.

Ros.   Well said.

Alv.   But how is it that the whole time I have been here you have not made one single request.

Ros.   What can I have to request of you beyond the continuance of your favors.

Alv.   The favors of a Spaniard are not so easily acquired. you are dignified and graceful and I could soon persuade myself to love you. but for you to become mine there are many further requisites.

Ros.   Favor me by mentioning in what I am deficient

Alv.   I would know in what degree of estimation you hold nobility.

Ros.   It is my divinity.

Alv.   I would know if you sufficiently despise low born and ignoble minds.

Ros   I detest, I abhor them.

Alv.   I must ascertain if you have the virtue to prefer noble blood to perishable beauty.

Ros.   I pray constantly to that effect.

Alv.   Then you are worthy of my choice I must now leave you.

Ros.   Why must you go so soon?

Alv.   I dare no longer trust to my hauteur.

Ros.   (I would fain try my powers that way) [puts on a grave face] and you think to retain this severity of manner.

Alv.   (She delights me!)

Ros.   But know proud Spaniard that from long protracted suffering will I teach you to extend your pity.

Alv   I will endure with rapture.

Ros.   Even with sighs shall thou fulfil my behest.

Alv. .   How sweet to die for one who can so well maintain her dignity.

Ros.   Begin then to fear me. Depart!

Alv.   I am compelled to obey.

Ros.   Not another look.

Alv.   Oh what a decree! what a refinement of severity! let the spirit of a martyr burn within and I will glory in my chains. (exit.)

Rosaura   (sola) Is it possible that A man can make such a fool of himself, why the creature['s] only delight seems in tormenting himself.

[sit*[s]* down] Heigho! What a morning this has been—four offers
in the space of a few hours might have harmed any young creature's brain—but thank heaven. I'm no longer a chicken and
must weigh the advantages on all sides. first Milord, that most
incomprehensible being, he would very possibly make an excellent husband, but then he is so cold and phlegmatic, his very
presence chills me—le petit maitre le Blan is amusing enough
for the moment, but such frivolity soon becomes wearisome. Don
Alvaro di Castiglia I fear would never forgive himself for having
degraded his illustrious house by marrying the Widow of a Venisian *[Venetian]* merchant. now I have past *[sic]* sentence upon
three out of the four. and who now remains . . . would that the
Italian were of a less jealous temperament! and yet tis said that
jealousy is the offspring of true love . . . that he loves me I can
no longer doubt. his every word and look confirms it—beside
this note that he this morning sent me is not this sufficient testimony such language flows but from a warm and tender heart. O
Alonso *[not in Goldoni; first name of Count, but not clarified
until fifth scene of third act]* forgive your Rosaura if she but for
a moment doubted thee. such cool deliberation on thy only fault
is but a poor requital of thy love. I'll suffer it no longer. [exit.]

Scene 3ᵈ
Rosaura's apartment, table with implements for writing

The Doctor and Eleanora. *[altered from ''Eleanor'' here and in remaining
text of second act, with both spellings used in third act]*

Doc.   This kind offer of our good friend Signor Pantalone is a most
          advantageous thing for you for consider if the Signor Stefanello
          [altered from earlier spelling ''Stefanelo''] was an opulent man
          how much more so must his brother be who inherits the greater
          part of the property.

Elea.   My dear father to tell the truth I have no further objection to this
          match, than the great disproportion of our ages.

Doc.   Do not let that be an obstacle, he is a well informed thoughtful
          old man and will treat you like a little Queen.

Elea.   As you seem to think it desirable I can no longer hesitate in
          accepting Signor Pantalone for it has ever been my delight im-
          plicitly to obey my father's will.

Doc.	Well said! my child! you are a blessing to your father. I will now go and immediately acquaint Signor Pantalone, before you alter your good resolution. (exit)
Ele.	It is a flattering prospect to be made a rich lady, and mistress of a house. But to have this old fellow for a husband is not quite so pleasant. Marionette I have good news for you I'm going to be married.
Mar.	You delight me but who is to be your spouse?
Ele	Signor Pantalone.
Mar.	And that you call good news! are you pleased? Are you contented?
Ele.	Do you not think it a good match.
Mar.	Yes. for a woman of sixty. but you who are a young girl—
Ele.	I thought so at first, but upon consideration of his wealth his age appears but of little consequence.
Mar.	It is of great consequence—it is of vital importance. Ask your Sister hear what she says, of a young girl marrying an old man. if I chose I could tell you all about it. I am not old yet I have had three husbands, but were I to marry again give me none of your grey hair'd gentlemen.
Ele	Certainly not provided you might have your choice.
Mar.	With your beauty and attraction I declare you almost deserve a Frenchman.
Ele	Find the Frenchman who would have me.
Mar.	Oh I could not wish for a more agreeable task. I'll find you one.
Ele	But besides being young, he must be handsome and rich.
Mon. *[sic]*	Of such, there is no scarcity in Paris.
Ele.	Should I not then go to Paris.
Mar.	No my dear young lady, they are arriving daily in Venice there is one I should particularly wish you to see. He met your sister at the ball last night, and has this morning payed *[sic]* her a visit.
Ele	But if he admires my sister he will not trouble himself about me
Mar.	Oh! these Parisians easily transfer their affections a sigh will bring them at your feet in an instant.

Ele.   You describe them as very inconstant.

Mar.   So long as your *[sic]* married what's that to you.

Ele.   But a husband's love.

Mar.   My dear how gothic! I declare you make me blush. But do you wish to see this Frenchman?

Ele.   There can be no harm in seeing him.

Mar.   Well then you leave the affair to me. I think I already see in your Sister a predisposition in favor of the Jealous Count. poor thing I pity her taste. Le Blan shall therefore be your prize. A Frenchman! Oh what a lucky girl.

Ele.   But the promise I made my father to marry Sig Pantalone.

Mar.   Tell him you have altered your mind.

Ele   He will accuse me of fickleness

Mar. .   Plead that it is the nature of your sex.

Ele.   He will scold me.

Mar.   Let him.

Ele.   He will threaten.

Mar.   Don't be frighten'd

Ele.   He will compel me by force.

Mar.   My dear the ceremony cannot be performed without you. Stand out firm.

Ele   I fear I shall not be able to resist.

Mar.   I will speak to your Sister we will both assist you.

Ele.   Dear Marionette I depend on you.

Enter Rosaura.

Mar.   Come Signora Rosaura to the assistance of your poor Sister. her father insists on her marrying Sig. Pantalone she abhors the idea, yet has not sufficient courage to disobey a parent's command.

Ele   Dear Rosaura I commend myself to you.

Ros.   At present retire to your chamber.

Ele.   But if I should meet my father what shall I say?

Ros.	Tell him that on such a subject you cannot decide without asking my advice.
Ele.	But he will say he is my father and has superior claim.
Ros.	Then say that I am the person who must supply your dowery. *[sic]*
Ele	Ah that reply will have more weight than any thing you have yet suggested. I know not how to thank you my dear Sister. (Marionette remember the Frenchman.) (aside) [exit
Mar.	Certainly a mother could not take more interest in the poor girl than you do my dear Mistress. But somebody calls, allow me to go and see who it is. (exit)
Ros	It is too barbarous a custom to dispose of females' hearts to the certain ruin of their happiness.

Enter Marionette

Mar.	Madam here is Monsieur le Blan's valet, come with a message from his master.
Ros.	Show him in.
Mar	Come Signor French valet.

Arlecchino enter*[s]* dressed as a French valet *[and]* comes forward making grotesque bows.

Ros.	Bravo! bravo! but I fear you will fatigue yourself speak if you have any thing to say from your master.
Arl.	Madam at the behest of my Master, I come to present you a Jewel. [Speaks with affectation]
Ros.	A Jewel for me.
Arl.	For you Ma'm. but before I give it you, that is to say before I present it you I ought to make a compliment of which I aspire I do not remember a word.
Ros.	Then I think you had better return to your master and get you*[r]* speech by heart.
Arl.	Well I thought I *[would]* have a try at it first, but in case I should fail master wrote down the grand compliment in the sacred depository (those were his very words) of this here bit of paper. [presents a note]

Ros.	(Reads) "Accept sovereign ruler of my soul this little token of adoration from thy most abject slave. Such is my form but who could do justice to this heart." what does this mean but perhaps the present will itself resolve this enigma.
Arl.	A Jewel, a precious invaluable Jewel. See here it is. [presents a portrait]
Ros.	Is this it?
Mar	Does the portrait of a Parisian appear insignificant in your eyes.
Arl.	Madame I pray you for a reply, on which depends the happiness of the master and the interest of the servant.
Ros	Wait an instant and you shall have one. [goes to the table and writes]
Mar.	Pray by what good fortune have you risen from waiter at an Inn, to the honor of valet to a Frenchman.
Arl.	Really I can hardly tell you neither shall care much about it if it can procure me the good graces of Signora Mar.
Ros.	Here is your reply it is unnecessary for me to direct it.
Arl.	I trust it is an agreeable one for you must know we I and my master made an agreement that my master was to pay me according to the nature of your reply.
Ros.	You have fulfiled [sic] your commission you may now depart.
Arl.	Good day to you ladies. [bows I wish you a good morning. [bows frequently] exit
Mar.	Well as I live there's another lackey running across the hall.
Ros.	What does he want let him come in
Mar.	O! It's Milord's servant.

Enter Birif [same in Goldoni]

Bir	Madame. (makes a low bow.
Mar	(Oh see what gravity)
Ros.	Whence come you Sir?
Bir.	Milord Runebif sent me as he was prevented coming himself. he send[s] you this trifle. [presents her a watch.]

Ros.	Oh how beautiful see Marionette what a magnificent watch. but did your master send me *[a]* message.
Bir	No Madam.
Ros.	Pray give him my compliments.
Bir	Madam (bows and is going)
Ros.	Favor me (presents him some money)
Bir.	You surprise me Madame. [refuses to take it. exit)
Mar.	The Italian would not have refused it.
Ros.	Neither I suspect would the Frenchman. but who comes here wrapt in a cloak.
Mar.	It is Arlecchino again but in the dress of a Spanish servant

Enter Arlecchino

Arl.	May the Heavens grant you a long life Donna Rosaura. [bows]
Ros.	What is all this acting? who do you now wish to represent, who sent you?
Arl.	Don Alvaro di Castiglia my master, he sends Donna Rosaura a treasure. Behold it (he bows again) stoop your head. This is the geneological *[sic]* Tree of Don Alvaro.
Ros.	This is not a present to be slighted [takes it] did he say nothing.
Arl.	Why yes he said something but I should quite have forgotten it. If I had not been prudent enough to write it down [gives her a note]
Ros.	Wait an instant and I will give you a reply. [goes to the table]
Mar.	Now do tell me what freak is this to change your dress.
Arl.	Obedience to my master's will
Mar.	Bless my heart, and you adopted his manners too.
Ros.	Here is my reply.
Arl.	I am your humble servant Donna Rosaura. [*[preceding single bracket seems to have been copied too soon and reappears in its proper place following Arlecchino's next line below]*
Ros.	Good day.

Arl.   Adieu Marionette [exit with great solemnity.] *["Addio, Mario-
                nette" in Goldoni]*

Ros   Come Marionette let us go and see how fares it with poor El-
                eanora

Scene 4th

Milord and the Count, the street.

Cou.   Milord how is it that you do not keep your engagement with
                Signora Rosaura.

[Milord passes without reply.]

Cou.   Truly she is a lady of very distinguished manners and deserving
                the attentions of so accomplished a gentleman as Milord Runebif.
                they do say that the condescending gracefulness (we will not call
                it Coquetry) of a fair Italian's manners but ill accord with an
                English gentleman's idea of Female propriety. Now I on the
                contrary think that the two extremes must counteract each other.
                suppose for instance an English host receiving an annual visit
                from his most particular friend, how cold and repulsive are his
                manners. whilst the fair Italian of course runs with open arms to
                welcome the the *[first "the" ends a line; second "the" begins
                the next line, indicating another copying error]* stranger the bo-
                som friend of her dear lord overpowering him with protestations
                of endless love and affection. What say you Milord to this picture
                of conjugal bliss? But I do wrong to detain you. will not Rosaura
                be expecting her sweet Lord? (The cold blooded rascal I had
                hoped by this bantering to have engaged him in a duel and so
                terminate either by his death or my own this world of uncertainty.

Birif and Foletto *[same in Goldoni]* enter

Bir.   Sir [presents my lord *[not "Milord"]* with a note.

Fol.   Most illustrious Count [the Count makes *[a]* sign for him not to
                speak. Foletto gives him a letter]

Mil   Have you done as I bid you?

Bir   Yes Sir.

Mil   Accepted? (to Birif

Bir   With thanks.

Mil.   You may go (gives him money) [Birif bows and Exit*[s]*.]

Count makes a sign to Foletto to to *["to" copied twice]* go he holds out his hand for money but the Count pushes it away.

Fol.   Oh delightful Italy, but detestable to serve [exit.]

Cou   (That fellow brought Milord some reply possibly it is some message from Rosaura) my friend I congratulate you. But how is it you manage the ladies run after you. Messages fly about Madam Ros.

Mil. .   Oh you mad fellow. [exit]

Cou.   I a mad fellow by heaven he shall pay for his insolence. I'll make the dumb rascal reply to the call of my sword. [grasps it] exit]

Don Alvaro enters from the opposite side.

Alv.   Arlecchino is I fear a faithless messenger. or else Rosaura is undeserving of my attention. such tardiness of reply is not to be endured by gentlemen of my descent—but perchance—the examination of my present yet detains her. there are twenty four generation*[s]*. A king is at the head, then follow many Princes and heros all deserving of attention. this delay is I see excusable. but here comes A*[r]*lecchino.

Enter Arlecchino.

Arl.   Donna Rosaura wishes you great happiness. (bows

Alv.   What said she to my tree?

Arl.   She kiss'd it over and over again, raised her eye brows and was breathless with wonder.

Alv.   Did you punctually deliver the compliment.

Arl   Oh to perfection.

Alv.   What was her reply?

Arl.   Here are the revered observations of Donna Rosaura. [bows and gives a note]

Alv.   My heart is prepare*[d]* for delight. [reads] "with many thanks I accept the portrait which you have deigned to send me." What's this?

Arl.   (aside) well now I am in for it. if I haven't changed the notes and given him the little Frenchman's reply instead of his own. But never mind a little spirit will carry me through and set all right again.)

Alv.	Why do you not answer when I speak to you. I tell you I do not understand this note.
Arl.	Is not the tree of your house the portrait of your grandeur?
Alv.	Oh I thought it must be so. [reads] for the respect I entertain for the original—for the original—how is that?
Arl.	Tell me who is first person in your tree?
Alv.	A King of Castiglia.
Arl.	See the pride of her heart how she piques herself on your noble descent.
Alv.	And not without reason. [reads] ''I cannot send you mine as I have none'' that does not look well—but to continue [reads] ''I will have this inestimable Treasure enchained in a locket of Gold'' the Devil what crammy tree into a Locket?
Arl.	Oh thats [sic] a little mistake. she means a Gold frame.
Alv.	[reads] ''and wear the Jewel next my heart.'' it is more than I could expect, to carry a thing of such magnitude about her person.
Arl.	Oh she's Poetic she does not mean actually to hang it round her neck but to have it always near her.
Alv.	Well I suppose that is her meaning. Adieu [is going]
Arl.	Cavalier
Alv.	What do you want?
Arl.	How's the memory?
Alv.	Who dare ask me such a question.
Arl.	True. then I suppose Spanish Dons like your Messeurs [sic] Francais pocket their promises.
Arl. [sic]	Oh! I had quite forgotten you. but you have served me faithfully and I must reward you according to deserts. here friend take a pinch of snuff from my snuff box. [earlier in the second act in Goldoni, Don Alvaro and Rosaura exchange snuff boxes, so Arlecchino is originally rewarded with snuff from Rosaura]
Arl.	I'm much obliged Sir. [tosses the contents into the Don's face and runs off. the Don follows. exeunt)

Scene 5th
A dressing Room
Le Blan discovered at a glass finishing his toilet.

Mons.   Upon my word these boots are more than one could have expected to have found in Italy but I shall never forgive my stupidity in not bringing with me three or four dozen pairs from Paris.
Heigho. I believe its *[sic]* time I left this place, my wardrobe's
woefully on the decline. my taste I fear also will become vitiated
by any longer familiarity with their horrible cut. how famously
I cheated the pretty Widow this morning, into a belief that this
poor sash was genuine Parisian. sweet confiding creature, she
believed in every word I told,—by the by I must hear what she
said to my portrait (rises and goes to the glass) of what she
<u>thought</u> of it there can be little doubt. Arlecchino!

Enter Arlecchino dressed as a French Valet bows.

Mons.   Bravo! bravo! with a little more of my tuition you may really
pass for a French man. but have you seen Madam.

Arl.   I have would I had not.

Mons.   Why do you say so?

Arl.   What beauty! what grace! what eyes! what a mouth! what a nose!
what a neck! [with affectation.]

Mon.   (One would think this fellow had been to Paris. that is exactly
the faults of our servants. They always fall in love with their
masters *[sic]* ladies (aside) Did you present the portrait.

Arl.   I presented it and she pressed it tenderly to her bosom.

Mons.   Hold! hold! I shall expire with delight.

Arl.   She could not cease from weeping on it.

Mons.   Sweet creature, did you recite my compliment.

Arl.   I recited it, accompanied with tears.

Mons.   Bravo Arlecchino did I not tell you your *[sic]* were born for this.
[kisses him]

Arl.   Sir do not be alarmed on hearing if she—Oh Heavens.

Mons.   Speak dear Arlecchino what did she do?

Arl.   Hearing those sweet words she fainted.

Mons.	You enchant me you beatify me, you raise me to the highest heaven of felicity. But tell me, what was her reply?
Arl.	(The Devil! what shall I do I have given it to the Spaniard) aside. She gave it me but . . . but.
Mons.	But what?
Arl.	I have lost it.
Mons.	Ah villain! rascal! that thou art to lose so precious a thing. by heavens I can scarcely refrain from running you through with this sword (draws his sword)
Arl.	I have found I've found it. (I had better give him the Spaniard's.) Hold. here it is
Mons	Sweet my Arlecchino solace of my woes. herald of my love. [embraces him]
Arl.	(I'm afraid I shall have some trouble in duping this good gentleman, he'll out with his sword again.
Mons.	Oh adored paper that pourest balm into my tortured breast. I open my bosom to receive thee. What delight rushes to my heart. Let me read. [reads] "I greatly admire the magnificent tree of your house." how the tree, she cannot mean my portrait.
Arl.	To be sure she does, are not you the only survivor of your family.
Mons.	Tis true.
Arl.	Well then dont [sic] you perceive the aptness of the simily? [sic]
Mons.	Ah Yes. Well no I should not have expected such a jeu d'esprit from an Italian lady.
Arl.	Oh I assure you they abound in wit.
Mons.	but to continue [reads] "and I perceive that you derive your origin from Princes and Heros." the devil she does. 'tis more than I ever discovered.
Arl.	And are you a Frenchman and at a loss for the meaning of that speech?
Mons.	I confess she puzzles me.
Arl.	Looking at your portrait "see," says she, "what a fine expression what a great and noble mien. you may tell at the first glance that he is the descendent of Princes and Heros."

Arl. *[sic]*	Ah you are the Prince of Interpreters. [kisses him] but let's on [reads] "if I might hope to be classed with those Heroines"—What Heroines?
Arl.	All those nymphs who adore you.
Mons.	You say well—no small number—an honorable assemblage truly to be admired so. [reads] "I should henceforth look upon myself as the most noble branch of our then enobled *[sic]* tree." What tree again. how proud she is of her simily. *[sic]*
Arl.	Then you understand. by being loved by you she will become noble and also her old father who is the tree of her house.
Mons.	Bravo. long live the great Arlecchino he deserves a boundless recompence. *[sic]*
Arl.	(Indeed he does) aside
Mons.	I cannot think what to offer you as a sufficient reward for so well executed an embassy.
Arl.	An Englishman on a similar occasion gave me a purse.
Mons.	A purse? tis not sufficient. you could not have done so much for him as you have for me, so extraordinary an obligation. But hold I have thought of a recompence *[sic]* deserving of your merits. Here I will divide with you the most precious jewel I have on earth. [gives him the back of R.letter] [exit]

Arlecchino stands staring after him with the bit of Paper in his hand. [Curtain drops]

Act the Third.
Scene 1ˢᵗ
Rosaura's Boudoir.
Rosaura and Marionette.

Ros.	Well now Marionette I suppose you will hardly give me the merit of inventing a scheme which would do credit to the spirited Dames of your nation.
Mar.	You know I always said you had more spirit than any Italian I ever met with.
Ros.	I am very anxious to make trial of the affections and fidelity of my four lovers. so at the Carnival Masquerades I propose disguising myself, and appearing before each of them as an as an *[copying error; "as an" ends one page and is repeated at the*

beginning of the next page] unknown admirer. I can adopt the dress, language, and national peculiarities of each nation and endeavor to appear as their countrywoman in this I flatter myself I shall succeed for I was always an excellent mimic. it is by these means only I can hope to discover by whom I am truly loved.

Mar.   The thought does not displease me, but I consider it more than probable that in the end you may not wish to marry either.

Ros.   Well the event will decide. in order to support these several characters, I have need of a little instruction. You can aid me in the French personage.

Mar.   And the English also having been three years in England. You must assume an awkward bashfulness in your deportment, a hesitating address and clumsy hobbling gait. these are the striking features of an English Female.

Ros.   Come come you are too severe

Mar.   By no means. I assure you it is a most faithful portrait. But will not your voice betray you?

Ros.   I can easily disguise that. [exeunt both]

Scene 2^d
Street before Rosaura's house

Mons. le Blan, and Don Alvaro each unperceived by the other reading Rosaura's note.

Mons.   (So my portrait she likens to the tree of my house, it is a comical simily.) *[sic]*

Alv.   (My genealogical tree is thus considered the portrait of my grandeur. That's very proper.)

Mons.   (My origin from Princes and Monarchs. surely the gipsey's *[sic]* not laughing at me.)

Alv. .   (To be sure the stock of a tree might be called the original.)

Mons.   ("If I might hope to be classed with all these Heroine*[s]*") *[previously, the note read, "classed with those Heroines"]* that is most inexplicable.

Alv.   My genealogical tree suspended from her neck. Oh preposterous!

Mons.   Arlecchino cannot have delivered his proper message.

Arl. *[sic]*   The servant has not interpreted rightly.

Enter Arlecchino

sees these two reading their notes goes up to them on tiptoe and snatches their notes from their hand*[s]* changes them and gives each his proper reply saying "By your leave Sirs." [exit]

Mons	[Reads] "I accept the portrait which you have deigned to send me, for the estime *[sic]* I entertain for the original" *[previously, the note read, "for the respect I entertain for the original"]* Ah there spoke my sweet Rosaura.
Alv.	[Reads] "I greatly admire the magnificent Tree of your noble house" *[previously, the note read, "your house"]* this is indeed the proper style of addressing me.)
Mons.	"I cannot send you mine in return as I do not possess one." *[previously, the note read, "I cannot send you mine as I have none"]* That's provoking.
Alv.	"And I perceive you derive your origin from Princes And Monarchs." *[previously, the note read, "And I perceive that you derive your origin from Princes and Heros"]* Tis well said.)
Mons.	I so greatly value this precious jewel, that I will have it enclosed in a locket of gold and wear it next my heart." *[previously, the note read, "I will have this inestimable Treasure enchained in a locket of Gold and wear the Jewel next my heart"]* Oh adorable creature! [kisses the note]
Alv.	"If I might hope to be classed among those heroines I should become the most noble branch of our then enobled *[sic]* tree" *[previously, the note read, "If I might hope to be classed with those Heroines I should hence forth look upon myself as the most noble branch of our then enobled tree"]* It would indeed be no small glory to her.
Mons	(That impudent rascal to withhold from me an instant such adorable intelligence.)
Alv.	Arlecchino must have given me at first a wrong reply.
Mons.	I lay a wager he gave me a note addressed to the Don.
Alv.	Perhaps he exchanged my note with some reply of Rosaura's to that frivolous Frenchman)

Mons.   My friend did you ever present Madame Rosaura with your gene-
          alogical tree.

Alv.   First tell me if you ever sent her your portrait.

Mons.   I will not deny it.

Alv.   I confess I did.

Mons.   I must then congratulate you on the esteem in which she holds
          your noble family.

Alv.   And I rejoice with you. that she received your portrait with so
          much courtesy.

Mons   You seek for possession of her favors.

Alv.   And you to gain her affections.

Mons   Then we are rivals.

Alv.   And consequently enemies.

Mons.   No my friend that need not follow.

Alv.   Don Alvaro di Castiglia could never endure for one to usurp the
          smallest portion of his lady's love.

Mons.   What then are your intentions?

Alv.   I intend that you shall herefore [sic] relinquish all pretention
          [sic] to Signora Rosaura.

Mons.   That will I do never!

Alv.   Our swords then must decide.

Mons.   Willingly I admit the trial.

Alv.   Let us retire to a more sequestered spot.

Mons.   I follow instantly.

Alv.   Now shall he suffer for his insolence [exit]

Mons   (solus) Hail to thee love hail beauteous Rosaura. fear not my
          angel. I come to lay my laurels at your feet. [is going]

[Marionette from the window]

[Mar.]   Ah Monsieur le Blan?

Mons   What Marionette.

Mar.   Would you wish to see Madame Eleanora?

Mons.	Would to heaven I could procure that pleasure.
Mar.	Then I'll make her come to the window. [puts her head in]
Mons	I'm all impatience to behold her . . . But Don Alvaro awaits me . . . and who is he? Am I to let skip the opportunity of an interview with a beautiful female merely for the satisfaction of fighting a madman. [Eleanora comes to the balcony. But Behold the orient Sun rising from the balcony of the East, but how far surpassing that dull orb is she who now presents herself before my dazzled eyes Alas Poor Rosaura hide your diminished head and crouch at the footstool of a superior divinity. Mademoiselle think not unworthily of a heart consecrated at the high altar of your sovereign beauty.
Ele.	Signor I have not the honor of knowing you.
Mons.	I am your most faithful adorer.
Ele.	How long have you been so?
Mons.	Since the dear moment when I first beheld thee.
Ele.	And were you so soon taught to love.
Mons.	Oh little needs there here instruction on so sweet a theme, to behold is to adore.
Ele.	I fear these are but idle words.
Mons.	O lady by the Heavens where in thou dwellest by the all radiant light of those sweet eyes by the veracity of a Frenchman do I sware *[sic]* I have thee with young love's wild devotion.
Ele.	Alas! these are but every day professions.
Mons.	O lady! lady! why thus incredulous—behold then a victim expiring before the altar of his divinity.
Ele.	Alas! poor Romeo. *[not in Goldoni]*
Mons.	And you deride my passion whilst I am drowned in bitter tears. [affects to weep]
Ele.	And can you weep. poor Soul I pity you.
Mar. *[sic]*	Would that the heat of these my suffocating sighs could melt the icy fetters of thy heart.
Ele. .	Methinks that in a slight degree I already feel their influence.

Mons.	Sayest thou so sweet lady then permit me to enter your presence there will I sigh and sigh till one by one each icy link shall melt away setting thy captive heart at liberty. then in this faithful bosom let the trembling fugitive find rest. [kneels]
Ele.	O rise! rise. I entreat you do I not see my father? yes tis he. I must away. exit]

Enter the Doctor.

Mons.	Oh heavens! she has disappeared and without bidding me one kind adieu, what unheard of cruelty.
Doc.	Who are you talking to?
Mons.	Behold in me a wretch suffering under the most severe bereavement. the light of my eyes, my soul, my Eleanor has fled.
Doc.	Am I to understand that your honor loves the lady who resides in this house.
Mons.	Oh! to distraction.
Doc	And pray may I ask how long you have been her admirer.
Mons.	Some few moments, since I beheld her radiant form at that balcony.
Doc.	I am all astonishment. that you could so soon fall in love.
Mons.	Oh we Frenchmen have so much vivacity, and such tender hearts. A look might prove fatal.
Doc.	And are your affections durable?
Mons.	Durable! they last as long as the little God of Love ordains, who is the sovereign of our hearts.
Doc.	Then if Love commands you tomorrow to forget Sig. Eleanora must you obey him.
Mons.	Helas! Oui. [not in Goldoni]
Doc	Oh! indeed! then I must go speedily and acquaint her of this charming versatility of affection in her most faithful adorer.
Mons.	Excuse me, why should she know it?
Doc.	It will no doubt greatly raise you in her esteem.
Mons.	I thank you for your kind intentions but excuse me when I desire that you will not acquaint her with this conversation or by heavens! this sword shall be your future confabulator. and pray may

I ask who are you? that you take so lively an interest in mine and Signora Eleanora's affairs.

Doc. Well to undeceive you know that I am her father.

Mons. Ah Monsieur le Docteur my excellent friend my revered father in law do me the favor to say which of your sweet daughters you will permit me to adore.

Doc. O Both if you will.

Mons. Ah Yes they are both so amiable, and do you know my dear friend a Frenchman has affections sufficient for a hundred. permit me to knock at this door.

Doc. It is my Daughter's house but however you may knock. [Monsieur knocks]

Mons. Oh happy father of two sovereign beauties. [the door is opened]

Mons. I follow you.

Doc It is not the custom of this country for fathers to open the door to their Daughters [*sic*] gallants. by your leave Sir. [pushes him back, goes in and shuts the door]

Mons. Monsieur! Monsieur! mon ami! my dear Doctor well well if he shuts the door I'll find my way in at another or if the worst comes to the worst I can but get in at the window. [exit]

Scene 3^d
The interior of a Caffé *["bottega" in Goldoni]* with seats
Milord and Count.

Cou Bring me Coffee *["caffè" in Goldoni]* [they bring coffee to Milord and Count.] Oh do not give Milord coffee he prefers the chocolate of the Ladies, what he gets at a Caffe *[accent mark is omitted]* does not please him. [Milord stoops his head and drinks]

Cou. Good Milord Would you not prefer a glass of liqueur it will raise your spirits give brilliancy

Milord [drinks again.]

Cou. This fashion of not answering when addressed is some thing quite new. its novelty is no doubt quite charming to the Italian ladies who have ever found in their Country men in such wearisome attention and politeness of manner.

[Milord looks fiercely at him]

Cou.   But what says our pretty Widow to this amiable excentricity *[sic]*
            of manner.

[Milord rises, and is going to leave the Caffé]

Cou.   Yes you do well to go and take the air.

Mil   Follow me Sir.

Cou.   By what authority do you command me?

Mil.   If you are a gentleman prepare to fight.

Cou.   Most willingly I obey that summons. [they come to front of shop]

Mil   Learn to say less and more to the purpose.

Cou.   Dictate not to me you cold blooded rascal.

Mil   Prepare. [draws his sword the Count does the same] we fight till
            blood flows.

Cou.   Come on [they fight the Count is wounded]

Mil.   See you bleed, I wish you no harm, let us desist I am satisfied.
            [replaces his sword] let us shake hands my friend. [offers his
            hand to the Count who repulses it fiercely, muttering]

Cou.   fool that I was to miss my aim. [exit]

Scene 4th
The outside of a Caffé *["caffettiere" in Goldoni]*
Don Alvaro.

Alv.   Le Blan not yet arrived the cowardly renegade. the thought of
            such a contest might well appal the Frenchman, but he who flys
            [sic] from the stroke of my sword deserves the chastisement of
            my whip waiter bring me coffee [he sits down at side table]

Arlecchino Enters

Arl.   [aside] now is the time to make peace with the Spaniard.) comes
            up to him Cavalier may the Heavens watch over you.

Alv.   Good day Arlecchino.

Arl.   I wish to speak with your Lordship if you will allow me.

Alv.   About what? do not fear.

Arl.   Oh concerning Donna Rosaura.

Alv.	Dear Arlecchino console me with some assurance of my sweet lady's love.
Arl.	She has sent me to invite you this evening to her supper, she was sitting at table as I may be, and hardly a word could her delicate lips utter besides the revered name of Don Alvaro di Castiglia.
Alv.	Sweet Rosaura dear Mistress of my heart. tell me then faithful herald of my happiness tell me what said she of her noble lord.
Arl.	If you allow me, I will accompany her words with the actions she made use of.
Alv.	Do. I grant thee leave that I may at once be transported into her sweet presence.
Arl.	Being at desert *[sic]* she took a biscuit precisely of the same sort as these [takes one] and bathing it three times in her wine as I may do in this coffee and eating it gently, just in the same elegant manner [he eats the biscuit] said, ''go seek Don Alvaro, and tell him—tell him—that—for him—I care not a fig. [runs out laughing]
Alv.	Oh the villanous *[sic]* knave stop him, stop the rascal that I may chastise him. Donna Rosaura is incapable of such a speech this insult has raised the thunderbolt of my anger.

Enter le Blan.

Mon.	Pray do not accuse me of . . .
Alv.	In good time thou comest, draw this instant [draws
Mons.	Sweet my Rosaura to thee do I consecrate my victim. [draws his sword]
Alv.	Back to hell from whence thou comest.
Mons.	Be thou then my guide. [they fight]

Rosaura masked as a French woman rushes between.

Ros.	Henri. *[no first name in Goldoni]* dear Henri desist! I intreat *[sic]* of you to desist. for my sake endanger not your sweet life.
Mons.	Fair mask I fight for my lady.
Ros.	And will you for an Italian through *[sic]* away that life on which alone the existence of one of your own Parisian women depends?
Mons.	But if my rival challenges me I cannot retreat.

Ros.   Your rival will cease to wish for your death when you no longer contend with his happiness.

Mon.   But who is my sweet monitor.

Ros.   My name I cannot reveal but that I love let these sighs alone proclaim. [kneels]

Mon   Rise! Rise! my treasure. I shall expire if I see you here longer.

Ros.   I cannot rise, whilst unpersuaded of your love.

Mon.   [Kneels by her side] Yes lovely creature I swear to love thee, I for ever, and vow eternal fidelity.

Ros.   Oh! that I cannot hope for.

Mon.   Beleive *[sic]* me my hope I will be thine only.

Ros.   Do you not fight for another.

Mon.   But I will leave her for you.

Ros.   Announce it to your rival.

Mon.   Wait one moment henceforward I am thine. [addresses Don Alvaro] My friend I am particularly anxious for a conference with this lady, henceforth Rosaura is yours. Will it please you an instant to suspend our duel?

Alv.   In vain do you hope by this artifice to avoid the encounter.

Mon.   I am a Gentleman and tho' I yeild *[sic]* up my pretentions *[sic]* to Rosaura know that we do not part without fighting. I demand but an instant to reply to that lady.

Alv.   The laws of the Cavalier are studied amongst us long before our alphabet. I will retire into the Caffé. [Replaces his sword and exit*[s]*]

Mon.   Madam behold me entirely your's. *[sic]* I yeild *[sic]* up Madam Rosaura because you command me Out of gratitude bless me with a sight of your face.

Ros.   At present I cannot.

Mon.   But when shall I hope for that delight.

Ros.   Circumstances will not permit me to make myself known to you at present but the time will come. intelligence reached me that you were in danger dear Henri. I heard no more. on the wings of love I flew to the spot were *[sic]* you and Don Alvaro were to meet and thank heaven in time to avert this calamity. with a grateful heart may I now again return to my solitary cell

Mons.   Lady you speak enigmas, surely so fair a form is not immured within a convent's walls.

Ros.   Hist! hist! [looks round fearfully] question me no further. I must away.

Mons.   Oh this is the height of torment. you are not happy. pour your laments into this faithful bosom. say is it some cruel parent's will that compels you to seek this seclusion. say but the word and this single arm moved by all potent love, would rescue you from the very jaws of Cerberus *[not in Goldoni]* himself.

Ros.   This is not the place to reveal my unhappy tale but meet me this evening in the little chapel of the convent of Santa Bianca. there at the foot of the Altar will I recall to your reason my form, one to whom in all the reverses of her fortune her Henri has ever been most dear.

Mon.   I am dying with impatience for that dear moment to arrive but will you leave me without some little token of affection?

Ros.   Such a thing might lead to discovery but by this ordinary locket *[Monsieur gives Rosaura a small bottle in Goldoni]* will I make myself known to you it contains my only treasure [shows it to le Blan who discovers it to be his own portrait]

Mon.   Ah delightful creature. [kisses it]

Ros.   Remember your appointment. [exit]

Mon.   Adieu my angel! but I fear she has too much of the saint in her composition. this meeting in convent chapels is no joke, it only brings a man into trouble. catch me at the foot of an Altar, no, no, she'll never do for me. besides I'm sure she's not French, not genuine Parisian at any rate. I'll back to Rosaura, so now once more to call out the Don. Don Alvaro!

Alv.   Who calls? [Comes forward]

Mon.   A thousand apologizes *[sic]* my dear Don for having so long detained you. but our conflict is quite at an end.

Alv.   But you still mind in your good resolution of yeilding *[sic]* up all pretension to the hand of Signora Rosaura.

Mon.   Upon my soul it was quite a mistake if I led you for a moment to suppose such *[a]* thing I am as ardent as I ever was to profess the affection of so sweet a lady.

Alv.   Then you are prepared to fight.

Mon.   With all my heart.

[they fight again, Rosaura masked as a Spanish lady enters.

Ros.   Gentlemen you but play with your swords.

Alv.   A spanish lady!

Mons.   Madam tis your eyes unnerve my arm.

Ros.   I know you not, it is with Don Alvaro di Castiglia I would speak.

Alv.   What do you desire of your servant?

Ros.   I would speak alone with you. desire that Frenchman to depart.

Alv.   In favor retire a moment.

Mons.   Certainment. *[French spelling is "certainement," but word is not in Goldoni]* (Surely all the women are run mad, thus ends our second encounter.) [exit]

Ros.   Don Alvaro you astonish me and would the whole of Spain be astounded to to *[copying error; "to" ends one page and is repeated at the beginning of the next page]* hear that unmindful of your great descent and lineage you are about to marry the Daughter of a Venisian merchant.

Alv.   Alas! I am covered with shame The voice of this lady produces in me a similar effect as did the enchanted spear of Rinaldo. *[not in Goldoni; a character from the epic poem* Jerusalem Delivered *by Torquato Tasso (1544–95)]* If there still remain a hope for me to escape this detested engagement.

Ros.   By great penance alone can you hope to absolve your indiscretion.

Alv.   Don Alvaro, who knows no other sovereign than his *[own]* kind, willingly submits himself to the grandeur of a heroine.

Ros.   Then sir the first punishment for your misheralded conduct, you shall love me without seeing me and obey me without knowing me.

Alv.   Oh that is too much!

Ros.	I shall follow you round the world still unknown to you, as a watch upon your conduct, give me a sign by which you may at my pleasure recognise me.
Alv.	Take this snuff box [gives her his box]
Ros.	It is perchance the keepsake of some fair one. *[Rosaura says this because in Goldoni, she and Don Alvaro exchange snuff boxes in second act]*
Alv.	It is an exchange of Rosaura's. I despise it. I pray you relieve me of the burden.
Ros.	We meet again this evening.
Alv.	Would that I might know your name
Ros	That time will come. [exit]
Alv.	She is no doubt some beauteous incognito of high birth come to Venice to see the honor of our illustrious house. I trust not without avail. exit.

Scene the 5th
An alcove in the public garden.
The Count, Arlecchino, by

Arl.	Excuse me for breaking in upon your solitude. I have some thing to tell you, Signora Rosaura has sent me to invite all the people at the Hotel to her conversazione *["conversazion" in Goldoni; "evening party"]* this evening.
Cou	The Devil she has. What! every one indiscriminately.
Arl.	I mean to say . . . but I am such a fool! [laughs] a joke I've been playing the Don has made me laugh so I cannot stop myself ha ha.
Cou.	How was that?
Arl.	I was bringing him a message from Sig Rosaura.
Cou.	What docs Don Alvaro hold correspondence with Signora Rosaura.
Arl.	O yes Sir, and she has sent me this evening to invite him
Cou	And does she exclude me?
Arl.	Oh no Sir here is your invitation [gives him a note]

Cou	Then shall I indure *[sic]* the sight of my three rivals.
Arl.	Oh never fear Sir, remember you are her Countryman.
Cou.	Alas! with her that has but little weight

Rosaura masked as an Italian enters and stands apart attentively viewing the Count.

Cou.	But who is that female who stands leaning against that tree she has long been observing us.
Arl.	Heaven knows. but I suppose she's all astonishment at seeing such a dolorous face in these times of rejoicing, good evening Count [exit]

Rosaura approaches

Cou.	And what will you of me lady masker. [Rosaura sighs] Ah had le Blan been here he might have listened to your sighs. but the days are gone when I could enjoy this revelry.
Ros.	Would you offend a lady with whom you are at present wholly unacquainted
Cou	Pardon Signora but masked and in this strange habit and Alone . . .
Ros.	Tis too true this disguise is to myself most distressing, but hear me a rumour is abroad that you, even my Alonso are on the eve of marriage, my faithful heart would not credit the tale yet still there arose a doubt and to relieve my mind from this horrible suspense I sought this interview, but one word from your sweet lips will restore my peace say, is it not a false report—why do you not answer—speak—I command you speak e'en tho your words strike daggers to my soul.
Cou.	Alas! would that I could persuade myself t'were true [sighs] But know that my life my soul are exclusively eternally Rosaura's.
Ros.	And sayest thou so to me villain [draws a stiletto from her bosom and rushes towards the Count, but falters drops the weapon the Count supports her in his arms he removes the mask and discovers Rosaura]
Cou.	Heavens! Rosaura!
Ros.	Oh let me away! let me away I am covered with confusion.
Cou	But one instant. say, is there still left me a ray of hope.

Ros.	Oh no no no. I am unworthy of your love. [turns away.]
Cou	[lets go of Ros. hand and seizes the stiletto] then let not this weapon again miss its aim.
Ros.	[looks round] Ah my stiletto! hold. Alonso I am undeserving such fidelity, but if by the offer of this hand I could hope for your forgiveness, take it. my heart has long been thine.
Cou	Ah do my senses deceive me or am I at once raised to this heaven of bliss in possession of the treasure for which I have so long sought and sued, and this at the moment when I fear'd it had been torn from my eager grasp. yes your eyes confirm my happiness, yet were not this a moment devoted to delight I would ask my sweet Rosaura if t'was not cruel in her thus . . .
Ros.	Yes yes I have trifled with your affections with blushes will I avow it, but a life of tenderest dearest love and obedience shall expiate my fault. I have this evening assembled the four *[should be "three" gentlemen rivals, as the Count is the fourth suitor]* gentlemen who you were pleased to term your rivals and intend giving them a decisive answer to their pretention. *[sic]* it grows late and I fear my absence will be observed let us go, my carriage is in attendance at the Southern gate. [exeunt.]

Scene 6th
A drawing room in Rosaura's chair*[s]* arranged for company
Eleanora and Marionette

Mar.	Well have you made up your mind. you know Signor Pantalone comes to night *[sic]* to receive his final answer.
Elea.	Oh yes I'm determined not to accept his offer.
Mar.	I commend your spirit, now tell me how you like le Blan.
Ele.	Oh I'm delighted with what I have yet seen of him his vivacity and easiness of manner are quite charming but I fear I must not beleive *[sic]* all he says.
Mar.	Pray why not?
Ele.	Oh he professed too much at first sight.
Mar.	Well but you will credit his actions so if he makes you an offer of his hand in marriage what can it signifies *[sic]* what he says.
Ele	But do you think that such a thing is probable.

Mar.	First tell me if you won't make any objection
Ele.	Certainly not. I don't know what lady could object to so very agreeable a gentleman.
Mar.	What reward will you make me, if I succeed in procuring you that good fortune.
Ele.	I would make your fortune.
Mar.	Well leave it to me. I'll manage this affair for you.
Ele.	But what will my sister say you know she must have first choice
M.	Oh she has four suitors to make choice from, besides I've a notion le Blan's no favorite there, we can but pity her taste. however we may make more certain of him on that account confide in me. I'm a woman of my word. I have made more matchs *[sic]* in this world than I have hairs on my head. But here comes your Sister, say no more about it. [enter Ros.]
Ros.	Well, sister you have made a remarkably expeditious toilet this evening
Ele.	I came in but a moment before you.
Ros.	Listen this evening shall I celebrate my marriage with the Count
Ele.	The Count. you have then made your election [looks at at *["at" copied twice]* Marionette who nods and smiles]
Ros.	Yes I have, but what my dear Sister will become of you?
Ele.	I may perhaps soon have a home of my own
Ros.	Say you so, do you then accept the proposals of Sig Pantalone.
Ele.	Heavens defend from such a thought.
Ros	On Whom then do you found your expectations. [Eleanora blushes and looks at Marionette]
Mar.	Bless my stars is it so difficulty *[sic]* a thing to find a husband for such a young Lady as Signora Eleanora.
Ros.	Hush somebody enters.

Enter the Count.

[kneels to Rosaura who extends him her hand he kisses it, then rising addresses Eleanora.]

Cou.	Sweet Eleanora grant the happy Alonso one sisterly embrace.

Ele.   I congratulate you on having gained the affections of so sweet a lady as my sister. and it will ever be my pride to name the Count di Bosconero by the dear title of Brother Alonso.

[The Count and Ros. talk apart.]

Mar.   [to Eleanor] Why you little gipsey. *[sic]* you were just going to let out our secret. you know that your sister will disapprove of the match and would very likely knocked *[sic]* the scheme on the head. pray keep your own counsel.

Enter Don Alvaro.

Alv.   I make my obeisance to Donna Rosaura

Ros.   I am the humble servant of Don Alvaro.

Alv.   Good evening to the whole party.

Ros.   Favor me [the Don seats himself next to Rosaura]

Alv.   I do not see my genealogical tree.

Ros.   It is in the anteroom.

Alv.   In the anteroom! such and *[sic]* object I think would by no means disgrace a drawing room. such thing*[s]* furnish conversation.

Mar.   Don't you think Don it would be better placed over the Street door, then you know people would learn what an honor you are to society.

Alv.   [Ah! the impertinent French woman.]

Enter Mons le Blan

Mons.   Madam Rosaura your most humble servant. Madmoiselle *[sic]* Eleanora I bow to your Sovereign Beauty. Friends I wish you a good evening. Oh Marionette quite well I hope. [all rise and bow]

Ros.   Monsieur le Blan take a seat.

Mon.   The seat is occupied which I could wish for. Mais n'importe. I will seat myself next to this lovely girl [seats himself next to Ele.] Madam Rosaura how have I offended you that you do not condescend to wear my portrait according to your gracious promise to me this morning.

Ros.   I will explain to you.

Mar.   Mistress, Arlecchino has just come to tell me that my lord Anglais and his servant have both left Venice.

Ros.   Oh this is sad intelligence. I had hoped he would have joined our party this evening. however I suppose some urgent business calls him hence. I must now gentlemen claim your attention for a few moments and will take this opportunity of replying to the flattering proposals which I have from each of you this day received. Don Alvaro, how ever my vanity might at the moment have been gratified by your noble offer my prudence soon suggested to me, the folly of incuring *[sic]* those censures which as the Daughter of a Venesian citizen must justly have been my due, for defaming the now spotless grandeur of your illustrious house. besides would it not in me be the hight *[sic]* of presumption to contend with the Spanish incognita who this evening appeared to you at the Caffé and to whom you presented the snuff box of the despised Rosaura—yet strange to say she once more begs your acceptance of it.

Alv.   How is this! is a gentleman of my descent thus to be trifled with. how came you by this box.

Ros.   I this evening received it from <u>him</u> to whom I would now restore it.

Alv.   Indeed! then you are the incognita.

Ros.   Most true, but I must yet trespass on your attention.

Alv.   Pardon me I cannot stay here to be insulted your conduct in this affair has been such as to impress my mind with an unalterable detestation of Italy and its inhabitants. I go never to return and as the deserved punishment for you unparalleled and a city I deprive you for ever of my protecting presence.

Ros.   It grieves me exceedingly to see Don Alvaro so much offended. my only consolation is that I feel I am undeserving of his censure. Mons le Blan I confess I was somewhat surprised to see you here this evening how is it that you neglect your engagement at the Altar of Santa Bianca. consider what a disappointment the fair sufferer will endure, not even the possession of your portrait will compensate for the absence of the original. I pray you do not let me any longer detain you, and permit me to return this precious Jewel. you will no doubt soon have an opportunity for presenting it to some fair lady more deserving than I feel myself to be.

Mons   Oh upon my word Madam you are much too severe. I assure you this was only a little affair en passant, nothing to be compared with the affection I bare *[sic]* for you and your Sister, and

I am sure sweet Mademoiselle Eleanor credits my assertion she is a lady of too much spirit to reject me merely because an elder Sister has set her the example.

Mar.   You must pop the question in plainer terms or she'll not understand you.

Mons   Yes yes she does, behold the mounting blush upon that cheek, would that I might interpret it as the harbinger of my future happiness, [kneels] say sweet lady could you ever love le Blan e'en teach your heart to prize the love the adoration that glows here.

Ele.   How hard it is to say you nay.

Mons.   Why impose upon yourself that task grant me but this little pledge [takes her hand] and our lives henceforth shall be one long continued joyous festival.

Ele.   With such a proposal who would not be delighted. I joyfully accept your offer.

Mons.   Thanks my Angel.

Enter Doctor and Pantalone.

Pan.   Well my friends I wish you all a good evening.

Doc.   But daughter how have you offended the Don Alonso. *[sic]* he passed us this moment demanding vengeance on all the Italian Damsels.

Mons.   Oh Monsieur le Doctour *[sic]* my most sincere friend my venerable father in law permit me a tender embrace. [embraces him] and communicate to you my happiness in having obtain*[ed]* the permission of marriage from your lovely daughter Eleanora.

Pan.   How! what new arrangement is this.

Ros.   I confess she has been somewhat precipitate but . . .

Doc.   Well well you know I have always allowed you to act for yourselves in such cases I only hope she may never live to repent of having refused the offer of Mr Pantalone my worthy friend here.

Pan.   I suppose I must appear agreable *[sic]* to this arrangement and make a virtue of necessity. I certainly did wish to marry Signora Eleanora, but it was with hopes that she would love me, and since she seems to prefer this young gentleman I will make no more ado about the matter. But wish you Sir and you Miss Nelly *[no nickname in Goldoni]* a long and happy life.

Mons   Bravo Long live Monsieur Pantalone.

Cou.   Gentlemen permit me now to address you. Signora Rosaura has at lenght *[sic]* by the offer of her hand consented to raise me to the highest altitude of bliss, and this evening we have chosen for the celebration of our nuptials allow me to solicit your attendance at the marriage feast.

Ros   To which request let me add my entreaties and by your presence pardon the stratagems of which Rosaura has been guilty in order to win her chosen lover!

CURTAIN.

V.

Transcription of Shorthand Notes in the Case of Jarman against Bagster

The manuscript of Dickens's transcription is found in the Guildhall Library, City of London, within a packet of various documents (Ms 20778).

William J. Carlton provides the following history of Charles Dickens's work on two court cases, Jarman vs. Bagster (Chapter V) and Jarman vs. Wise (Chapter VI):

> Among the cases which came before the ecclesiastical courts of Doctors' Commons shortly after the young shorthand writer had installed himself in Bell Yard were two which, though commonplace enough in themselves, are of peculiar interest as illustrating Dickens' method of turning to account even the most trivial incidents which came under his observation in the course of his daily work. They arose out of a disturbance in the vestry-room of the venerable church of St. Bartholomew-the-Great, Smithfield. Objection had been taken by some of the parishioners to the levying of a poor rate, an altercation ensued, and proceedings were instituted against two of the aggrieved ratepayers by one of the churchwardens, Charles Jarman, the proctor engaged to act on the plaintiff's behalf being Dickens' co-tenant, [Charles] Fenton. The suits were heard separately in the Consistory Court of London before Dr. Stephen Lushington, who delivered judgment against each of the delinquents on 18th November, 1830. Charles Dickens was present on this occasion, the two judgments were taken down in court by his nimble pen, and Dickens' transcripts from his shorthand notes are still preserved. . . .   (57–58)

Dickens was age 18 at the time.

Carlton is the first to report, "Apart from their value as examples of Dickens' activity as a professional stenographer, these documents are of considerable literary importance, for they constitute the actual record of incidents which furnished the material for one of the most entertaining of the *Sketches by Boz*, that entitled 'Doctors' Commons' " (61). The originally published text of "Doctors' Commons" from *The Morning Chronicle* is provided in Appendix B, and it significantly differs in places from Dickens's subsequent reworking of the text for publication in book form.

Content that is not in Dickens's handwriting is presented in *italics without brackets*. Dickens ends each manuscript page with a catchword (the first word of the next page). Each catchword is presented in **boldface**. Insertions by Dickens while he was proofreading his manuscript are <u>underlined</u>. Words written and then stricken by Dickens are presented as originally written, but with a line placed through each such word. Corrections and notes are *[italicized within brackets]*.

Consistory
The office of the Judge Promoted by—
Jarman against Bagster
Sentence
18 November 1830
C Fenton

In the Consistory Court of London
Second Session Michaelmas Term 1830
Thursday November the 18ᵗʰ "
The Office of the Judge promoted by
Jarman against Bagster
Fenton   Dyke
Copy from Mr. C Dickens' Shorthand Notes
Sentence of the Judge Dr. Lushington

It appears to the Court that it is first necessary to consider the nature of
the charges **which** which have been made in the present suit,—whether they
are in themselves such as supposing them to be proved would require the
Court to interpose its authority according to the forms and usage of the
Ecclesiastical law; and whether the evidence which has been adduced is sufficient to substantiate those charges.

Now the Citation, the contents of which have been read in the first instance
undoubtedly calls upon the Defendant in the Cause to answer especially for
quarrelling chiding and brawling by words, in the Vestry Room and for creating a riot and disturbance therein. It has been contended on behalf of the party
proceeded against that in point of fact, it is a simple Citation for brawling; and
that the riot and disturbance, can be considered only as incidental to and
consequent upon, the brawling previously set forth in the Citation. Now, upon
looking at the Articles, if any doubt at all had existed, **as** as to the true intent
and meaning of the Citation, I am of opinion that that *[sic]* doubt was not
effectually removed, as soon as the very articles were given in, for these
articles do charge two offences in themselves perfectly distinct, one offence
being that, of rushing into the room and conducting themselves in a violent
and improper manner, and the other offence being that, of using words which
the law denominates brawling. Now, not only are these offences distinct in
themselves, but they are said to have taken place at different times. The
offence charged in the 3ʳᵈ Article being that of having rushed into the room
despite the interference of the Beadle, this being at the commencement,—the
rushing into the Vestry Room,—the use of brawling words at the period when
he was about to quit it. I certainly am of opinion that it is perfectly competent
on this Citation, for the Promoter to proceed on both these charges, and I
think no doubt can be entertained,—provided the evidence substantiates the
averments contained in the ~~charges~~ articles,—that **the** Court would be under
the *[second "the," following inserted text after first "the"]* necessity of
pronouncing that both these articles are proved, and to proceed accordingly.
The question therefore eventually comes to this, whether, the evidence is or
is not sufficient to establish these articles in proof, and if it is, whether, any,
or all the numerous circumstances introduced into this case, ought to have

the effect or operation on the mind of the Court, with respect to the Sentence which it is to give.

Now, the Court has heard a great deal relating to the history of this Parish, which it appears to me has a very remote bearing indeed upon the subject which the Court is called upon to determine. The Court has not to determine whether there is, or is not, by law a Select Vestry—the Court has not to adjudicate on the question, whether, the Overseers in former times have or have not exercised the powers entrusted to them in a proper or improper manner,—the Court has nothing to do with the proceedings in Parliament,—the Court has no concern whatsoever with proceedings of that description, and I think that none of of these circumstances have any such material connection with any part of the case, that it becomes the duty of the Court in the slightest degree to examine them with any minuteness. I shall confine myself to such parts of the evidence as I think necessarily ought to be discussed and considered, in order to arrive at the only true conclusion in the cause, namely, whether the Articles are, or are not proved.

It appears that the Vestry,—calling itself a Select Vestry, whether it were so by law or not, is a matter with which the Court has no concern, had to choose Overseers, or rather to recommend the choosing of Overseers in a manner different from that which had usually been adopted in the Parish before, and it appears that these Overseers found it necessary to make a poor rate, for the purpose of maintaining the poor of the Parish. In order to do so they were desirous of having the aid and assistance of those who had past *[sic]* through the office, and they wished to **take** take the benefit of their advice on this subject,—they were desirous not only of doing this, but, that public notice also should be given of their intention to make a rate from the circumstance of the making a rate being rendered a matter of publicity it must be inferred that the intention was that persons who had any interest in that rate might come forward and state their objections to it. Now the notice is attached to the evidence of a person of the name of Davis examined in this cause, and is as follows "The

"Churchwardens and Overseers of this Parish *[lines end where Dickens ended them]*

"will meet at the Vestry Room on Tuesday in the evening

"evening next the 6th to start at 6 oclock *[sic]*

"to make a rate for the relief of the poor."

Now I am unable from from any consideration which 1 can give this paper,— to come to the conclusion, that this was in any way whatsoever a calling of a Vestry. It does not appear to me, that any individual on hearing this paper read or on perusing it, could come in his own mind to the determination, that this was a Vestry Meeting; and I find that this does not seem to have been **the** the judgment of one witness at least examined in the cause,—because Mr. Mitchell on interrgatory *[sic]*, expressed his opinion, that the individuals who did come to this meeting, and who afterwards entered the Vestry Room, did not come in consequence of this notice,—that is to say, admitting they were summoned to attend a Vestry. Now, it would have been a matter rather singular undoubtedly, if it had been the intention of the officers of this Parish to change the ancient system which so long had prevailed in this Parish, it would have been a most extraordinary mode of departing from that system, if they had carried that determination into effect by a notice in itself of so ambiguous a nature, nay it was a matter of so much importance,—in consequence of the alteration in the system which had been pursued for such a length of time,—that it must have been made matter of very great previous description, and must have been made matter of publicity and notoriety, in point of fact, if the Select Vestry, had intended to surrender the powers they exercised, **and** and to throw the concerns of the Parish open to a general Vestry. I cannot therefore bring my mind to believe, there was anything in this notice, or in the publication of it at the time, which could possibly give the Parishioners any intimation, that the Vestry would be open for the attendance of those who had not heretofore been considered as having a right to attend there. Now, if this be so, still less do I think, that, the circumstances which attended the holding of the meeting tend in any degree, to have deceived the persons, who so came, into any such notion, for, it appears that from the commencement, the door was shut,—it appears that all persons who had not belonged to the Select Vestry, and who were not Overseers were in point of fact at the commencement of the meeting excluded. It appears, that a person of the name of Curtis, came in with a view of objecting to the rate, which had been made,—his objections were made,—he **then** then went out to these persons,—the objections were taken into consideration,—he returned into the room, it is announced to him that his objections to the rate are considered good; and he again went out. Now, it does appear to me, that the persons outside the door, must of necessity almost from these facts and circumstances, have been perfectly satisfied, that, there was no intention that they should be called into that room as vestrymen, by the notice in question. But I think the very fact of a list having been handed, of the names of persons evidently intending to object to the rate as it had been made, heretofore, and as they expected it would have been made again, it is quite impossible to conceive even, that, these parties when they gave in that list, had any such understanding. Now, under these circumstances this Mr. Curtis having retired, there being no Vestry at all, neither any notice of a Vestry, nor any Vestry de facto held, which must I think have been perfectly well known to all the parties concerned, it appears that at that time this Mr. **Curtis** Curtis having entirely withdrawn, the Beadle, a person of the name of Davis, was directed to call in the first person on the list of the name of Wise. Now, when this is done, it appears by the whole of the evidence, that, Mr. Bagster, as well as the other persons concerned, despite all the exertions the Beadle could make, forced their way into the Vestry Room; and I find in answer to the 11th interrgatory *[sic]*, Mr. Curtis, states that they were forbidden by the Beadle, to enter. Indeed it is perfectly clear from the evidence of every witness in this case, that they did effect their entrance into the Vestry Room by force, and by overpowering the exertions of the Beadle to the contrary. Now, then the question comes to this, whether under the circumstances of overpowering the Beadle by force, which must necessarily be attended with riot and disturbance, to a certain extent, is this, or is this not, an Ecclesiastical Offence, when such riot and disturbance took place, in the Vestry Room on consecrated ground. Now, was this at all requisite for the purpose of preserving **any** any asserted or claimed rights on behalf of the persons not hitherto admitted to the Vestry? It has been agrued, that, this proceeding was similar to those which have taken place in other Parishes. I apprehend there is no doubt if any person having a right to enter a Vestry Room is excluded, he has a right of action against the individual excluding him, and could recover damages for being so excluded, but, I am by no means satisfied that in order to obtain any such right, it is necessary by force to obtain entrance into the room, and remain in it, despite the remonstrances of those who happen to be in it. I apprehend, all these parties could have attained all their legal remedies, in the same force and with the same efficacy, if they had remonstrated against being so excluded; and afterwards commenced their action against the parties who had actually excluded them, or by whose authority they had been kept out. I cannot think therefore, that, the excuse of maintaining the asserted right on **the** the part of these individuals can possibly operate on the present occasion. And then really the question does come to this, there are many Vestries which are called Select in the City of London, and other places, whether legally so, or not the Court has really nothing to do with, but is it right, or is it fit that persons who question the legality of these Select Vestries should attempt to enforce their claims by force and violence. If I could conceive that these individuals had merely in entering the room caused that same degree of noisy confusion, which frequently happens from a crowd pressing in, when there is no opposition, then the circumstances would be in a very different aspect: but here it is quite evident that the parties were forewarned that they were to be excluded from entering that room as a body—despite that warning, despite the exertions of the Beadle to the contrary, they do overcome the efforts of that Beadle, they enter the room by force, they persist in remaining when remonstrated with, the consequence **is** is, all the proceedings of that meeting though it is not a Vestry meeting, are entirely put an end to. Now, I am of opinion that whatever may be the rights of the parties of this Parish,—I wish it to be distinctly understood I am not in any degree giving an opinion whether a Select Vestry be legal or not,—or whether those persons have a right to attend or not, but I am of opinion whether they have the right or not, they committed an illegal act in persisting to enter it in the riotous and disorderly manner in which they conducted themselves. I therefore think, that with respect to that Article of the Allegation which charges these persons with behaving in a riotous tumultuous & disorderly manner in the Church, I think, I shall be under the necessity of saying, that the Article is proved. And, the Court cannot but consider what would be the consequence, if it were to do otherwise,—it inevitably must be this, that wherever there is a contested right respecting a Select Vestry by the inhabitants, those who think they have a fair claim **in** in point of law to enter that meeting, will endeavour to obtain it by force of arms; and the Church must remain, a constant scene of disturbance and riot, it being the bounden duty of this Court, as I apprehend, to preserve a place consecrated to the worship of God, from any such contamination.

Now, I come to consider the second offence, that of brawling under the Statute, the Statute requiring the offence charged to be proved by the testimony of two witnesses. The offence,—namely,—that of calling Mr. Jarman a liar,—no person can scarcely doubt—,— provided it be established by satisfactory evidence,—but that it must be considered as brawling in this case. With respect to the provocation which might have been given, it may be a subject for consideration here after, if the Court should think it necessary. Now, I must recollect, that, this is a criminal suit, and that the offence is charged under the Statute, the offence is not charged,—if I may use the expression,—**at** at Common Law, because, if the offence had been charged at Common Law, it would have given the Court a wider discretion with respect to the extent of proof that might be necessary in order to establish the offence: but, being charged under the Statute, then all the enactment of that Statute must be completely fulfilled, before the Court can possibly venture to say that the offence charged has been proved according to the directions of that Statute. Now, let us see, whether there are two witnesses deposing to the brawling; there is one admitted on all hands, namely the first witness examined John Davis. The question then is simply this, whether, the evidence of Mr. Clarke the second witness, can be considered as such testimony, as that which the Statute requires. Now, the way in which Mr. Clarke gives his evidence is as follows, it is of consequence that the Court should notice it. He says

"Among other things Mr. Jarman said
"Mr. Bagster I am surprized to see you here **after**
"after the observation that you made when
"I applied to you for the Church rate
"upon which the said Samuel Bagster asked what
"was that" Mr. Jarman replied "that you

''could wish to see the Church burnt down''

''The Deponent understood Bagster to say ''you are a liar''

Now here comes the word ''understood,'' a term certainly the most indefinite possible, a term which I can never conceive to be in the slightest degree equivalent to a direct deposition of the fact which the witness is called upon to prove. ''The Deponent'' understood Bagster to say ''you a liar'' *[sic]* but ''being unwilling to believe that Mr. Bagster

''had made use of such an expression *[t]*he

''Deponent enquired of a person standing by

''if such were the case.''

Now, what does this come to? he doubts the accuracy of his own hearing, and endeavours to obtain information from a third party, whether or not he was accurate in his apprehension, and he was assured he was. Why, the whole of this amounts to neither more nor less than hearsay, he doubts his own impression in the first instance, and the doubt which **was** was impressed upon his mind, is removed by nothing but hearsay from an individual not produced in the cause. He goes on & says afterwards, to the best of his knowledge and belief, the words were used, but he will not undertake to swear it was so. Now, I conceive under the terms of the Statute it is indispensably necessary he should swear positively & the Court is not at liberty to consider this the evidence of such a second witness as the Statute necessarily requires. I am therefore of opinion, that, with respect to the charge of brawling, it is not satisfactorily proved, by the evidence produced in this Cause. If it had been proved by the testimony of two lawful witnesses, which the Statute re-quires,—unquestionably it would have been my duty to have considered, whether, there had not been some provocation afforded to this gentleman which might in some degree diminish the offence charged, and without in the slightest degree meaning to attribute to Mr. Jarman, that, he really and truly made the charge against Mr. Bagster, of any intention that he wished the Church of St. Bartholomew **really** really burnt down, yet, I must say even if such an expression had on a former occasion escaped the lips of Mr. Bagster, I cannot see that it was either very proper or advisable for Mr. Jarman to have taunted him with the use of such an expression. Every man must feel, that taunts of that kind, must call for a contradiction, or expressions of a similar nature by way of contradiction or answer. It is not necessary however to enter into that question, because I am satisfied the charge is not legally proved. It remains only therefore for the Court to consider, what should be its sentence under these circumstances of part of the Articles being proved, and a part not being proved.

Now, under all the circumstances, the Court is of opinion that it ~~would go far enough~~ will do justice by pronouncing that part of the Articles, that is to say, the whole of the Articles are proved, with the exception of the 4th Article.

The Court thinks it is not necessary that it should decree any suspension from entering the Church; and the Court **is** is further of opinion, that, it will go far enough to prevent a recurrence of any proceedings of this nature, by condemning the party proceeded against in £20, nomine expensarum. At the same time admonishing that individual in future not to forget that whatever may be the nature of the rights he claims, as the degree of provocation he thinks he receives, he must recollect—as well as every one of the Parishioners, that when they enter a place consecrated to the worship of God, it is their duty to restrain their tempers and passions, and to behave themselves with that decorum, required by the Sanctity of the place in which they are assembled.

x^{d}
C Dickens *[signature]*
Short hand Writer
5 Bellyard
Doctors Commons.

VI.

Transcription of Shorthand Notes in the Case of Jarman against Wise

The manuscript of Dickens's transcription is found in the Guildhall Library, City of London, within a packet of various documents (Ms 20778).

See introductory content to preceding case of Jarman vs. Bagster (Chapter V). Content that is not in Dickens's handwriting is presented in *italics without brackets*. Dickens ends each manuscript page with a catchword (the first word of the next page). Each catchword is presented in **boldface**. Insertions by Dickens while he was proofreading his manuscript are <u>underlined</u>.

Corrections and notes are *[italicized within brackets]*.

Consistory
The office of the Judge Promoted by—
Jarman against Wise
Sentence
18 November 1830
C Fenton

In the Consistory Court of London
Second Session Michaelmas Term 1830
Thursday November the 18ᵗʰ " " "
The Office of the Judge promoted by
Jarman against Wise
Fenton   Dyke
Copy from Mr. C Dickens' Shorthand Notes
Sentence of the Judge Dr. Lushington

The Court has already expressed its opinion on the general circumstances attending the transactions **which** which gave rise to this Suit, for to a certain extent undoubtedly they are admitted to be precisely the same as those of the last case: the first point therefore to which the attention of the Court must be directed, is, whether there be anything in the conduct of Mr. Wise or the other party in the cause which could give rise to any particular distinction. Now, on behalf of Mr. Wise, it has been contended by his Counsel firstly, that the forcible entry into the Vestry Room is not proved, and secondly that the Brawling may be proved, but that there are very many circumstances in the case, which tend to mitigate the offence, and it has also been contended that the motives of the party proceeding, are not unimpeachable. It has been stated that in some instances the Ecclesiastical Court, is in the habit of considering what are the motives by which parties promoting the office of the Judge are actuated. At the same time it must be remembered, that it is a matter of very considerable difficulty to ascertain with accuracy the motives which operate on the minds of parties. It may frequently happen in complicated cases **of** of this description, a man may in some degree be instigated by feelings of which the Court could not altogether approve,—and at the same time it may occur that he may have a conscientious conviction that there is a certain degree of necessity for his instituting a proceeding of this description. I confess that upon the present occasion, I have very great difficulty in coming to any satisfactory conclusion as to what the real motives of the parties were in instituting these proceedings: but, unless I saw it established by the clearest and most indisputable evidence, that this prosecution was instituted from bad or improper motives, I take it that the rule of law, as well as the rule of charity prevents me from attributing any such intention. Beyond all doubt, the Promoter had a right to come to this Court, for the law would not have provided a punishment against offences of this description, unless it were the wish, and intention of those who framed it, that the Promoter, should apply to this Court in order to prevent a repetition **of** of such disgraceful proceedings. Now, with respect to the third Article, which alledges *[sic]* the forcible entry, the learned Counsel, has put this fact to the Court,—that Mr. Wise was invited to enter the Vestry Room, he having been called in by the Beadle, his name being first on the list,—and it certainly does appear, that he was so invited, and was so admitted into the room. Now, whatever may have been the intention of the party to have forced an entrance into that room, which may perhaps be argued from previous circumstances, I certainly agree with the learned Counsel who offered this argument, to the extent of saying, it is not proved that he made a forcible entry into this room: but however as soon as he did effect an entry, the whole conduct of this gentleman as it appears to me, was altogether of that description, which deserves the severest reprehension of this Court. The whole of the language he used, as appears by the evidence of **the** the witnesses in the cause, was not merely a brawling, but was actually calculated to excite a breach of the peace, and produce consequences which every man must deplore. But, Mr. Wise himself actually appears to have been perfectly aware of the probable effect of the language he used, and in fact to have calculated on a breach of the peace, as the almost necessary consequence of it. Now, I find on reverting to the evidence of Mr. Benjamin Clarke that he expresses himself in the following manner*[.]* He says, on the 4th Article, the Church warden having previously left the chair "Immediately

"after the adjournment of the said meeting *[lines end where Dickens ended them]*

"as aforesaid the Overseers and Select

"Vestrymen thought it right to retire which

"they accordingly did, thinking that those
"parties who had occasioned the disturbance
"found that no business would be transacted
"they would follow. The Churchwardens
"of course remained, they could not leave
"the Church till it was cleared. The Deponent
"was the last of the Vestrymen who retired and
"hearing angry and provoking words passing and
"it being his impression that it was the
"object of those who uttered them, one of **whom**
"whom was the said Richard Wise to provoke
"the Churchwardens (Charles Jarman the party
"promoting the Office of the Judge in this Cause,
"and the said Mr. John Dawkins) to commit
"a breach of the peace, he the Deponent re-
"turned into the said Vestry Room where
"he found Wise who continued in persisting
"to remain. The said Charles Jarman
"reasoned with the said Richard Wise
"who expressed a positive determination not
"to go out but to provoke a breach of the
"peace rather than do so. He did not say
"(as the Deponent heard) anything further
"than that, sooner than he would go out he
"would provoke a breach of the peace. He
"moreover in a loud insulting tone of voice
"called the said Charles Jarman "a Drunken
"Churchwarden." He also made use of a
"similar expression to John Dawkins then
"Upper warden of the said Parish. He the
"said Richard Wise also addressing himself
"to the said Charles Jarman said "You are
"a pretty fellow—for a Churchwarden only
"a Journeyman Wollen [*sic*] Draper, or the Journeyman
"to a Wollen [*sic*] Draper,"—or words to that effect[.] **Now**

Now, it appears to me, that howsoever this gentleman may have obtained his entrance into that Vestry Room,—admitting it to have been as has been pleaded properly; indeed on the invitation of the persons there assembled,—that his conduct when he did obtain that entrance, was the very reverse & possibly I think the very language he used, his express declaration that he would not leave the room,—and that he would provoke a breach of the peace, does seem to amount to the terms of the articles <u>viz</u>., that he conducted himself in a violent and outrageous manner on the said occasion, and by such his conduct created a riot and disturbance. I am of opinion therefore, that, the third Article is proved. With respect to the 4th, there is no doubt according to the depositions of all parties that the brawling has been proved, I think I may say it was of a very gross description, utterly uncalled for by any thing which appears in evidence to have occurred. It must have given great provocation to the parties, for the words used did not arise in consequence of any discussion as to the rights of the parties, but, they are words of personal abuse addressed to **the** the Churchwardens themselves, and as far as appears, by the absence of all evidence in the case to support it, is utterly destitute of all foundation. Being of opinion therefore that the charges are substantiated it only remains for the Court to consider the sentence which it feels to be its duty to pronounce; and considering that this is a proceeding so far as relates to brawling,—under the Statute, established by the evidence, the Court feels itself under the necessity of suspending this person from entering the Church, and the Court can exercise no discretion except as to the period of time, I shall content myself with suspending him for the term of one fortnight. The only remaining question is, whether, under all the circumstances, the Court ought not to condemn this person in full costs, and in strict justice the Court is very much inclined to think it ought to go the whole length of condemning him in the whole costs, for I am very much of opinion, that the principal part of the disturbance was **occasioned** occasioned by this individual, and that worse language was used by him than had been admitted. At the same time however, considering the commotions which have taken place in this Parish, the jarring opinions which appear to have prevailed in it and the general irritation which unfortunately has been occasioned by the conflicting claims of these parties, the Court is inclined not to go the whole length which the Statute empowers it to do.

The King's Advocate   I trust the Court will excuse my interruption. I hope it will not forget, the great length of the interrogatories which have been administered by the Defendant in this Cause.

Dr. Lushington   The Court is perfectly aware, Sir Herbert Jenner, of the length of the interrogatories, but on the other hand it cannot help looking at the number of witnesses which has been produced on the part of the Promoter. I must consider that the remedy which the law at present affords for the purpose of preventing disturbances in the Church ought not to (as it is in the opinion of many persons) be made so exceedingly onerous, as, that the punishment inflicted on the guilty party should be **even** even greater than the offence itself. The expense of these proceedings when it falls on the shoulders of those convicted under this Statute, is so heavy, as in many instances to be in no proportion to the guilt committed. <u>and,</u> it would be in direct opposition to all general rules and principles, on which punishment is inflicted if such were to be the case <u>in the present instance</u>. The legislature in providing for offences of this description, had no other object in view, than the interest of the public at large,—it did so for the purpose of preventing the commission of the like offences in future; but if the punishment were to be more than adequate to the offence, this jurisdiction would in the public opinion be considered oppressive and unjust. Therefore considering that eight witnesses have been examined on the part of the Promoter, notwithstanding my being of opinion that some of the interrgatories *[sic]* which have been addressed to them have a very remote bearing on the question at issue, I shall content myself with condemning the Defendant, in the sum of £35, nomine expensarum.

x^{d}
C Dickens *[signature]*
Short hand Writer
5 Bellyard
Doctors Commons.

VII.

Acrostic

Dickens contributed four original poems to Maria Beadnell's album (Chapter VII through Chapter X), placing quotation marks around each title, with the exception of his first contribution, simply titled Acrostic. The album is found in the Charles Dickens Museum, London (no call number).

In 1831, Dickens wrote of himself in "The Bill of Fare" (Chapter XI), "He lost his [heart] twelve month ago, from last May." This would date his courtship of Maria from May 1830, and his acrostic poem in her album from either 1830 or 1831, the latter year provided by Dickens at the conclusion of his second entry in the album, "The Devil's Walk" (Chapter VIII). Accordingly, Dickens's first poem for Maria was written when he was age 18 or 19.

My life may chequered be with scenes of misery and pain,
And 't may be my fate to struggle with adversity in vain:
Regardless of misfortunes tho' howe'er bitter they may be,
I shall always have one retrospect, a hallowed one to me,
And it will be of that happy time when first I gazed on thee.

Blighted hopes, and prospects drear, for me will lose their sting,
Endless troubles shall harm not me, when fancy on the wing
A lapse of years shall travel o'er, and again before me cast
Dreams of happy fleeting moments then for ever past:
Not any worldly pleasure has such magic charms for me
E'en now, as those short moments spent in company with thee;
Life has no charms, no happiness, no pleasures, now for me
Like those I feel, when 'tis my lot Maria, to gaze on thee.

VIII.

"The Devil's Walk."

"The Devil's Walk," titled with quotation marks and a period, is from Maria Beadnell's album, found in the Charles Dickens Museum, London (no call number).

This poem is neither a parody of Percy Bysshe Shelley's "The Devil's Walk" nor a parody of any portion of the various versions of "The Devil's Thoughts" (also known as "The Devil's Walk") coauthored by Samuel Taylor Coleridge and Robert Southey. Rather, Dickens adopted the subject of the Devil's wanderings and reflections in an odd combination of praise for Maria as a symbol of Satan's heavenly loss, and condemnation of current religious and political events which Dickens rejects but Satan supports. Dickens was especially knowledgeable of political events of the day, having started employment as a reporter for the *Mirror of Parliament* in early 1831.

Dickens dated his poem November 1831, when he was age 19. Words which Dickens underlined are so noted.

While sitting one day in his well aired halls
Of which we've often heard tell,
The Devil determined to make a few calls
To see if his Friends were well:
So he put on his best and himself he drest
In his long tailed coat of green
And he buttoned it tightly o'er his chest
Least his own Tail should be seen.

To the House of Lords the Devil went straight
To learn the state of Nations,
And with mixed feelings of pleasure and hate
He heard their deliberations;
For he saw a few Nobles rich and proud
War 'gainst the people and Prince,
And he thought with pain tho' he laughed aloud
Of the Wars in Heav'n long since.

Then to Irving's Chapel[8] he gaily hied
To hear the new "unknown tongue"
And he welcomed with great pleasure and pride
The Maniacs he'd got among:
For it always fills the Devil with glee
To hear Religion mocked,

And it pleases him very much to see
Sights at which others are shocked.
                              Then

Then away to Bristol[9] he quickly walked
T'indulge in meditation,
And he gaily laughed as he slowly stalked
O'er a scene of desolation.
He honored the hand that had done the deed
Vowed that an ''Anti'' he'd be,
Then back to London he started with speed
His old friend Sir Charles[10] to see.

The Devil was walking up Regent Street
As some other great folks do
When a very old friend he chanced to meet
Whom it pleased him much to view.
Let those describe his great pleasure who can
On the Member for Preston[11] spying
He took off his hat for he envied the Man
His pow'r of deceit and lying.

As the Devil was passing I won't say where
But not far from Lombard Street,[12]
He saw at a window a face so fair
That it made him start and weep
For a passing thought rushed over his brain
Of days now beyond recal,
He thought of the bright angelic train
And of his own wretched fall.

A dim cold feeling of what he had been
Wrung from him a bitter groan
He gazed and thought of the Angels who sing
Surrounding Heaven's High Throne.
He thought of the time,—the happy time,—
When among them he had been
And he madly cursed the impious crime
Which plunged him in pain and sin.

This feeling vanished as soon as it came
And he turned to walk away

But sought for this Album to find the name
Of her he'd seen that day.
He cast his eye swiftly o'er these few lines
To drive away thoughts so sad
And he said with glee "they're worthy of me
For I'm sure they're <u>devilish bad</u>."

<u>Novr</u>. 1831.   C.D.

IX.

"The Churchyard."

"The Churchyard," titled with quotation marks and a period, is from Maria Beadnell's album, found in the Charles Dickens Museum, London (no call number). Count de Suzannet places "The Churchyard" in the "tombstone" category of poetry, popularized by Thomas Gray in his poem "Elegy Written in a Country Church-yard" in 1751. He finds "an original touch in young Dickens's handling of the theme: the humble unadorned graves of the Christian poor contrasted with the mausoleums of the ungodly rich" (163).

Dickens dated his poem November (with the month underlined) 1831, when he was age 19.

How many tales these Tombstones tell
Of life's e'er changing scene,
Of by gone days spent ill or well
By those who gay have been;
Who have been happy, rich, and vain,
Who now are dead, and cold,
Who've gone alike to dust again
The rich, poor, young, and old.

Here lies a Man who lived to save
Of Worldly gain a store;
—It has not saved him from the grave
He ne'er can use it more.
A marble Tablet tells his fame
To those who shall survive;
—It tells us not who blest his name
While he remained alive.

Now mark the contrast.—Near this mound
Lie the remains of one
With whom no fault was ever found,
Who spotless as the Sun
Fulfilled his Christian duties here,
Both cheerfully and well
But no rich velvet deck'd his Bier
No lines his virtues tell.

And is it so! Is man so vain,
To riches such a Slave
As to take his pride of gold, and gain
E'en with him to the Grave!—

Why let him take it.—Let him see
If 'twill avail him there,
Where we must all one dread day be,
Where all Men must appear.

Here sleeps a girl.—A year ago
Bright, beautiful, and gay,
Peaceful, and happy, then, but oh!
How soon such days decay:
They changed to times of shame and grief
And this the mournful token
Death was to her a glad relief
For her young heart was broken.

Aye—broken.—let the Rouè[13] smile
And let him boldly speed
Exulting in his shameless guile
To boast of such a deed.
Let him boast gaily among men
—They'll hear without surprize
And let him boast if he can when
On his death bed he lies.

In truth it is a manly deed
With woman's heart to trifle,
To break the bent and bruised reed
And with neglect to stifle
The feelings man himself has raised
Which he can't prize too high.—
To leave the object he has praised
Alone to weep and die.

But why pursue this painful theme
Or longer here remain
The dead sleep sound; they cannot dream
               of
Of sorrow, grief, or pain.
From Man to GOD they will appeal
Where no man can dissemble
There will the wronged for justice kneel
There will the Tyrant tremble.

Novr. 1831.   C.D.

X.

"Lodgings to Let"

"Lodgings to Let," titled with quotation marks by Dickens, is from Maria Beadnell's album, found in the Charles Dickens Museum, London (no call number). Dickens's text is placed in the album on a right-hand page as poetic commentary on a watercolor illustration which Dickens's good friend and future brother-in-law Henry Austin affixed to the corresponding left-hand page.

Count de Suzannet explains, "The drawing for *Lodgings to Let* represents an open window framed in an attractive setting of brick, woodwork and green shutters. By the window, a handsome young woman may be observed busily rinsing a bottle and glasses in a wash-tub. Behind the lifted sash a printed notice has been affixed: 'Lodgings to let' (ingeniously inserted through a slit at the back of the sheet)" (164).

As Dickens's poem is, of course, best understood in the context of Austin's drawing, a facsimile of the later can be viewed in an issue of *The Strand Magazine* (Darwin 578).

Although Dickens does not date "Lodgings to Let," he locates it in the album between his November 1831 dated poem "The Churchyard" and his transcription of "Written in an Album by T. Moore,"[14] signed C. D. and dated 1831, making him age 19 at the time of its composition. Words which Dickens underlined are so noted.

Lodgings here! A charming place,
The Owner's such a lovely face
The Neighbours too seem very pretty
Lively, sprightly, gay, and witty
Of all the spots that I could find
This is the place to suit my mind.

Then I will say sans hesitation
This place shall be my habitation
This charming spot my home shall be
While dear "Maria" keeps the key,
I'll settle here, no more I'll roam
But make this place my happy home.

A great advantage too will be,
I shall keep such good company,
So good that I fear my composing
Will be considered very prosing
Still I'm most proud amongst these pickings
To rank the humblest name,—Charles Dickens.

XI.

The Bill of Fare

"The Bill of Fare" was composed in 1831, when Dickens was age 19, and also recited by Dickens during the same year at a dinner party hosted by Maria Beadnell's parents (*Letters* 1: 16). Dickens had borrowed Maria's sister Anne Beadnell's album, prior to the dinner, either to compose the poem directly in the album, or, more likely, to copy it into the album from a manuscript (*Letters* 7: 778). Although both manuscript and album are now lost, "The Bill of Fare" is preserved in three different transcriptions, none in Dickens's handwriting.

According to Rosenbaum and White's *Index of English Literary Manuscripts*, the copy held by the Huntington Library, Art Collections, and Botanical Gardens (HM 17514) is in Maria Beadnell's handwriting (711). The *Index*, however, is in error. Both the Huntington Library copy and the Charles Dickens Museum, London (no call number), copy are in the handwriting of Mrs. Margaret Lloyd, Maria's other sister. The copy held by Yale University Library's Beinecke Rare Book and Manuscript Library (Osborn d 122) is in an as yet unidentified handwriting.

At least one transcription must have been made from either Dickens's original manuscript or Anne's album. All three transcriptions contain identical footnotes, which provide a more detailed account of some of Dickens's comments. Such explanatory footnotes serve no purpose and make no sense if Dickens composed them himself, wrote them in the album, and later interrupted his reading of the poem aloud in order to explain meanings of selected lines already known by his audience. The footnotes do make sense if they were added at least after Dickens had become known as an author in 1834, or more probably after Dickens had become famous as an author in 1836. Mrs. Margaret Lloyd's copy in the Charles Dickens Museum, London, has an 1839 watermark.

Differences are found among the three transcriptions. The primary text presented here is from the Charles Dickens Museum, London. Variations which appear in Yale University Library's copy are **noted in boldface**, while other variations which appear in the Huntington Library's copy are *noted in italics*. Words stricken by Dickens are printed with a line through them. It is not possible to reconstruct Dickens's original text and punctuation, as any transcription from any source could contain copying errors.

Dickens reveals in a letter to Maria (*Letters* 7: 777–78; see Appendix C) that this poem consists of at least three stanzas. Although the three transcriptions are not in agreement as to where a third stanza begins, it is not difficult to establish a total of three stanzas for the entire poem. Dickens's letter to Maria is understandable only in the context of the poem's final stanza. His comment "I do not think what I write" refers to the line "I think rather more from the head, than the heart," meaning he actually writes from the heart. His comment "I allude particularly to the last four lines" directs Maria to his concluding words "His death wasn't sudden; he had long been ill, / Slowly he languished, and got worse, until / No mortal means could the poor young fellow save / And a sweet pair of eyes sent him home to his grave."

Walter Dexter wrote an entire chapter on the identification of those present in the poem and at the actual dinner during which Dickens read his poem aloud. His commentary is excerpted in Appendix D.

Dickens composed "The Bill of Fare" in the style of Oliver Goldsmith's "Retaliation," which is reproduced in Appendix E.

The Bill of Fare
By Charles Dickens.
Imitated from Goldsmith
To Miss Maria Beadnell
This trifle is dedicated by the Author

As the great rage just now is imitation
'Mong high born and low, throughout the whole nation,
'Mong high born & low throughout the whole nation
'Mong high-born & low, throughout the whole nation,
I trust 'twill excuse the few following lines,
Of which I'll say nothing, but that these poor rhymes,
As you might expect in degenerate days
Like these, are entitled to no share of praise
Because they are novel;—the ground work at least,
Is a copy from Goldsmith's ever famed Feast.
"And a bad one it is too,"—you'll say I fear,
But let me entreat you, don't be too severe.—
If in a fair face, 'twill elicit a smile:—
If one single moment 'twill serve to beguile—
I shall think on it with great satisfaction,
Et cet'ra,—and so forth:—now then to ~~begin~~ action—
Et cet'ra & so forth; now then to action—
Et cet'ra,—& so forth:—now then to action!—

Without further preface to waste the time in
We'll set to at once,—if you please we'll begin.
We'll say a small party to dinner are met
And the guests are themselves about to be eat
And the guests themselves are about to be eat
Without saying grace, (I own I'm a sinner),
We'll endeavor to see what we've for dinner.
We'll endeavour to see what we've for dinner.
Mr. Beadnell's a good fine Sirloin of beef,
Mr. B—dn—l's a good fine sirloin of beef
Though to see him cut up would cause no small grief.

And then Mrs. Beadnell, I think I may name,
And then Mrs. B—dn—l I think I may name
As being an excellent <u>Rib</u> of the same.
The Miss B's are next, who it must be confessed,
The Miss B's are next who it must be confest
Are two nice little Ducks; and very well dressed.
Are two nice little ducks, and very well drest.
William Moule's of a Trifle, a trifling dish.
W—m M—e of trifle a trifling dish
Mr. Leigh we all know is a very great Fish.
Mr. L—h we all know's a very great fish;
Mrs. Leigh a Curry, smart, hot and biting,
Mrs. L—h a curry, smart, hot & biting,
Mrs. Leigh a curry, smart, hot, & biting,
Although a dish that is always inviting.
For cooking our meat we utensils won't lack;
So Miss Leigh shall be called a fine <u>roasting Jack</u>
So Miss L—h shall be called a fine roasting jack
A thing of great use when we dine or we sup,
A patent one too! never wants winding up.
Mr. Moule's a bottle of excellent Port:
Mr. M—e's a bottle of excellent port;
Mrs. Moule of Champagne,—good humor's her forte.
Mrs. M—e of champagne,—good humour's her forte;
The Miss M's of Snipe are a brace if you please;
And Joe is a very fine flavored Dutch Cheese.
And Joe is a very fine flavoured Dutch cheese.
Mrs. Lloyd and her Spouse are a nice side dish—
Mrs. L—d and her spouse are a nice side dish
Some type of their most happy state I much wish
(Some type of their most happy state I much wish
(Some type of their most happy state I much wish
To produce: let me see,—I've found out one soon)
Of honey, and sweets in the form of a <u>Moon</u>!
Of honey & sweets in the form of a moon;
Of Honey & sweets in the form of a <u>Moon</u>;
Arthur Beetham—this dish has cost me some pains—
A—r B—m—this dish has cost me some pains
Is a tongue with a well made garnish of brains.
M'Namara, I think must by the same rule
M'N—a I think must by the same rule
Be a dish of excellent Gooseberry-Fool.

And Charles Dickens, who in our Feast plays a part,
And C—s D—s, who in our feast plays a part
Is a young summer cabbage, without any heart.
Not that he's <u>heartless</u>: but because as folks say,
He lost his a twelve month ago, from last May.
Now let us suppose that the dinner is done
And the guests have rolled on the floor one by one.
And the guests have roll'd on the floor one by one:—
I don't mean to say they're at the completion
Trying the famed City cure for repletion.
Trying the fam'd city cure for repletion;
Nor do I by any means raise up the question
Whether they owe their deaths to indigestion.
We'll say they're all dead: it's a terrible sight
But I'll dry my tears, and their epitaphs write.

[no break for a new stanza here]
[no break for a new stanza here]
Here lies Mr. Beadnell, beyond contradiction.
Here lies Mr. B—l beyond contradiction
An excellent man, and a good politician;
His opinions were always sound and sincere
Come here! ye reformers, o'er him drop a tear
Come here, and with me weep at his sudden end,
Ye who're to ballot and freedom a friend.
Ye who're to ballot & freedom a friend.
Come here all of ye who to him ever listened,
Praise one rare quality—he was consistent.
And if any one can say so much for you,
We'll try to write on you an epitaph too.
He was most hospitable, friendly and kind
He was most hospitable, friendly, & kind;
An enemy, I'm sure, he's not left behind.
And if he be fairly, and all in all ta'en,
"We never shall look upon his like again."
Here lies Mrs. Beadnell, whose conduct through life
Here lies Mrs. B—l whose conduct through life
As a mother, a woman, a friend, a wife
I shall think, while I profess recollection
Can but be summ'd up in one Word—<u>Perfection</u>.
Can but be summed up in one word—Perfection.
Can but be summ'd up in one word—P E R F E C T I O N.

Her faults I'd tell you beyond any doubt,
But for this plain reason,—I ne'er found them out:
Her character from my own knowledge I tell,
For when living she was, I then knew her well.
It chances to've been by the fates brought about,
That she was the means of first bringing me out.
All my thanks for that and her kindness since then
All my thanks for that & her kindness since then
I'd vainly endeavor to tell with my pen:
I'd vainly endeavour to tell with my pen:
I think what I say—I <u>feel it</u>, thats better,
Or I'd scorn to write of these lines one letter.
Or I'd scorn to write of these lines on letter.
Excuse me, dear reader, for pause now I must
Here two charming sisters lie low in the dust
But why should I pause? do they want my poor aid
To tell of their virtues while with us they stayed.
Can a few words from me add a hundredth part
To the regret felt for them in every heart?
No! No! 'tis impossible, still I must try,
To speak of them here, for I <u>can't</u> pass them by.
And first then for Anne I'll my banner unfurl—
A truly delightful, and sweet tempered girl,
And whats very odd, and will add to her fame,
Is this one plain fact—she was always the same.
She was witty, clever,—you liked what she said;
Without being <u>blue</u>, she was very well <u>read</u>.
Her favorite Author, or else I'm a fibber,
And have been deceived, was the famed <u>Colley</u> Cibber[15]
I dont think dear reader 'twill interest you,
But still if you please keep that quite <u>entre nous</u>
I grow tedious, so of her I'll not din more,—
Oh!—she sometimes dressed her hair a la chinoise
Oh!—she sometimes dressed her hair à la Chinois.—
Oh!—she sometimes drest her hair <u>a la Chinois</u>.
Ladies if you want this fashion to follow
And I know where you the pattern can borrow
Don't look in ''the fashions'' 'mong bows & wreathings
Don't look in ''the fashions'' 'mong bows and wreathings
You'll find it on any antique China tea things.
But who have here? Alas what sight is this!
But who have we here? alas what sight is this!

But who have we here? alas what sight is this!
Has her spirit flown back to regions of bliss?
Has Maria left this world of trouble and care
Has Maria left this world of trouble & care
Because for us she was too good and too fair,
Because for us she was too good & too fair.
Has Heaven in its jealousy ta'en her away
As a blessing too great for us children of clay.
All ye fair and beautiful sadly come here,
All ye fair & beautiful, sadly come here,
And Spring's early flowers, Strew over her bier
Fit emblems are they of life's short fleeting day
Fit tributes are they to her mem'ry to pay;
For though blooming now they will soon be decayed
They blossom one moment then wither and fade.
I linger here now; and I hardly know why
I've no wish, nor hope now but this one—to die
I've no wish, no hope now, but this one—to die
I've no wish, no hope now, but this one,—to die.
My bright hopes and fond wishes were all centered here
My bright hopes & fond wishes were all centered here
Their brightness has vanished, they're now dark and drear.
Their brightness has vanished, they're now dark & drear.
Their brightness has vanished, they're now dark & drear.
The impression that mem'ry engraves on my heart
The impression that Mem'ry engraves in my heart
The impression that Mem'ry engraves in my heart
Is all I have left, and with that I ne'er part.
Is all I have left, and with that I'll ne'er part:—
Is all I have left, & with that I ne'er part.
I might tell you much, and I say it with a sigh
I might tell you much, and I say't with a sigh,
I might tell you much, & I say't with a sigh,
Of the grace of her form, and the glance of her eye
Of the grace of her form, & the glance of her eye;
I might tell of happy days now pass'd away
I might tell of happy days now passed away
Which I fondly hoped then would never decay
But 'twere useless—I should only those times deplore
I know that again I can see them no more.
But what's this small form that she folds to her breast
As if it had only laid down there to rest?

Poor thing is it living? ah no it's dead quite
It is a small dog liver-colored and white,
It is a small dog, liver coloured and white.
It is a small dog, liver-colored & white.
Dear me now I see—'tis the little dog that,
Would eat mutton chops, if you cut off the fat
So very happy was its situation
An object it was of such admiration
That I'd resign all my natural graces,
E'en now, if I could with ''Daphne'' change places.
William Moule next alas with the dead lieth here,
W—m M—e next alas with the dead lieth here
And his loss we shall never recover I fear.
And his loss we shall ne'er recover I fear:
No more shall the young men, among whom am I,
Regard with great envy his elegant tie.
No more shall the girls, with anxiety, wait
At a party, and mourn that he came in late.
Though it was not his fault, it must be confessed
Though it was not his fault, it must be confess'd
We knew very well that he lived ''in the west.''[16]
And men of great fashion now never go out,
'Till long after twelve when engaged to a rout
No more shall he waltz an hour with one lady
To the delight of his tut'ress Miss A. B.
Who no more shall turn to me and whispering low,
Who no more shall turn to me, & whispering low,
Say, ''doesn't he waltz well? I taught him you know''
No more shall he curse all the City Folks' Balls
And vow that he never will honor their Halls
No more from the ''London,''[17] will he be turned back
No more from ''The London'' will he be turned back
No more from ''The London'' will he be turned back
Because of his wearing a kerchief of black
No more when we sit round the blithe supper table,
Shall he hush to silence the prattling babel
By—when a lady, a speech made upon her,
Rising to return us her thanks for the honor
No more—but I think I'll use that phrase no more
I feel that I can't this loss enough deplore.
I feel that I can't enough this loss deplore.
I feel that I can't enough this loss deplore

Momus and Bacchus both be merry no more
Momus & Bacchus, both be merry no more,
Your friend Mr. Leigh lies dead on the floor.
Your friend Mr. L—h now lies dead on the floor.
Your friend Mr. Leigh now lies dead on the floor.
Weep both of ye, each hide your sorrowful head,
For he isn't dead drunk, but he's really dead.
We shall never again see his good humored face
We shall never again see his good humoured face
We shall never again admire the grace
With which he would drink off his bottle of wine
Or with which he'd ask you next Sunday to dine
Or with which next Sunday he'd ask you to dine.
We shall never again laugh aloud at his fun
We shall never in turn amuse him with a pun.
In his Will I hope as a legacy that
He's left me that elegant, pretty dress hat,
The shape, make, and color of which were so rare;
The shape, make and colour of which were so rare
The shape, make, & color of which were so rare;
And which on all extra occasions he'd wear.
I really do his loss most deeply regret,
As the kindest, best tempered man, I e'er met.
As the kindest best temper'd man I e'er met.
I'm as hale and as hearty as any man here
I'm as hale and as hearty as any one here,
I'm as hale and as hearty as any one here,
So I'll help to carry him to his new bier
Mrs. Leigh's life, alas, has come to an end:
Mrs. L—h's life, alas, has come to an end [this line starts a third stanza]
Mrs. Leigh's life, alas has come to an end:— [this line starts a third stanza]
But I cant speak of her, I fear to offend.
I don't think the truth need her feelings much gall,
But if I can't tell it, I wont write at all.
If 'twere not for the lesson that I've been taught
I'd have painted her as in justice I ought.
I'd say she was friendly, good hearted, and kind
I'd have said she was friendly, good hearted, & kind
I'd have said she was friendly, good hearted, kind,
Her wit I'd have praised and intelligent mind
'Bout scandal, or spreading reports without heed,
Of course I'd say nothing, how could I indeed?

Because if I did I should certainly lie,
And my remarks here, doubtless, would not apply
And my remarks doubtless here would not apply.
So as I fear either to praise or to blame,
I will not her faults, or her virtues here name.
And Mary Anne Leigh's death I much regret too,
And M—y A—e L—h's death I much regret too,
Though the greatest tormentor, that I e'er knew.
Whenever she met you at morn, noon, or night,
To tease and torment you was her chief delight
To tease & torment you, was her chief delight;
To each glance or smile, she'd a meaning apply
On every flirtation she kept a sharp eye.
Though,—tender feelings I trust I'm not hurting,—
She ne'er herself much objected to flirting.[18]
She to each little secret always held the candle,
And I think she liked a small bit of scandal.
I think too that she used to dress hair well,
I think, too, that she used to dress her hair well
I think, too, that she used to dress her hair well,
Although Arthur said—but that tale I wont tell.
Although A—r said—but that tale I won't tell.
In short though she was so terribly teasing
So pretty she looked, her ways were so pleasing
That when she had finished I used to remain,
Half fearing, half hoping, be teased again.
Half fearing, half hoping, to be teased again.
Half fearing, half hoping, to be teased again.
Here lies Mr. Moule, at whose plentiful board
Here lies Mr. M—e at whose plentiful board
We often have sat, and where with one accord
Mirth, pleasure, good humor, and capital wine
Mirth, pleasure, good humor & capital Wine,
Seemed always to meet, when one went there to dine.
Seem'd always to meet when one went there to dine.
To his friends he was always good humored and kind
To his friends he was always good-humored & kind
And a much better host 'twould be hard to find.
If he for an instant his good humor missed
I've heard it would be at a rubber of whist.
At least, I've sometimes heard his partners say so:
Though of course I myself this fact cannot know.

His hospitality deserved great credit
Indeed I much wish all men did inherit
That merit from him; I'm sure it is needed,
That some should prize it as highly as he did.
I think his opinions were not always quite
So kind, or so just as they should be of right.
However that question I'll not travel through.
'Twould not, I think, become me so to do.
Some others in this point like him we may see,
So I will say requiescat in pace.
Mrs. Moule, alas, lieth here with the dead
Mrs. M—e, alas, lieth here with the dead;
Her good temper vanish'd her light spirits fled
I'd say much of her, but all knew her too well,
To leave any thing new for me here to tell.
So I'll only say—in thus speaking of her
I'm sure all she e'er knew will concur
If kindness and temper as virtues are held
If kindness & temper as virtues are held
She never by any one yet was excelled.
Louisa Moule's next—I can't better call her
L—a M—e's next—I can't better call her
Than the same pattern—N. B. a size smaller.
Here lies Fanny Moule, of whom't may be said
Here lies F—y M—e, of whom't may be said
That romance or sentiment quite turned her head
Her chief pleasure was, but I cannot tell why,
To sit by herself, in a corner and sigh.
You might talk for an hour to her thinking she heard,
And find out at last she had not heard a word.
She'd start, turn her head,—the case was a hard one—
And say with a sigh "dear! I beg your pardon"
Whether this arose from love, doubt, hesitation,
Or whether, indeed, 'twas all affectation
I will not by my own decision abide;
I'll leave it to others the point to decide
Thus much though, I will say, I think it is droll
That one who so pleasing might be on the whole,
Should take so much trouble—it must be a toil—
All her charms and graces entirely to spoil.
Here lies honest Joe, and I'm sure when I say
Here lies honest Joe, & I'm sure when I say

That he'd a good heart there's no one will say nay.
The themes of all others on which he would doat
Were splendid gold lace, and a flaming red Coat
Were splendid gold lace & a flaming red Coat;
His mind always ran on battles and slaughters
His mind always ran on battles & slaughters,
Guards, Bands, Kettle Drums, and splendid head quarters
Guards, Bands, Kettle-drums & splendid Head Quarters.
I've heard that the best bate to catch a young girl
I've heard that the best bait to catch a young girl
Is a red coat, and a mustachio's curl
Is a red coat & a mustachio's curl;
Bait your hook but with this, and Joe would soon bite
Bait your hook but with this, & Joe would soon bite
Hint at it, he'd talk on from morning to night
In portraits of Soldiers he spent all his hoard
You talked of a Penknife—he thought of a Sword.
Inspecting accounts he ne'er could get through,
His mind would revert to some former <u>review</u>
He ne'er made a bill out, smaller, or larger,
But he thought he was then mounting his <u>charger</u>
He ne'er to the Counting House trudged in a heat
But he thought of forced marches and a <u>retreat</u>
But he thought of <u>forced marches</u> & a <u>retreat</u>
And ne'er from the play to his home went again
But trembling he thought of the roll call at <u>Ten</u>
But trembling he thought of the roll call at <u>TEN</u>.
But fallen at last is this "gay young deceiver"
A prey to death and a bad <u>scarlet fever</u>
Here lies Mrs. Lloyd I am sorry to say
Here lies Mrs. L—d; I am sorry to say
That she too from us is so soon snatched away
That her fate is most hard it can't be denied,
When we think how recently she was a bride
That she became one is no source of surprise
For if all that's charming in critical eyes
Is likely to finish a dull single life,
I'm sure she ought t've been long since a wife
I'm sure that she ought t've been long since a wife.
I'm sure that she ought t've been long since a wife
Though we lament one so pleasing and witty,
Though we lament one so pleasing, so witty,

Though we lament one so pleasing, so witty,
And though her death we may think a great pitty
And though her death we may think a great pity,
I really myself do quite envy her fate,
And I wish when with death I've my tête a tête,
He'd do me the favor to take me away
When my prospect here, were bright blooming and gay
When my prospects here were bright, blooming & gay,
When my prospects here were bright, blooming & gay,
When I'm quite happy, ere with sorrows jaded,
I wish for my grave, when my hopes are faded.
When I might be certain of leaving behind
Those who would ne'er cease to bear me in mind
She's gone and who shall now those sweet ballads sing
She's gone and who now shall those sweet ballads sing
Which still in my ears so delightfully ring
"We met" "Friends depart" I those sweet sounds retain,
And feel I shall never forget them again.
And I feel I shall never forget them again:—
And I feel I shall never forget them again.
And down here Mr. Lloyds remains lie beside
And down here Mr. L—d's remains lie beside
Those of his so recently blooming young bride
I'm sorry he's dead, for I knew him to be,
Good humored, most honest, kind hearted & free
Good humoured, most honest, kind hearted, and free.
That he was consistent I ne'er had a doubt
Although scandal said & 'twas whispered about
Although scandal said, and 'twas whispered about
Although scandal said, & 'twas whisper'd about,
That when he last Summer from Paris came home
(I think 'twas his marriage induced him to roam)
He his principles changed—so runs the story,
Threw off the <u>Whigs</u>, and became a staunch <u>Tory</u>
Threw off the <u>Whigs</u>, & became a staunch Tory.
But be that as it may, I think its but fair
To say that I know he enjoyed the <u>fresh air</u>.
And is Arthur Beetham for the first time hushed
And is A—r B—m for the first time hushed?
And is Arthur Beetham for the first time hush'd?
And has he returned to his original dust
Has he gone the way of all flesh with the rest

In spite of the great care he took of his chest[19]
At our snug coteries will he never make one
Will he never again gladden us with his fun
Poor fellow! I fear now's he laid in the Earth
Poor fellow! I fear, now he's laid in the earth,
That of our amusements we'll all find a dearth
And yet he'd his faults,—to speak without joking
He had a knack of being very provoking.
So much so that several times t'other day
I devoutly, heartily wished him away
But after I'd done so, my conscience me smote
And here perhaps, a couple of lines, I may quote,
Missing his mirth and agreeable vein
I directly wished we had him back again
And does McNamara with the dead recline
And does M'N—a with the dead recline?
And does M'Namara with the dead recline?
Poor Francis, his waistcoats were wond'rously fine
He certainly was an elegant fellow
His Coats were well made, his gloves a bright yellow,
Florists shall hold up his Pall by the corners
Morgan[20] and Watkins[21] shall be his chief mourners
Morgan & Watkins shall be his chief mourners—
Morgan, & Watkins shall be his chief mourners.
Last here's Charles Dickens, who's now gone for ever
Last, here's C—s D—s, who's now gone for ever;
It's clear that he thought himself very clever.
To all his friends faults;—it almost makes me weep
He was wide awake—to his own fast asleep!
Though blame he deserved for such willful blindness
He had one merit,—he ne'er forgot kindness.
Perhaps I dont do right to call that a merit
Which each human creature's bound to inherit
But when old death claimed the debt that he owed him
He felt most grateful for all that was showed him
His faults, and they were not in number few,
His faults—and they were not in number a few,
His faults, & there were not in number few
As all his acquaintance extremely well knew,
Emanated—to speak of him in good part,
I think rather more from the head, than the heart.
His death wasn't sudden; he had long been ill,

Slowly he languished, and got worse, until
Slowly he languished & got worse, until,
No mortal means could the poor young fellow save
And a sweet pair of eyes sent him home to his grave.

                                         Finis
                                ["Finis" omitted]

XII.

O'Thello

Dickens's father, John Dickens, wrote a note which had been attached to a manuscript page from Act 1, Scene 4, reading, "This manuscript is in the hand writing of Mr Charles Dickens, forming a portion of one of the 'Parts' in a Burlesque Burletta on 'Othello,' written by him for representation in his own family in the year 1833."

Dickens would have been age 20 or 21 at the time of his humorous adaptation of Shakespeare's tragedy. The only manuscript pages which survive are those which contain the part of "The Great Unpaid," performed by John Dickens. Presumably Dickens made at least two manuscript versions of this home theatrical, a complete version from which he directed his play, and acting copies containing only the parts needed by each performer.

The manuscript for Act 1, Scene 2, is found in the Rosenbach Museum and Library (EL3 f.D548 MS8). A portion of the right margin has been torn off, removing the last letter of the words "enter" and "join" in the stage directions at the top of the page. The manuscript of what is tentatively identified here as a continuation of Act 1, Scene 2, is found in Yale University Library's Beinecke Rare Book and Manuscript Library, along with Act 1, Scene 3, unidentified Act and Scene A, and unidentified Act and Scene B (MS Vault Shelves Dickens). The manuscripts of Act 1, Scene 4, and Act 2, Scene the Last, are found in the Morgan Library and Museum, within a collection of documents related to Dickens's theatricals (MA 109).

Words which Dickens underlined are so noted.

For examples of and notes concerning original lyrics to the airs which Dickens borrowed for *O'Thello*, see Appendix F.

O'Thello

(Part of The Great Unpaid)

Act 1. Scene 2

Discovered at table on opening of Scene

G U.   Begin the business
         (Brab rushes in and says "Ruin! Confusion!"

G U   What charge can warrant such a gross intrusion?

Brab—Warrant

G U.   You're not warranted
         In making noise enough to wake the dead.
         Tell us (first having made a proper bow)
         What is the meaning of this precious row.

Brab—stol'n my daughter

G U.   Who has done this?

Brab—O'Thello

G U   Call the man in

         (Music: wait till he comes in & music stops)
         And now command silence

         What can you say Sir in your own defence?

The number 1 is recorded at the bottom of this page, with a half circle over the 1. The following text is possibly a continuation of Act 1, Scene 2; the number 2 is recorded at the bottom of this page, with a half circle over the 2.

(When O'Thello says "all my eye" start suddenly as if surprised)

Brab—or gin and cloves

G. U.   Silence! On such assertion I can't act
         To say he did, is no proof of the fact.
         O'Thello, if you can, prove these are flams.
         Did you to gain her love use any drams?

O'Th—to embrace

(After they have embraced come forward & say)

G U.   Good! There's no more business now to bore us
         So I propose we have a jolly chorus.

Grand chorus

Solo. The Great Unpaid
       Air—''away with melancholy—''
Away with grief. Be jolly
Nor grave night charges bring
of drunken freaks and folly
But merrily merrily sing fal! la!
What's the use of repining
at magistrates odd law?
can we prevent their fining?
Then merrily merrily sing fal la

Chorus   Away with grief & c

Act 1 Scene 3

at ''That is the Moor I know him by his knock.'' Ente[r]
with O'Thello. Shake hands with the company and joi[n]
in following''

Chorus

Air—''Gold's but dross''—Robert le diable

G U.   Bring the porter in the Pewter
            And be sure they draw it mild

E argo.   If he suspects his wife he'll shoot her
            And I am for vengeance wild.

Cass.   Let's be happy
                Lots of baccy
            Let the cheerful smoke abound

Desd   Dancing lightly
                Gaily Sprightly
            Let the merry song go round.

G U.   Right fal la ral la ral lide

E argo.   Right fal la ral liddle dol de

Cass   Right fal la ral la ral lide

Desd   Right fal la ral liddle dol de

Cho: Right fal la ral & c

        (at end of chorus go out with the rest)

Act 1. Scene 4

(after the fight enter with O'Thello. Quick Music. Sit
down in Great Chair. When O'Thello says "But never more
be officer of mine" come forward and say

G U.   Serve him well. Tomorrow bring him over
              And I will fine him as he's half seas over.

Grand Chorus

G U.   Begone Dull Mike. I view you with detestation

Cho   begone Dull Mike. You've lost your situation

Cass   My wife will die, and so shall I
              If you don't let me stay

G U.   You very well know that's all my eye
              So Take yourself away.

Cass   ⎰ My wife will die and so shall I
                  If you don't let me stay

Cho   ⎱ His wife will die he says oh cri!
                  If he isn't allowed to stay

Cass   My wife will die and so shall I
              If you don't let me stay

Cho: You very well know that's all my eye
              So take yourself away   (Repeated)

Act 2 Scene the last

(at Emilia's crying out Murder! Run in and go with
Brabantio up to the Couch; remain there administering
restoratives until Roderigo and the remainder of the
Dram: falls: run out after E. Argo; then come forward
with Brabantio

Brab—So T'is, leave her.

G U.   Torture him well as soon as he comes back

Brab—Jug of <u>sack</u>

G U (solus) And in his absence, to secure the Moor
              We just mount guard before the bedroom door.
                  (draw chair to centre Swing and sit there)

O'th—disarm me

G U.   I'm glad to hear it 'Gad he's quite alarmed us

E argo—better go

G U.   Rod'rigo, see the villain is secured
In the lock-up-house let him be immured.

[Unidentified Act and Scene A]

Brab—wish you joy

Medley chorus

Solo. Desdemona

Air "There's na luck about the house"

oh! let us pass a merry night
Our house is rather small
But being recovered I invite
all present to a Ball.
There is some cold duck in the house
There's wine enough for all:
Likewise some spirits & some grouse
So we'll enjoy the ball

Cho.   Oh Let us pass & c

Solo. E. Argo

I feel all of a quiver
With grief & shame I shiver
    Bring a cigar
    Bring a cigar
It's balmy smoke I love

[Unidentified Act and Scene B]

Solo—Cassio

Air "When in death I shall calm recline"

When in sleep I shall calm recline
Oh take me home to my "Missus" dear

Tell her I've taken a little more wine
Than I could carry, or very well bear.
Bid her not scold me on the morrow
For staying out drinking all the night
But several bottles of Soda borrow
To cool my coppers and set me right.

Solo.—The Great Unpaid

Air—Merrily oh

Merrily ev'ry heart will bound here
    Merrily oh Merrily oh!
If with success our piece is crowned here
    Merrily oh! Merrily oh!
If our humble efforts meet with yr applause
and your smiles grace us, we have gained our cause
Merrily every heart will bound here
(Chorus Repeat the whole   Merrily oh! Merrily oh

XIII.

Private Theatricals Regulations

The manuscript for Dickens's "Private Theatrical Regulations" is found in the Morgan Library and Museum, within a collection of documents related to Dickens's theatricals (MA 109). Although the manuscript is in the handwriting of Henry Austin, secretary of Dickens's amateur acting company, Dickens signs his name to the text and writes "Stage Manager" next to his name.

On 7 October 1833, when Dickens was age 21, he wrote to Miss Urquhart, a friend who had already appeared with him in his amateur theatrical performance of *Clari* on 27 April 1833.[22] The letter informed her, "In forwarding the inclosed play for your perusal, and in requesting your acceptance of the part of Laura, I am desired by Mr. Dickens to call your attention to the accompanying Regulations, which have been drawn up with the view of preventing any misunderstanding, and in the hope of rendering our undertaking conducive to our own amusement, and that of our friends" (*Letters* 1: 31). Dickens refers to himself in the third person, as he had his letter signed by Henry Austin, in the latter's capacity as secretary.

1. Mr. Dickens is desirous that it should be distinctly understood by his friends that it is his wish to have a Series of Weekly Rehearsals for some time, experience having already shewn that the Rehearsals are perhaps the most amusing part of private Theatricals. This is rendered indeed unavoidable in the present case, it being yet impossible to say at what precise period the rooms used on the last occasion can be appropriated to the reception of the Audience & Performers—The probability however is, that they will be sufficiently clear to admit of the Stage being filled up about Christmas—

2. It is earnestly hoped that Ladies & Gentlemen who may have somewhat inferior parts assigned them in any piece will recollect the impossibility of giving every performer a principal character, and that they will be consequently induced rather to consult the general convenience and amusement than individual feeling upon the subject. The same observation will apply to the filling up of Chorusses & c—

3. Suggestions relative to the Costume of Characters, alterations in any part of the Dialogue, introduction of Songs & c if made on a Rehearsal Night to the Manager, will be immediately attended to, & if it be deemed advisable, adopted.

4. It is scarcely necessary to add that a punctual attendance at Rehearsals, and an early knowledge of the several parts, are most especially necessary—

5. It is proposed that a Rehearsal shall take place every Wednesday at 7 oClock for 8 precisely. Early notice will be given of the First Rehearsal which is only delayed until the various Characters are accepted—

	Henry Austin	Secretary
	Charles Dickens	Stage Manager
Principal Scene Painters	— Mr. Henry Austin	
	and	
	Mr. Milton	
Stage Carpenter & Mechanist	— Mr. Boston	

APPENDICES

A. Description of Canon's Housekeeper in The Adventures of Gil Blas, *translated by Tobias Smollett*

Book II, Chapter I

Fabricius conducts Gil Blas, and introduces him to the Licentiate Sedillo. The Situation of this Canon. A Description of his Housekeeper.

We were so much afraid of being too late, that we made but one leap from the alley to the house of the old licentiate. We knocked at the door, which was opened by a girl ten years old, who passed for the housekeeper's niece, in spite of scandal; and, asking if the canon could be spoke with, Dame Jacintha appeared. She was a person already arrived at the age of discretion, but still handsome; and, in particular, I admired the freshness of her complexion. She wore a long gown of coarse stuff, with a large leathern girdle, from one side of which hung a bunch of keys, and from the other a rosary of great beads. As soon as we perceived her, we bowed with profound respect, and she returned the salute very civilly, but with a modest deportment and downcast eyes. . . .

I have already observed that Dame Jacintha, though somewhat superannuated, had still a fres[h]ness of complexion: true, indeed, she spared nothing to preserve it; for, besides a glyster which she took every morning, she swallowed during the day, and when she went to bed, some excellent jellies of her own composing, and slept soundly all night, while I watched my master: but that which, perhaps, contributed more than any thing to preserve her colour from fading, was an issue [incision made to produce a discharge of blood (?)], which Inesilla told me she had in each leg.[23]

B. "Doctors' Commons" by Charles Dickens

(as originally published in *The Morning Chronicle*, 11 October 1836)

SKETCHES BY "BOZ."—No. III.
(NEW SERIES.)

DOCTORS' COMMONS.

Walking, without any definite object, through St. Paul's Church-yard, a little while ago, we happened to turn down a street entitled "Paul's-chain," and keeping straight forward for a few hundred yards, found ourself, as a natural consequence, in Doctors' Commons. Now, Doctors' Commons being familiar by name to everybody as the place where they grant marriage-licenses to love-sick couples, and divorces to unfaithful ones; register the wills of people who have any property to leave, and punish hasty gentlemen who call ladies by unpleasant names; we no sooner discovered that we were really within its precincts, than we felt a laudable desire to become better acquainted therewith; and as the first object of our curiosity was the Court whose decrees can even unloose the bonds of matrimony, we procured a direction to it, and bent our steps thither without delay.

Crossing a quiet and shady court-yard, paved with stone, and frowned upon by old red-brick houses, on the doors of which were painted the names of sundry learned civilians, we paused before a small, green-baized, brass-headed-nailed door, which, yielding to our gentle push, at once admitted us into an old quaint-looking apartment, with sunken windows, and black carved wainscoting, at the upper end of which, seated on a raised platform, of semi-circular shape, were about a dozen solemn-looking gentlemen, in crimson gowns and wigs. At a more elevated desk, in the centre, sat a very fat and red-faced gentleman, in tortoise-shell spectacles, whose dignified appearance announced the judge; and round a long green-baized table below, something like a billiard-table without the cushions and pockets, were a number of very self-important-looking personages, in stiff neckcloths and black gowns with white fur collars, whom we at once set down as proctors. At the lower end of the billiard-table was an individual in an arm-chair, and a wig, whom we afterwards discovered to be the registrar; and seated behind a little desk, near the door, were a respectable-looking man, in black, of about twenty stone weight or thereabouts, and a fat-faced, smirking, civil-looking body, in a black gown, black kid gloves, knee shorts, and silks, with a shirt-frill in his bosom, curls on his head, and a silver staff in his hand, whom we had no difficulty in recognizing as the officers of the Court. The latter, indeed, speedily set our mind at rest upon this point, for advancing to our elbow, and opening a conversation forthwith, he had communicated to us in less than five minutes that he was the apparitor, and the other the court-keeper; that this was the Arches Court, and therefore the counsel wore red gowns, and the proctors fur collars; and that when the other Courts sat there, they didn't wear red gowns or fur collars either; with many other scraps of intelligence equally interesting. Besides these two officers, there was a little thin old man, with long grizzly hair, crouched in a remote corner, whose duty our communicative friend informed us was to ring a large hand-bell when the Court opened in the morning, and who, for aught his appearance betokened to the contrary, might have been similarly employed for the last two centuries at least.

The red-faced gentleman in the tortoise-shell spectacles had got all the talk to himself just then, and very well he was doing it, too, only he spoke very fast, but that was habit; and rather thick, but that was good-living. So we had plenty of time to look about us. There was one individual amused us mightily. This was one of the bewigged gentlemen in the red robes, who was straddling before the fire in the centre of the Court, in the attitude of the brazen colossus, to the complete exclusion of everybody else. He had gathered up his robe behind, in much the same manner as a slovenly woman would her petticoats on a very dirty day, in order that he might feel the full warmth of the fire. His wig was put on all awry, with the tail straggling about his neck, his scanty gray trowsers and short black gaiters, made in the worst possible style, imparted an additionally inelegant appearance to his uncouth person; and his limp, badly-starched shirt-collar almost obscured his eyes. We shall never be able to claim any credit as a physiognomist again, for, after a careful scrutiny of this person's countenance, we had come to the conclusion that it bespoke nothing but conceit and silliness, when our friend with the silver staff whispered in our ear that he was no other than a doctor of law, an ecclesiastical dignitary in the cinque ports, a not very distant relation to a commissioner of lunacy, and heaven knows what besides. So of course we were mistaken, and he must be a very talented man. He conceals it so well though—perhaps with the merciful view of not astonishing ordinary people too much—that you would suppose him to be one of the stupidest dogs alive.

The gentleman in the spectacles having concluded his judgment, and a few minutes having been allowed to elapse, to afford time for the buzz in the court to subside, the registrar called on the next cause, which was "the office of the Judge promoted by Bumple against Sludberry." A general movement was visible in the court at this announcement, and the obliging functionary with the silver staff whispered us that "there would be some fun now, for this was a brawling case." We were not rendered much the wiser by this piece of information till we found by the opening speech of the counsel for the promoter that, under a half obsolete statute of one of the Edwards, the court was empowered to visit with the penalty of excommunication any person who should be proved guilty of the crime of "brawling," or "smiting" in any church, or vestry adjoining thereto; and it appeared, by some eight-and-twenty affidavits, which were duly referred to, that on a certain night, at a certain vestry, meeting in a certain parish particularly set forth, Thomas Sludberry, the party appeared against in that suit, had made use of and applied to Michael Bumple, the reporter, the words "You be blowed;" and that on the said Michael Bumple and others remonstrating with the said Thomas Sludberry on the impropriety of his conduct, the said Thomas Sludberry repeated the aforesaid expression, "You be blowed;" and furthermore, desired and requested to know whether the said Michael Bumple "wanted anything for himself," adding, that if the said Michael Bumple did want anything for himself, he the said Thomas Sludberry "was the man to give it him;" at the same time making use of other heinous and sinful expressions, all of which, Bumple submitted, came within the intent and meaning of the Act; and therefore he, for the soul's health and chastening of Sludberry, prayed for sentence of excommunication against him accordingly. Upon these facts a long argument was entered into on both sides, to the great edification of a number of persons interested in the parochial squabbles, who crowded the court; and when some very long and grave speeches had been made *pro* and *con*, the red-faced gentleman in the tortoise-shell spectacles took a review of the case, which occupied half an hour more, and then pronounced upon Sludberry the awful sentence of excommunication for a fortnight, and payment of the costs of the suit. Upon this Sludberry, who was a little, red-faced, sly-looking, ginger-beer seller, addressed the Court, and said, that if they'd be good enough to take off the costs, and excommunicate him for the term of his natural life instead, it would be much more convenient to him; for he never went to church at all. To this appeal the gentleman in the spectacles made no other reply than a look of virtuous propriety; and Sludberry and his friends retired. As the man with the silver staff informed us that the Court was on the point of rising, we retired too—pondering, as we walked away, upon the beautiful spirit of these ancient ecclesiastical laws, the kind and neighbourly feelings they are calculated to awaken, and the strong attachment to religious institutions which they cannot fail to engender.

We were so lost in these meditations, that we had turned into the street and run up against a door-post, before we recollected where we were walking. On looking upwards to see what house we had stumbled upon, the words "Prerogative-office," written in large characters, met our eye; and as we were in a sight-seeing humour, and the place was a public one, we walked in, without more ado.

The room into which we walked was a long, busy-looking place, partitioned off, on either side, into a variety of little boxes, in which a few clerks were engaged in copying or examining deeds. Down the centre of the room were several desks, nearly breast high, at each of which three or four people were standing, poring over large volumes. As we knew that they were searching for wills, they attracted our attention at once.

It was curious to contrast the lazy indifference of the attorneys' clerks, who were making a search for some legal purpose, with the air of earnestness and interest which distinguished the strangers to the place, who were looking up the will of some deceased relative; the former pausing every now and then with an impatient yawn, or raising their heads to look at the people who passed up and down the room; the latter stooping over the book, and running down column after column of names in the deepest abstraction. There was one little dirty-faced man in a blue apron, who, after a whole morning's search, extending some fifty years back, had just found the will to which he wished to refer, which one of the officials was reading to him in a low hurried voice from a thick vellum book with large clasps. It was perfectly evident that the more the clerk read, the less the man with the blue apron understood about the matter. When the volume was first brought down, he took off his hat, smoothed down his hair, smiled with great self-satisfaction, and looked up in the reader's face with the air of a man who had made up his mind to recollect every word he heard. The first two or three lines were intelligible enough; but then the technicalities began, and the little man began to look rather dubious. Then came a whole string of complicated trusts, and he was regularly at sea. As the reader proceeded, it was quite apparent that it was a hopeless case, and the little man, with his mouth open and his eyes fixed upon his face, looked on with an expression of bewilderment and perplexity irresistibly ludicrous. A little further on, a hard-featured old man, with a deeply-wrinkled face, was intently perusing a lengthy will, with the aid of a pair of horn spectacles, occasionally pausing from his task, and slily noting down some brief memorandum of the bequests contained in it. Every wrinkle about his toothless mouth, and sharp keen eyes, told of avarice and cunning. As he leisurely closed the register, put up his spectacles, and folded his scraps of paper in a large leathern pocket-book, we thought what a nice hard bargain he was driving with some poverty-stricken legatee, who, tired of waiting year after year, until some life-interest should fall in, was selling his chance, just as it began to grow most valuable, for a twelfth-part of its worth. It was a good speculation—a very safe one. The old man stowed away his pocket-book in the breast of his great-coat, and hobbled away, with a leer of anticipation. That will had made him ten years younger at least.

Having commenced our observations, we should certainly have extended them to another dozen of people at least, had not a sudden shutting up, and putting away of the worm-eaten old books, warned us that the time for closing the office had arrived, and thus deprived us of a pleasure, and spared our readers an infliction. We naturally fell into a train of reflection as we walked homewards upon the curious old records of likings and dislikings; of jealousies and revenges; of affection defying the power of death, and hatred pursued beyond the grave, which these depositories contain: silent but striking tokens, some of them, of excellence of heart, and nobleness of soul; melancholy examples, others, of the vast passions of human nature. In short, the subject obtained such complete possession of us, that if we fail to write a whole paper about it one of these days we shall be rather surprised.[24]   BOZ.

C. Dickens's Personal Commentary on "The Bill of Fare"

(written to Maria Beadnell in late 1831)

My dear Maria.—(I fear I ought to say "Miss Beadnell" but I hope you will pardon my adhering to the manner in which I have been accustomed to address you.) I have taken the opputunity [*sic*] of returning your sister's Album [obviously containing "The Bill of Fare]. . . .

   I hope you will like the Lines. I do not <u>think</u> what I <u>write</u> you know.—I allude, particularly to the <u>last four Lines</u> of the <u>Third Verse</u>.[25]

D. Commentary on "The Bill of Fare"

(from Chapter II of *The Love Romance of Charles Dickens*
by Walter Dexter)

Together with the letters from her ardent lover, Maria preserved all her life a copy (in the handwriting of John Dickens, the father of Charles), of a parody of "Retaliation," written by Charles Dickens, which the author refers to as "Goldsmith's ever famed Feast," and entitled by him "The Bill of Fare."

Interior evidence shows this to have been written in the second half of 1831, when Dickens had known the Beadnell family for about a year and a half.

It forms an excellent introduction to the Beadnell Circle which opened an entirely new world to the ambitious young man who, six years before, had been a drudge in a blacking warehouse near Charing Cross, while his father was in the Marshalsea Debtor's Prison. Fortunately that nightmare was of short duration; three years of schooling had followed; then eighteen months as office boy to a firm of solicitors in Gray's Inn.

At the time Dickens first met Maria he was about eighteen years of age, and was following a little better employment as a reporter in the courts of Doctors' Commons where by the aid of one of his mother's relatives, he shared part of a little office in Bell Yard, Carter Lane.

In "The Bill of Fare" we are introduced to the whole of the company which, on occasions, assembled in the spacious rooms over Smith, Payne and Smith's Bank at No. 2 Lombard Street, London.

George Beadnell, the father, was manager of the bank, and he had three daughters. The eldest, Margaret, had married David Lloyd, a tea merchant, on April 20th, 1831, and "The Bill of Fare," therefore, refers only to the remaining daughters as "The Miss B's," who were "two nice little Ducks, and very well dressed." The elder of them was Anne, "a truly delightful and sweet tempered girl," whose favourite author, "was the famed *Colley* Cibber," a jest at her engagement to Henry Kolle, Dickens's friend, through whom, no doubt, he had obtained entrée to the family. Maria, the youngest daughter, who was, in fact, a year older than Dickens, is described as "too good and too fair" for this world, and the young man bursts into ecstasies over "the grace of her form, and the glance of her eye," the lady on whom his "bright hopes and fond wishes were all centered."

These lines were not written in retrospect, but it is interesting to note how prophetic they were.

George Beadnell is described as "an excellent man," with a spouse who could be "summed up in one word—Perfection."

Among the guests we find first the Moule family. Mr. Moule, "at whose plentiful board we often have sat," lived in Pound Lane, Lower Clapton. Mrs. Moule "never by any one yet was excelled." There were two daughters, Louisa and Fanny, the latter a retiring girl, whose chief pleasure was "to sit by herself in a corner and sigh," "romance or sentiment" having "quite turned her head." Joe Moule, their brother, was destined for the army.

Next comes the Leigh family, one of whom was to play a large part in the drama of Dickens's lost love.

Mr. John Porter Leigh, "the kindest and best-temper'd man I e'er met," was a corn-dealer of Lea Bridge Road, and evidently a man after his (Dickens's) own heart, fond of a joke and a glass. But not so his wife, whom he feared "either to praise or to blame;" or his daughter Mary Anne, "the greatest tormentor that I e'er know," and a great flirt, as we shall have occasion to see later on. Of David Lloyd's recent marriage to Margaret Beadnell, and their honeymoon in Paris, there is a mention—they are "a nice side dish," and Dickens takes the opportunity of mentioning in parenthesis, "Some type of their most happy state I much wish."

Arthur Beetham was a young surgeon, who unfortunately died in 1834, and the remaining bachelor of the party, not counting the narrator himself, was a certain Francis M'Namara, "an elegant fellow" with waistcoats "wondrously fine."

These, then, were the folk with whom Dickens was associating in 1830–1, types which a diligent reader of *Sketches by Boz* will readily see were, a few years later on, translated into his first published work.

Of Dickens himself, these lines clearly show his state of mind; "a young summer cabbage" who had lost his heart "twelve months ago from last May" (i.e. May 1830) wide awake to his friends' faults, "to his own fast asleep." But, as he confesses in the concluding lines, his faults emanated "rather more from his head than his heart," "and a sweet pair of eyes sent him home to his grave."[26]

E. "Retaliation" by Oliver Goldsmith

(published 1774)

OF old, when Scarron his companions invited,
Each guest brought his dish, and the feast was united;
If our landlord supplies us with beef, and with fish,
Let each guest bring himself, and he brings the best dish:
Our Dean shall be venison, just fresh from the plains;
Our Burke shall be tongue, with a garnish of brains;
Our Will shall be wild-fowl, of excellent flavour,
And Dick with his pepper shall heighten their savour:
Our Cumberland's sweet-bread its place shall obtain,
And Douglas is pudding, substantial and plain:
Our Garrick's a salad; for in him we see
Oil, vinegar, sugar, and saltness agree:
To make out the dinner, full certain I am,
That Ridge is anchovy, and Reynolds is lamb;
That Hickey's a capon, and by the same rule,
Magnanimous Goldsmith a goosberry fool.
At a dinner so various, at such a repast,
Who'd not be a glutton, and stick to the last?
Here, waiter! more wine, let me sit while I'm able,
Till all my companions sink under the table;
Then, with chaos and blunders encircling my head,
Let me ponder, and tell what I think of the dead.

   Here lies the good Dean, re-united to earth,
Who mix'd reason with pleasure, and wisdom with mirth:
If he had any faults, he has left us in doubt,
At least, in six weeks, I could not find 'em out;
Yet some have declar'd, and it can't be denied 'em,
That sly-boots was cursedly cunning to hide 'em.

   Here lies our good Edmund, whose genius was such
We scarcely can praise it, or blame it too much;
Who, born for the Universe, narrow'd his mind,
And to party gave up what was meant for mankind.
Though fraught with all learning, yet straining his throat
To persuade Tommy Townshend to lend him a vote;
Who, too deep for his hearers, still went on refining,

And thought of convincing, while they thought of dining;
Though equal to all things, for all things unfit,
Too nice for a statesman, too proud for a wit:
For a patriot, too cool; for a drudge, disobedient;
And too fond of the *right* to pursue the *expedient*.
In short, 'twas his fate, unemploy'd, or in place, Sir,
To eat mutton cold, and cut blocks with a razor.

   Here lies honest William, whose heart was a mint,
While the owner ne'er knew half the good that was in't;
The pupil of impulse, it forc'd him along,
His conduct still right, with his argument wrong;
Still aiming at honour, yet fearing to roam,
The coachman was tipsy, the chariot drove home;
Would you ask for his merits? alas! he had none;
What was good was spontaneous, his faults were his own.

   Here lies honest Richard, whose fate I must sigh at;
Alas, that such frolic should now be so quiet!
What spirits were his! what wit and what whim!
Now breaking a jest, and now breaking a limb;
Now wrangling and grumbling to keep up the ball,
Now teasing and vexing, yet laughing at all!
In short, so provoking a devil was Dick,
That we wish'd him full ten times a day at Old Nick;
But, missing his mirth and agreeable vein,
As often we wish'd to have Dick back again.

   Here Cumberland lies, having acted his parts,
The Terence of England, the mender of hearts;
A flattering painter, who made it his care
To draw men as they ought to be, not as they are.
His gallants are all faultless, his women divine,
And comedy wonders at being so fine;
Like a tragedy queen he has dizen'd her out,
Or rather like tragedy giving a rout.
His fools have their follies so lost in a crowd
Of virtues and feelings, that folly grows proud;
And coxcombs, alike in their failings alone,
Adopting his portraits, are pleas'd with their own.
Say, where has our poet this malady caught?
Or wherefore his characters thus without fault?

Say, was it that vainly directing his view
To find out men's virtues, and finding them few,
Quite sick of pursuing each troublesome elf,
He grew lazy at last, and drew from himself?

   Here Douglas retires, from his toils to relax,
The scourge of impostors, the terror of quacks:
Come, all ye quack bards, and ye quacking divines,
Come, and dance on the spot where your tyrant reclines:
When Satire and Censure encircl'd his throne,
I fear'd for your safety, I fear'd for my own;
But now he is gone, and we want a detector,
Our Dodds shall be pious, our Kendricks shall lecture;
Macpherson write bombast, and call it a style,
Our Townshend make speeches, and I shall compile;
New Lauders and Bowers the Tweed shall cross over,
No countryman living their tricks to discover;
Detection her taper shall quench to a spark,
And Scotchman meet Scotchman, and cheat in the dark.

   Here lies David Garrick, describe me who can,
An abridgment of all that was pleasant in man;
As an actor, confess'd without rival to shine,
As a wit, if not first, in the very first line:
Yet, with talents like these, and an excellent heart,
The man had his failings, a dupe to his art.
Like an ill-judging beauty, his colours he spread,
And beplaster'd with rouge his own natural red.
On the stage he was natural, simple, affecting;
'Twas only that when he was off he was acting.
With no reason on earth to go out of his way,
He turn'd and he varied full ten times a day.
Though secure of our hearts, yet confoundedly sick
If they were not his own by finessing and trick,
He cast off his friends, as a huntsman his pack,
For he knew when he pleas'd he could whistle them back.
Of praise a mere glutton, he swallow'd what came,
And the puff of a dunce he mistook it for fame;
Till his relish grown callous, almost to disease,
Who pepper'd the highest, was surest to please.
But let us be candid, and speak out our mind,
If dunces applauded, he paid them in kind.

Ye Kenricks, ye Kellys, and Woodfalls so grave,
What a commerce was yours, while you got and you gave!
How did Grub-street re-echo the shouts that you rais'd,
While he was be-Roscius'd, and you were be-prais'd!
But peace to his spirit, wherever it flies,
To act as an angel, and mix with the skies:
Those poets, who owe their best fame to his skill,
Shall still be his flatterers, go where he will.
Old Shakespeare, receive him with praise and with love,
And Beaumonts and Bens be his Kellys above.

   Here Hickey reclines, a most blunt, pleasant creature,
And slander itself must allow him good-nature:
He cherish'd his friend, and he relish'd a bumper;
Yet one fault he had, and that one was a thumper.
Perhaps you may ask if the man was a miser?
I answer, no, no, for he always was wiser:
Too courteous, perhaps, or obligingly flat?
His very worst foe can't accuse him of that:
Perhaps he confided in men as they go,
And so was too foolishly honest; Ah, no!
Then what was his failing? come tell it, and, burn ye!
He was, could he help it? a special attorney.

   Here Reynolds is laid, and, to tell you my mind,
He has not left a better or wiser behind:
His pencil was striking, resistless and grand;
His manners were gentle, complying and bland;
Still born to improve us in every part,
His pencil our faces, his manners our heart:
To coxcombs averse, yet most civilly steering,
When they judg'd without skill he was still hard of hearing:
When they talk'd of their Raphaels, Corregios, and stuff,
He shifted his trumpet, and only took snuff.[27]

F. Examples of Original Lyrics for Airs in O'Thello

"Away with Melancholy"

Away with melancholy,
Nor doleful changes ring,
On life and human folly
And merrily merrily sing,
          Fal la.

Chorus

For what's the use of sighing,
While time is on the wing,
Can we prevent its flying,
Then merrily merrily sing,
          Fal la.

Come on ye rosy hours,
Gay smiling moments bring
We'll strew the way with flowers,
And merrily merrily sing,
          Fal la.[28]

"Gold's but Dross"

By simply naming the various airs selected for *O'Thello*, Dickens indicated that his amateur acting company already knew these melodies. "Gold's but Dross," however, was apparently not an old song, as Dickens associates it with *Robert le Diable*, a successful French opera by Giacomo Meyerbeer, first performed in Paris on 21 November 1831 (Scribe and Delavigne 31). In Act I, Scene VII, Section 98, Robert and the Chevaliers sing, in part, "Gold is an illusion, / Let's know how to use it: / Is not the true good on earth pleasure?" and these lines are repeated throughout the scene (Scribe and Delavigne 40, 43–44).

In January 1832, the first English version was produced at London's Adelphi Theatre. However, this cannot be the version from which Dickens selects an air. *The Athenaeum* reports:

> The race which we announced as about to take place, between majors and minors, for the opera of 'Robert le Diable,' has been decided, as to order of priority, in favour of the Adelphi. The order of merit must stand over to be adjudged—not to the swiftest, but to the most worthy. The piece produced at this house, on Monday last, under the title of 'Robert le Diable, the Devil's Son,' is the opera of Meyerbeer, without the music.[29]

The next produced English translation, this time with music, premiered at Drury Lane Theatre under the title *The Demon; or, the Mystic Branch* in February 1832. Its unpublished manuscript, titled *The Demon Duke; or, The Mystic Branch: An Opera, In 3 Acts,* does not indicate the authorship. The following lyrics are located in Act I, Scene I of the manuscript, which is dated 14 February 1832:

> Gold is only a bubble
> Unless it bliss can buy
> The best relief from trouble
> Is it not pleasure and joy?[30]

Yet another translation opened one day later at Theatre Royal, Covent Garden, but under the title *Robert the Devil or The Fiend-Father; A Grand Romantic Opera in Three Acts* by Michael Rophino Lacy. Lacy's published version provides the following translation, also in Act I, Scene I:

> Gold's a vanishing treasure;
> The wise still make it fly;
> While gold brings hours of pleasure,
> To lose it never sigh![31]

It appears, then, that someone independent of the three London productions translated the original French as ''Gold's but Dross,'' possibly kept Meyerbeer's music, and then published sheet music for household use. If so, it seems likely that this as yet unlocated sheet music contained a subtitle or otherwise linked the air to Meyerbeer's *Robert le Diable* to promote sales. What is certain is Dickens and his acting company were sufficiently familiar with ''Gold's but Dross'' for Dickens to provide new lyrics to the air and expect his performers to be able to sing it.

''Begone Dull Care'' [altered to ''Begone Dull Mike'' by Dickens]

Begone, dull care, I prithee begone from me,
Begone, dull care, for you and I shall never agree,
Long time thou hast been tarrying here,
And fain thoa would'st me kill,
But I [in] faith dull care,
Thou never shall have thy will.

Too much care will turn a young man grey,
Too much care will turn an old man to clay,
My wife shall dance and I will sing,
So merrily pass the day,
For I hold it one of the wisest things,
To drive dull care away.[32]

"There's Nae Luck about the House" [by William Mickle]

And are you sure the news is true?
And are ye sure he's weel?
Is this a time to think of wark!
Mak haste, lay by your wheel;
Is this the time to spin a thread
When Colin's at the door!
Reach me my cloak, I'll to the quay
And see him come ashore.
For there's nae luck about the house,
There is nae luck at aw;
There's little pleasure in the house
When our gudeman's awa.

And gie to me my bigonet,
My bishop's satin gown;
For I maun tell the bailie's wife
That Colin's come to town.
My Turkey slippers maun gae on,
My stockings pearly blue;
'Tis aw to pleasure my gudeman,
For he's baith leel and true.
                              For there's nae luck & c.

Rise, lass, and mak a clean fire side,
Put on the muckle pot,
Gie little Kate her button gown,
And Jock his Sunday coat;
And mak their shoon as black as slaes,
Their hose as white as snaw,
It's aw to please my ain gudeman,
For he's been lang awa.
                              For there's nae, & c.

There's twa fat hens upo' the bauk
Been fed this month and mair,
Mak haste and thraw their necks about,
That Colin weel may fare;
And mak the table neat and clean,
Let every thing look braw,
For wha can tell how Colin fared

When he was far awa.
Ah, there's nae, & c.

Sae true his heart, sae smooth his speech,
His breath like cauler air,
His very foot has music in't
As he comes up the stair!
And shall I see his face again,
And shall I hear him speak!
I'm downright dizzy wi the thought,
In troth I'm like to greet.
For there's nae, & c.

If Colin's weel, and weel content,
I hae nae mair to crave—
And gin I live to keep him sae,
I'm blest aboon the lave.
And shall I see his face again,
And shall I hear him speak!
I'm downright dizzy wi the thought,
In troth I'm like to greet.
For there's nae, & c.[33]

"Legacy" [by Thomas Moore; titled "When in Death I Shall Calm Recline"
by Dickens]

When in death I shall calm recline,
O bear my heart to my mistress dear.
Tell her it liv'd upon smiles and wine
Of the brightest hue, while it linger'd here.
Bid her not shed one tear of sorrow
To sully a heart so brilliant and bright;
But balmy drops of the red grape borrow,
To bathe the relic from morn to night.

When the light of my song is o'er,
O bear my harp to your ancient hall;
Hang it up at some friendly door,
Where weary travelers love to call.
And should some bard that roams forsaken
Revive its soft notes when passing along,

O! let one thought of its master awaken
Your warmest smile for the child of song.

Take this cup that is now o'erflowing,
To grace your revel when I am at rest:
Never, O never, its balm bestowing
On lips that beauty hath seldom blest.
But should some warm devoted lover,
To her he loves, once bathe its brim,
O then my spirit around shall hover
To hallow each drop that forms for him.[34]

"Merrily Oh"

Merrily every bosom boundeth,
    Merrily oh, merrily oh!
Where the song of freedom soundeth,
    Merrily oh, merrily oh!
There the warrior's arms shed more splendour,
There the maiden's charms shine more tender,
Every joy the land surroundeth,
    Merrily oh, merrily oh!

Wearily every bosom pineth,
    Wearily oh, wearily oh!
Where the band of slavery twineth,
    Wearily oh, wearily oh!
There the warrior's dart has no fleetness,
There the maiden's heart has no sweetness,
Every flower of life declineth,
    Wearily oh, wearily oh!

Cheerily then from hill and valley,
    Cheerily oh, cheerily oh!
Like your native mountains sally,
    Cheerily oh, cheerily oh!
If a glorious death, won by bravery,
Sweeter be than breath sigh'd in slavery,
Round the flag of freedom rally,
    Cheerily oh, cheerily oh![35]

G. Early Writings Falsely Attributed to Dickens by John Payne Collier

1. Sweet Betsy Ogle

Only one verse of "Sweet Betsy Ogle" was published by John Payne Collier in 1872. He attributed its composition and recitation to Dickens in what was purportedly Collier's personal diary from 1832–33 (4: 14). Arthur Freeman and Janet Ing Freeman reveal Collier's fabrication of this "diary" (1: 303) and further note how Collier "would consciously imitate and (at last) fabricate popular ballads all his adult life" (1: 177). In fact, Collier composed in his own handwriting an entire "Sweet Betsy Ogle" ballad and later placed his manuscript in a personal copy of his published "diary," precisely at the location of the verse he selected to be presented as a Dickens original.[36]

Collier also sought a share of personal credit for Dickens's being hired as a newspaper reporter where Collier himself was employed. He continued in his "diary" that "I have mentioned hereafter the trifling part I took in the appointment to a reportership on the *Morning Chronicle* of one of the greatest wits and novelists of our age. He subsequently sent me a kind note of acknowledgment, which I fear I destroyed, not guessing the eminence at which the writer afterwards arrived" (4: v). However, Collier erred in the timeline of his "diary" regarding Dickens's employment. While he writes of his "trifling part" and "little hesitation in recommending him to the proprietor of the *Morning Chronicle*" as occurring in July 1833 (4: 14), Kaplan dates Dickens's actual application for a reporting position on the newspaper as August 1834 (60). Clearly, then, Dickens's "kind note of acknowledgement" to Collier never existed.

[Stanza 1, as published in Collier's "diary"]

Sweet Betsy Ogle,
In her bird's-eye fogle,
Is round my heart-strings twined and twisted:
No voice is clearer;
If you should hear her,
Pray, don't go near her;
Her looks can never be resisted.

[Alternate version of Stanza 1 by Collier, from his complete manuscript]

Sweet Betsy Ogle
In bird's-eye fogle
Is in my heart-strings twined and twisted.
No voice is clearer,
If you should hear her,
O, don't go near her,
Her eyes can never be resisted.

[Stanza 2 by Collier, handwritten in margin of page 14, *Diary* Part IV]

Cock-sparrows listen,
Her bright eyes glisten,
Stones kiss the shoes she has her feet on
If thunder lour
And milk turn sour
She has the power.
By one sweet look the milk to sweeten.

[Alternate version of Stanza 2 by Collier, from his complete manuscript]

The sparrows listen
When her eyes glisten;
Stones kiss the shoes she has her feet in:
If thunder lower,
And milk turn sour,
She has the power
By one mere look the milk to sweeten.

[Stanzas 3–7 by Collier, from his complete manuscript]

Her foot and ankle
In my breast rankle;
To all her charms I am a martyr.
Black is her stocking;
It may be shocking,
But I'm not mocking,
To say how blest must be her garter.

As she goes tripping,
O'er kennel skipping,
The very stones with joy behold her.
They fain would stop her,
But 'tis improper:
I'd give a copper,
If I were they, and might be bolder.

And then her bosom
Is such a blossom,
A very bou-quet for our noses:
Her lips and cheeks

Who ever seeks,
For weeks and weeks,
Will revel in a bed of roses.

I follow after,
Though by her laughter
She knows full well the love I harbour:
What I'm afraid is,
Like other ladies,
She thinks my trade is
No better than a penny barber.

But no—God bless her!
I'm a professor,
And six-pence is my lowest fee, sir.
Though I'm above her
I do so love her,
Beyond all other,
Were I the King, I'd marry she, sir.

2. The Turtle Dove

"The Turtle Dove" was unsigned advertising copy commissioned by Robert Warren, a London manufacturer of boot blacking. The text below appeared on the front page of the 13 March 1832 issue of the *True Sun*. John Payne Collier attributed the last stanza to Dickens in 1872, in a fabricated diary for the years 1832–33 (see introduction to Appendix F, Part 1, Sweet Betsy Ogle). Collier claimed that on 24 July 1833, Dickens's uncle, John Barrow, "referred me jocosely to the rhymes (possibly his [i.e., Dickens's]) which accompanied the wood-cut advertisements of Warren's blacking, containing the figure of a dove, which, looking at a polished boot, and mistaking the reflection of itself for the real appearance of its mate, had gone on thus, in the person of the writer and supposed spectator of the amorous, but disappointed interview:

> I pitied the dove, for my bosom was tender;
> I pitied the sigh that she gave to the wind;
> But I ne'er shall forget the superlative splendour
> Of Warren's Jet Blacking, the pride of mankind."[37]

An examination of the original and complete advertisement reveals Collier's falsity in his second effort to demonstrate that he was among the first to recognize Dickens's talent before Dickens had written or published his first sketch in December 1833. No such woodcut of a dove and a shiny boot accompanies the advertisement, although Collier's description of the fictional illustration does match the content of the *entire* jingle. It is clear, then, that Collier had searched through period newspapers for something other than another ballad like "Sweet Betsy Ogle" to attribute additionally to

Dickens, so that he could assert "I thought the lines very laughable and clever for the purpose" and "I was of opinion that I ought to see more of the young man" (4: 13).

John Drew collected and republished the advertising jingles published by Robert Warren in the *True Sun* between March and May 1832, including among the rest, of course, "The Turtle Dove." It seems likely that Drew has not seen Collier's manuscript for "Sweet Betsy Ogle" inserted in the Folger Shakespeare Library copy of his printed diary or recognized the falsity of Collier's statements regarding his having aided Dickens's reporting career with a position on the *Morning Chronicle* in the fabricated *Old Man's Diary*. While Drew acknowledges that Collier and his diary "could be deemed unreliable," he generally seems to reject this likelihood and concludes only somewhat tentatively that "the balance of probabilities, at time of writing, comes down in favour of Dickens's authorship and involvement in the series [of jingles]" (xi).

The Turtle Dove

Air—"Jessy of Dumblain."

As lonely I sat on a calm summer's morning,
To breathe the soft incense that flowed on the wind;
I mus'd on my boots in their bright beauty dawning,
By Warren's Jet Blacking—the pride of mankind.

In their bright jetty gloss, ev'ry feature divinely
Was shewn, and appear'd with rich lustre to glow;
No high-polish'd glass could have shewn them so finely,
As Warren's Jet Blacking, the pride of the beau.

On a maple-tree near sat a turtle bewailing,
With sorrowful cooings, the loss of her love;
Each note that she utter'd seem'd sadness exhaling,
And plaintively echo'd around the still grove.

When lo! in my boots the lone mourner perceived
Her form, and supposed that her lover was there;
Even I, that the vision was real, half believed—
The Blacking reflected her image so clear.

She hover'd around, at the figure still gazing—
Anxiety seem'd but to heighten her woe:
She perch'd on the boot with a courage amazing,
And fondled the vision that bloom'd in its glow.

How wild were her cries, when the fairy illusion
She found but a cheating and transient shade;
Like Hope's airy dreams but a faded delusion,
That shone in the bloom Warren's Blacking displayed.

I pity'd the dove, for my bosom was tender—
I pity'd the strain that she gave to the wind;
But I ne'er shall forget the superlative splendour
Of Warren's Jet Blacking—the pride of mankind.

3. Untitled Monopolylogue

A monopolylogue is an invention of actor Charles Matthews (1776–1835), in which one actor plays the part of every character. The untitled monopolylogue ("like those of [Charles] Matthews") presented here is Collier's own handwritten composition, complete with his notations in which he experimented with altering various words and lines.[38] He later placed his monopolylogue in a personal copy of his published fabricated diary for the years 1832–33 (see introduction to Appendix F, Part 1, Sweet Betsy Ogle), among his fabricated set of pages about Dickens.

Collier's decision not to publish some or all of the monopolylogue in his "diary" is readily explained. First, he had already chosen an excerpt from his own "Sweet Betsy Ogle" as a fictitious example of what he claimed to have heard Dickens sing as a Dickens original. Second, he had already chosen an excerpt from the newspaper advertisement "The Turtle Dove" as a fictitious example of what he claimed to have heard Dickens's uncle recite as possibly a Dickens original. Collier was considering a third fictitious example, this time one supposedly given to him by someone else who knew Dickens at the time.

Collier chose Vincent George Dowling (1785–1852), founder and editor of *Bell's Life in London*, and then added a vertically placed notation, where it would fit in the left margin, reading, "V. Dowling gave me this song & said it was written by C. Dickens." However, Dowling's association with Dickens did not begin until 1835, when Dickens started providing *Bell's Life in London* with twelve sketches, to be published under the pseudonym Tibbs (Slater xxiv). Collier's "diary" was written to end two years earlier, prior to Dowling's business association with Dickens. So, Collier recognized this timeline error prior to the publication of his "diary," filed his unused monopolylogue, and never had further occasion to publish any of it as another Dickens original, courtesy of Collier.

Come bustle, Corderoy,
No time to lose, my boy;
Our neighbours all forward are stepping
Make holiday for one day,
You know 'tis Easter-Monday
Let's be off to the Forest of Epping

Mount your Nag,
Do not lag,
Or I'm certain that the stag
Will be turn'd out before we can get there:
All the fun will be done
If you do not cut and run
Hang the shop board. Lord, how can you set there?
Now your goose is no use;
Put on your mink so spruce,
Lay by all your needles and thread, sir.—
Here's your horse, legs across;
You will find a number worse:
See, this is the tail, that's the head, sir.

Spoken. "It's too bad, Mr Cordovan: you are always leading my little ninth part of a man into danger and mischief: you'll be death of my Corderoy one of these days."—["]Danger and mischief Mrs Corderoy! Where's the harm of going a hunting once a year?"—"Mrs C. my dear; hold your tongue: I shall do as I like; shan't I Cordovan? If I am but the ninth part of a man, I am man enough for you any day."—"Any day you may be: instead of going to hunt stags, you should look after your horses at home."—"Say what you like, I will go to the Easter hunt; shan't I Cordovan? G—d, my life I forgot my spurs: what shall I do for spurs?"—"Spurs? stick a couple of needles through the back of your boots."—"An excellent thought! Now then we are off"—"You are not on yet. Stop, neighbour: you are getting up on the wrong side: you'll have your face to the tail."—["]Why that's true. Good bye wife; but bless me, if I have not taken my yard-measure instead of a riding whip"—"No matter: We have not time to stay and change it now": so

Heigh down, ho down,
Derry, derry, down down,
We are off to the Forest of Epping.

Through Mile-end, Stratford, Bow
This pair of sportsmen go,
And join the procession of Cocknies:
Some gallop and some trot,
Some can ride, but most can not,
And 'tis very hard riding with knock-knees.
At the gate they must wait,
While some the toll debate,
Or because the new trap of Mr Gunter

Is inclos'd twixt the post
And a drag drawn by a ghost
Of a steed that has once been a hunter:
But at last they got past
Though the[y] fear'd they should stick fast,
And arriv'd at the Forest light-hearted;
Where the crowd halloo'd loud
That the stag "with antlers proud,"
Would without more delay be uncarted.

(Spoken) "Off she goes!—Hark forward!"—"Stop! gentlemen, for heaven's sake, stop! Do not gallop before the dogs! let them be laid on first."—"Aye, aye Tom Moody is right: give the stag a fair start & the dogs after him"—"But there's five or six will keep on"—"Let 'em: it isn't their fault: they can[']t hold their horses:"—"Now the hounds have got the scent: all right! He's over, hark forward!"—"Hunting is a noble sport & what a fine field of horses, ponies and donkeys!"—"Aye and there goes Mr Gunter's drag and horse: nothing can stop him."—["]Stop him! Yes he's stopped now; at least the drag is, on one side of the hedge, & the old hunter scampering away with the shafts at his heels on the other"—"Tally ho! He's over! Poor Mr Jinkin, he's off in a quag, and Lollypop has been pulled out of his saddle by a bough, while Mr Frizzle is hanging like Absolum, by the hair of his head from another."—"There's the danger of Macassar"—"Now they're off again, with

Heigh down, ho down,
Derry, derry, down down,
Oh the fun in the Forest of Epping!

The stag took the water
In quite another quarter,
And few at the capture were present:
Mr Corderoy and friend
Were not, you may depend,
For both now found riding unpleasant
Both their breeches
Lost some stitches
With leaping hedges, ditches
I mean breeches that nature bestow'd, sir;
And Cordovan's steed
Which was not the finest breed
Contriv'd to get rid of his load, sir.

They both of them began
To think enough they'd ran,
Since both had lost plenty of leather;
But rising high in stirrups,
They gave their horses chirrups,
And both go to London together.

(Spoken) ["]You may call hunting a noble sport, if you will: I had rather hunt fleas on my shop-board"—"I never call'd it a noble sport & we did not see much of it after the start."—"I call it cruel: I feel it now: it is cruelty to animals"—["]What makes you wince so? Come along: can't sit up-right?["]—"You don't seem to like it much neither; and though you only walk your horse you rise in your stirrups as if you were in full trot."—"As I live, here's a spread in the road! nine out of that broken-down donkey-cart."—["]One man has broken his leg: how lucky it was a wooden one."—"Hollow, Corderoy, where are you now?"—["]Here, on the ground, and I wish I had never got off it."—"But you got off your horse at all events, & no bones broken"—"No, but the stupid beast has broken both his knees."—"And you have been macadamising the road with your head."—"If I had not luckily pitched upon it, I might have hurt myself."—"Well lead your poor lame horse the rest of the way: we have not far to go now, and I'll make it easy for you with Mrs Corderoy["]:

Then heigh down, ho down,
Derry, derry, down down
And home from the Forest of Epping.

NOTES

1. See Dickens, *Dickens to His Oldest Friend* 10 for a facsimile of the playbill.
2. See Dexter, "One Hundred Years Ago" 46–47, which includes a facsimile of the letter.
3. Dexter, "The Early Work of Dickens" 147.
4. Valentine 2; "First Work by Dickens" 3; "Dickens Play Recovered" 11.
5. Unpublished letter; photocopy held by Robert C. Hanna; location of original unknown.
6. Unpublished letter, photocopy held by Robert C. Hanna; location of original unknown.
7. See Dickens, *Dickens to His Oldest Friend* 10 for a facsimile of the playbill.
8. Edward Irving, a controversial preacher from Scotland, began preaching in London in 1822. Even his excommunication in 1830 on charges of heresy had little

impact on his popularity. Some members of his congregation began speaking in tongues, while others interpreted the unknown utterances. Irving set aside times for speaking in tongues, and Dickens might be referring to a woman who disrupted a prayer meeting with an unauthorized outburst on 30 October 1831. See Oliphant 130–31.

9. Bristol was the location of three days of rioting, starting on 29 October 1831. Riots had already occurred across the country following the defeat of a voter enfranchisement and representation Reform Bill by the House of Lords on 8 October 1831. The Bristol Riots were the worst, with prisoners released from jail, over one hundred houses burnt down, and twelve deaths. See Stevenson 288–93.

10. Sir Charles Wetherall, Member of the House of Commons who had voted against the voter and representation Reform Bill in April 1831. His return to Bristol on 29 October 1831, to open the city's Assize Courts as the Recorder of Bristol, was met with the pelting of his carriage with stones, followed by violence in the courtroom and the commencement of three days of rioting. See Stevenson 291–92.

11. As the voter and representation Reform Bill of 1831 was written to "preserve some popular constituencies, like Preston," the Member for Preston could claim to favor reform, as the Reform Bill's passage would be inconsequential to his seat in the House of Commons. See O'Neill and Martin 546.

12. Maria Beadnell and her family lived at No. 2, Lombard Street, London.

13. *Sic*; correct spelling is roué, a rake.

14. Dickens seems to have recorded the poem by Sir Thomas Moore (1779–1852) from memory, as he shortens and paraphrases its actual title, "Written in the Blank Leaf of a Lady's Commonplace Book," and misrecords the first line as "Here is one spot [actually "leaf"] reserved for me."

15. Poet Laureate from 1730–57, whose first name rhymes with Anne Beadnell's fiancé's last name, Henry William Kolle.

16. Transcript references a footnote here: "N.B. The purlieus of Tottenham Court Road!!!" **"The purlieus of Tottenham Court Road."** *"The purlieus of Tottenham Court Road!"*

17. The London Tavern, which contained a full-sized ballroom, near Leadenhall Street and Gracechurch Street, on the west side of Bishopsgate. See King 382–83.

18. Transcript references a footnote here: "A singular fact!" **"A singular fact."** *"A singular fact."*

19. Transcript references a footnote here: "The reason assigned by Mr. A. B. [Arthur Beetham] for constantly wearing his Coat buttons up to his chin was his extreme anxiety to preserve his Chest from cold."

20. Transcript references a footnote here: "a celebrated glover." **"A celebrated glover (?)"**

21. Transcript references a footnote here: "a celebrated Tailor." **"A celebrated tailor (?)"**

22. See Dickens, *Dickens to His Oldest Friend* 10 for a facsimile of the playbill.

23. Smollett 1: 115, 124.

24. Dickens, "Doctors' Commons" 3.

25. Dickens, *Letters* 7: 777–78. All underlined words are as they appear in the original.

26. Dexter, *The Love Romance of Charles Dickens* 23–26.

27. Goldsmith 87–93.

28. Bodleian Library Ballads Catalogue. Harding B 25(91). <http://www.bodley.ox.ac. uk/ballads/ballads.htm>.

29. "Adelphi Theatre" 68.

30. *The Demon Duke; or, The Mystic Branch: An Opera, In 3 Acts* [unpublished ms], 14 February 1832, p. 498; Old Dominion University PR1271.E49 no. 348. Note that in the original manuscript the title does not contain any punctuation.

31. Lacy 13.

32. National Library of Scotland. L.C.Fol.178.A.2(256). <http://www.nls.uk/>.

33. Mickle 62–64.

34. Bodleian Library Ballads Catalogue. Johnson Ballads 893. <http://www.bodley.ox. ac.uk/ballads/ballads.htm>.

35. Bodleian Library Ballads Catalogue. Harding B 28(124). <http://www.bodley.ox. ac.uk/ballads/ballads.htm>.

36. Folger Shakespeare Library, ms tipped into vol. 4 at pp. 14–15 (W.b.507).

37. Collier 4: 13.

38. Folger Shakespeare Library, ms originally tipped into vol. 4 at pp. 14–15, now catalogued as a separate document, as Collier decided against excerpting from or referring to the ms in *An Old Man's Diary* [Y.d.341 (150)].

WORKS CITED

"Adelphi Theatre." *Athenaeum* 28 January 1832: 68.

Alexander, Christine. "The Juvenilia of Charles Dickens: Romance and Reality." *Dickens Quarterly* 25 (March 2008): 3–22.

Bodleian Library Ballads Catalogue. Harding B 25(91). <http://www.bodley.ox.ac.uk/ ballads/ballads.htm>.

———. Harding B 28(124). <http://www.bodley.ox.ac.uk/ballads/ballads.htm>.

———. Johnson Ballads 893. <http://www.bodley.ox.ac.uk/ballads/ballads.htm>.

Carlton, William J. *Charles Dickens: Shorthand Writer*. London: Cecil Palmer, 1926.

Collier, John Payne. *An Old Man's Diary, Forty Years Ago*. 4 vols. London: Thomas Richards, 1871–72. [The actual copy consulted was owned by Collier and is now held by the Folger Shakespeare Library (W.b.507 vol. 4). "Sweet Betsy Ogle" is a page tipped in between pages 14–15, while the Untitled Monopolylogue (Y.d.341 [150a-c]) was originally also tipped in between pp. 14–15 but is now stored separately by the Folger.]

Darwin, Bernard. "New Discoveries of Charles Dickens: His Earliest Writings in Maria Beadnell's Album." *Strand Magazine* 84 (1935): 574–79.

The Demon Duke; or, The Mystic Branch: *An Opera, In 3 Acts* [unpublished ms], 14 February 1832, p. 498; Old Dominion University PR1271.E49 no. 348.

de Suzannet, A. ''Maria Beadnell's Album.'' *Dickensian* 31 (1935): 161–68.

[Dexter, Walter.] ''The Early Work of Dickens.'' *Dickensian* 24 (1928): 147–54.

———. *The Love Romance of Charles Dickens: Told in His Letters to Maria Beadnell (Mrs. Winter)*. London: Argonaut, 1936.

———. ''One Hundred Years Ago: Dickens's School Days in London.'' *Dickensian* 22 (1926): 45–47.

Dickens, Charles. *Dickens to His Oldest Friend*: *The Letters of a Lifetime from Charles Dickens to Thomas Beard*. Ed. Walter Dexter. London: Putnam, 1932.

———. [BOZ]. ''Doctors' Commons.'' *Morning Chronicle* 11 October 1836: 3.

———. *Letters of Charles Dickens*. Pilgrim Edition. Ed. Madeleine House et al. 12 vols. Oxford: Clarendon, 1965–2002.

———. [unsigned]. ''Our School.'' *Household Words* 4 (11 October 1851): 49–52.

''Dickens Play Recovered.'' *Morning Post* 15 July 1926: 11.

Drew, John M. L. *'The Pride of Mankind': Puff Verses for Warren's Blacking with Contributions Attributed to Charles Dickens*. Oswestry, Shropshire: Hedge Sparrow, 2005.

''First Work by Dickens.'' *Daily Express* 15 July 1926: 3.

Forster, John. *The Life of Charles Dickens*. 3 vols. London: Chapman and Hall, 1872–74.

Freeman, Arthur, and Janet Ing Freeman. *John Payne Collier: Scholarship and Forgery in the Nineteenth Century*. 2 vols. New Haven: Yale UP, 2004.

Goldoni, Carlo. *Il servitore di due padroni/La vedova scaltra*. Milano: Mondadori, 1993.

Goldsmith, Oliver. *The Complete Poetical Works of Oliver Goldsmith: Oxford Edition*. London: Henry Frowde, 1906.

Hanna, Robert C. *Dickens's Nonfictional, Theatrical, and Poetical Writings: An Annotated Bibliography, 1820–2000*. New York: AMS, 2007.

Kaplan, Fred. *Dickens: A Biography*. New York: William Morrow, 1988.

King, Alec H. ''The London Tavern: A Forgotten Concert Hall.'' *Musical Times* 127 (July 1986): 382–85.

Lacy, Michael Rophino. *Robert the Devil, or The Fiend-Father: A Grand Romantic Opera in Three Acts (The Music by Meyerbeer)*. London: Thomas Hailes Lacy, n.d.

Langton, Robert. *The Childhood and Youth of Charles Dickens*. Manchester: Privately Published, 1883.

Mickle, William Julius. *The Poetical Works of William Julius Mickle, Collated with the Best Editions: by Thomas Park, Esq.* London: Stanhope, 1808.

National Library of Scotland. L.C.Fol.178.A.2(256). <http://www.nls.uk/>.

Oliphant, Mrs. [Margaret]. *The Life of Edward Irving, Minister of the National Scotch Church, London*. Vol. 2. London: Hurst and Blackett, 1862.

O'Neill, Mark, and Ged Martin. "A Backbencher on Parliamentary Reform, 1831–1832." *Historical Journal* 23 (1980): 539–63.

Rosenbaum, Barbara, and Pamela White, comps. *Index of English Literary Manuscripts* vol. 4, part 1. London: Mansell, 1982.

Scribe, Eugène, and Germain Delavigne. *Robert le Diable* [libretto] in *L'Avant Scène Opéra* 76 (June 1985): 31–69.

Slater, Michael, ed. *Dickens' Journalism: Sketches by Boz and Other Early Papers 1833–39*. Columbus: Ohio State UP, 1994.

Smollett, Tobias, trans. [Lesage, Alain-René]. *The Adventures of Gil Blas, of Santillane*. 2 vols. Lions: Cormon and Blanc, 1815.

Stevenson, John. *Popular Disturbances in England, 1700–1832*. London: Longman, 1992.

"The Turtle Dove." *True Sun* 13 March 1832: 1.

Valentine, E. S. "Charles Dickens, Playwright at Sixteen." *New York Herald/New York Tribune Magazine* 23 May 1926: 2.

Yapp, K. F. "Dickens's Recipe for Brewing a Punch." *Dickensian* 1 (1905): 205–06.

Recent Dickens Studies: 2007

Natalie McKnight

The following is a review of articles, book chapters, and books of liter-
ary criticism on Charles Dickens published in 2007. It shows that Dick-
ens scholarship continues to thrive, that most if not all of it makes
worthwhile contributions to the field, and that new historicism continues
to predominate as a critical approach. I've organized the review around
the following headings: (1) Influences on Dickens/Dickens's Influence;
(2) Science, Medicine, and Technology; (3) Gender Studies; (4) Post-
Colonial Studies; (5) Other Interdisciplinary Approaches: Perfor-
mances/TV/Film, Art, Social Science, Philosophy/Theology, Cultural
Studies, Journalism; (6) Travel Writing; (7) Language, Style, Structure,
and Genre; (8) Studies of Individual Works; and (9) Bibliographic,
Biographic and General Reference Works. The review ends with a few
summary comments about the quality of the year's publications on Dick-
ens. While I tried to be as comprehensive as possible, I apologize in
advance to anyone whose work I inadvertently left out.

When I first began this project I must confess I had fears of finding myself
after several months like Richard Carstone in *Bleak House*—feverish and
muddle-headed poring over the endless Jarndyce documents (784; ch. 51).
But, thanks to the insights, sound research, and clear writing of most of the
scholars covered in this review, I found myself instead more like David
Copperfield enjoying the company of his old friends Tom Jones, Peregrine
Pickle, Robinson Crusoe, and co. (66; ch. 4). For I did rediscover Dickens
characters (and settings and narrative voices) in new lights through many of
the studies covered below. And many of these works have enriched my

Dickens Studies Annual, Volume 40, Copyright © 2009 by AMS Press, Inc. All
rights reserved.

understanding of Victorian culture in general, from studies of the Indian Mutiny, dustmen, and volcano panoramas to works on female friendships, homoeroticism, and popular radical literature in the nineteenth century. It's an embarrassment of riches, one I feel honored to have been asked to peruse.

I have used the following nine categories to organize my review of Dickens scholarship from 2007: (1) Influences on Dickens/Dickens's Influence; (2) Science, Medicine, and Technology; (3) Gender Studies; (4) Post-Colonial Studies; (5) Other Interdisciplinary Approaches: Performances/TV/Film, Art, Social Science, Philosophy/Theology, Cultural Studies, and Journalism; (6) Travel Writing; (7) Language/Style/Structure/Genre; (8) Studies of Individual Works; and (9) Bibliographic, Biographic, and General Reference Works. Naturally, some works could easily fall into more than one category, but when this was the case, I simply tried to list studies under the most representative grouping. I limited my coverage solely to works published in 2007, for I found if I exceeded this boundary, I opened a Pandora's Box of problems. What would my boundaries be, if they weren't the confines of the year? This necessitated refraining from reviewing some recent excellent contributions to Dickens studies, but the study had to start and stop somewhere and the most objective adjudicator in this decision was the calendar.

1. Influences on Dickens/Dickens's Influence

Robert Tracy offers an illuminating analysis of the influence of W. C. Macready on *Nicholas Nickleby*. The connections go well beyond Dickens's dedication of the novel to Macready. Tracy emphasizes the importance of Dickens using the term "Esquire" in the dedication, since it asserts "his friend's right to be considered a gentleman," a sensitive point for Macready, for he felt embarrassed by the dubious social status of his acting profession (which had also been his father's profession). Through this dedication, then, Dickens offers public confirmation of the status Macready aspired to. Tracy points out that Nicholas Nickleby shares Macready's desire to be seen as a gentleman and "the difficulty of asserting that right when society sees only that he is poor" (162). Dickens continues the parallels between Macready and Nicholas by using some of his friend's theatrical experiences in his depictions of the theatrical escapades of Nicholas and Smike; Tracy provides particularly astute analysis in this section.

In "Affecting Tales in *David Copperfield*: Mr. Peggotty and *The Man of Feeling*," David Paroissien defends Dickens against charges of over-sentimentality by placing his style in context with the popular "novel of sentiment" of the times. In particular, Paroissien compares sentimental passages in *David Copperfield* to Henry Mackenzie's *The Man of Feeling* (1771). This is the kind of influence that the average reader of Victorian literature would not be aware of, which makes the essay particularly worthwhile. Dickens owned Mackenzie's collected works, and he mentions the writer in his preface to *Nicholas Nickleby*, in fact comparing himself to him. Paroissien traces intriguing similarities between Mackenzie's chapter 26 "The Man of Feeling in a Brothel" and the story of Emily's seduction and recovery from *David Copperfield*. Mackenzie's fallen woman is also named Emily, and her father responds much as Mr. Peggotty does in *David Copperfield*. In fact, as Parois-sien states, "so similar are the reactions of the father and the uncle to misfortune one might plausibly suggest that Dickens found the germ of Mr. Peggotty's 'long journey' in search of his orphaned niece in Captain Atkins's dogged pursuit of his daughter." But Paroissien notes a key difference: "Into Mackenzie's climactic bout of weeping . . . Dickens intrudes something bolder and far more disturbing. Before Little Emily is delivered into her uncle's arms, she must face an extraordinary encounter with Rosa Dartle, whose expression of sexual jealousy casts the reunion between uncle and niece in a distinctly modern light" (201). Paroissien concludes that Dickens "borrowed selective features of the novel of sentiment and improved them almost beyond recognition" with complex emotional, psychological material (202).

John Bowen offers a touching tribute to the influence of Dickens on American author Bret Harte in "Dickens, Bret Harte and the Santa Cruz Connection." Forster quotes Harte's poem "Dickens in Camp" in his biography of Dickens. The poem shows "how a reading of *The Old Curiosity Shop* influences for the good the rough men [of a logging camp]" (203). Dickens had praised Harte's work, in particular "the Luck of the Roaring Camp" and "The Outcasts of Poker Flat." In May 1870, Dickens wrote to Harte saying " 'how highly he thought of his work' and 'asking him to contribute to *All the Year* Round . . . and bidding him . . . to visit him at Gad's Hill' " (204). The letter was crossing the Atlantic when Dickens died. Bowen notes that Harte was probably at Santa Cruz when Dickens wrote him, and so he sees this moment as the "true beginning of the Dickens Project at Santa Cruz" which has had such great and lasting success (205).

Holly Furneaux explores Dickens's and Wilkie Collins's mutual influence in "A Distaste for Matrimonial Sauce: The Celebration of Bachelorhood in the Journalism and Fiction of Collins and Dickens." As Furncaux states, the essay "focuses on [Collins's] celebratory bachelor pieces for Dickens journals *Household Words* and, later, *All the Year Round*, and examines Dickens's tactical interspersion of Collins's valorization of the unmarried man with his serialized, fictional ruminations on the same theme. Far from repressing such material, Dickens as editor prominently positioned Collins's often controversial paeans to the joys of unmarried life, strategically deploying Collins's pieces to support and recommend the treatment of bachelorhood in his own part-published novels'' (22). The essay nicely counters prevailing beliefs that Dickens repressed Collins's more provocative material and also opposes traditional portraits of Dickens as defender of hearth and home. In fact, Furneaux argues that ''on issues of sexuality, Dickens's fiction supported, promoted, and even went beyond Collins's exploration of alternative desires and lifestyles'' (23). She maintains that Dickens positioned Collins's celebrations of bachelorhood so as to ''prime readers for a more favorable reception of the provocative figure of the volitionally single male'' in his own work (29). In addition, she sees in Dickens a general anxiety over the figure of the unmarried man as a threat to bourgeois values. However, in stating that Jarvis Lory ''presents a very rare example of bachelorhood positively represented'' Furneaux may have pushed her point too far, since some of Dickens's most appealing male characters are bachelors, for example: Pickwick, Brownlow, the repentant Scrooge, Captain Cuttle, Sol Gills, Jarndyce, and Grewgious (29). In spite of this reservation, Furneaux's overall argument is well supported and offers an intriguing perspective on the issue of influence within the context of simultaneous, contiguous publications.

Tracing a much earlier influence, Stephen Bertman in ''Dante's Role in the Genesis of Dickens's *A Christmas Carol*,'' analyzes parallels between the *Divine Comedy* and Dickens's first Christmas book. Bertman points out that both works are ''framed by key Christian holidays,'' both use divisions of three (heaven, hell and purgatory for Dante; three ghosts for Dickens), both involve the use of spiritual guides, both track ''the spiritual trajectory of a single flawed human being,'' and both ''encourage us to rise above selfishness'' (167). Bertman discusses Dickens's familiarity with Dante (who is mentioned in *Pictures from Italy* and *Little Dorrit*, for instance). The article makes a sound argument and gives new reason to appreciate the power and economy of *The Carol*.

Sally Ledger's excellent *Dickens and the Popular Radical Imagination* explores Dickens's debt to the popular radical writings and illustrations of the early nineteenth century, a ''hitherto more or less occluded relationship'' (2). Proposing ''an altogether less respectable, more truly disruptive, more *popular* radical genealogy'' for Dickens than what has previously been presented, Ledger argues that it was ''blazingly clear'' to Dickens's contemporaries that he was ''a radical political writer,'' but that this perception has been undermined by subsequent critics who have overemphasized his commitment to middle-class values (2). Ledger begins her study with a chapter on popular radical culture in Regency England, focusing particularly on the pamphlets of William Hone and William Cobbett, illustrated by George Cruikshank, in response to the Peterloo Massacre and the Queen Caroline affair (the Queen was on trial at the time for alleged adultery and radical pamphlets defended her).

Chapter 2 examines "Nineteenth-century show trials," arguing that "in developing set-piece trial scenes in his novels, Dickens drew on both popular and radical cultural histories of the legal process from the late eighteenth and early nineteenth centuries . . . [and] borrowed from both 'official' and unofficial texts, and from both high—and low-cultural fields, thereby effectively reaching out to an extraordinarily wide readership" (41). Ledger examines show trials in *Oliver Twist*, *Bleak House*, and *Pickwick Papers* and reveals a deeper, more radical satire in the Bardell trial in *Pickwick Papers.* In addition she sees *A Tale of Two Cities* as "an apotheosis of Dickens's embroilment with both theatre and law [that] deploys the ingredients of popular and radical culture to play off the loquaciousness and legalese of London's Old Bailey justice against the more cursory justice of the French Revolutionary Tribunal" (59). In this sense, the novel critiques English culture as much as French, seeing it as not that much different from pre-revolution France.

In chapter 3, "Dickens, popular culture and popular politics in the 1830s: *Oliver Twist*," Ledger finds the roots of Sikes and Nancy in Hone's melodrama *The Power of Conscience: Confession of Thomas Bedworth*, which Cruikshank illustrated as he would later illustrate *Oliver Twist*. This chapter argues that the paternalism of *Oliver Twist* continues into *A Christmas Carol* but is finally jettisoned in *Barnaby Rudge* and *The Chimes*. This theme of paternalism is also prominent in chapter 4 "Christmas is cancelled: Dickens and Douglas Jerrold Writing the 1840s," which states that both Dickens and Jerrold were "equally earnest in their denunciation of contemporary theories of political economy" and that Dickens made his most radical statement in *The Chimes* (107). One might contest Ledger's assertion that Dickens abandoned paternalism at this point, since vestiges of it persist right through *Our Mutual Friend* and *Drood*, but, certainly, the overall trend she notes is there.

Chapter 5, "Popular and Political Writing in the Radical Press: From Douglas Jerrold to Ernest Jones, Chartist" traces "the significant continuities that existed between the literary and journalistic projects of Chartism, of Dickens, and of Douglas Jerrold in post-Reform Britain." In chapter 6, "*Household Words*, Politics and the Mass Market in the 1850s" Ledger counters the usual perspective that Dickens designed *Household Words* to pacify readers, unlike cheap radical publications of the times. Instead, Ledger argues that Dickens's intent was "to bridge . . . the incipient chasm that was opening up between popular and radical culture from the 1840s onward. By determinedly pursuing a broad popular readership at the same time as promoting a politics of social reform, and by insisting on sustaining an inclusive conception of 'the People,' Dickens's journalism persists with an older conception of 'popular' culture (a culture 'of' the people) that was gradually being superseded, from the 1840s, by a commercial culture produced 'for' a mass-market populace" (171). Her argument here, as elsewhere, convinces, yet it is somewhat marred by the odd error she makes in referring to *Hard Times'* Stephen Blackpool dying in a "factory accident" when in fact he falls down an old mine shaft (189).

The final chapter, "Flunkeyism and Toadyism in the age of machinery: from *Bleak House* to *Little Dorrit*," posits Bleak House as an ironic commentary on the Crystal Palace, the Houses of Parliament, and by extension all of England. She concludes by again affirming Dickens's alliance with "the People" in *Little Dorrit*: "the discrepancy between the critical and the public reception of *Little Dorrit* would seem to suggest that the intelligentsia of the 1850s was somewhat out of step with the cultural interests and political concerns of 'the People' whom Dickens was addressing. It is utterly characteristic of the novelist himself that he was not" (232). Ledger's book is a must-read for Dickens scholars and Victorian scholars in general. Her research is extensive and illuminating, her writing lively and detailed, and the accompanying illustrations are highly entertaining.

2. Science, Medicine, Technology

Science seems to be a growing area of interest in Dickens studies. Trey Philpotts explores Dickens's perspective on inventors in the informative "Dickens, Invention, and Literary Property in the 1850s," published in the March *Dickens Quarterly*. Philpotts contends that the customary identification of the inventor Doyce from *Little Dorrit* with Dickens as an inventor of fictional worlds is misleading. For Philpotts notes that "an article in *Household Words*, published only two years before *Little Dorrit*, argues that mechanical invention and literary creativity are two very different modes of production, and thus should be treated differently by the law" (18). The article he refers to, "Patent Wrongs" by Henry Morley, states that "the distinction between literary and mechanical invention is a simple but important one: the writer is more closely bound to his creation than the mechanical inventor, whose work may well have proceeded by way of successive stages over a number of years, and have been influenced by the contributions of many other people" (18–19). It is odd to think that Morley, and Dickens for that matter, did not see that the author drew from the contributions of past authors just as the inventor drew from past inventions, yet it is clear they did not.

Philpotts shows that the distinction between invention and authorship was influenced by Thomas Talfourd (a Whig MP) who had pushed for legislation to extend copyright coverage from "28 years or the life of the author to the life of the author plus 60 years" (19). Talfourd contrasted invention and authorship by suggesting that if mechanical inventions " 'were not hit on

this year by one, [they] would probably be discovered the next year by another,' '' but it would be absurd to argue that if Shakespeare hadn't written
his plays someone else would have come up with them sooner or later (20).
It's a sound argument and one that Dickens applauded, praising Talfourd in
his dedication to *The Pickwick Papers*. Philpotts goes on to show that the
Patent Law Amendment of 1852 took care of the needs of patent reformers;
however, inventors at times held up progress by maintaining exclusive rights
(24). He concludes, ''What fundamentally mattered was not the patent law,
or some supposed analogy between the mechanical inventor and literary artist,
but a much more immediate issue: the failure of Great Britain to make use
of its wealth of material inventions at a time of national crisis''—that is,
during the Crimean War (25). Philpott's essay is well-researched and provides
an illuminating context for the character of Doyce as well as for broader
issues of creative rights in relation to the needs of the nation.

In '' 'Quite a Tonic in Himself': Charles Dickens and Healthcare,'' Doug
Lowe, the manager of the Clinical Audit and Effectiveness Department of
Northern Devon Healthcare Trust, shows how Dickens anticipated ''the core
philosophical underpinning of EBM [Evidence-Based Medicine]'' (116).
EBM, a practice that has had growing influence in Great Britain since the
1990s, involves '' 'integrating individual clinical expertise with the best available external clinical evidence from systematic research' '' (qtd. in Lowe
116). Lowe notes Dickens's regular reading of *The Lancet* as well as his
advocacy of pediatrics as a specialty and his support of the Great Ormond
Street Children's Hospital. But it is Dickens's 1851 *Household Words* story
''Birth, Mrs Meek, of a Son'' that draws Lowe's particular attention. In this
story the baby in question, Augustus George, deteriorates under the constant
administration of castor oil and opium that he receives from his grandmother,
Mrs. Bigby, and the nurse-midwife, Mrs. Prodgit. Lowe indicates that the
child mortality statistics used in the story reflect those of Charles West, ''the
driving force behind the establishment of Great Ormond Street Hospital in
1852'' (117). Dickens, Lowe argues, incorporates statistics along with the
baby's specific clinical case to criticize the lack of professionalism in healthcare and the over-reliance on unproven traditional practices.

Lowe also discusses Sarah Gamp as another and more extensive characterization of poor healthcare practices of the day but adds that it wasn't just
midwives who bore the brunt of Dickens's satire—incompetent doctors
abound as well, such as the ineffective Parker Peps in *Dombey and Son*, the
drunken Dr. Haggage in *Little Dorrit*, and the dishonest Dr. Jobling in *Martin
Chuzzlewit*. But Dickens's treatment of healthcare practices grew more positive as the practices themselves became more professional, according to Lowe,
who notes the good care Johnny receives in the Children's Hospital in *Our
Mutual Friend* as well as Dickens's favorable comments on the East London

Hospital for Children in "A Small Star in the East" (120). (He might also have mentioned Maggy's praises of a hospital as an " 'Ev'nly place' " in *Little Dorrit* [117; I, ch. 9].) Lowe concludes by stating that Dickens's perspective on healthcare has too often been seen as exclusively negative, and he hopes his article may balance that perspective, as indeed it does.

Katherine Byrne focuses on a particular aspect of healthcare, tuberculosis, as both a physical phenomenon as well as a "symbol of the destructive power of capitalism" and "a means of resisting and disrupting its progress" in *Dombey and Son* (2). In "Consuming the Family Economy: Tuberculosis and Capitalism in Charles Dickens's *Dombey and Son*," Byrne points out that tuberculosis disrupted Thomas Malthus's understanding of disease as a " 'positive check to population' " (qtd. in Byrne 2), since tuberculosis, unlike other more contagious diseases, tended to strike not the most vulnerable members of the population, such as infants, the elderly and the infirm, but people in the prime of their lives, and it caused a very slow decline, which created "a further drain on society's resources" (2). Tuberculosis, in other words, was not very Malthusian or very Darwinian; it seemed to serve no productive purpose. Byrne emphasizes the "traditional link" between tuberculosis (i.e., "consumption") and consumerism. Increase of trade, which brought a wider range of people together, contributed to the spread of the disease. Anxieties about the effects of growing consumerism and lifestyles of " 'Riot, Luxury, and . . . Excess' " fed beliefs that trade was linked to the spread of tuberculosis (qtd. in Byrne 3). Byrne goes on to show how the "destructive economic impact of tuberculosis forms a central concern in *Dombey and Son*" through the death of Paul (4). Byrne sees Paul's death as an indictment of capitalism and consumerism in general. Lest this seem like a trendy argument, Byrne repeatedly notes the eighteenth-century roots of the debate about "pathologized consumerism" (5). Dombey's business feeds upon consumerism, which Dickens depicts as diminishing human relationships to basic monetary transactions. Tuberculosis also offers a fitting counter to materialistic culture, for it has been traditionally seen as a "spiritualized disease" (10): "the tuberculosis victim is not only physically unable to labour, but also traditionally thought to be spiritually heightened by their disease so as to be above such earthly, mundane concerns as the desire to consume" (10). Hence, it is fitting that Paul's tuberculosis (and Byrne offers a convincing diagnosis of his condition) results in the "breakdown of patriarchal inheritance. . . . [which] foreshadows the financial decay of the firm, and as the Dombey empire is symbolic of the whole economic world . . . this can be read as an assessment of the ability of disease to disrupt, thwart and consume the powers and progress of capitalism" (8). Tuberculosis, then, is both the result of and a check to capitalism, in Byrne's well-argued essay.

Adelene Buckland explores connections between popular scientific shows in London and Dickens's fiction in " 'The Poetry of Science': Charles Dickens, Geology, and Visual and Material Culture in Victorian London.'' Buckland notes that most studies of Dickens and science have focused on his reactions to *Origin of Species* (1859) and therefore do not deal with the effects of natural history on earlier moments in his career. While I can think of several exceptions to this statement just within the last few years, Buckland's focus on the scientific panorama, diorama, and cyclorama and other exhibitions in the 1840s and 1850s does offer a unique and informative perspective on several Dickens works. Catastrophism was popular at the time—the belief that the history of the earth evolved as a series of catastrophes, and these catastrophes explain ruptures in the geological record and the disappearance of various species. Because of the popularity of this belief, and its intrinsic drama, it was natural that catastrophes would form a major part of scientific shows in London. Buckland's descriptions of these shows (accounts drawn mostly from Richard Altick's 1978 *The Shows of London*) are worth reading for their own sake, even without following any particular connection to Dickens. She discusses the "Ascent of Mont Blanc" panorama at the Egyptian Hall, which included depictions of Vesuvius during the time that the original was experiencing earthquakes (an article about the earthquakes appeared in *Household Words* for 29 May 1858). Earlier, in the 1840s, the Colosseum at Leicester Square presented a cyclorama (a 360–degree panorama) that recreated the 1755 Lisbon earthquake, including "rumbling floors, violent light, and sound effects" (681). Buckland goes on to show how Dickens used the diorama as "a structural device in his chapter "A Rapid Diorama" in his 1846 travel book *Pictures from Italy*, while also writing positively about dioramas and panoramas in "Extraordinary Traveller," a *Household Words* article from 1850. In this essay Dickens extols these shows as a means for the masses to "travel" to places they normally would not be able to reach. Dickens could see in these devices the kind of popular, democratic, and positive form of entertainment that he, too, tried to provide in his writings.

Buckland traces Dickens's use of earthquake imagery in *Dombey and Son* in his description of the effects of the railroad—"progress and catastrophe are inseparable in the endlessly shifting urban world Dickens depicts," Buckland argues (685). She also links the popular geological exhibits to the dinosaur that famously appears in the first chapter of *Bleak House* and to overall themes of the novel. She writes that

catastrophe is both one of the novels' structural pleasures, and gives a cultural warning: when Krook arrested the flow of information he exploded; the lack of awareness of the 'connections' between all the characters has led directly to

the volcanic slum at Tom-all-Alone's and to Judy Smallweed's 'geologic age.'
The remaking of worlds in the cyclical, progressive history of *Dombey and Son*
is reforged in the popular-scientific world of *Bleak House* as an almost mythic
form of retributive punishment for the excesses of urban culture.   (689)

By the time Dickens writes *Our Mutual Friend*, the panorama and diorama
have ceased, Darwin has published *Origin of Species*, and London seems like
a "post-catastrophic space: there is no longer any sense that the world can
be exploded and made new" (689). Buckland's intelligent analysis of scientific shows and publications and their effects on Dickens's fiction provides
intriguing insights on specific Dickens works, the changing worlds of his
novels, and popular Victorian culture.

Jonathan Taylor's *Science and Omniscience in Nineteenth-Century Literature* traces similarities between science's belief in and efforts toward omniscience and omniscient literary narratives of the nineteenth century. Taylor
begins by citing Pierre Simon Laplace's *Philosophical Essay on Probabilities*
(1812) and his description of a scientific omniscience, the ideal scientific
intelligence that could explain all. Laplace admits that such omniscience
will never be entirely possible but presents probability theory as "a radical
alternative to omniscient certainty" (3). Taylor remarks that Laplace's position shares more in common with quantum physics, which disrupts the "linear
model" most scientists support that moves from classical to quantum physics
(2–3). "This is the context in which the following books' apparently 'transhis-
torical' focus can be understood and justified," Taylor argues. "Rather than
standing as a straightforward example of how the past has been superseded
by the present," Taylor continues, "Laplace can be taken instead as an
example of the persistence and recurrence of certain debates, images, themes
and questions in scientific discourse 'across' history" (4). Taylor states, "this
book attempts to trace different kinds of narratives, in which the past is not
merely superseded by the future, but engages with that future in a two-way
debate. According to these alternative narratives, literary and scientific texts
do not merely exist as artifacts, reflecting their historical moments; they might
also anticipate future scientific developments, or look back to past themes
and debates" (4–5).

Taylor divides the book into three sections: section 1, "On History, Chaos
and Carlyle"; section 2, "On Cosmology, Heresy, Abbot and Poe"; section
3, "On Microcosms, Macrocosms, and the Music of the Spheres." His
"Afterword," "On Demonic Omniscience and Dickens," really should be
considered its own chapter, not merely an "afterword." Laplace serves as a
useful jumping-off point for Taylor's analysis of various takes on omniscience, but it would have been helpful if Taylor had provided more evidence
to show that the figures he covers were familiar with Laplace's work; without

such evidence the science/arts connection seems somewhat insubstantial. His comments on omniscience in Dickens are intriguing, however. For example, Taylor argues that the shift in *Old Curiosity Shop* from a first- to a third-person narrator enacts "the historical movement from the more personal modes of narration prevalent in the 1830s novels, to the objective omniscience which . . . became the dominant mode of narration in later Victorian fiction" (148). Moreover, Taylor strengthens the connection to Laplace's writings on omniscience and probability by showing how the narrator of the novel "is constantly engaged in investigating probabilities" (153). Gambling and gaming tables naturally abound because of the grandfather's addiction, but all the characters "weigh up probabilities in order to understand the world" (157). He cites Audrey Jaffe's comment, "Quilp is a substitute in the text for the missing omniscient narrator" (160). Taylor concludes, "As an 'Evil Power,' who enjoys playing and 'cheating at cards,' Quilp foreshadows the God of twentieth-century science" (162). A Dickens scholar can't help but wish that Taylor had extended his discussion beyond *The Old Curiosity Shop*, but then Dickens is not his main focus, and if anything Taylor has been perhaps a bit overly ambitious in what he has attempted to cover. The framework he establishes of a general yearning for omniscience but a realization that probabilities may be the best we can have, and his ideas about scientific progress not necessarily being as linear as we often tend to believe, offer stimulating and useful contexts for readings of nineteenth-century literature, ones that can be applied more systematically to other works of Dickens and fellow Victorian authors.

3. Gender Studies

Sharon Marcus's *Between Women: Friendship, Desire, and Marriage in Victorian England* provides one of the most rewarding studies of the year, with chapters on "Friendship and the Play of the System," "Just Reading: Female Friendship and the Marriage Plot," "Dressing Up and Dressing Down: The Feminine Plaything," "The Female Accessory in *Great Expectations*," "The Genealogy of Marriage," "Contracting Female Marriage in *Can You Forgive Her?*" and a concluding chapter on Woolf and Wilde. The title of the book responds to Eve Kosofsky Sedwick's *Between Men: English Literature and Male Homosocial Desire*. Marcus also draws on Adrienne Rich's notion of a lesbian continuum that suggests that "women might not have experienced the panic around boundaries between homo- and heterosexuality that men did" (10). Since Marcus states that her response to this assertion is "Yes, but . . . " she then lists a series of qualifications which she goes on to explore in her study—that is, were the forms of women's love interchangeable? Was love between women essentially less interesting than that between men? And, "aren't we beginning to see that some relationships between Victorian men enjoyed the fluidity Sedwick considered the monopoly of women?" (10)

The originality of Marcus's book rests on her intelligent probing of assumptions about women's sexuality and friendships as well as her reliance on sources that she feels have not been emphasized sufficiently in past gender studies that have "depended disproportionately on trial records and medical sources that foreground pathology and deviance" (13). Marcus emphasizes everyday social relationships documented by diaries, letters, memoirs, magazines, and, of course, literature. Abandoning the assumption that heterosexuality was dominant "allows us to use these sources to make new distinctions . . . between how women wrote about friends and lovers . . . [and] new connections . . . between femininity and homoeroticism, or between female marriages and marriages between men and women" (14). She examines how women who were not lesbians could be as enticed by images of desirable women as much as men or lesbians were. "I now grasped," Marcus writes, "that our contemporary opposition between hetero- and homosexuality did not exist for Victorians, and that Victorians were thus able to see relationships between women as central to lives also organized around men" (19).

Marcus concludes her excellent introduction, which reads like a manifesto, by stating that her book "offers a history of sexuality and gender that does not focus on power differences or oppositions between polarized genders and antithetical sexualities. Instead it explores what remains to be seen if we proceed without Oedipus, without castration, without the male traffic in women, without homophobia and homosexual panic" (21). One of the many things to admire about her study is its boldness and its undermining of conventional thinking on sexuality without appearing contentious.

Chapter 1, "Friendship and the Play of the System," suggests that the importance of female friendships has often been ignored in Victorian studies, and she asserts that Victorian society actually promoted such friendships as a natural step on the path toward marriage (26). Even obvious lesbian relationships were tolerated more widely than has often been supposed, certainly more than male and female lovers living together outside of wedlock. Marcus examines the relationships between Rosa Bonheur and her companion Natalie Micas and between Frances Power Cobbe and Mary Lloyd as examples. She relates these real life examples to literature by questioning, "If the Victorian novel worked to reproduce gender norms, and if female friendship was one of the relations that defined normative femininity, how did novels incorporate those female friendships into courtship narratives?" (76). Marcus answers her own question in part by noting that "almost every Victorian novel that ends in marriage has first supplied its heroine with an intimate female friend'' (76). The stability of female friendships provides a ''spring-board for the adventures that traditionally constitute our notion of the narrata-ble'' (79). Marcus sees David Copperfield's progress toward a successful marriage as being ''inseparable from the story of the friendship that forms between his first and second wives'' (88). Agnes advises David on his court-ship and marriage, and Dora herself regrets not having known Agnes sooner, for she is sure the relationship would have made her a better wife. Dora then bequeaths David to Agnes on her deathbed (90). David in turn learns from Dora and Agnes's friendship how to be a better companion in a marriage.

Chapter 3 explores the eroticism of dolls and fashion plates and the ways in which both appeal to women's voyeurism. These topics then inform chapter 4's analysis of Miss Havisham and Estella, who, like ''girls in children's books[,] sequester themselves with a doll who represents both a daughter and a mother'' (161). Marcus argues that desire between women is the ''form of desire that most distinguishes the novel'' but that it is ''oddly absent from critical readings'' (166). ''Throughout the novel,'' Marcus continues, ''Pip attempts to merge with a female couple that simultaneously solicits and ex-cludes him by identifying him with both its members'' (168). Marcus insists that Miss Havisham and Estella merely represent an intensified version of the Victorian ideal mother/daughter relationship with ''the maternal determi-nation to make a daughter an irresistible marriage prospect'' (170). Although her argument here is fairly persuasive, Marcus seems to ignore the more twisted aspects of Miss Havisham's manipulation of Estella for revenge.

Marcus continues by stating that *Great Expectations* shows how ''a man's desire for a woman is shaped by his identification with the desire between women woven into the fabric of the family, everyday life, and consumer culture—the very stuff of the Victorian novel'' (170). By watching Estella, Pip concludes that he, too, must be dolled up to be loved. Marcus counters Freud's theory of penis envy with her own theory—envy of femininity—with Estella's refined femininity making Pip see his masculinity as ''undesirable as manual labor'' (172). ''Pip learns,'' Marcus states, that ''to gain access to a woman he must embrace the path of femininity and transform himself into a female accessory'' (173). She remarks that Pip is ''loyal to consumer society's credo that when the going gets tough, the tough go shopping'' (182). He ''fully embraces the accoutrements of fashion culture and doll fiction'' along with ''their dynamics of pain, pleasure, and objectification. . . . [so that] the punishment scenarios that dominated Victorian fashion discourse, pornography, and doll literature surface in *Great Expectations* as recurring scenes of chastisement and humiliation'' (185–86). Occasionally Marcus pushes her argument too far, as when she says that Miss Havisham turns Estella into a dildo, but by and large her arguments are sound and defended with meticulous research and expressed in clear and lively writing. In her conclusion, Marcus states that "the most surprising commonality this book has found between Victorian society and our own . . . [is that] in the past as in the present, marriage and family, gender and sexuality, are far more intricate, mobile and malleable than we imagine them to be" (262).

Carolyn W. De La L. Oulton explores similar territory in *Romantic Friendship in Victorian Literature*. But while Marcus focuses exclusively on women's relationships and finds in general a greater openness to a range of female intimacies than one might expect, Oulton looks at same-sex romantic friendships of both men and women and finds anxieties about such intimacies and clear cultural proscriptions on them. Romantic friendships, according to Oulton, are distinguished from regular friendships by their intensity, intimacy, and the "startling rhetorical expression" such friends gave to their love and their dependence on one another (1). Oulton persuasively argues that it was the very restrictiveness of Victorian society—the clear cultural mores about what one could and could not do—that allowed for such intense expressions of friendship that one finds in letters and novels. By the 1890s sexologists were beginning to increase the general awareness of sexual motivations, rendering romantic friendships more problematic; in 1897, for instance, Havelock Ellis wrote in *Sexual Inversion* that " 'conventional propriety recognizes a considerable degree of physical intimacy between girls, thus at once encouraging and cloaking the manifestations of homosexuality' " (2). But Oulton suggests that such studies merely reinforced "an already present fear of the intrusive elements" of romantic friendships (2).

Oulton's book includes the following chapters: "Ennobling Genius: Writing Victorian Romantic Friendship," "Extraordinary Reserve: The Problem of Male Friendship," "A Right to Your Intimacy: The Ends of Female Friendship," "Tenderest Caresses: Romantic Friendship and the Satirists," and "Sinister Meaning: Crises at the *Fin de Siècle*." She offers fairly substantial sections on *David Copperfield* in chapter 2 (on male friendships) and on *Bleak House* in chapter 3 (on female friendships). Exploring the relationship between David Copperfield and Steerforth, Oulton sees in David "an innocent enthusiast" with an "artless passion" for the more "worldly" Steerforth (46). She argues that Dickens, like Tennyson in *In Memoriam*, carefully delimits the friendship between David and Steerforth, indicating "Dickens's awareness of the dangers inherent in romantic friendship" (46). According to Oulton, Steerforth is David's "bad angel" and his removal is necessary for David to achieve self-esteem and self-mastery (69). In analyzing *Bleak House*, Oulton focuses on the friendship between Esther and Ada and sees, at least on the surface, the typical Victorian pattern of a female protagonist moving from an intense female friendship to marriage (86). Yet Oulton traces complications in this typical trajectory: Ada's marriage ends with Richard's death, and so the female friendship outlasts marriage. The narrative sets the reader up to expect Ada's and Richard's marriage to be the culmination of the plot, but Dickens undermines these expectations and reverses Ada's and Esther's roles, leaving Esther the married one in the end and Ada a "desexed housekeeper to Jarndyce" (91). "The final pages of the book," Oulton writes, "firmly reinforce the triumph of this ostensibly marginalized figure [Esther] by humiliating her potential rival [Ada]," thereby suggesting that the "central friendship [is] more fraught than Esther herself would have the reader believe" (92–93).

Oulton concludes the book by reemphasizing that "the course of literary romantic friendships itself points to the largely unspoken rules that are assumed to govern them"—for instance, that the friendship shouldn't persist after marriage and that there should be no "erotic exchange or even acceptance of such a possibility" (155). Throughout her study, Oulton presents original, close readings and a fine analysis of the myriad of contradictions presented by the peculiarly Victorian romantic friendship, which was "dangerously unrestrained but simultaneously proscriptive, sacrosanct but transient and frequently satirized," contradictions that "exemplify the preoccupations of the age that was finally to disavow [romantic friendship]" (157).

The Literary Mother: Essays on Representations of Maternity and Child Care, edited by Susan C. Staub, includes Melissa Klimaszewski's "The Contested Site of Maternity in Charles Dickens's *Dombey and Son*." Klimaszewski explores "the ambiguous status and pivotal role of the nursemaid" in *Dombey and Son* and the "complex of social and textual relations surrounding motherhood and mother substitutes in nineteenth-century Britain" (138). According to Klimaszewski, nursemaids were essential to middle-class homes, yet they also presented a challenge to control of the home. *Dombey and Son* adds to these anxieties about the influence of nursemaids the further concern that the wet nurse may wield an influence on the business world, breaking down strict private/public and female/male dichotomies that defined Victorian society (139). As Klimaszewski puts it, "nursemaids are hired to form the bodies and minds of those who are already expected in many ways to be their social superiors. The breastfeeding wet nurse, through her close physical contact with a higher class infant, raises these concerns to a fever pitch" (141). Dombey tries to limit Polly Toodle's potential for contaminating his son Paul by renaming her, setting strict boundaries, and watching her intently in the glass conservatory. Despite his efforts, his son bonds with Polly, and Dombey's firing of her hastens his son's death. Susan Nipper, Klimaszewski argues, pushes the challenge to Dombey even further, ultimately confronting him more directly and aggressively than any other character in the book. Klimaszewski's reading highlights important tensions in the novel and places them within the context of Victorian middle-class domestic patterns. Brief references to maidservants in other Dickens novels would have strengthened her assertions about Victorian anxieties about nursemaids, but perhaps such an analysis is best left to a book-length study.

Laurence Talairach-Vielmas, in *Moulding the Female Body in Victorian Fairy Tales and Sensation Novels*, analyzes how Victorian fairy tales and fantasies offer a new perspective on constructions of femininity. He sees fantasy and sensation novels, which he finds to be similar, as revealing through their distortions of reality the "contradictory discourses" concerning the feminine ideal that were exacerbated by the rise of capitalism (5). Talairach-Vielmas sees urbanization as presenting a challenge to the Angel in the House ideal of femininity: "the Angel gradually left her safe haven, stepped outside the house unchaperoned, and traveled to the urban centre, her shopping excursions upsetting traditional gendered spheres" (6). Victorian fairy tales reflect these changes, since many of them emphasize the molding of the female body and "register fears concerning the management of female appetites and feature heroines eager to consume goods" (8). Women fashioning themselves as objects on the market reflects the rise of capitalism and consumerism. The author presents a clear thesis for the book:

> From examples of little girls being literally and physically moulded to the pattern of ideal femininity in Victorian fairy tales and fantasies to sensational heroines turning themselves into attractive objects to seduce men, the study embarks on an expedition through the looking-glass, into a realm where women debunk definitions of femininity privileged by men, and illuminates the changes which the rise of consumer culture entailed in the construction of ideal femininity.   (15)

Chapter 6 focuses on the use of fashion plates in Dickens's *Bleak House* and M. E. Braddon's *Lady Audley's Secret*. Talairach-Vielmas sees Lady Dedlock as objectified through the house's many mirrors and through her "British Beauty" plate, a portrait that was part of a collection of artistic renderings of aristocratic ladies. This portrait reduces her to a series of commodities (shawl, fur, bracelet, etc.) and then ultimately serves as a mug shot to be used in tracing her (118–19). Lady Dedlock turns into a series of signs that others try to read to interpret her past and present. He sees similar commodification of women in Braddon's *Lady Audley's Secret*. His reading in this chapter is sound and illuminating, although his reasons for grouping sensation fiction in with fairy tales is not always clear. Perhaps the category of fairy tales/ fantasies/ and sensation novels is really too broad to hold together. He concludes, "Victorian fairy tales, fantasies, and sensation novels . . . investigate the way women were led to conform to and to mould themselves in accordance with the dominant representations, ultimately questioning the possibility for woman to be anything but reflection" (173).

Holly Furneaux's "Charles Dickens's Families of Choice: Elective Affinities, Sibling Substitution, and Homoerotic Desire" examines "one particularly rich strategy through which Charles Dickens and his contemporaries articulated the queer possibilities inherent within the putatively heterosexual family: in-lawing, in which prohibited desire for a member of the same-sex is quite transparently redirected . . . to an opposite-sex sibling.'' Furneaux focuses on *Pickwick Papers*, *Oliver Twist*, *Nicholas Nickleby*, *Martin Chuzzlewit*, *Bleak House* and *A Tale of Two Cities* in this well-argued essay. While her approach shares some similarities with Marcus's book on female friendship, Furneaux examines exclusively homoerotic relationships in Dickens and considers how they challenge familiar domestic expectations, while Marcus often posits female friendships, homoerotic or not, as upholding Victorian domestic ideals, which she sees as less limiting than often supposed (153).

Furneaux argues that adoptive father-types such as Mr. Pickwick and Mr. Lorry exemplify ''the many structures of affinitive kinship in which marriage is deprivileged as just one possible choice in determining family'' (154). These guardians ''denaturalize'' parenting, according to Furneaux, who feels that ''such elective practices of guardianship, through which . . . nurturing becomes a masculine role and maternity is pluralized . . . demonstrate Dickens's fascination with the possibility of diverse gendered roles within the family'' (154).

Tracing the ''slippage of desire'' from a brother to a sister, Furneaux reveals how Dickens ''complicates gendered boundaries, showing the proximity, rather than the opposition of masculinity and femininity'' (157). Here she acknowledges her debt to the work of Sedgwick, Judith Butler, and Sharon Marcus. Furneaux examines how male characters in Dickens often shift their affections from a male friend to his sister, or a female friend to the friend's brother, and the various parities, physical and emotional, between siblings that made such a shift likely. Her first examples, however, deal with shifting between members of the same sex, such as Jonas's sudden transfer of attention from Charity to Mercy in *Martin Chuzzlewit*, or Dora transferring David to Agnes in *David Copperfield*. She then goes on to see vestiges of this pattern in the relationships of Sam Weller and Pickwick and Ben, Bob, and Arabella in *Pickwick Papers*; in David, Steerforth, and Emily's love triangle in *David Copperfield*; and in Smike, Nicholas, and Kate in *Nicholas Nickleby*. Occasionally, I found myself wondering if a man couldn't fall in love with a friend's sister or a woman with a friend's brother without the feeling being considered homoerotic transference, but in general Furneaux's argument is well supported and contextualized, and her overall point that Dickens affirms ''families of choice'' is, I think, indisputable (191).

4. Post-Colonial Studies

Both post-colonial studies that I will review here focus on the same subject—the Indian Mutiny of 1857. Christopher Herbert, in *War of No Pity:*

The Indian Mutiny and Victorian Trauma, argues that too much of "Mutiny literature" has been overly influenced by anti-imperialism and that such "doctrinaire" analysis tends to miss the complexity of a subject that is so rife with "ambivalence, self-contradiction, rhetorical ruses and pitfalls, cognitive and textual dissonance, and unconscious displacements" (17). Dickens's own responses to the mutiny certainly match Herbert's description, as we see in chapter 5, which focuses on *A Tale of Two Cities*. In this chapter, Herbert argues that the Indian rebellion made a " 'terrible break' " in British culture that reveals itself, among other ways, through a change in the English novel (205). The novel had flourished in the 1850s, but after the Mutiny it gave way to "trashy-seeming, indecent 'sensation fiction' in the early 1860s" (205). This occurred, Herbert posits, because the realism that had made the British novel so powerful to that point could not capture the surrealistic nightmares of the Mutiny. Herbert speculates that the "deepest component of the Mutiny trauma . . . may have been the shock given to the British national conscience by revelations of British cruelties perpetrated in India and by the spectacle of the rabid vindictiveness of the British public during . . . the early months of the war" (208). (Earlier he suggests that the British response to the trauma can be compared to that of the U.S. following 9/11 and that in both cases the worst part is the shock at our own atrocities [18]).

Herbert first discusses Dickens's "The Perils of Certain English Prisoners," indicating that Dickens had revealed in letters that the story was a response to the Mutiny. While acknowledging the racism of the piece, Herbert feels that the story is of such poor quality that no one should take it too seriously: "The artistic crudeness of the tale seems almost like a rhetorical method designed to advertise the crudeness of the jingoistic response to the Mutiny" (212). This may be reaching too far to defend Dickens against charges of racism; Herbert makes better arguments in analyzing *A Tale of Two Cities* as a far more significant response to the Mutiny, and one worthy of much more serious examination in the context of this traumatic event. (Herbert mentions Grace Moore and William Oddie as previous scholars who have made brief connections between the Mutiny and *A Tale of Two Cities* but states that the connections have not yet been thoroughly explored [213]). As he puts it, "Not to stress this linkage is to deprive the novel of its immediate historical anchorage and to deprive the literary history of the Mutiny of one of its cardinal texts" (213). Herbert sees France's revolutionaries as representative at first of the Indian mutineers, but then "the great program of executions they undertake, by means of the feverishly active guillotine . . . - corresponds . . . not to any actions of the Indian mutineers but to the mass hangings and prolonged mass executions carried out in India *by the British*" (233). Dickens uses the French Revolution, in other words, to examine both sides of the Mutiny. Herbert refers to a letter from the *Times*, in August 1857, that makes the same connection between mutineers and the victims of the French Revolution, describing prisoners hanged daily " 'like a reign of terror . . . for the natives' " (qtd. in Herbert 233). Dickens's intense depiction of the revolutionary horrors may have been fueled, Herbert believes, by Dickens's recognition of similar fury in himself, which he hoped to eradicate.

Priti Joshi's "Mutiny Echoes: India, Britons, and Charles Dickens's *A Tale of Two Cities*" takes a similar, if more qualified perspective on the relationship between Dickens's novel and the Mutiny. Joshi and Herbert's works were probably in press at about the same time, and so, unfortunately, neither was able to respond to the other's perspective on this comparison. Like Herbert, Joshi situates her argument in the context of Grace Moore's and William Oddie's earlier suggestions about the influence of the Mutiny (a term Joshi puts in quotation marks) on Dickens's novel. But unlike these studies, Joshi aims "to broaden the scope" of the comparison "in order to develop an account of Dickens's thinking about identity and Otherness" (54). Joshi contrasts Dickens's critique of British bureaucracy in his novels of the 1850s with his much more conservative journalism and short fiction of the same period, often set in non-British locales, where a protagonist's "identity *as a Briton* leads [him] to act nobly and valiantly" (54). These pieces reflect a desire for a "simple, uncomplicated world," Joshi argues, and they "indicate that the flip side of Dickens's critique of British institutions and bureaucracy was both an anxiety about the enervating influence of prosperity and domesticity and, as antidote, the craving for a landscape in which the hero is unfettered and free to express himself as British" (54). According to Joshi, *A Tale of Two Cities* navigates these divergent impulses, while it aids in the formation of a British national identity, a subject of particular interest in the post-"Mutiny" years (55).

Joshi, like Herbert, offers a vivid summary of the events leading up to and following the Indian rebellion, and both accounts are worth reading for their own sakes. After her summary, Joshi argues that for Dickens, the "Mutiny" consolidated his "sometimes inchoate and dispersed sentiment into a celebration of British valor that laid to rest ghosts of disunity that had marred the national self-image and that Dickens had been repudiating in his fiction" (66). Joshi suggests but then rejects simplistic analogies between the mutineers and the French revolutionaries, or between the East India Company and the French elite. Instead, Joshi maintains that the novel is Dickens's response to the "cultural anxieties of the 1850s, especially the desire for national glory and triumph" (80). So the novel is not *about* the Indian "Mutiny" but the events of 1857 do "animate" the work (80). Joshi sees Miss Pross as part of Dickens's attempt to establish a national identity in her willingness to make "The Crossing [of the Channel] and a Sacrifice [her potential self-sacrifice in fighting Mme. Defarge]" (81). Sydney Carton offers the best example of Crossing and Sacrifice, of course. "As in Dickens's short fiction," Joshi notes, "here too national identity is awakened via Sacrifice in a hostile, foreign land *and* through an investment in domesticity—a domesticity that, presided over by the gentle, golden-tressed Lucie, insistently announces itself as Britain" (82). While Herbert's reading of *A Tale of Two Cities* (see above) seems determined to redeem Dickens at least in part from his early racist and jingoistic comments about the Indian Mutiny, Joshi's interpretation of the novel seems just as determined not to exonerate Dickens. Both studies are intriguing, richly contextualized, and soundly argued, but one can't help but wish that each writer could have responded to the other.

5. Other Interdisciplinary Approaches

TV/Film/Performances

In 2007 Shari Hodges Holt published an intriguing analysis of the 1998 film *Great Expectations*, entitled "Dickens from a Postmodern Perspective: Alfonso Cuaron's *Great Expectations* for Generation X." I remember feeling somewhat guilty about enjoying Cuaron's film because it took such liberties with Dickens's text but not quite enough liberties to make it seem entirely new. The film takes place in the 1990s in Florida's Gulf Coast and New York; Pip becomes Finnegan Bell, an aspiring artist; Magwitch is a mob hitman. But Holt's fine analysis has helped me to accept my own somewhat embarrassed appreciation of the film by underscoring how it "demonstrates the particular relevance of Dickens's Victorian narrative for postmodern generations" (69). Holt sees the work as a " 'nostalgia film,' " using Fredric Jameson's term for "a postmodern cinematic genre in which the 'desperate attempt to appropriate a missing past is now refracted through the iron law of fashion change and the emergent ideology of the generation' " (71). The film's "cultural pastiche" and its mixing of high and low cultures indicate its postmodern style; Holt, referring to Jay Clayton's "Dickens and the Genealogy of Postmodernism" and *Charles Dickens in Cyberspace: The Afterlife of the Nineteenth Century in Postmodern Culture*, finds this style to be in tune with key elements of Dickens's text. Clayton sees Wemmick as a truly postmodern character, not Pip, but Holt points out "the striking similarities between the narrative of Pip's disillusionment and the cultural experience of the first truly postmodern generation, the generation that American sociologists and demographers have deemed 'Generation X' . . . [which] is marked by disenchantment" (73).

But Holt sees more in common between Pip and Generation X-ers than disillusionment. She also refers to sociological studies that indicate the trauma

Generation X experienced in coming of age in a period of unprecedented drug and alcohol use, high divorce rates and abortions, an economic recession, and an overall loss of the idealism of the 1960s, producing in the generation a sense of worthlessness and lack of purpose similar to what Pip seems to feel as a boy and young man (74). Both tend to respond to their condition by embracing consumerism. And both ultimately have to confront the emptiness of their dreams and must struggle to find a new identity among "the myriad possibilities" represented by the "X" of "Generation X" (77). The comparison may seem a bit forced in this brief summary, but Holt makes a persuasive case, nicely contextualized with both Dickens scholarship and sociological studies; the comparison helps to show why Dickens's novel makes such a successful framework for "a late-twentieth-century tale of self-discovery" (77). Holt sees the film playing with the postmodern idea of identity as a patchwork of various representations and points out the film's emphasis on mirrors, portraits, and celebrity culture. She offers a particularly fine reading of the film's final scene and how it picks up on the light/shadow imagery of Dickens's second ending to suggest the possibility of a reunion between Finn and Estella.

In "Boz on the Box," Robert Giddings offers a thorough and helpful "Brief History of Dickens on British Television." Many readers will be familiar with some of the broadcasts included in this survey, but most will probably find, as I did, descriptions of presentations I was never aware of (this will be particularly true of readers outside the U. K.). For instance, Giddings states that the BBC's 1967 *Great Expectations* written by Hugh Leonard and directed by Alan Bridges is "a remarkably adult treatment. . . . [and] has not been surpassed" (102). Giddings notes that the BBC focused on producing classics as serials in response to the competition it faced from commercial television after 1955. Would that commercial television always produced such quality side-effects! Not all versions receive Giddings's praise, of course. He refers to the "Heritage Britain" stage of television productions in the 1970s when classics "were not so much brought to life as exhibited lying in state" (103). Some but not all of these productions were also shown in the U.S.'s Masterpiece Theater series. Giddings notes the 1977 *Hard Times* as an exception to the "Heritage Britain" style and calls it a "landmark production" (104). Other highpoints for Giddings are the 1982 *Nicholas Nickleby* (a film of the stage version) and the 1985 *Bleak House* (105). In 1998 the BBC-1's classic serials unit shut down, but by then the "Pride and Prejudice Effect" was in full swing. This effect was produced by the popularity of Andrew Davies's 1995 film version of the novel (and one could argue the effect really began the year before with his surprisingly popular version of Eliot's *Middlemarch*). The popularity of these productions led to competing commercial and BBC-filmed classics, referred to as the "Battle of the Bodices" (106). These productions tended to be coproduced with American companies and involved "additional merchandising" such as computer games, clothing, tourism and so forth. Other highpoints for Giddings are the 1999 versions of *Oliver Twist* and *David Copperfield*, as well as Andrew Davies's 2005 *Bleak House*. When Giddings interviewed Davies about the latter production, Davies bemoaned Dickens's perverse tendency " 'to spawn one group of characters after another, instead of getting on with the story,' " and explained how he searched for the "spine" of the story (in the case of *Bleak House*, Esther's " 'journey of. . . . self-discovery' ") in order to hold the film together (110). Giddings's article brings many productions to light that probably have been forgotten or are unknown to many. Upon reading it, I found myself itching to go to the BBC site and start ordering.

Art

Leon Litvack's "*Dickens's Dream* and the Conception of Character," analyzes Robert William Buss's unfinished watercolor of Dickens "dreaming" his own characters. The painting shows Dickens apparently in a trance and seated in a chair several feet away from his desk, with smoke from his cigar swirling about him along with images of characters he created. Litvack examines how the painting relates to contemporary ideas about the creative process, how it compares to other portrayals of Dickens, and what it tells us about Buss's feelings about Dickens. Buss had a complicated relationship with the novelist: he had produced illustrations for the third number of *Pickwick Papers*, but the publishers found his work inadequate and replaced him with Phiz. "Given these circumstances," Litvack remarks, "it is interesting that he continued to admire Dickens's humour and moral vision throughout his life, and that, elderly and ailing, he decided to paint this large, detailed *capriccio* image of Dickens surrounded by his characters" (5). Litvack notes that Buss draws from a "common trope in Victorian painting and illustration . . . with precedents stretching back to the Renaissance . . . . these images emerged from a religious context, portraying the author at the moment of divine inspiration" (15). Litvack analyzes images with similar compositions that pay tribute to Tennyson, Hans Christian Andersen and Edwin Landseer, as well as other portraits of Dickens that surround him with a swirl of characters. Buss's composition seems to capture truths about Dickens's creative process, particularly his claim in a letter to Forster that he did not really invent his characters—he just saw them and wrote them down (11). And the title of the painting reflects Dickens's use of the word "dream" to refer to thinking or imagining (12).

Litvack concludes with an intriguing comment about the effect of Buss's painting, stating that it can . . . be read as a completion of Dickens's work: aside from Paul Dombey and Little Nell, the other characters who appear in colour all come from *Edwin Drood*; perhaps by deciding to complete these first, Buss conveyed a sense of fulfillment of Dickens work. It is a souvenir, a remembrance, a work of homage, which reveals a great deal about what Buss thought of Dickens, and confirms how the recognition of pervasive Dickensian images provides visual pleasure.

(31)

The essay provides rich insights into this particular painting, as well as an illuminating context for Victorian portraits of artists.

Alexander Bove reflects on both dreams and portraits in "The 'Unbearable Realism of a Dream': On the Subject of Portraits in Austen and Dickens." Bove argues that "while any representation is to some extent historically determined by ideologies, social and economic structures, and aesthetic values, mimetic representation, with its aesthetic of immediacy and realism, is as such all the more constrained by these historical determinants" (655). Bove sees a tension between "representation and nature, between sign and referent, that marks the mimetic project of bourgeois realism in the nineteenth century" and reveals not only a "crisis of representation" but one of subjectivity as well (655). To illustrate his point, Bove analyzes the scene from *Pride and Prejudice* in which Elizabeth examines Darcy's portrait and one from *David Copperfield* in which David views a portrait of Rosa Dartle. Bove thinks that portraits get referred to so often in nineteenth century novels partly in response to the novelistic emphasis on "mimetic characterization" (657). Bove argues that Elizabeth comes to understand Darcy through his letter ("his own linguistic representation of his character") and his portrait viewed at his estate (660); both serve to rewrite Elizabeth's and the readers' misinterpretations of him.

While Austen seems ultimately to affirm the power of mimesis in this scene, Dickens in *David Copperfield* undermines "the illusion of mimesis implicit in portraiture . . . [by] inflicting a wound, a scar, upon the face of mimesis itself" (663). Bove indicates how portraits served as signs of "bourgeois comfort," but maintains that Rosa's undermines such connotations with "uncanny associations of death and doubling disruptive to bourgeois identity" (666). He notes that the portrait seems aggressive in the small bedroom in which David is placed, and its " 'startling' " effect, mentioned twice, seems to threaten David's ego. In the scene in which David confronts the portrait, he states that the scar was not shown in the painting, but that his mind placed it there; Bove sees this as "a struggle for autonomy" between the image and language, whereas in Austen the two worked in tandem (670). Rosa's image follows David into his dream where it merges with his own identity "until the loosening of the distinction between identities shakes the very *terra firma* of the reality principle'' (671). The distinguishing characteristics of Rosa—''her scar and her irony''—are depicted as being beyond the capacity of mimesis (673).

Bove ultimately sees Rosa as a double for both David and Dickens, and he refers to her fearful reality, quoting Chesterton's reference to '' 'the unbearable realism of a dream' '' (676). Bove concludes,

> Dickens, in a period when the visual arts had first discovered the powerfully subversive potential of distortion in caricature..., found a powerful tool in expressive (overdetermined) distortion as a way of circumventing this complicity between mimesis and bourgeois ideology. The scar inflicted upon mimesis is thus not simply an aggressive gesture but a means of... subverting the mimetic bind on subjectivity in order to achieve an expressiveness repressed by the very form of realism.   (677)

While some readers may find passages in this essay overdetermined by theory, and others might wish Bove had incorporated more examples to support his larger arguments about mimesis and bourgeois identity, his readings of these crucial scenes and his analysis of tensions between verbal and visual portraits and mimesis and subjectivity are highly original and nuanced.

Beryl Gray analyzes Phiz's illustrations in ''Man and Dog: Text and Illustration in *The Old Curiosity Shop*.'' Focusing in particular on illustrations of Quilp and Jerry the dog-trainer (one ''a kind of dog, the other . . . a master of dogs''), Gray shows Phiz's ability to ''penetrate, and to conspire with, Dickens's imagination'' (125). Gray is particularly good at pointing out the pathos of scenes (some illustrated, some not) of Jerry and his dogs, ones that are often underappreciated as they get overshadowed by scenes dominated by the spectacularly hideous Quilp. As Gray notes, Browne makes Jerry look like Sikes from *Oliver Twist*, which underscores similarities in their characters (133). The essay offers insightful analysis of both the illustrations and a vivid, albeit unillustrated scene of pathos with Jerry and the dogs.

Philosophy/Theology

In *Ethics and the English Novel from Austen to Forster*, Valerie Wainwright claims that the ethics of literary works used to be a dominant focus of earlier literary criticism but that the subject went out of fashion. It may, however, be coming back into vogue, given recent trends in Dickens scholarship and literary studies in general. Perhaps the return to ethics is a response to the glaring lack of ethics seen in political and business leaders, or perhaps it marks a growing desire to make literary criticism more widely relevant after decades of studies that speak primarily to a diminishing number of readers. In any case, several works this year productively embrace the topic.

Wainwright's aim "is to return to and revise arguments concerning the ethics of a sequence of remarkable novels of the long nineteenth century, taking into account new research on key moments in the debates of modernity." Wainwright feels that modern ethics have privileged "personal flourishing," and that "the novelists who contributed brought to this debate a shrewd understanding of the manifold difficulties that might complicate the realization of such an ideal" (2–3). The ethics Wainwright analyzes are modern as is her critical approach, informed as it is by new historicism. Wainwright devotes chapters to *Mansfield Park*, *North and South*, *Hard Times*, *Middlemarch*, *The Return of the Native*, and *Howard's End*, plus an afterward on Bruce Chatwin's *Utz*.

Wainwright argues that Dickens's ethics were influenced by the "ideals of the Cambridge Platonists, whose work was at the very time being published by his friend Edward Tagart" (31). The Platonists felt that our ability to act ethically was due to good will, not our capacity to reason. According to Wainwright, *Hard Times* shows that "for Dickens the will functions best when it is connected to and guided by the power of sight: a power which is to be discerned in a mix of acute perception and sympathetic attention" (31). It also works best in the company of loyalty and love, and Wainwright points to Sissy and Rachael from *Hard Times* and Dorothea from *Middlemarch* as examples of characters who act ethically out of "a strongly felt sense of the abiding meaningfulness of certain connections" (31). In her reading of *Hard Times*, Wainwright sees Dickens as a critic of liberalism, an "angry liberal," attacking through Bounderby and Gradgrind an ideology "that can serve as a justification for an excess of self-interest" (49). She feels the novel emphasizes much more than the need for amusement and imagination; it reveals how "the good will powers a vitally effective moral life," and the good will is fueled by "accurate perception and lasting emotive attachments" (106, 108).

Hard Times, according to Wainwright, explores the limits of both communitarian and liberal ethics, communitarians believing in the goodness of communal life, and liberals finding that such a life encroaches on their personal freedoms. Wainwright argues, "as a social idea the circus stands for communal practices set in contrast with the aggressively libertarian drives of . . . characters . . . for whom the family counts for little or nothing," such as Bounderby and Gradgrind (110). Wainwright should probably mention that the circus seems to fall between the two polarities she emphasizes, offering the community of a family but with a much greater openness to personal liberties and aberrance. Wainwright contextualizes her argument with the sermons and publications of Edward Tagart, minister at a Unitarian chapel that Dickens attended on occasion. Tagart promoted the importance of good will in leading an ethical life, countering J. S. Mill's notion that the will was nothing but " 'nervous energy' " (115). Drawing from Tagart, Dickens reveals the importance of the will in his characterizations of Sissy and Rachael.

Wainwright suggests that Dickens finds a compromise between liberals and communitarians "through his representation of effective moral agency" and in doing so "registers his distance from all those who, like John Stuart Mill, found the Christian ideal essentially a doctrine of passive obedience. . . . In his moral agents, opposing characteristics are paradoxically reconciled . . . spontaneous and self-disciplined, they are both free and yet obedient" (121). Wainwright's study offers not only good readings of Dickens; it also offers insights on what it means to be "good" in general in response to the demands of one's community and the demands of oneself.

In *Moral Taste: Aesthetics, Subjectivity, and Social Power in the Nineteenth-Century Novel*, Marjorie Garson analyzes the conjunction of "taste" and morality, showing how various fictional works from the nineteenth century imply that good taste is a sign of good morals. She demonstrates that "the contradictions in the discourse of taste account for a wider range of meanings in even the best-known texts than has always been recognized" (4). The book includes the following chapters: "The Discourse of Taste in *Waverley*," "A Room with a Viewer: The Evolution of a Victorian Topos," "Resources and Performance: *Mansfield Park* and *Emma*," "The Improvement of the Estate: J. C. Loudon and Some Spaces in Dickens," "Charlotte Brontë: Sweetness and Colour," "*North and South*: 'Stately Simplicity,' " and "The Importance of Being Consistent: Culture and Commerce in *Middlemarch*."

The chapter on Dickens is lengthy and presents fascinating material on nineteenth-century landscaping practices and writings. She focuses in particular on J. C. Loudon, a famous landscaper and horticultural writer whose *The Suburban Gardener and Villa Companion* (1838) played a significant role in shaping middle-class tastes (178). Garson examines how Loudon casts light on domestic spaces in several Dickens novels. While she can't argue a direct influence, she makes a convincing case that it would have been likely Dickens knew or at least knew of Loudon and probably knew Loudon's wife, who edited *The Ladies' Companion*. She also draws connections between Edward Kemp's mocking of lower-class gardening vulgarities in *How to Lay Out a Garden* and Dickens's portrayal of Wemmick in *Great Expectations*. Kemp decries gardeners who try to crowd too much into a small space, who indulge in the sham of artificial ruins, who construct bridges to span puddles, etc.—the passages sound like fairly accurate descriptions of Wemmick's "estate." In fact, since the connections between Kemp and Dickens's Wemmick are more striking than those between Loudon and Dickens, it is a particular shame that Garson doesn't specify the publication date of the first edition of Kemp's book, which was 1858, so that readers can determine the likelihood of an influence on *Great Expectations* (1860–61). The edition she cites was published in 1860, meaning it came out at the same time as *Great Expectations*, making the argument for influence a little more dubious. Although the Kemp passages suggest the clearest link to Dickens, Garson argues that "what makes Loudon particularly relevant to Dickens is his claim about the sufficiency of small properties. . . . that domestic happiness does not take wealth, that the influence of the domestic angel can make the most modest home into a haven of harmony" (208). This is a philosophy Dickens certainly embraced. Garson is right to suggest that "Dickens is hostile to the discourse of taste in general, which he finds narrowly and invidiously prescriptive. In particular, he has no use for the kind of tastefulness that would inhibit the exuberance and vitality of ordinary people" (208). If anything, Dickens seems to be writing deliberately to counter the taste discourse and its snobbish mockery of cockney gardening practices. When he tries to take up the discourse of taste seriously, he veers into false sentimentality (208).

According to Garson, "whether or not Dickens read Loudon, the 'small-is-sufficient' discourse so important to the *Villa Companion* shapes the contrast, in *Bleak House* (1853) and *The Tale of Two Cities* [sic] (1859), between the modest and happy domestic establishment and the doomed chateau, while the small yet supposedly sufficient properties of James Carker in *Dombey and Son* (1848), John Wemmick in *Great Expectations* (1860–61), and Noddy Boffin in *Our Mutual Friend* (1864–65) are certainly conceived in response to the discursive tradition to which Loudon contributes" (209). Garson makes excellent observations in this lengthy chapter, and the passages from nineteenth-century landscape and gardening books offer fascinating contexts for Dickens. Yet some may feel that a little less on landscaping and a little more analysis of other Dickens spaces would have been intriguing and helpful. I would, for example, have particularly liked her to comment on the Plornishes' Happy Cottage in *Little Dorrit* or on Tartar's garden in *Drood*.

Kathleen Poorman Dougherty examines Scrooge's abrupt change of character in "Habituation and Character Change." Dougherty contrasts Scrooge's transformation with Aristotle's belief that character is formed gradually, through habit. Yet we seem to be able to accept the idea of sudden changes in literary characters, which to Dougherty suggests that such changes must make intuitive sense to us. Dougherty compares two such cases of rapid character change, Euripides' Hecuba and Dickens's Scrooge, an odd pairing, to say the least, but an interesting one as the two characters move in opposite directions in their changes. Dougherty argues that "it is perfectly plausible for such rapid character transformations to occur, because certain radical experiences may require a completely new interpretation of the world and necessitate a different form of engagement with it" (295). While Hecuba's suffering reduces her from a good woman to a vengeance machine, Scrooge's experience with the ghosts effects a transformation from a money-making machine into a good man. The ghosts show Scrooge how to feel again, which allows him to return to the human race, but Hecuba has experienced so much tragedy that she becomes hollowed out, reduced solely to the desire for revenge.

Dougherty looks at how a traditionalist (one who follows Aristotle's belief in character change through habit) might argue that these aren't real changes and that Scrooge and Hecuba merely act out facets of their personalities that were always there but latent. But Dougherty feels "the problem with such a response is that it forces us to deny that character is ever deep and abiding" (303) because the traditionalist view turns character into a matter of "a chance amalgamation of personality and social circumstance" (303). I can see her point here, yet the same objection could be made to her argument that dire circumstances can change character—doesn't that also mean that character isn't deep and abiding and that it is vulnerable to circumstance? However, Dougherty offers a more effective response to the traditionalist position, the idea that these abrupt character changes may not in fact be so abrupt: "what we witness as rapid character change is simply the culmination of a long, drawn-out process" (304). We may not see the gradations of the "internal struggle" the character undergoes, but that does not mean these things aren't there (304). She admits, however, that this interpretation, while intriguing, may work better for Hecuba than Scrooge. The best compromise between a traditionalist position and belief in rapid character change can be found through the concept of practical wisdom, Dougherty finds. Practical wisdom comes in part through good judgment, which does accrue gradually, thereby allowing for the traditionalist's belief in habituation. But judgment does not operate in a vacuum—it responds to "understanding what Aristotle might call 'the universal' or the general principle" that enables one to discern right from wrong, and "it is this conceptual understanding that can change rapidly culminating in a character change" (305). Dougherty does a fine job of situating her analysis in a philosophical context and neatly dissecting the influences on character, but her essay is somewhat marred by too much plot summary. Considering that she is comparing two such diverse texts, however, some plot summary was certainly necessary.

Paul Saint-Amour also analyzes the ethics of *A Christmas Carol* in " 'Christmas Yet to Come': Hospitality, Futurity, the *Carol* and 'The Dead.' " Saint-Amour's comparison between Dickens's Christmas story and Joyce's brought out so many intriguing similarities I wondered why I had never thought of them in tandem. His essay posits both stories as "serious meditations on the ethics of hospitality" (93). Joyce's story focuses on "three forms of hospitality: the social codes of invitation and limited welcome; the ethics of limitless welcome to the absolute stranger; and the call within cosmopolitan political philosophy for a universal right of hospitality" particularly in the context of occupied Dublin (93). Saint-Amour points out that

Dickens in his preface to the *Carol* refers to it as a "Ghostly little book" but that the story turns out to be more of a guest than a "*gast*" (94). Dickens asks the reader to host his little book, Saint-Amour argues, "framing the act of reading as an act of hospitality." At the same time, the story hosts the readers, an act of reciprocal hospitality. Saint-Amour refers to Derrida's delineation of two forms of hospitality, one conditional, one unconditional. Conditional hospitality refers to "codified obligations . . . extended to a guest, stranger, or foreigner possessed of a social status," whereas unconditional hospitality refers to the " 'Law' of hospitality, 'just hospitality,' " extended to "a figure who lacks that status: the figure of the absolute other" (95). He further distinguishes the two hospitalities by clarifying that "absolute hospitality forgoes or even abjures the logic of reciprocity, exchange, and rights on which conditional hospitality is premised" (95). Unconditional hospitality, by overturning the rules of conditional hospitality, has the potential to transform the host. The host sees his home anew through the visitor, by entering it " 'from the inside *as if* he came from the outside' " (95).

The *Carol*'s Ghosts effect just such a transformation with Scrooge. Saint-Amour admits that Scrooge seems an unlikely candidate to play host to anyone, but states "if some achieve hospitality on their own, others have it thrust upon 'em" (96). One might argue that being forced to receive visitors is hardly playing the role of host, but Saint-Amour predicts this objection, pointing out that Marley's Ghost proffers Scrooge the hope that he might be different in the future, indicating that while the visitation has been involuntary, the choice to become a better man will be volitional. Scrooge learns to become a "willing host" in response to his early forced hosting. Saint-Amour offers insightful comments on the introduction of the Ghost of Christmas Present, where Scrooge "enters his own home thanks to the visitor and is emancipated by virtue of being, paradoxically, his guest's hostage" (96). As much as Dickens plays with Scrooge as host and guest, the two roles are not interchangeable, as Saint-Amour asserts: "*A Christmas Carol* testifies to the difference of the other even as it insists that 'mankind was my business' . . . in other words, that social life . . . is none other than the encounter with radical alterity" (97). Ultimately, after hosting ghosts and facing his own corpse, Scrooge discovers "*that he himself is the ghost*" (98). In other words, he recognizes the other in himself.

Saint-Amour continues his argument with an examination of Joyce's "The Dead" where the theme of hospitality is more overt, with the setting being a holiday party and Gabriel's after-dinner speech focusing on the topic of hospitality. Saint-Amour sees Dickens's three ghosts echoed in Gabriel's three unsettling encounters: one with Lily, one with Molly Ivors, and finally the climactic one with his wife Gretta, in which she undermines his understanding of her by telling him about her first love, Michael Furey, who died for love of her. Gabriel abandons his plans of making love to his wife, and comforts her as she cries instead. Just as the *Carol* leads to a profound recognition of the other, even within the self, so "The Dead" shows "that extreme alterity can take the form of an intimate whose disclosures vandalize the portrait of our intimacy; it suggests, by extension, that radical hospitality can be asked of us not only by the absolute stranger but also by the intimate who comes bearing absolutely strange news" (103). Saint-Amour's comparison of these two works is mutually illuminating, and his use of hospitality theory provides a lens that yields insightful readings of these two frequently analyzed works.

In "*Nicholas Nickleby* and the Discourse of Lent," Leona Toker argues that Dickens reveals "his intuitive insight into the structures of meaning around the corruption of Lent" (19). Toker sees Lent, with its fasting, not as the opposite of carnival with its feasting and revelry, but as "its second self: both stage the blurring of borderlines between the individual and his or her environment—carnival on the basis of excess and Lent on the basis of lack" (19). Lent only has meaning if its fasting is not enforced and is limited in time. Fasting that is forced is a corruption of Lent. Toker draws connections between Dickens's depictions of such corruptions in *Oliver Twist* and *Nicholas Nickleby* and the "motifs of hunger" in "the literature of concentration camps—in particular, the memoirs of Soviet concentration camps" (21). Reading Dickens in relation to this literature, Toker argues, "one is struck by the way in which the intuition of a young artist of genius reveals *the deep structure* of the social evil that he attacks" (21). Toker proceeds to trace connections among Yorkshire schools, prisons, and concentration camps, but readers may find these comparisons a bit stretched, since she never fully justifies invoking Lent to describe situations where people are not fed properly. In other words, the Lent/poorly fed boys connection seems shaky enough, but then to see meaningful connections between such scenes and concentration camps stretches the line of argument to the breaking point. I'm intrigued by Toker's original comparison, but I think she simply lacked sufficient space and time to realize it fully. She does make interesting points about how Dickens uses hunger as a way to bring about key meetings and coincidences. And her observation that "*the answer to hunger is fasting*" presents a tantalizing philosophical perspective on the will, which she relates to Nicholas's story by describing various scenes where he and other characters willingly accept privation.

Social Studies Approaches

This is a broad category in itself, within the broader category of "other interdisciplinary approaches." The works I discuss here draw on law, sociology, psychology, and urban reform. Most use these disparate disciplines wisely, instead of being used by them. In other words, information and theories from the social sciences for the most part actually do cast new light on Dickens texts in these studies, although occasionally the material meant to cast light ends up casting a shadow instead.

In *The Novel of Purpose: Literature and Social Reform in the Anglo-American World*, Amanda Claybaugh sets out to "sketch the ways in which the nineteenth-century novel was shaped by reformist writings" (2). Claybaugh sees Harriet Martineau as influencing other Victorian authors to write "the novel of purpose," which was the term used at the time for a work of fiction meant, like reformist writings, to "act on its readers—and, through its readers, the world" (7–8). Novels of purpose did much to raise the status of the novel in general, revealing the form to be much more than a source of frivolous entertainment. Claybaugh devotes chapters to "Social Reform and the New Transatlanticism," "The Novel of Purpose and Anglo-American Realism," "Charles Dickens: A Reformer Abroad and at Home," "Anne Brontë and Elizabeth Stoddard: Temperance Pledges, Marriage Vows," "George Eliot and Henry James: Exemplary Women and Typical Americans," "Mark Twain: Reformers and Other Con Artists," and "Thomas Hardy: New Women, Old Purposes."

In chapter 3, "Charles Dickens: A Reformer Abroad and at Home," Claybaugh makes the odd statement that Dickens became a reform novelist slowly only after five novels, a comment that seems to ignore the clear reformist impulses of *Oliver Twist* and *Nicholas Nickleby*. She goes on to admit that the early novels have reformist scenes, "but Dickens himself did not understand these scenes to be reformist at the time he wrote them" (53). While one may jump to point out the obvious social critique against the New Poor Law in *Oliver Twist* and the overt attack on Yorkshire schools in *Nicholas Nickleby*, Claybaugh sees these novels as arguing *against* reform, by which she means official reforms, and *in favor of* personal charity. Reform works at a distance, charity up close. I think Claybaugh missteps in insisting on this dichotomy, for often Dickens seems to be advocating both, as in *Nicholas Nickleby* where he celebrates the personal charity of Nicholas and the Cheerybles while also advocating the reform of Yorkshire schools. Claybaugh sees Dickens contrasting his subjective approach in "A Visit to Newgate" to the assumed objectivity of reformist writings (i.e., impressions vs. numbers), but that also seems to be a false dichotomy since reformist writings did not rely solely on numbers, nor did Dickens rely solely on his personal, subjective impressions. It is a shame that Claybaugh gets sidetracked by these false dichotomies, for she offers a wealth of interesting contextual materials here.

Claybaugh seems on firmer ground in her analysis of *American Notes* and the role that Dickens's American travels played in making him a more conscious reformist writer. She brings out an interesting irony: Dickens, who was advocating for copyright reform at the time, plagiarizes from the writings of two American reformers, Samuel Gridley Howe and Theodore Weld, in *American Notes*. Dickens borrows freely from Howe's reports for the Perkins Institute for the Blind and equally freely from Weld's antislavery pamphlet *American Slavery As It Is*, in both cases without citation. But she emphasizes these lapses not to suggest Dickens's hypocrisy in plagiarizing while advocating copyright reform. Such borrowing was normal in reformist writing, she indicates (75). Instead, Claybaugh points out Dickens's use of these reformers "to draw attention to what these borrowings show us about his involvement in an Anglo-American culture of reform" (71).

Dickens was able to circumvent the South's ban on antislavery pamphlets by placing within *American Notes* the one Weld had written; *American Notes* then gets reprinted and disseminated in the U.S., even in the South, its antislavery pamphlet intact. Weld's pamphlet reprinted the advertisements of slave masters looking to reclaim maimed runaway slaves. The descriptions of the slaves, with the details about scars, missing limbs, and other dismemberments, revealed the guilt of the very masters who wrote them in order to retrieve their "property." These advertisements, appearing in the context of Dickens travel narrative, provide a glaring testimony against slavery, one needing little authorial intervention. His inclusion of the ads served its purpose: "Southern readers were shocked to see what their own newspapers looked like through unfamiliar eyes, as their indignant reviews of Dickens's book made clear. Reprinting proved to be a powerful technique of defamiliarization" (79). Claybaugh suggests that Dickens later withdrew from Anglo-American reform after this out of disgust with American manners and piracy but also because of a need to draw limits on the ever-growing demands for his own philanthropy. "National boundaries," Claybaugh argues, "offered what he had been looking for . . . a way of delimiting connections that could otherwise ramify beyond action or even comprehension. For Dickens, the withdrawal to the nation was what enabled reform" (84). In spite of my reservations about early statements in this chapter, Claybaugh's analysis in general is penetrating and far-reaching, particular read in the context of the book's opening chapters.

Olga A. Stuchebrukhov explores how nationalism shaped the fiction and nonfiction of Dickens and Dostoevsky in *The Nation as Invisible Protagonist in Dickens and Dostoevsky: Uncovering Hidden Social Forces Within the Text*. While numerous other critics have emphasized similarities between these two authors, Stuchebrukhov draws on Marxist historian Benedict Anderson's theory about the novel's link to nationalism to show how Dickens, through allegory, and Dostoevsky, through symbolism, constructed images of the ideal nation. She focuses in particular on Dickens's *Bleak House, Household Words*, and *All the Year Round* and Dostoevsky's *The Devils* and *The*

Diary of a Writer. Stuchebrukhov sees *Bleak House* as "an embodiment of political middle-class nationalism" and an allegory "of Esther Summerson's progress from an illegitimate child to the 'queen' of middle-class virtues that are presented by Dickens as the national norm" (7). She distinguishes between cultural nationalism and state nationalism and sees the union of Esther and Woodcourt as exemplifying "a well-balanced nation-state that fuses the masculine domain of the state with the feminine domain of the nation into the pastoral idyll of Esther's Bleak House" (7). In analyzing Dickens's *Household Words* and *All the Year Round*, Stuchebrukhov demonstrates how he posited France as a model for a "well-balanced nation-state," whereas Great Britain lacks such balance due to aristocratic control and *laissez faire* economics (8). Stuchebrukhov's writing is clear, amply supported, and persuasive throughout. I found her section on the beginnings of national identity and nationalism in Great Britain to be particularly helpful material that is not often covered in Dickens criticism.

In "Lowell Revisited: Dickens and the Working Girl," Chris Louttit offers an excellent analysis of Dickens's Lowell chapter of *American Notes* in the context of "six reports made by the Children's Employment Commission 1842–43." Louttit sees Dickens's response to Lowell women factory workers as being shaped by his reaction to the first report in the series (7 May 1842) that "provoked public concern about children and women at work in mines and factories across the land" (28). Another influence on this chapter was Lord Ashley's Mines and Collieries Bill. Dickens wrote a letter to the *Morning Chronicle*, 25 July 1842, in response to this bill, specifically attacking "the practice of women working underground 'by the side of naked men . . . and harnessed to carts in a most revolting and disgusting fashion'" (29). Louttit remarks that Dickens probably wrote the Lowell chapter of *American Notes* a week after he had written the letter to the *Morning Chronicle* about the mine bill, suggesting an immediate influence that has not previously been noted. In this context, the Lowell chapter is "an actively motivated account of an ideal alternative to the sufferings endured by those women 'out of sight in the dark earth,'" and he suggests the influence of the Lowell experience on later female characters such as Lizzie Hexam, a woman who is able to work and maintain her virtue and dignity (34–35). Louttit's revelation of these likely influences adds to our understanding of Dickens's positive reactions to the Lowell factories, as well as to his subsequent characterizations of women.

Hisup Shin examines the influence of sanitation reports on Dickens's fiction in "What Creeps Out of Holes: The Figuration of Filth and the Urban Everyday in Chadwick's Sanitary Report and Dickens' Later Novels." Shin sees *Our Mutual Friend* as presenting a cityscape "whose rhythms of life echo the way money is being unceasingly circulated to an effect of social and ideological numbness. . . . [in a] self-perpetuating web of financial investment that sets the tone of everyday life in the novel'' (314). Shin sets against this financial circulation ''an extending cluster of filthy objects and people . . . [that] accompany and complicate the financial cycle of the city'' (315). Shin notes Dickens's comparison of the circulation of money to trash blowing in the wind, which underscores that ''everything, even rubbish,'' becomes a financial matter, as Boffin's lucrative dust mounds show. In this cityscape, currency becomes trash, and trash becomes currency, a connection many have noted and that Carlyle had made earlier in *Latter-Day Pamphlets* (1850).

Shin focuses on the influence of Edwin Chadwick's *Report on the Sanitary Conditions of the Labouring Poor of Great Britain* on Dickens's depiction of the city. Chadwick's report suggested systems for underground sewage, street cleaning, and safe water supplies, among other sanitary issues, all to be organized under one administrative body. His plans also called for the use of sewage for farm manure (a practice that is actually coming back into vogue today as planners strive for more efficient and ecological practices in the face of concerns about pollution and dwindling water supplies). ''In ridding the city of pollution,'' Shin finds, ''Chadwick's sanitary vision provides a prototype for Dickens' 'recycle-able' city, by converting it into the de-corporealized, exchangeable form of produce'' (319). Filth in Dickens ''repeatedly comes across as a crucial ingredient in reinforcing his totalizing social vision'' (319). Shin examines Dickens's comparison in *Our Mutual Friend* between London and Paris, where '' 'wonderful human ants creep out of holes and pick up every scrap' '' and sees how in this image Dickens undermines to a degree Chadwick's vision of the sanitary, orderly city (320–21). Shin contrasts Dickens's description of wonderful human ants to Chadwick's horrified description of chiffoniers or rag pickers. Dickens's ''way of relating the complex image of urban heteronomy . . . posits an open-ended frame that weaves signs of filth and poverty'' that stand in contrast to Chadwick's vision of organized sanitation (340). In *Bleak House* Esther's appreciation of the '' 'extraordinary creatures in rags, secretly groping among the swept-out rubbish' '' can be seen as indicative of Dickens's own ''open-minded'' and ''egalitarian'' attitude toward the streets (341). Shin offers perceptive readings in this essay as well as important contextual information about Chadwick, but the essay would be stronger with more coverage of Chadwick's relationship with Dickens, which was extensive and complicated, since Dickens had combated him over the New Poor Law but worked with him on sanitation reforms dear to both men. This context really needs to be delineated in order to fully appreciate the complexity and ironies of Dickens's attitude toward filth, rag pickers, and the like.

Kieran Dolin's ambitious *A Critical Introduction to Law and Literature* suggests that literature ''has something to offer the law in its resolution of social conflicts'' (3). Dolin includes chapters on ''Renaissance Humanism and the New Culture of Contract," "Crime and Punishment in the Eighteenth Century," "The Common Law and the Ache of Modernism," "Rumpole in Africa: Law and Literature in Post-Colonial Society," and "Race and Representation in Contemporary America" but makes reference to Dickens particularly in the chapter on "The Women Question in Victorian England." Dolin relates the famous divorce case of Caroline Norton (granddaughter of playwright Sheridan), whose husband physically abused her, tried to mortgage her trust fund, separated her from her children, and publicly and falsely accused her of adultery. As Dolin states, "unable to contract, unable to sue, deprived of the right to her own earnings and unable to divorce, Norton was clearly 'excluded from [legal] discourse and imprisoned within it' " (125). Her case relates to Dickens, Dolin shows, as Dickens covered the story in the *Morning Chronicle* and then parodied it in the trial in *Pickwick Papers*, mocking in particular the lame proof Norton's husband used in court to indicate her adultery. Dolin traces further connections in Norton's use of a quotation from Dickens in her epigraph to *English Laws for Women* (133), and in Dickens's artist friend Maclise's using Norton as a model for his *Spirit of Justice* painting in the House of Lords chamber. Dolin sees a deeper similarity between Norton and Dickens, however, since both use "the body of the victim as a sentimental spectacle, mobilizing reform through the cultivation of pity" (135). Like Norton, Dickens reveals a primary concern that always "lay in the human consequences of the law, rather than in the content or rationale of legal rules" (137). An interesting reading of *Bleak House* follows with an assessment of the national jaundice that the Jarndyce case implies. Dolin concludes that in his treatment of trials "Dickens pioneered the legal trial as an allegory of modern society," one influencing later authors such as Kafka and Gaddis (138). While there is not much new interpretation of Dickens here, the book provides useful contexts in its articulation of key legal cases and trends affecting the literature of four centuries.

The next works I'll discuss draw more from sociology and psychology in their analyses of Dickens. Donna Tussing Orwin's *Consequences of Consciousness: Turgenev, Dostoevsky, Tolstoy* examines how these three writers helped to shape the Russian concepts of the self. In chapter 8, "Childhood in Dickens, Dostoevsky and Tolstoy" Orwin posits Dickens as a "common denominator" between Dostoevsky and Tolstoy in their depictions of childhood and the transition from childhood to adulthood (140). Both Tolstoy and Dostoevsky believed in "the natural goodness of children" and both use Dickens as a model for this idea, as well as a model for the portrayal of unhappy children. Dickens has such a striking influence in these portrayals because he was one of the first to place a child at the center of an adult narrative. Dostoevsky, Orwin indicates, borrowed Nell's name for his character Nelli, the orphan of *The Insulted and the Injured*. Frequently the two authors have been compared to Dickens's disadvantage as Dostoevsky's Nelli strikes most readers as more realistic, but Orwin indicates that Dickens's characterization is more realistic than often supposed since it shows "the almost irresistible effect of outside evil on healthy souls" (144). As for Tolstoy, he was deeply influenced by *David Copperfield* in writing *Childhood*. While Tolstoy and Dostoevsky went beyond Dickens in terms of psychological realism in their depictions of "the damaged psyche of the abused child" (148), both "learned more about the psychology of childhood in Dickens than is usually understood" (157). Many Dickensians will of course be aware that Dickens was an influence on Tolstoy and Dostoevsky, but Orwin's study will advance our understanding of this influence by referring to specific characters and passages in lesser-read works by these great Russian writers.

Rachel Ablow's *The Marriage of Minds: Reading Sympathy in the Victorian Marriage Plot* analyzes "the implications of the common Victorian claim that novel reading constitutes a way to achieve the psychic, ethical, and affective benefits also commonly associated with sympathy in married life: like a good wife in relation to her husband, novelists and critics claimed, novels could 'influence' readers and so help them resist the depraved values of the marketplace" (2). Ablow clarifies that she is "less interested in sympathy as a feeling . . . than in sympathy as a mode of relating to others and of defining a self''; she also investigates the implications of ideas about the marriage of minds in ongoing debates about marriage law (2, 16).

Ablow devotes her first chapter to *David Copperfield*, with subsequent chapters focusing on Emily Brontë's *Wuthering Heights*, George Eliot's *Mill on the Floss*, Wilkie Collins's *The Woman in White*, and Trollope's *He Knew He Was Right*. These novels allow Ablow to explore a spectrum of attitudes toward novels and marriages as developers of sympathy. Ablow admits that "it is always dangerous—and usually misleading—to use a single text to stand for the ethos of an entire period," but she might have added that it is also dangerous to allow one novel to stand for a writer's entire oeuvre. That would be my chief objection to her approach in this book—it would have been helpful to use a greater range of examples from these authors' writings. That said, she generally makes well-supported arguments, with each chapter offering a very helpful, clearly delineated thesis statement. In the chapter on Dickens, she argues that his characters and his "privileged status in readers' hearts and homes reflects the novelist's attempt to define a new aesthetic organized around feelings commonly identified with domesticity" (19). In particular, she makes the truly unique claim that "Dickens is the paradigmatic wifely novelist of the nineteenth century . . . and *David Copperfield* is the novel in which he explains and defends that characterization most clearly" (19). Like a good Victorian wife, Dickens, she argues, seeks to influence his readers by winning their love for him and his characters. "The goal of the wifely text," Ablow continues, "is to help us see ourselves in new ways: as endlessly improvable, limitlessly lovable, and as capable of enormously virtuous yet profitable acts of generosity" (21). Her analogy is fascinating—and illuminating—yet it does not acknowledge the subordination implicit in the wife's role, a subordination that would be unappealing to Dickens, the master of control. Ablow sees in David Copperfield's attachments to Steerforth and Dora the replication "of contemporary notions of 'female influence' " (29), but instead of his influence being a counter to worldly ambition, like a good wife's should be, his serves more as an "alibi" for his ambitions, which seem "undertaken exclusively for love" (29). While David is often mistaken about these two characters, his noble affection for both has beneficial effects, "even as it makes the interiorities of the beloved objects largely irrelevant" (37).

Ablow argues against numerous readings that suggest that the novel traces David's epistemological evolution—the development of his ability to see and understand others more clearly. Instead, she suggests that Dickens provides David with a character he cannot mistake, one with no interior to misread—Agnes (38). She becomes the image not only of the ideal wife but also of the ideal text "in relation to whom the goal is not understanding of some hidden interiority, but attachment to something like a directional signal or a narrative arc," particularly as David/Dickens describes his ultimate image of her as " 'pointing upward' " (43). "In Agnes and David's relationship," Ablow concludes, "Dickens argues for according the novel form a role that is not just analogous to that of the wife, but that might serve as a substitute for it" (43). While the chapter loses some of its focus in passages on Rosa Dartle, in general Ablow draws an intriguing analogy here between the role of the novel and the role of the ideal wife. In subsequent chapters, she sees much more problematic and at times pessimistic attitudes toward sympathy.

In " 'Subject to the scepter of imagination': Sleep, Dreams, and Unconsciousness in *Oliver Twist*," David McAllister explores 'the importance of sleep and unconsciousness throughout the novel" and suggests that Dickens's descriptions of sleep were influenced by Robert Macnish's *The Philosophy of Sleep* which Dickens had consulted to try to make sense of his dreams of his sister-in-law, Mary Hogarth, after her sudden death (1). McAllister draws upon David Paroissien's comparison in *The Companion to Oliver Twist* between Macnish's work on sleep, and Dickens's sleep scenes. Dickens owned the book and clearly read it, for he refers to it in a letter in 1851, but Paroissien shows through the *Oliver Twist* analysis that Dickens had probably read the work by 1837.

McAllister extends this analysis by connecting Dickens's reading of Macnish's work to the dreams he had of Mary Hogarth. McAllister notes the precision of Dickens's descriptions of semiconscious states and how they serve to heighten the surrealism of scenes such as Fagin's inspection of his treasure (8). McAllister contrasts this scene with the "nonspecific descriptions of sleep in the early numbers of *Oliver Twist*" and, in fact, in early scenes in *Pickwick Papers* as well (9). In earlier descriptions, sleep appears as an "absolute state, without any of the gradations from broken to complete" that we find in *Oliver Twist* (10). McAllister points out that the first descriptions in Dickens of sleep as a state with gradations appear in the July 1837 numbers of both *Oliver Twist* and *The Pickwick Papers* (with a description of Pickwick's semiconscious state in his first night in the Fleet). That a change in his depictions of sleep should appear simultaneously in both novels suggests to McAllister that Dickens probably read Macnish's book in May or June 1837, that is, in the month or two following Mary Hogarth's death, when he was haunted by recurring dreams of his sister-in-law. This is good close reading and good detective work on McAllister's part as well as good use of material from *The Companion to Oliver Twist*. McAllister's essay not only demonstrates Dickens's evolving understanding and use of sleep states; it also shows how much can still be unveiled by close attention to writing/publication dates and the other biographical events of the moment.

Normally, I would have limited this review to studies in English, but I've made an exception for Nathalie Vanfasse's *Charles Dickens Entre Normes et Deviance*. Vanfasse is such a clear and cogent writer that even a rusty French reader such as myself found her book relatively easy to read and rich with insights. Vanfasse sees the Victorian fascination with all that is abnormal and deviant as a natural reaction to the era's pressure to uphold social norms. This pressure was fed by the era's belief in progress, which led to the idea that deviance could not only be understood but also contained. Vanfasse notes in Dickens's writing a curious blend of celebration and subversion of Victorian orthodoxy; he evokes the norms of the period while also apologizing for them, leading to the "pluridimensionnel" quality Michael Hollington refers to in his preface to the book. Vanfasse includes chapters on "Conventions socials," "Formes et exigencies littéraires" (with sections on "Poésie et chansons populaires," "Le modèle théâtral," and "Formes et conventions romanesques"), and "Autres exigencies artistiques" (with sections on visual arts and realism). According to Vanfasse, Dickens's attitude toward realism was ambiguous: he supported the idea of it, but did not follow it in his own writing. Dickens demonstrates the limits of realism in grotesque scenes and characters and idiosyncratic uses of language (232). In doing so, he allies himself more with earlier Romantic writers than with the realist, rationalist writers coming into vogue at the time. His imagination seems to transcend reality, Vanfasse asserts, creating visionary fictions with the capacity to suggest "l'inconnu et l'indéfini" (237). Vanfasse's study provides a nuanced analysis of conformist and subversive impulses in Dickens with the kind of substantial context that gives her interpretations credibility.

Cultural Studies

In this section I look at works that examine various strands of Victorian culture—some offer general studies of the period, while others evoke the times by tracing one subject (such as memory) or one figure (such as the dustman). All include substantial references to Dickens. Cora Kaplan's lively *Victoriana: Histories, Fictions, Criticisms* discusses the increased interest in things Victorian in the past 40 years. Kaplan asserts that "the variety and appeal of Victoriana over the years might better be seen as one sign of a sense of the historical imagination on the move, an indication that what we thought we knew as 'history' has become, a hundred years after the death of Britain's longest-reigning monarch, a kind of conceptual nomad, not so much lost as permanently restless and unsettled" (3). What Kaplan says here about history might also be said about Dickens criticism over the past one hundred years, for it keeps discovering and rediscovering and reknowing the author and his works. Kaplan's chapter one focuses on *Jane Eyre*, chapter 2 on "Biographilia" (our love of life stories), chapter 3 on pastiches of Victorian fiction such as A. S. Byatt's *Possession* and Michel Faber's *The Crimson Petal and the White*, and the last chapter on Jane Campion's film *The Piano*. In the chapter on biographies, Kaplan discusses Peter Ackroyd's study of Dickens, suggesting that its "over-idealizing identification . . . occasionally tips into its opposite, revealing the biographer's envy and competitiveness" (50). Kaplan defends the comment about the biography's idealizing tendencies by suggesting that Ackroyd failed to deal sufficiently with Dickens's racist comments or the implications of his journalism in general, but she never really justifies the accusation about Ackroyd's "envy and competitiveness." She sees the biography as yielding more to Romantic impulses than to the expectations of modern readers (which, on a side note, may be one of the reasons *this* reader liked it). She suggests that our disillusionment with politicians makes us turn more and more to read about authors whose works hold up over time. While Kaplan's criticisms of Ackroyd can seem harsh at times, the book offers an intriguing if somewhat quirky cross-reading of our culture's translation of Victorian culture.

Julian Wolfreys, in *Dickens to Hardy*, offers

> close and contextual readings of a small number of broadly canonical early to mid-Victorian novels. The focus of these readings is on their middle-class protagonists, audiences and authors in order to construct a case about the ways in which middle-class history in the nineteenth century is the locus and site of struggle for emerging discourses of identity and modernity—and indeed, of modern identities themselves. (1)

As part of his exploration of identity, he examines inventions that shaped perceptions of reality, such as telescopy and microscopy. Part 1 focuses on "Cultural Memory," with chapter 1 being devoted to *Pickwick Papers*. Wolfreys notes the repeated images of vision in the novel and then goes on to analyze its ironic and parodic elements, calling it a hybrid in its indebtedness to past novels combined with its prefiguring of modern uses of fragmentation and self-referentiality. "The 'novelty' of this production," Wolfreys asserts, "announces itself internally through the narrative's estranging pastiche of the old" (19). In the gap between old and new the novel articulates a "cultural consciousness mediating the moment of its coming into being. . . . It is, in effect, a cultural *roman à clef*, staging a moment of being English" (19). Occasionally readers may find that Wolfreys becomes more enamored of theory than of the text he is analyzing, and one might wish for more concrete examples to tie to his abstractions. His concluding remarks are good, however: "*Pickwick* is a virtual catalogue of the passing of particular social behaviours. . . . the modernity of *The Pickwick Papers* is signaled in its acknowledgement of the materiality and temporality of being; and . . . we receive it not simply as a collection of comic misadventures, but also as a heterogeneous collection of *memento mori*. Or, as the title has it *posthumous papers*" (44, 49).

When I first picked up Jane Berard's *Dickens and Landscape Discourse*, I thought it might cover territory similar to that in Garson's *Moral Taste* (see above)—that is, the influence of nineteenth-century landscaping practices and texts on Dickens's fiction. But Berard focuses more on landscape as a "cultural construct" created by Dickens "to shape his narrative and his characters and to validate the importance of place, of physical settings in his novels" (9). According to Berard, "Dickens . . . searches for freedom and meaning in the landscape and finds them missing. . . . Dickens succeeds in expressing the allure of industrialized landscapes, while castigating their squalor and the dehumanization of their constituents" (32). Berard references Romantic writers' and Victorian painters' perspectives on landscape, as one might expect, but what one might not anticipate from the title of the book is that Berard focuses her analysis primarily on *Martin Chuzzlewit*, with brief references to contiguous works, such as *American Notes*. The title suggests a more comprehensive examination of landscape in Dickens. Another source of confusion is her protean use of the term "landscape" to refer to everything from scenes of nature to industrial landscapes to social/cultural/political landscapes so that eventually I really couldn't tell what she meant by the term. In addition, long stretches of the book go by with very little reference to Dickens. While Berard presents interesting contextual materials about hill forts and "the geopolitical landscape of Wiltshire," the connections between these passages and Dickens's texts need to be made clearer. Equally distracting are certain inaccuracies in her analysis of Dickens's reactions to the United States. For instance, in her eagerness to show that Dickens was disappointed in Niagara Falls and saw in it a symbol of "the power relations within capitalism" (a strange reading that she does not fully explain), she states that Dickens had described the falls in a letter to Henry Austin as "'nothing but water.'" This is very misleading, since Dickens is actually quoting his servant Anne when he writes these words and is clearly making fun of her for refusing to look closely at any American scene whatsoever (51–52).

Brian Maidment's *Dusty Bob: A Cultural History of Dustmen, 1780–1870* is a fine example of just how illuminating a cultural study can be if it is thoroughly researched, clearly presented, and rife with fascinating details. Perhaps not all readers will want to know this much about dustmen, but I found the book to be a highly entertaining and informative read. Maidment begins by emphasizing that dust for Victorians was a reminder of that which we came from and would return to, "a *memento mori* of the most dramatic kind" (2). This alone gives dustmen a kind of fascination, as if they were so many grim reapers regularly visiting Victorian domiciles. Maidment locates the cultural figure of "Dusty Bob" as originating in Pierce Egan's picaresque novel *Life in London* (1820–21), but the figure got picked up in theatricals and popular songs in which the dustman was often depicted as a lusty character with his sidekick "African Sal" or "Black Sal," a black servant. Maidment suggests that the dustman "was used by Regency and early Victorian society as a means of exploring, and, in a limited way, of rendering less troublesome some of its deepest anxieties and fears" (6). The figure was also an outlet for "the repressed and anxious genteel or professional spectator" (8).

Naturally, Maidment examines *Our Mutual Friend*'s Boffin, stating that he is "the single most powerfully imagined exposition of the complex interdependence between dust, wealth, health, happiness, contamination and redemption" (10). He also sees Boffin as "a cultural anachronism characteristic of a mid-Victorian regret for the loss of the picturesque and the triumph of urban anxiety" (14). Maidment includes interesting descriptions of the dustman's work, and he shows the value of the dustman's collections, with "breeze" (residue from charcoal) being used for brick-making, cinders for heating kilns, bones for china, and rags for paper (17). In chapter 7, "Dust Commodified and Categorized: Mayhew, Dickens and the Investigative Impulse, 1840–1900," Maidment discusses Dickens's preoccupation with dust and waste in both *Household Words* and *All the Year Round*, as well as in *Our Mutual Friend*, for which he sees Charles Dance's play *The Dustman's Belle* (1846) as a likely source, with its themes of "inheritance, concealment, corruption and redemption" (206). Ultimately, Maidment sees the dustman as a "powerfully carnivalesque riposte to the gentility of early Victorian society" (217).

Journalism

John Tulloch does a fine job of analyzing Dickens's strengths as a journalist in "Charles Dickens and The Voices of Journalism." The editors of the book in which it appears set out to identify "some of the elements that make up the journalistic imagination" and at the same time explore "the reasons why it has so long been devalued and misunderstood" (1). Tulloch picks up on the editors' point about journalism being undervalued in the opening comments of his essay, in which he argues that journalism in Britain has less status than in America where its "secure role . . . is embedded in the First Amendment" (59). But, for Dickens, journalism was "training for writing novels" (59), and Tulloch reminds readers (citing John Drew) how much of Dickens's publications could be considered journalism because they appeared in newspapers, journals, or other serial publications. His publications also bear the mark of journalism due to their topicality, particularly their concern for ongoing social problems. Tulloch helpfully delineates a range of possible journalistic voices, including the controversialist, the social investigative, the observer, the mimic, and the campaigner, all of which he explains, and he shows that Dickens "displayed an assured control" of most of them and "an extraordinary ability to switch between them" (64). Tulloch's anatomy of these journalistic voices will help readers to a greater appreciation of Dickens's nonfictional writings.

6. Travel Writing

The December *Dickens Quarterly* contains two fine articles concerning Dickens's *Pictures from Italy*, both based on papers originally delivered at the Genoa Dickens conference held earlier in the year (which itself received rave reviews from attendees). In "Reluctant Source: Murray's Handbooks and *Pictures from Italy*," Eleanor McNees traces the influence of John Murray's popular *Handbooks for Travellers*, first published in 1836, on Dickens's travel narrative. McNees argues that "Dickens deliberately set out to write a travel book against the guidebook genre, one that would substitute a 'series of faint reflections—mere shadows in the water, for Murray's practical advice to prospective British tourists" (211). According to McNees, these travel works appeal to very different readers—Murray's aims at middle-class voyagers looking for "safe passage through a foreign country" while Dickens targeted travelers with "a romantic yearning to resist the beaten track" (211). In spite of these differences, the works share distinct similarities. *Pictures from Italy* tends to rely on the travel routes that Murray used, and it "closely paraphrases the *Handbooks*' descriptions of particular sites and specific paintings" (212).

McNees sees Murray as providing Dickens with a "solid platform from which to perform the rebellious role of traveler" (224). Overall, McNees provides a very useful context for a better understanding of Dickens's impressionistic *Pictures*.

John M. Drew looks at the context of the initial publication of Dickens's Italian travel narrative as a series of columns in the *Daily News*, published under the title "Traveling Letters. Written on the Road." Drew situates this serial publication in the context of the *Daily News* as a "newly launched newspaper" and the "key cultural and political concerns" of the time (230). In doing so, Drew hopes to "restore an overlooked dimension to a text usually viewed as a series of letters addressed to friends and commenced over 18 months previously" (230–31). These "Traveling Letters" began with the very first edition of the paper; eight were published in all, comprising about a third of *Pictures from Italy*. Drew sees in the Brave Courier of *Pictures* links to both Sam Weller and Mark Tapley, placing Dickens himself in the role of Martin or Pickwick. Dickens's somewhat paternalistic relationship to "the Brave" reflects his hope that *The Daily News* will contribute to " 'social improvement' and mutual friendliness amongst the classes" (235).

Drew also considers another influence on *Pictures*, Dickens's "hidden rivalry" with Francis Mahony, who served as the anonymous correspondent from Rome for the *Daily News*. Mahony's reports focused more on politics and were meant to "dovetail with, and be subordinate to, Dickens's more personal and familiar material" (237). Like Dickens, Mahony republished his reports in book form; his was entitled *Facts and Figures from Italy . . . Addressed During the last Two Winters to Charles Dickens, Esq., Being an Appendix to His "Pictures."* Dickens did not appreciate Mahony passing off his book as a collaborative effort and refused to write a preface for it, penning instead a perfunctory "Notice" (237). Mahony returned the "favor" by including in the volume a brief critique of *Pictures* that implies that Dickens's depiction of Italy is superficial (238). Drew ends with an analysis of Dickens's writing style in his Travelling Letters compared to the style of the writing surrounding it in *The Daily News*: "against a uniformly drab background of turgid, formal, diegetical narrative," Dickens's descriptions, with their experimental uses of language to evoke the sensations of travel, appear "brilliant" and put a "strangely literal spin on the very concept of 'traveling letters' " (242). As Drew states, "all Dickens's works published originally in installments have been revitalized and illuminated by the vigorous reinsertion of their particular webs of text into the fabric of their original publishing medium," and that statement is certainly true of what his own study accomplishes (241).

Dickens on France: Fiction, Journalism and Travel Writing, edited by John Edmondson, includes nonfictional writings by Dickens on France, such as

"Travelling Abroad" and "Our French Watering-Place," as well as introductions and extracts from novels (*Dombey and Son*, *Little Dorrit*, and *Tale of Two Cities*). It contains the following chapters: "London to Paris by Train: Crossing the Channel to Calais," "On the Road: Through France to Switzerland," "Holidays in Boulogne," "Going North: Country Ways, Traveling Players, Fun at the Fair," "An Awakening in a Sleepy Town," "A Flâneur in Paris: City Life (and Death)," "Going South: Lyon, the Rhône, and Avignon," "From Travelogue to Fiction," "The French Revolution," "Slaughterhouses, Railway Catering, and Other French Lessons," and "Language Skills and the English." Edmondsun asserts that the works collected in the book demonstrate that Dickens had "an instinctive affinity with French life and culture," feelings that deepened as he "became increasingly familiar with the country and its people" (vii). Each chapter begins with an introduction that explores "the nature of Dickens's relationship with France and the reasons for his attraction to it." For instance, Edmondson suggests that Dickens loved Parisians not only for their love of art and their intelligence but also for their "respect for individuality and tolerance of the unusual" and their "readiness and ability . . . to make the most of life" (viii, xi). For Edmondson, "It is . . . his [Dickens's] preoccupations with what lies beneath the surface of the places and people he encounters, and with this own psychology and situation as traveler and outsider, that give Dickens's travel-related writing on France depth and longevity, rendering it of much more than just historical interest for the contemporary reader" (xiv). Edmondson justifies pulling all these writings together in their own volume because the collection "demonstrates the many ways in which his responses to the country and its people provided inspiration for his work, enriched his understanding and . . . influenced his ideas" (xviii). Of course *Dickens in France*, a slim volume published by In Print Publishing in 1996, does much the same thing. But Edmondson's book is more comprehensive in its readings and notes, and the introductions are more extensive (with helpful publication histories in each introduction), so that it does add to what has already been published on this subject.

7. Language/Style/Structure/Genre

In "Dickens and Personification" John Reed analyzes how Dickens's use of personification put him outside the growing trend toward realism in fiction. "What figurative device is less conducive to realism," Reed asks rhetorically, "than personification, so deeply connected to unrealistic genres such as allegory and fable?" (3). Reed sees Dickens's use of personification as an "implied resistance" to realism that when used along with de-animation emphasizes ''the way in which human existence may be perceived as hyper real'' (3). His use of these devices, Reed argues, allowed him to ''exceed the limits of realism and to stimulate a similar kind of animating activity in his readers'' (4). Reed suggests that Dickens's use of this literary technique was a conscious resistance to realism and part of his larger project of encouraging ''fancy'' in an increasingly utilitarian world, and he notes that personified objects in Dickens are often mirrored by de-animated characters, such as the wooden Dombey vs. the suave wooden midshipman over the door of Sol Gill's shop. In his analysis of these two figures, Reed underscores that Dickens's use of personification here is not just an exercise of fancy but an expression tied to the deeper themes of the novel. In his concluding sentences, Reed writes, ''Dickens was trying to demonstrate his narrative control over his readers by exceeding the self-imposed limits of literary realism, and employing techniques related to emotions deeply embedded in the human imagination. He did not want to be a mere realist, master though he was of many of its techniques. He wanted rather to be something closer to a magus'' (15). Reed's article is by no means the first defense of Dickens's departures from realism, of course, but he adds keen insights to the ongoing dialogue about the issue, particularly in his analysis of the connections between personification, de-animation, and central themes of the novel.

George Goodin published a two-part essay in issues 3 and 4 of *Dickens Quarterly* entitled ''The Uses and Usages of Muddle.'' Goodin borrows the term ''muddle'' from *Hard Times*' Stephen Blackpool and uses it to refer to the ''incoherence, illogicality, confusion, and vagueness'' that distinguish the speech of so many Dickens characters. Goodin analyzes the tradition of seeing artful and artless stupidity as a defense mechanism, and he goes on to suggest how much muddle there is in everyday conversation since the majority of people don't listen well, and good conversation relies on building on the comments of the other speaker. Goodin then examines the causes of muddle and suggests that some characters choose incoherence, such as Mrs. Nickleby, who in her garrulous, nonsensical monologues can dominate without appearing to bully (142). The essay is at its most interesting when it reveals such hidden motivations or causations in muddle; it's at it least so when it starts seeming more like a long list of examples. One of the purposes of muddle, Goodin suggests (citing Garret Stewart), is to allow characters to '' 'retreat' '' from their own pronouncements without appearing to do so (203). Ultimately, Dickens's use of muddle ''suggests a skepticism evident throughout Dickens's work about the power of language and the human intellect'' (208), and Goodin quotes Coleridges's comment on Milton's *Paradise Lost*: '' 'the grandest efforts of poetry are when the imagination is called forth, not to produce a distinct form, but a strong working of the mind, still offering what is still repelled' '' (208). Although Goodin offers many good observations, he could have situated his argument more thoroughly in the context of past Dickens studies of the same subject (for instance, Robert Golding's *Idiolects in Dickens*, 1985).

Barry Tharaud examines the structure of *Pickwick Papers* in "Form as Process in *The Pickwick Papers: The Structure of Ethical Discovery*." Tharaud surveys various arguments for seeing coherent structure in the novel, then proposes "to examine a different sort of form that is a process of discovery in the reader's mind" (145). "This process of discovery," Tharaud argues, "develops as in a Platonic dialogue or an Emerson essay: an idea or condition is examined from various points of view, each of which is incomplete but which furthers our understanding of the problem and makes us more aware of its complexity" (145). Tharaud sees the episodic structure of the novel as "ideally suited to a process of intellectual examination and discovery." The particular subjects of the novel's Platonic dialogue Tharaud sees as "the nature of moral behavior . . . the nature of friendship and the limits of human perception" (145–46). According to Tharaud, Dickens posits imagination and memory as the chief instruments of morality, and reason must be wedded to feeling for morality to hold true, sentiments that ally him with the Romantics, of course. Tharaud's argument is clearly presented and well defended and concludes with the following observation about Pickwick: "Pickwick's too-empathetic concern for good deeds can itself be an obstruction to morality. It is only after Pickwick overlooks his exalted standards of justice and is genuinely concerned for the happiness of individuals whom he loves that he becomes truly charitable, a *true* philanthropist" (157).

Matthew Bevis explores the relationship between pubic speaking and literature in *The Art of Eloquence: Byron, Dickens, Tennyson, Joyce*. "This book explores," Bevis explains, "how four writers responded to a debating, parliamentary people, and examines the ways in which they and their publics conceived the relations between political speech and literary endeavor" (3). Specifically, Bevis is interested in how these writers used a " 'literary' detachment that could gain critical purchase on political arguments" (5). Chapter 2, "An Audience with Dickens," describes how Dickens can be considered an orator since he often composed out loud. According to Bevis, "Dickens declines to write parliamentary or electioneering novels [as others such as Trollope had], yet his ear is always close to this ground" (89). Bevis refers to Dickens's early experience as a Parliamentary reporter and an early writing "A Parliamentary Sketch" and how these exert an influence on his fiction (89–90). His first novel, *Pickwick Papers*, clearly demonstrates this influence. As Bevis states, "the 'entry' from the Transactions of the Pickwick Club is, as contemporary reviewers observed, an entry into the House of Commons" (93). Bevis makes fine comparisons between Pickwick's and Smorltork's exchange and "a renowned discussion in the Commons between

Brougham and Canning" about Catholic Emancipation (93). Bevis notes, too, the similarities between Pickwick's triple clause structure and Brougham's (94). He also observes that when Brougham retracted some of his remarks he said that "his allusion to his adversary was meant in a 'political' and not a 'personal' sense," just as Blotton and Pickwick in the opening scene of the novel retract their insults to each other by claiming they were meant in a "Pickwickian" sense. While Dickens was influenced by Parliament, Parliament in turn was influenced by Dickens; Bevis quotes a *Fraser's* account of an MP who said that since the first number of *The Pickwick Papers*, " 'we had not been treated with a single scene of this kind, formerly so common, in which honourable Members, after accusing each other of falsehood, swindling, or some other little irregularities of a similar kind, ended the affair amicably, at last, by declaring that these terms were only meant to apply 'in a Parliamentary sense' " (95). Brougham was chairman of the "Society for the Diffusion of Useful Knowledge," which sounds much like Pickwick's plans for "the advancement of *knowledge*, and the *diffusion* of learning" (96).

Bevis traces Dickens's continuing satires on Brougham in *Oliver Twist* in which Bumble adopts some Broughamesque lines. But Bevis indicates that Dickens became increasingly disillusioned about politics. Asserting that Dickens turns "away from an emphasis on direct political intervention and toward a focus on the indirect power of social attitudes," Bevis points out that Dickens hoped *Household Words* might make " 'every man in England feel something of the contempt for the House of Commons' " that he himself had (106, 112). The last section of the chapter examines how oratory comes full circle with Dickens as he turns his books, influenced by oratory, into oratory in his public readings. Through these readings, Bevis argues, Dickens hoped to show "how the ills of society could be overcome by the reforming efforts of honourable citizens outside Parliament" (135). The connections Bevis makes throughout this chapter between Dickens's works and specific figures and exchanges in Parliament, in addition to being amusing, help to illuminate specific passages in the novels while also underscoring the importance of this influence on Dickens's life as a writer in general.

In "Lives Unled in Realist Fiction," Andrew Miller looks at fictional lives mirrored by alternative (what he terms "optative") lives in other characters, focusing in particular on Henry James and Dickens. Finding that in Dickens's fiction "optative regret does dominate" (121), Miller sees Dickens's fascination with such doubling as having its roots in his own realization of where his childhood experiences of poverty and neglect might have led. Miller quotes Dickens's comment " 'But for the mercy of God . . . I might easily have been, for any care that was taken of me, a little robber or a little vagabond' " (120). Miller examines optative regret in Edith, Dombey, Sr.,

Florence, and Carker, all of whom at various times in *Dombey and Son* indulge in musings on how they might have been, and he argues that such optative ideas or "lateral prodigality," seem to be "an intrinsic feature of . . . [realist] fiction" (122). Miller examines how the family particularly encourages thoughts of lives that might have been since comparisons to children's, parents', and siblings' lives are inevitable. Miller concludes, "Within the domestic world that Dickens and James both study . . . it seems we deny our passion by sacrificing others, our children first of all—which sacrifice, in turn, calls forth the spectral host of lives we have not led, and consigns us to their unhappy company" (132). Miller's essay adds an intriguing dimension to studies of the doppelganger, suggesting that in realist fiction imaginary doppelgangers exert at least as much influence as actual characters.

In "Local Speech, Global Acts: Performative Violence and the Novelization of the World," Mario Ortiz-Robles questions how the realist novel, which is meant to capture everyday experiences in their local and temporal specificity, can at the same time demonstrate "a remarkable formal portability, traveling virtually intact across cultures and languages and beyond historical circumstances" (1). "How can the novel be at once local, insular, even provincial, and yet worldly, universal, global?" Ortiz-Robles inquires (1). One answer, he suggests, emerges from the form/content relationship, with the content of the realist novel being local but its form universal. In musing on this idea, he considers the related notion, posited by Benedict Anderson and Franco Moretti, that realist novels serve in nation-building—through the novel "the modern nation state could be symbolically grasped by its citizens" and divergent communities could develop a loyalty to the nation (2).

Ortiz-Robles extends Anderson's and Moretti's arguments by exploring the performative aspects of novels that enable them to accomplish such nation-building. The novel, he argues, can and should be seen as a "performative speech act" (3), a linguistic phrase distinguished from constative language. "Performative speech acts," he explains in an end note, "are utterances that do something in or by the saying of something and constative speech acts are utterances that describe or constate something to which true/false criteria can then be applied" (11). Ortiz-Robles points out that most major events in most novels are initiated by performative speech acts, and he turns to *Bleak House*, among other novels, for examples. He sees the Jarndyce case as the result of a "mind-numbingly repetitive, self-propagating iterative chain of discrete performative acts whose cumulative force . . . amounts to little more than institutional inertia" that drives characters to madness and suicide (5). Instead of seeing *Bleak House*, both the novel and the actual house, as representing the nation, "a performative reading pursues a logic of iteration in which form and content become indistinguishable. . . . the content/form doublet collapses under the pressure of novelistic representation as it tries to suppress or displace the performative force of its own discourse" (6). Here Ortiz-Robles's argument itself begins to collapse under the weight of theory and abstractions unsupported by sufficient references to the novel. Yet he concludes with intriguing comments: "The realist novel can thus be said to assemble the conditions of possibility of a global subject: the 'ideal reader' of the novel becoming a subject who is 'at home' in the 'world republic' of the (global) novel precisely by being 'at home' nowhere, and particularly in the temporal and spatial certainties that, according to Anderson and Moretti, the novel seems to guarantee" (11).

Albert D. Pionke focuses on Dickens's delineation of "acceptable and unacceptable forms of secrecy" in "Degrees of Secrecy in Dickens's Historical Fiction." Pionke suggests that Dickens may have had difficulty in suggesting the boundaries of acceptable and unacceptable secrecy as his own position as a novelist implicated him in the creation and revelation of secrets (35). In comparing secrecy in *Barnaby Rudge* and *A Tale of Two Cities*, Dickens's two historical fictions, both of which demonstrate the author's preoccupation with delineating good vs. bad secrecy, Pionke sees *Barnaby Rudge* as implicitly exploring the relation between secrecy and power and suggests that the novel posits personal secrecy as better than institutional secrecy, even though Mary Rudge's secret about her husband and Dolly's about Hugh's attacking her lead to later calamities (39–40). The women are exonerated, though, since their intentions are good. But this places the omniscient narrator as "ultimate arbiter of judgment" which leaves readers without much reason to believe they could make such a judgment, thereby undermining Dickens's "general concern in all his novels to show the power that individuals have to effect social change" (41).

Pionke continues by examining how invested *A Tale of Two Cities* is in secrecy, with its early comment about " 'every beating heart . . . [being] a secret to the heart nearest it' " (43). But he points out that Victorians would have been "prejudiced against practices of secrecy" because of their "obsession with truth-telling and their related tendency to conflate concealment of any kind with dishonesty" (44). Dickens navigates between this aversion to secrecy and the knowledge that everyone keeps secrets by trying to distinguish between "privacy and conspiracy," aligning privacy with "the English domestic circle surrounding Lucie and . . . conspiracy, with the web of Revolution knitted in France by Madame Defarge" (44, 45). But this two-nation dichotomy breaks down through various doublings, and both nations engage in spying. The division between privacy and conspiracy breaks down even further in the conclusion of the novel, as Pionke shows: "Carton's vision of future bliss [upon facing execution] is enabled by practices of secrecy not unlike those of the novel's conspirators. Moreover, this final scene is made possible only by the exposure of Carton's last, most private thoughts; thus, in a final confusion of categories, privacy as a separate, superior form of secrecy can only be secured by its own violation'' (47). ''Ultimately,'' Pionke concludes, ''both historical novels fail in their attempts to distinguish good from bad secrecy—*Barnaby Rudge* because the criterion for judging acts of concealment relies on a fantasy of omniscience, and *A Tale of Two Cities* because the private must be exposed before it can be approved'' (49). Pionke's comparison of these two works reveals the deep connections between these historical fictions and provides good insights into Dickens's complex attitude, and Victorian attitudes in general, toward secrecy.

8. Studies of Individual Works

David Copperfield

Alan P. Barr examines *David Copperfield* as a novel that ''elegizes the loss of innocence and its enthusiasm'' in ''Mourning Becomes David: Loss and the Victorian Restoration of Young Copperfield'' (63). While David also mourns numerous deaths in the novel, it is the loss of innocence that is most pervasive. Barr draws connections between the novel and Tennyson's *In Memoriam* and Wordsworth's ''Tintern Abbey,'' icons of nineteenth-century mourning, one for a lost loved one, one for innocence (63). (Barr acknowledges that Jerome Buckley made similar comparisons in 1984 [71].) In *David Copperfield* these two types of losses are linked—it is the losses of his mother, baby brother, Dora, Steerforth, and Ham that lead to the subsequent loss of innocence. Barr analyzes how Dickens uses fairy-tale images to indicate ''how the subtext is one of surviving the loss of innocence in a world that confusingly resembles a dark, uncertain, and dangerous woods'' (63). Like a true Romantic, David finds ''healing in Nature'' when he journeys to the Alps. But mourning doesn't really end, Barr notes, drawing from Freud, until the mourner attaches himself to a new object of love, and for David that is Agnes. The novel, according to Barr, suggests the necessity of disciplining one's heart—those who don't do so end up like Steerforth and Emily, yet doing so ''exacts the price of ecstasy'' (76). I found Barr's essay intriguing as I tend to see *Great Expectations*, the more cloaked autobiographical novel, as being the elegiac one with *David Copperfield* casting a stronger note of optimism and belief in progress and self-improvement, but Barr makes a good case for seeing *Copperfield* as deeply elegiac in spite of its happier ending.

Barr's second essay on *Copperfield* in 2007 confronts the intersection of class issues and art in ''Matters of Class and the Middle-Class Artist in *David Copperfield*.'' Barr sees David's progress toward becoming an artist as an extended critique of middle class-mores concerning work, marriage and family. Dan Peggotty undermines prevailing notions of what it means to be a "gentleman," since he seems to embody a kind of nobility that many lack who are gentlemen by class (56). Uriah Heep continues the undermining of middle-class virtues through his loathsome, unctuous emphasis on being humble and working hard (59). Barr sees David's success as an artist as disconnected from the middle-class emphasis (and even David's own emphasis) on the importance of hard work, since diligence alone won't necessarily bring success in this area. According to Barr, "the world of *David Copperfield* is better at lampooning passionate involvement than at affirming its value" (66). Barr concludes, "Dickens, an artist solidly entrenched within an undeniably vibrant, but chafing bourgeois society, is exasperated and partially alienated by it. But, as his own vitality and humor suggest, he is tentatively hopeful that from David's artistic achievements and modest, orderly domicile progress may be made toward greater civility and emotional expansiveness" (66).

In "Professions of Labour: *David Copperfield* and the "Dignity of Literature," Richard Salmon explores how Dickens addressed the status of writers in this novel as part of the "Dignity of Literature" debate that occurred mainly between 1848 and 1851 and centered on the "publication of William Thackeray's semi-autobiographical novel about the moral and cultural development of a young bohemian writer, *The History of Pendennis*" (35). The Romantic perspective posed writing as semi-mystical, but Salmon begins his article with a quotation from Marx and Engels stating that " 'the bourgeoisie has stripped of its halo every occupation hitherto honoured and looked up to with reverent awe. It has converted the physician, the lawyer, the priest, the poet, and the man of science into its paid wage-labourers' " (35). Writers, too, were being seen as mere wage-laborers by some, including, at times, Thackeray. Salmon seeks to complicate the usual perspective that Dickens upheld the dignity of authors in *Copperfield* in opposition to Thackeray's position. Instead, Salmon argues that Dickens's novel "may also be read as a negotiation of the process by which the 'poet' is converted to the function of 'wage-labour' within modern culture." Salmon suggests that the " 'bourgeois pseudo-religiosity' of nineteenth-century professional ideology, which, according to Marshall Merman, was not yet apparent to the authors of *The Communist Manifesto*, co-exists in Dickens with an apprehension of the materiality of literary production as 'demystified' as that which he would have discerned in Thackeray" (36).

Salmon reviews the context of the debate and the scholarship that has analyzed *Copperfield* as in part a response to *Pendennis*, one that shows Dickens supporting the dignity of writers and Thackeray portraying them as hacks. He then goes on to suggest that this clean binary is misleading because "both texts ultimately subscribe to the proposition, formulated by Marx and Engels, that the conversion of the 'poet' into a 'paid wage-labourer' is the necessary cost of the formation of the modern professional author" (38).

This is not hard to prove in terms of Thackeray, since his position is clear, as it was to his contemporaries. Salmon indicates as much by quoting Dickens's obituary of Thackeray, where he states that the writer " 'too much feigned a want of earnestness, and . . . made a pretence of undervaluing his art, which was not good for the art that he held in trust' " (42). Dickens demonstrates his own earnestness and valuing of art in his portrayal of David Copperfield with his dutiful and intense work ethic. Yet this portrayal doesn't negate the fact that Dickens, like Thackeray, undermined the Romantic image of authorship "with a more prosaic model of disciplined mental labour" (42). Salmon indicates a point of similarity between the novels that has often been overlooked: "the governing trope of Pen's literary career—putting 'Pegasus in harness'—might also serve as an appropriate metaphor for the narrative trajectory of David's professional apprenticeship" (42). Salmon notes that while David promotes hard work as the key to success, his seems to come with very little labor; this and the fact that he can conduct his work at home shows writing to be "labour without alienation" (43). He concludes that "in this novel, Dickens strives to formulate an ideal of literary 'professional labour,'" in which both halves of the felt oxymoron undergo a process of revision. This ideal finds its most appropriate expression in David's determination "[n]ever to put one *hand* to anything, on which I could throw my whole self . . . a sublation of the metonymic 'hand' of alienated labour into the unified 'self' of the bourgeois professional, which explicitly renounces the 'affect[ed] depreciation' of literary work which Dickens discerned in Thackeray's *Pendennis*" (49). I admire Salmon's ability to deflate false dichotomies in this essay and in the process to delineate the complexities of Dickens's attempts to uphold the dignity of literature.

Great Expectations

In addition to Shari Hodges Holt's article on Alfonso Cuaron's film version of *Great Expectations* (discussed above under "Other Interdisciplinary Approaches—TV/Film/Performance"), two other works on the novel deserve notice. Ian Brinton's *Great Expectations*, part of the Continuum Reader's Guides, offers helpful critical and historical contexts for an informed reading of the novel. Brinton's chapters are: "Contexts," "Language, Form, and Style," "Reading *Great Expectations*, Critical Reception and Publishing History," "Adaptation Interpretation and Influence," and "Further Reading." Brinton begins with biographical information, emphasizing the importance of Gad's Hill to Dickens, and his experience in the blacking factory as a youth, and connects these pieces of information to the "nostalgic quality which haunts the opening pages of *Great Expectations*, accompanied by a sense of both fear and loss" (3). In general, Brinton is impressively efficient and clear in quickly surveying the major works and life events and the inter-sections between them. Chapter 2 was a little disappointing, for it is entitled ''Language, Form, and Style'' but deals almost exclusively with prison imag-ery. Subsequent chapters provide a good survey of the novel's critical recep-tion and a brief survey of literary criticism (nothing on gender studies, though, which seems an odd gap), and also a very good discussion of the illustration history (which relied mostly on Philip Allingham's work) and an analysis of the different endings (which relies chiefly on Edgar Rosenberg). Brinton uses his sources well to guide readers, although better coverage of issues of style and gender would have been helpful

In ''Dickens's Hamlet Burlesque,'' Daniel Pollack-Pelzner amusingly ana-lyzes Wopsle's absurd performance of Hamlet in *Great Expectations*. Pollack-Pelzner states that he is ''interested in the specific vulnerabilities of *Hamlet* that open it to a performance like Wopsle's'' (103). Clearly Dickens is poking fun at contemporary theatrical conventions in the scene (even typical gestures of his acting friend Macready), but, according to Pollack-Pelzner, *Hamlet* is ''as much its target as Wopsle'' (104). The flip side of the bardolatry of the eighteenth and nineteenth centuries was bard-burlesquing. Anything treated with such reverence and seriousness naturally becomes open to mockery, and that was certainly the case with Shakespeare. Dickens himself penned and produced a Shakespearian burlesque called ''O'Thello (the Irish moor of Venice)'' (105). Pollack-Pelzner also notes the burlesque hybrid of *Midsum-mer Night's Dream* and *Hamlet* in the *Pickwick Papers'* chapter ''Strongly Illustrative of the Position, that the Course of True Love is Not a Railway'' (105). He suggests that ''we might read Wopsle's butchery of *Hamlet* as an analogue to the mechanical's travesty of *Romeo and Juliet* in their 'most lamentable comedy . . . of Pyramus and Thisbe' '' (105) and that the catcalls of Wopsle's audience reflect the wry comments of Hippolyta in response to the mechanicals' performance. Pollack-Pelzner describes Wopsle's absurdly drawn-out death scene in which he dies '' 'by inches from the ankles up-ward,' '' but then he comments that this is not much more protracted than what Shakespeare actually wrote, with Hamlet receiving his mortal wound in ''Act Five, Scene Two, Line 306 . . . but [not dying] until fifty-seven lines later, after Laertes proclaims 'Hamlet, thou art slain' (thirteen lines in), Ham-let announces 'I am dead, Horatio' thirty-two lines in, and Hamlet repeats 'O, I die, Horatio' (fifty-one lines in). . . . a sonorous counterpart to Bottom's death throes as Pyramus: 'Now die, die, die, die, die' '' (106). Pollack-Pelzner makes numerous witty and relevant observations about *Hamlet's* vulnerability to burlesque all the while underscoring the rich meta-theatrical quality of Wopsle's performance—after all, ''we are watching Pip watch an audience watch Wopsle play Hamlet. But his is not an unprecedented scene, for we are used to watching Hamlet watch Claudius watch the Player King play King

Hamlet'' (104). His essay performs what should be criticism's chief function: it makes one newly appreciate the text at hand, in this case, particularly its humor.

Hard Times

In ''The Muddle and the Star: *Hard Times*,'' Wendy S. Jacobson suggests that Stephen and Rachael transcend the circus/Gradgrindery dichotomy that has been focused on so much by critics. Jacobson refers to Northrop Frye's comment that Dickens's novels are neither Romantic nor realistic but instead are ''fairy tales with plots that offer themselves as portraits of the real'' (Jacobson 144). She goes on to examine the Biblical allusions that accrue around the narration of Stephen Blackpool's story, underscoring Stephen's progress from ''early muddle and despair ultimately to light and faith,'' as exhibited in his dying speech when he states that he has found comfort in staring at a star and thinking of Rachael and that both have helped clear away the muddle in his mind (145). According to Jacobson, the term ''fancy,'' so important to this novel, to Dickens in general, and to criticism of Dickens, shifts from its association with the circus to an association with religious faith ''through the imagery of light that has rendered Rachael holy in Stephen's deeply troubled heart'' (146). Stephen sees her as an angel after she has saved his wife from drinking poison (and saves Stephen from the complicity of which he would have been guilty), and in his tribute to her, says ''I nevermore will see or think o'anything that angers me, but thou, so much better than me, shalt be by th'side on't. And so I will try . . . t'trust t'th'time, when thou and me at last shall walk together far awa', beyond the deep gulf'' (150). Jacobson argues that ''no other character's interiority is offered in quite the same detailed way, and though other characters have a struggle, only Stephen dies, and his death . . . implies martyrdom'' (152). Stephen's martyrdom brings all the social classes together, so that the novel, as Jacobson suggests, quoting Stanley Friedman, '' 'finally stresses not the differences that divide the social classes but the kinship that unites' '' (154). Fancy (or imagination—she uses the terms interchangeably here) brings much more than the amusement and escapism of the circus: without it ''there is no love, or faith, and without faith, the mechanistic greed of the industrial wasteland will for ever 'monotonously' go 'up and down like the head of an elephant in a state of melancholy madness' '' (154). Jacobson does a fine job of weaving Stephen and Rachael's story into the thematic contrasts of circus vs. Grandgrind, fancy vs. utilitarianism, and her indication that fancy is essential, even to religious faith and love, deepens the implications of the term and the novel in general.

Little Dorrit

Peter Orford suggests that Dickens's experiences in Italy play a key role in his narration of the Dorrit's journey abroad in "An Italian Dream and a Castle in the Air: The Significance of Venice in *Little Dorrit*." More specifically, Orford argues that Dickens's perspective on Venice "may inform our understanding of William Dorrit's path to self-acceptance" (157). Dickens chose Venice as "backdrop for the delusion" of Dorrit, Orford indicates, because it seemed to "present a world of illusion and fantasy" to underscore Dorrit's retreat into his own "castle in the air" (165). In his travel writings, Dickens called Venice " 'a strange Dream upon the water' " (165), and Dorrit experiences it as a dream as well. But later, when he returns to Italy, he cannot maintain the dreamy castle in the air. Orford sees Dorrit's subsequent illness as in fact a sign that he is finally returning to himself. No longer able to keep his prison past at bay with his airy castle dreams, Dorrit becomes the man he had been and reconnects with Amy. His confusions about his whereabouts in the end seem more like self-awareness to Orford than delusion.

The Mystery of Edwin Drood

It was a particularly auspicious year for studies of *The Mystery of Edwin Drood*. Fortunately, scholars are focusing not just on the mystery of the story and how Dickens might have concluded it had he lived. Scholarship on the novel is increasingly revealing the richness of the text as it stands—the beauty and resonance of the language, the complex symbolism, the appeal of its diverse and well-delineated characters.

In "The *Drood* Remains Revisited—the Sapsea Fragment," Arthur Cox revises the statement he originally made about the fragment in 1966 in *Dickens Studies*. Forster in his *Life* suggests that the fragment, called the "Sapsea Fragment" since it included that character from *Drood*, was written by Dickens to slow down the plot of his last novel, which he felt had advanced too quickly. Cox's close reading of the fragment, as well as his detailed descriptions of the physical characteristics of the manuscript (the size of the paper, the number of pages and lines, the color of the ink) are impressive. Cox previously argued that Dickens had probably written the fragment upon learning that "the first two numbers of *Drood* were . . . twelve printed pages too short," but he now argues that Dickens would have had very little time at this point (December 1869) to compose the fragment and must, instead, have written it "during the gestation-period" of the novel (91, 93). One of the mysteries of the fragment is that in itself it is fragmented; given the page numbers on it, it appears that the first five pages must be missing. Cox suggests in this article that Dickens may have introduced Sapsea's infamous, self-aggrandizing epitaph to his wife and some conversation about it in these missing five pages. He surmises that Forster may have withheld these pages since they duplicate material in chapter 4 and "he knew that any duplication in the Fragment of material in the novel would compromise the effect of that passage in the larger and more important work" (96). Cox seems to be going out on a limb a bit in this suggestion, but he has built such sturdy scaffolding throughout the essay that one does not feel his conjecture is without support.

In "The Book of Jasper," Bert Hornback responds to Robert Tracy's essay "Jasper's Plot: Investing *The Mystery of Edwin Drood*," published in *Dickens Quarterly* in 2006. Tracy's article suggested that Jasper could be considered the narrator of *Drood*; Hornback extends Tracy's argument (which, I agree, was very compelling) by showing how like Dickens it would be to pose as Jasper in constructing the narrative voice. "It is Jasper who creates Jasper for us," Hornback writes. He agrees with Tracy's point that Jasper projects a demonic version of Neville for his own purposes, thereby revealing him as narrator in the act of character-making. Ultimately, Hornback sees the novel as addressing the importance of observing well, and to do this one must step outside oneself. Hornback also sees the novel as more complete than usually supposed since Jasper does get punished—his punishment is his entrapment in his own self (83–84). Hornback's and Tracy's arguments are both intriguing, and both present new ways of thinking about a mystery that continues to mystify.

The Dickens Magazine, a relative newcomer to the field of Dickens-related journals, focused on *The Mystery of Edwin Drood* in issues 1–4 of series 4 (which began in 2006 but finished in 2007, which is why I'm including it in this review). Each series centers on one Dickens novel and features chapter summaries (effectively penned by David Parker in this volume) and articles on various biographical and contextual matters that serve to illuminate the text, including ones on other Victorian authors and writers in the style of Dickens. The issues also include ample, well-produced, and highly interesting illustrations and photographs. Each series ends up serving as a helpful guide to a novel. This series offers a wealth of interesting and illuminating articles. For example, "Dickens and Colonialism" by Alan Dilnot suggests that the narrator is "extremely sympathetic to the Landless twins and especially indignant at the racial prejudice against them" (9). In "The Detective Novel Post-*Drood*" Kim Edwards explores how indebted modern detective novels are to Victorian fiction. Philip Allingham, in a four-part essay on Luke Fildes's illustrations for *Drood*, offers detailed analysis of the illustrations and examines ways in which they reflect but also sometimes differ from Dickens's text. "Victorian Missionary Hudson Taylor 1832–1905" by George Gorniak describes the widespread influence of Taylor's China Inland Mission (founded in 1865), which led to the establishment of "120 mission stations, seven hospitals [and] 128 opium refuges for the cure of addicts" (32). The series as a whole is very readable, informative, and entertaining and a welcome addition to Dickens studies.

A Tale of Two Cities

Charles Dickens's A Tale of Two Cities, edited with an introduction by Harold Bloom, is an updated edition of his former collection of essays on this novel and is part of Bloom's Modern Critical Interpretations. The volume includes essays on "Dickens and the Catastrophic Continuum of History in *A Tale of Two Cities*," by J. M. Rignall; "The 'Angels' in Dickens's House: Representation of Women in *A Tale of Two Cities*," by Lisa Robson; "A Sisterhood of Rage and Beauty: Dickens' Rosa Dartle, Miss Wade, and Madame Defarge," by Barbara Black; "*Hard Times* and *A Tale of Two Cities*: The Social Inheritance of Adultery," by Hilary M. Schor; essays by John Reed, Carolyn Dever, Bjørn Tysdahl, Catherine Waters, Tom Lloyd, and John B. Lamb, as well as an introduction by Harold Bloom. All the essays have been previously published between 1984 and 2006, so I will not review them specifically here. But the book as a whole offers an excellent range of topics and approaches from esteemed scholars, and so it is well worth looking into.

9. Bibliographies, Biographies, and Other Reference Works

First I must begin by thanking Diana Archibald for her thorough, balanced and engagingly written "Review of Dickens Studies—2005" in the 2007 *Dickens Studies Annual*. I know all Dickens scholars, like myself, will profit from her assessments of recent scholarship, and I found myself returning to her essay numerous times as a model for this one. My thanks also to other previous "Review" authors, whose work helped me shape my own, Goldie Morgentaler and Robert Garnett in particular.

One of the most comprehensive and useful reference works of 2007 is Robert C. Hanna's *Dickens's Nonfictional, Theatrical, and Poetical Writings: An Annotated Bibliography 1820–2000*, which is part of the series of annotated bibliographies edited by Duane DeVries. I know I'm hardly the first to say it, but scholars owe a debt of gratitude to DeVries for this monumental undertaking which has proven to be so indispensable to Dickens research. Hanna's volume maintains the high standards of the series with its extensive coverage, sensible organization, and efficient—often lively—annotations with effective use of quotations to capture the gist and flavor of the works. (Trey Philpotts points out in a review in the March 2008 *Dickens Quarterly* that Hanna missed some relatively recent articles in his annotations, but I must admit I would not have caught these omissions myself.) The book is divided into four parts and an index: Part I covers criticism of Dickens's nonfictional works, Part II annotates studies of his personal writings and speeches, Part III focuses on studies of his plays, and Part IV annotates works on his poetry. Hanna includes information on the location of original manuscripts for each work and the letters that are relevant to it. Since Dickens's poetry and plays are some of his less read works, the annotated bibliography may open up relatively new territory for scholars. Hanna says as much in his introduction, where he points scholars to Dickens's poetry as a subject scantly covered. One tends to think of annotated bibliographies chiefly in terms of their usefulness—which is great—but Hanna's actually affords pleasure, as in reading his annotation of Bernard Shaw's criticism of *Sketches by Boz* in which he quotes Shaw as saying:

> "No equally gifted man was ever less of an artist and philosopher than [Dickens] was in 1835 when in his 23rd year, he wrote the *Sketches by Boz* in a fashion which Bulwer Lytton or Macaulay would have been ashamed of in their teens. He had a shabby genteel knowledge of society, a Londoner's knowledge of outdoor incident, and a reporter's knowledge of public life, besides his genius, which enabled him to succeed easily in spite of the inadequacy of the rest of the equipment." (62)

Now there's a quotation that captures the voice and spirit of Shaw, while also capturing paradoxical qualities of Dickens.

Michael Slater's *Charles Dickens* is a brief but amazingly thorough biography written initially for the *Oxford Dictionary of National Biography*. "The emphasis of this short life, "Slater writes, "falls upon Dickens's career as a phenomenally productive and phenomenally popular writer . . . while as much attention as possible is also paid to the main events in his personal life, such as his very public separation from his wife in 1858, as well as to his crowded and richly documented social life, his astoundingly extensive and unremitting charitable activities, and his hugely successful second career as a public reader of his own work" (ii). Readers will immediately feel in good hands with this book, given Slater's stature as a scholar, and he doesn't disappoint. While much of the ground he covers is, of course, familiar to Dickens scholars, Slater does more than simply rehash the known details. For instance, he advances lesser known material when he comments on Dickens's "ecstatic but veiled references to Nelly" (i.e., the actress Ellen Ternan with whom he was involved) in *The Lazy Tour of Two Idle Apprentices*, and when he makes connections between Dickens's own marital woes and the story he included in *The Lazy Tour* about the man who wills his feeble wife to death (65). His coverage of Dickens's paying for homes for Ellen under the name "Mr.

Tringham" also seems impressively detailed for a volume of this size. In spite of the evidence he puts forth here, Slater cautions that it is still a "matter of debate" whether Dickens and Nelly really consummated their relationship and reminds us that there is "no hard evidence for the existence of [their] ill-fated putative infant," although much detailed and clever commentary has been brought to bear on the issue. Also intriguing is the alternative story of Dickens's death that Slater finds in Claire Tomalin's *Invisible Woman* (88). In this version, Dickens falls ill, not at home at Gad's Hill as is usually reported, but while visiting Ellen, who escorts him back to Gad's Hill in a closed cab. Slater brings his study right up to the present in his description of the thriving Dickens industry, with several journals devoted to the studying of his works and the term "Dickensian" well ensconced in our everyday vocabulary (with all its many, often contradictory meanings). He ends with a wonderful quotation from a gasman that worked the lights at Dickens's public readings, who said about Dickens " 'the more you want out of the Master, the more you will get out of him,' " a statement that nicely fits the subject of Dickens scholarship as much as it fits the Inimitable (104). My one complaint about this little biography is that its sources are listed all on one page with no line breaks between each citation, making them very difficult to read.

Paul Davis's *Critical Companion to Charles Dickens: A Literary Reference to His Life and Work*, a revision of *Dickens A to Z* with updated entries and expanded critical analyses, offers an impressively comprehensive guide "to the works themselves, to Dickens and the Victorian context in which he worked, and to the vast body of criticism and scholarship about the novels" (ix). The volume includes parts on "Biography," "Related People, Places and Topics," and "Works A–Z" (synopses, commentary, extensive character descriptions, and references to adaptations and further readings). He also includes as appendices a chronology and a bibliography of secondary sources. Throughout the book, the writing is clear and efficient, and the material covered is extensive; this continues to be an extremely helpful, easy-to-use reference work

Donald Hawes's *Charles Dickens* is another introductory guide with chapters on biography and on the major works. Interspersed with discussions of each of the novels (usually three works per chapter), Hawes also includes chapters on relevant issues such as "Social Class in Victorian England," "Prison and Crime," "Dickens and Education," "Medicine, Doctors, Nurses and Hospitals," "Dickens and Christmas," etc. The topics of these chapters make sense, and they are clearly written and informative (although sometimes a bit thin), yet the ordering of them is peculiar—why place "Prison and Crime" after a chapter on *Nicholas Nickleby*, *The Old Curiosity Shop*, and *Barnaby Rudge*? Why not right before the chapter on *Great Expectations*,

Our Mutual Friend, and *The Mystery of Edwin Drood*? And the chapter "Dickens and Christmas" would have been better placed before or after the one that includes analysis of *A Christmas Carol*, instead of seven chapters later. It probably would have made more sense to place these topical chapters in a separate section of the book. The ordering is not a big problem; it just seems to imply that a subject like prisons has more to do with *Barnaby Rudge* than with *Little Dorrit* or *A Tale of Two Cities*, which is debatable, since prisons and crime are subjects with relevance to almost every novel in Dickens's oeuvre. The coverage of prison reform is also a bit weak nor is much history of criticism offered here. The book summaries are amazingly efficient (sometimes almost dizzying, as in the whirlwind tour of *Bleak House*). Hawes has pulled together much useful material; I particularly like his description of the fates of Dickens's children and their descendents, which is a subject less frequently covered. I was also pleased to see that he draws examples from some of the lesser known short fiction and gives these works their due.

The last two works I will focus on don't fit as precisely into this category as the others, but they seem to belong here more than anywhere else, for both present biographical readings of Dickens. In "Charles Dickens: Genius and Human Circumstances," Robert Lapides aims to counter prevailing cultural assumptions that genius is a mysterious, inexplicable quality. "Belief in genius is our cultures' secular faith," Lapides suggests (9). He does not entirely dismiss the notion that genius is at least in part inexplicable, but he suggests that "extraordinary creativity is a function of character, that it originates in exceptional early experience, and that it continues to grow with boldly courageous activity," a theory he then applies to an analysis of how Dickens's early experiences influenced his creative genius (8). He begins with a survey of recent biological studies of possible genetic links to genius, which is fascinating material not usually found in articles on Dickens. Surprisingly, "DNA research has found nothing to support the heritability of differences in mental ability. . . . the leading geneticist R. C. Lewontin . . . argued strenuously that superior mental ability has no more a genetic than a divine origin" (9). On the other hand, psychological evidence points to a high correlation between genius and hard work, persistence, and determination. Lapides quotes R. A. Ochse, author of *Before the Gates of Excellence: The Determinants of Creative Genius*, who states that " 'the most salient and most consistent characteristic of creative achievers is persistent enthusiastic devotion to work' " (10). It almost sounds like something Dickens, or David Copperfield, would say of himself. Lapides proceeds to use these studies to suggest that Dickens, instead of needing to transcend his early negative experiences to become a great novelist, found that those very experiences are what forged "his driving need for ever-greater success" (14). (Of course, Dickens himself recognized this in the biographical statement he gave to Forster). But Lapides also analyzes specific characteristics of Dickens's parents that influenced his creativity as well—for instance, the fact that "both his parents were highly expressive and verbally adept" (11). It is illuminating to read an analysis of Dickens in the context of recent scientific and psychological studies on creativity and genius. Perhaps it is yet another indication of Dickens's genius that he understood, sans science and psychology, that he owed the best he had to offer to the worst he had experienced.

Finally, Rosemarie Bodenheimer's *Knowing Dickens* presents what I might call a biography of Dickens's mind. What did Dickens know? What can we know about him? How much of what he reveals in his writings was he conscious of and in control of? These are the questions Bodenheimer sets out to answer as she explores "the revealing and concealing intelligence that lurks somewhere—but where, exactly?—in Dickens's writing" and attempts "to capture something of that knowing Dickens that eludes us" (2). Bodenheimer herself struggles to categorize her work, as I did for this study, suggesting that it "makes its home in the gap between the chronological imperatives of biography and the literary imperatives of criticism, following some representative clusters of thought and feeling that link Dickens's ways of talking in letters with his concerns in fiction and journalism" (2).

Bodenheimer includes chapters on "What Dickens Knew," "Language on the Loose," "Memory," "Another Man," "Manager of the House," and "Streets." "Language on the Loose" examines Dickens's parodies of himself through his "hyperbolic talkers"; "Memory" dissects his most overtly autobiographical writings; "Another Man" looks at male rivals and doubles in Dickens's life and fiction; "Manager of the House" explores Dickens as home-maker—a constructor of his own and fictional homes; and finally "Streets" analyzes the connections between Dickens's perambulations and his writing process (15). In each chapter Bodenheimer draws from novels, letters, and nonfiction to capture a sense of the "inner dynamic" that shaped Dickens's life and writings (14). She succeeds admirably in this project.

For me, "Memory" and "Another Man" are the best chapters. In "Memory" Bodenheimer offers intriguing insights into the autobiographical fragment that Dickens gave to John Forster, and in "Another Man" she analyzes his use of "the other"—in life, fiction, theatricals and readings—to test "the limits of the self" (125). Frankly, I didn't think it was possible to say anything new about the autobiographical fragment, but she does through a finely nuanced reading of the rhetoric of the piece in relation to his other writings. She is particularly good at assessing how Dickens fluctuates between parody and pathos in his fictional projections of his traumatic childhood experience of being sent to work in a blacking factory when his father was imprisoned for debt. (He plays the experience for pathos with David Copperfield and for parody with Bounderby). Also illuminating is her analysis of the contrasts between Dickens's firm statements of knowledge and conviction in the autobiographical fragment versus his admission that he can never fully express how he felt at the time he worked in the factory. Bodenheimer asserts that such fluctuations indicate Dickens flailing around to find a suitable explanation and ending for his tale of trauma, the kind of satisfactory conclusion that is only ever available in fiction.

Bodenheimer's approach in this book is fascinating but ephemeral—sometimes it's hard to remember what is meant to hold the study together—that is, her analysis of just how knowing Dickens was, and how much we can know him. So, at times, we seem to get bits and pieces of observation and interpretation—but they are brilliant bits, even when the center hasn't always held. My only other objection to the book is her use of ''Bibliographic Notes'' (i.e., prose descriptions of sources related to each chapter) instead of precise citations, which makes it difficult to track the origins of specific ideas. But these objections do not diminish the overall effectiveness of this study, which manages to shed new light on what might seem to be familiar territory.

Conclusion

In coming to the end of this project, I have mixed feelings. First, to be honest, I will be glad to read something other than Dickens criticism for a while. Second, to continue the honesty, I doubt that I'll ever be as on top of Dickens criticism again. For years I have suspected that I was falling woefully behind in trying to keep up with Dickens scholarship; I now know for certain that I was right. Without an assignment such as this one, one that requires putting most other scholarly work on hold, it really is not possible to keep up with the industry of Dickens scholarship, unless one is retired or independently wealthy and can afford to devote oneself to it full time. This fact makes reviews and annotated bibliographies increasingly important in guiding scholars to what is worthwhile, to what they need.

After reviewing a year of scholarship, I'm pleased to say that one critical trend persists and that is the popularity of new historical approaches. New historicism always holds out the promise of bringing new information to bear on familiar texts, not just more idiosyncratic readings that may or may not have their roots in the text or the times. Even when it goes awry, and it does, at least for me, when contexts weigh far more heavily than the literary texts being analyzed, new historicism still almost always presents intriguing new material. New historicism also speaks to a wider range of readers than certain esoteric, jargonistic theoretical approaches we've witnessed over the past forty years, and I think this is a particularly important concern in literary criticism focused on a writer like Dickens, who was deeply devoted to communicating intimately with as large an audience as possible.

Finally, I have good news and bad news. The good news is that most of the works on Dickens from 2007 are really worth reading. The bad news is—most of the works on Dickens from 2007 are really worth reading. I hope you agree.

WORKS CITED

Ablow, Rachel. *The Marriage of Minds: Reading Sympathy in the Victorian Marriage Plot.* Stanford: Stanford UP, 2007.

Allingham, Philip V. "Luke Fildes's Illustrations: Parts 1–4." *The Dickens Magazine* 4.1–4 (2006–07): 12+.

Archibald, Diana C. "Recent Dickens Studies—2005." *Dickens Studies Annual* 38 (2007): 143–203.

Barr, Alan P. "Matters of Class and the Middle-Class Artist in *David Copperfield.*" *Dickens Studies Annual* 38 (2007): 55–67.

———. "Mourning Becomes David: Loss and the Victorian Restoration of Young Copperfield." *Dickens Quarterly.* 24.2 (June 2007): 63–77.

Berard, Jane H. *Dickens and Landscape Discourse.* New York: Peter Lang, 2007.

Bertman, Stephen. "Dante's Role in the Genesis of Dickens's *A Christmas Carol. Dickens Quarterly* 24.3 (Sept. 2007): 167–75.

Bevis, Matthew. *The Art of Eloquence: Byron, Dickens, Tennyson, Joyce.* New York: Oxford UP, 2007.

Bloom, Harold, Ed. *Charles Dickens's A Tale of Two Cities.* Updated edition. Bloom's Modern Critical Interpretations. New York: Infobase, 2007.

Bodenheimer, Rosemary. *Knowing Dickens.* Ithaca: Cornell UP, 2007.

Bove, Alexander. "The 'Unbearable Realism of a Dream': On the Subject of Portraits in Austen and Dickens." *ELH* 74.3 (2007): 655–79.

Bowen, John. "Dickens, Bret Harte and the Santa Cruz Connection." *The Dickensian* 103.3 (Winter 2007): 203–05.

Brinton, Ian. *Dickens's Great Expectations.* New York: Continuum, 2007.

Buckland, Adelene. " 'The Poetry of Science': Charles Dickens, Geology, and Visual and Material Culture in Victorian London." *Victorian Literature and Culture* 35.2 (2007): 679–94.

Byrne, Katherine. "Consuming the Family Economy: Tuberculosis and Capitalism in Charles Dickens's *Dombey and Son.*" *Nineteenth-Century Contexts* 29.1 (March 2007): 1–16.

Claybaugh, Amanda. *The Novel of Purpose: Literature and Social Reform in the Anglo-American World.* Ithaca: Cornell UP, 2007.

Cox, Arthur J. "The *Drood* Remains Revisited—the Sapsea Fragment." *Dickens Quarterly* 24.2 (June 2007): 86–102.

Davis, Paul. *Critical Companion to Charles Dickens: A Literary Reference to His Life and Work.* New York: Facts on File, 2007.

Dilnot, Alan. "Dickens and Colonialism: Helena and Neville Landless." *The Dickens Magazine* 4.1 (2006–07): 8–9.

Dolin, Kieran. *A Critical Introduction to Law and Literature.* Cambridge: Cambridge UP, 2007.

Dougherty, Kathleen Poorman. "Habituation and Character Change." *Philosophy and Literature* 31 (2007): 294–310.

Drew, John. M. "Pictures from *The Daily News*: Context, Correspondents, and Correlations." *Dickens Quarterly* 24.4 (Dec. 2007): 230–46.

Edmondson, John, ed. *Dickens on France: Fiction, Journalism and Travel Writing.* Northampton, MA: Interlink Books, 2007.

Edwards, Kim. "The Detective Novel Post-*Drood.*" *The Dickens Magazine* 4.4 (2006–07): 26–27.

Furneaux, Holly. "Charles Dickens's Families of Choice: Elective Affinities, Sibling Substitution, and Homoerotic Desire." *Nineteenth-Century Literature* 62.2 (Sept. 2007): 153–92.

———. "A Distaste for Matrimonial Sauce: The Celebration of Bachelorhood in the Journalism and Fiction of Collins and Dickens." *Wilkie Collins: Interdisciplinary Essays.* Ed. Andrew Mangham. Cambridge: Cambridge Scholars Publishing, 2007. 22–32.

Garson, Marjorie. *Moral Taste: Aesthetics, Subjectivity, and Social Power in the Nineteenth-Century Novel.* Toronto: U of Toronto P, 2007.

Giddings, Robert. "Boz on the Box: A Brief History of Dickens on British Television." *The Dickensian* 103.472 (Summer 2007): 101–15.

Goodin, George. "The Uses and Usages of Muddle (Part 1)." *Dickens Quarterly* 24.3 (Sept. 2007): 135–44.

———. "The Uses and Usages of Muddle (Part 2)." *Dickens Quarterly* 24.4 (Dec. 2007): 201–10.

Gorniak, George. "Victorian Missionary Hudson Taylor, 1832–1905." *The Dickens Magazine* 4.4 (2006–07): 30–32.

Gray, Beryl. "Man and Dog: Text and Illustration in *The Old Curiosity Shop.*" *The Dickensian* 103.472 (Summer 2007): 125–43.

Hanna, Robert C. *Dickens's Nonfictional, Theatrical, and Poetical Writings: An Annotated Bibliography, 1820–2000.* New York: AMS, 2007.

Hawes, Donald. *Charles Dickens.* New York: Continuum, 2007.

Herbert, Christopher. *War of No Pity: The Indian Mutiny and Victorian Trauma.* Princeton: Princeton UP, 2008.

Holt, Shari Hodges. "Dickens from a Postmodern Perspective: Alfonso Cuaron's *Great Expectations* for Generation X." *Dickens Studies Annual* 38 (2007): 69–92.

Hornback, Bert. "The Book of Jasper." *Dickens Quarterly* 24.2 (June 2007): 78–85.

Jacobson, Wendy S. "The Muddle and the Star: *Hard Times.*" *The Dickensian* 103.472 (Summer 2007): 144–56.

Joshi, Priti. "Mutiny Echoes: India, Britons, and Charles Dickens's *A Tale of Two Cities.*" *Nineteenth-Century Literature* 62.1 (2007): 48–87.

Kaplan, Cora. *Victoriana: Histories, Fictions, Criticism.* New York: Columbia UP, 2007.

Keeble, Richard, and Sharon Wheeler, eds. *The Journalistic Imagination: Literary Journalists from Defoe to Capote and Carter.* New York: Routledge, 2007.

Klimaszewski, Melissa. "The Contested Site of Maternity in Charles Dickens's *Dombey and Son.*" *The Literary Mother: Essays on Representations of Maternity and Child Care.* Ed. Susan C. Staub. Jefferson, NC: McFarland, 2007. 138–58.

Lapides, Robert. "Charles Dickens: Genius and Human Circumstances." *Encounter: Education for Meaning and Social Justice* 20.2 (Summer 2007): 8–15.

Ledger, Sally. *Dickens and the Popular Radical Imagination.* New York: Cambridge UP, 2007.

Litvack, Leon. "*Dickens's Dream* and the Conception of *Character.*" *The Dickensian* 103.1 (Spring 2007): 5–36.

Louttit, Chris. "Lowell Revisited: Dickens and the Working Girl." *Dickens Quarterly* 24.1 (March 2007): 27–36.

Lowe, Doug. " 'Quite a Tonic in Himself': Charles Dickens and Healthcare." *The Dickensian* 103.2 (Summer 2007): 116–24.

Maidment, Brian. *Dusty Bob: A Cultural History of Dustmen, 1780–1870.* New York: Manchester UP, 2007.

Mangham, Andrew, ed. *Wilkie Collins: Interdisciplinary Essays.* Cambridge: Cambridge Scholars Publishing, 2007.

Marcus, Sharon. *Between Women: Friendship, Desire, and Marriage in Victorian England.* Princeton: Princeton UP, 2007.

McAllister, David. " 'Subject to the Sceptre of Imagination': Sleep, Dreams, and Unconsciousness in *Oliver Twist.*" *Dickens Studies Annual* 38 (2007): 1–17.

McNees, Eleanor. "Reluctant Source: Murray's Handbooks and *Pictures from Italy.*" *Dickens Quarterly* 24.4 (Dec. 2007): 211–29.

Miller, Andrew. "Lives Unled in Realist Fiction." *Representations* 98 (Spring 2007): 118–34.

Orford, Peter. "An Italian Dream and a Castle in the Air: The Significance of Venice in *Little Dorrit.*" *The Dickensian* 103 (Summer 2007): 157–65.

Ortiz-Robles, Mario. "Local Speech, Global Acts: Performative Violence and the Novelization of the World." *Comparative Literature* 59.1 (Winter 2007): 1–22.

Orwin, Donna Tussing. *Consequences of Consciousness: Turgenev, Dostoevsky, Tolstoy.* Palo Alto, CA: Stanford UP, 2007.

Oulton, Carolyn W. De La L. *Romantic Friendship in Victorian Literature.* Burlington, VT: Ashgate, 2007.

Parker, David. Chapter Synopses for *The Mystery of Edwin Drood. The Dickens Magazine* 4.1–4 (2006–07): 2+.

Paroissien, David. "Affecting Tales in *David Copperfield*: Mr. Peggotty and *The Man of Feeling.*" *The Dickensian* 103.3 (Winter 2007): 197–202.

Philpotts, Trey. "Dickens, Invention, and Literary Property in the 1850s." *Dickens Quarterly* 24.1 (March 2007): 18–26.

Pionke, Albert D. "Degrees of Secrecy in Dickens's Historical Fiction." *Dickens Studies Annual* 38 (2007): 35–53.

Pollack-Pelzner, Daniel. "Dickens's Hamlet Burlesque." *Dickens Quarterly* 24.2 (June 2007): 103–10.

Reed, John R. "Dickens and Personification." *Dickens Quarterly* 24. 1 (March 2007): 3–17.

Saint-Amour, Paul K. " 'Christmas Yet to Come': Hospitality Futurity, the *Carol,* and "The Dead.' " *Representations* 98 (Spring 2007): 93–117.

Salmon, Richard. "Professions of Labour: *David Copperfield* and the 'Dignity of Literature.' " *Nineteenth-Century Contexts* 29.1 (March 2007): 35–52.

Shin, Hisup. "What Creeps Out of Holes: The Figuration of Filth and the Urban Everyday in Chadwicks' Sanitary Report and Dickens' Later Novels." *Nineteenth-Century Literature in English* 11.1 (2007): 311–46.

Slater, Michael. *Charles Dickens*. VIP series. Oxford: Oxford UP, 2007.

Staub, Susan C., ed. *The Literary Mother: Essays on Representations of Maternity and Child Care*. Jefferson, NC: McFarland, 2007.

Stuchebrukhov, Olga A. *The Nation as Invisible Protagonist in Dickens and Dostoevsky: Uncovering Hidden Social Forces Within the Text.*" Lewiston, NY: Edwin Mellen, 2007.

Talairach-Vielmas, Laurence. *Moulding the Female Body in Victorian Fairy Tales and Sensation Novels*. New York: Ashgate, 2007.

Taylor, Jonathan. *Science and Omniscience in Nineteenth-Century Literature*. Brighton: Sussex, 2007.

Tharaud, Barry. "Form as Process in *The Pickwick Papers*: The Structure of Ethical Discovery." *Dickens Quarterly* 24.3 (Sept. 2007): 145–58.

Toker, Leona. "*Nicholas Nickleby* and the Discourse of Lent." *Dickens Studies Annual* 38 (2007): 19–33.

Tracy, Robert. "W. C. Macready in *The Life and Adventures of Nicholas Nickleby.*" *Dickens Quarterly* 24.3 (Sept. 2007): 159–66.

Tulloch, John. "Charles Dickens and the Voices of Journalism." *The Journalistic Imagination: Literary Journalists from Defoe to Capote and Carter.* Ed. Richard Keeble and Sharon Wheeler. New York: Routledge, 2007.

Vanfasse, Nathalie. *Charles Dickens Entre Normes et Déviance*. Preface de Michael Hollington. Aix-en-Provence: Publications de l'Université de Provence, 2007.

Wainwright, Valerie. *Ethics and the English Novel from Austen to Forster*. Burlington, VT: Ashgate, 2007.

Wolfreys, Julian. *Dickens to Hardy, 1837–1884: The Novel, the Past and Cultural Memory in the Nineteenth Century*. New York: Palgrave-Macmillan, 2007.

INDEX

(Page numbers in italics represent illustrations)

433